Multifamily Housing Development Handbook

ULI Development Handbook Series

 Urban Land Institute

About ULI–the Urban Land Institute

ULI is the preeminent multidisciplinary real estate forum that facilitates the open exchange of ideas, information, and experience among local, national, and international industry leaders and policy makers dedicated to creating better places. Its mission is to provide responsible leadership in the use of land to enhance the total environment.

ULI sponsors education programs and forums to encourage an open international exchange of ideas and sharing of experiences; initiates research that anticipates emerging land use trends and issues and proposes creative solutions based on that research; provides advisory services; and publishes a wide variety of materials to disseminate information on land use and development. Established in 1936, the Institute today has more than 16,000 members and associates from more than 60 countries representing the entire spectrum of the land use and development disciplines.

Richard M. Rosan
President

For more information about ULI and the resources that it offers related to multifamily housing and a variety of other real estate and urban development issues, visit ULI's Web site at www.uli.org.

Cover photo: Site 17, Seattle, Washington. Eduardo Calderon, photographer. Courtesy of GGLO Architecture and Interior Design.

Project Staff

Rachelle L. Levitt
Senior Vice President, Policy and Practice
Publisher

Gayle Berens
Vice President, Real Estate Development Practice

Jo Allen Gause
Senior Director, Residential Development

Adrienne Schmitz
Associate Director, Residential Development
Project Director

Nancy H. Stewart
Director, Book Program

Eileen Hughes
Managing Editor

Barbara M. Fishel/Editech
Manuscript Editor

Helene Y. Redmond/HYR Graphics
Book Design/Layout

Meg Batdorff
Cover Design

Diann Stanley-Austin
Director, Publishing Operations

Maria-Rose Cain
Word Processing

Recommended bibliographic listing:

Schmitz, Adrienne, et al. *Multifamily Housing Development Handbook.* Washington, D.C.: ULI–the Urban Land Institute, 2000.

ULI Catalog Number: M27
International Standard Book Number: 0-87420-869-6
Library of Congress Catalog Card Number: 00-109220

Books in the ULI Development Handbook Series

Business and Industrial Park Development Handbook, 1988
Downtown Development Handbook, Second Edition, 1992
Mixed-Use Development Handbook, 1987
Office Development Handbook, Second Edition, 1998
Residential Development Handbook, Second Edition, 1990
Resort Development Handbook, 1997
Shopping Center Development Handbook, Third Edition, 1999

Authors

Principal Author and Project Director

Adrienne Schmitz
ULI–the Urban Land Institute
Washington, D.C.

Primary Contributing Authors

Kenneth Beck
Auerbach Realty Group Southwest
Santa Monica, California

Stephen Blank
ULI–the Urban Land Institute
Washington, D.C.

Karen Danielsen
National Association of Home Builders
Washington, D.C.

Libby Howland
Writer/Editor
Takoma Park, Maryland

Oliver Jerschow
Planning Consultant
Toronto, Ontario

Jennifer Nevitt
YieldStar.com
Charlotte, North Carolina

Phillip Payne
Boddie-Noell Properties
Charlotte, North Carolina

Richard B. Peiser
Harvard University, Graduate School of Design
Cambridge, Massachusetts

G. Ronald Witten
M/PF Research
Dallas, Texas

Contributing Authors

Michael Baker
ABT Associates
Bethesda, Maryland

John Byrne
Queensland Department of Housing
Brisbane, Queensland, Australia

Cheryl Downey
Consultant
Long Beach, California

Steven Fader
Steven Fader Architect
Los Angeles, California

Terry Lassar
Communications Consultant
Portland, Oregon

Joseph Petersen
Village Green Residential Properties, Inc.
Farmington Hills, Michigan

Cary Roth
Stanford University Graduate Housing Operations
Stanford, California

Mary Boehling Schwartz
U.S. Census Bureau
Suitland, Maryland

Marc Weiss
Center for National Policy
Washington, D.C.

Acknowledgments

The Urban Land Foundation (ULF), as part of its commitment to support ULI's core research program, provides major funding for the new and revised editions of the ULI Development Handbook Series. The *Multifamily Housing Development Handbook* was funded in part by grants from ULF. Leadership of the National Multi Housing Council also provided funding. The Urban Land Institute gratefully acknowledges these contributions.

Like all ULI handbooks, this one is the product of the collective effort of many minds and hands. Although it is impossible to mention everyone who participated in this project, a number of individuals deserve special acknowledgment and thanks.

First, special recognition goes to the individuals who drafted major portions of various chapters. Richard Peiser and Kenneth Beck wrote Chapter 5 while they were at the University of Southern California. Phillip Payne of Boddie-Noell Properties and Stephen Blank, a ULI Senior Resident Fellow, wrote Chapter 7. Jennifer Nevitt of YieldStar.com deserves credit for Chapter 8. Writer Libby Howland drafted Chapter 9. Oliver Jerschow, while a researcher at ULI, wrote chapter 10, and Ron Witten of M/PF Research, wrote Chapter 12.

The authors of the case studies—Michael Baker, John Byrne, Karen Danielson, Cheryl Downey, Steve Fader, Oliver Jerschow, Terry Lassar, Cary Roth, Mary Schwartz, and Samia Wilson—deserve recognition for their thorough research. We also thank the multifamily housing developers, architects, and designers who cooperated with the case study authors, providing the written materials, data, and photographs needed for each case study. Many of the feature boxes came from original text written by Joseph Petersen and Eric Adams. Others were written by Margaret Allen, Alan Segan, and Mitchell Vexler.

We would like to thank the Urban Land Institute staff for its skill and dedication in bringing this book together. A book of this size and scope requires the talents of many individuals, and they all deserve thanks. First, credit goes to Lloyd Bookout, who initiated the project and developed the book's concept. Thanks go to Gayle Berens and Jo Allen Gause, who provided direction throughout the book's lengthy production. Richard Haughey jumped right in on his first day of work and reviewed the entire book, offering valuable comments and additions. Stephen Blank and Dean Schwanke double checked text and calculations, and Leslie Holst helped with last-minute research.

We thank the editorial staff for ensuring that the information was clearly written and presented, making it most useful to our audience. We would like to thank Barbara Fishel for editing the entire text, Helene Redmond for her excellent job of designing and laying out the entire book, Eileen Hughes for managing the editorial process,

Diann Stanley-Austin for handling the printing schedule, and Meg Batdorff for designing the cover.

And to all others who had a hand in this book, we offer our appreciation.

Adrienne Schmitz
Principal Author and Project Director

Contents

Foreword

This handbook is part of the ULI Development Handbook Series, a set of volumes on real estate development that traces its roots back to 1947, when ULI published the first edition of the *Community Builders Handbook*. That edition was revised and updated several times over the following 25 years, and a replica of the original edition is being reissued this year. In 1975, ULI initiated the Community Builders Handbook Series with the publication of the *Industrial Development Handbook*. A number of titles were published in this series over a period of years, covering industrial, residential, shopping center, office, mixed-use, downtown, and recreational development. The publication of the *Resort Development Handbook* in 1997 marked the complete redesign of the handbook series and its renaming as the ULI Development Handbook Series.

This is the first edition of ULI's *Multifamily Housing Development Handbook*. Previously, the topic of rental housing was covered briefly in the *Residential Development Handbook*. But because developing, marketing, and managing multifamily rental housing is so different from developing and selling owner-occupied housing, ULI decided that multifamily rental housing merits its own text.

The objective of this handbook, as with all the handbooks in the series, is to provide a broad overview of the land use and real estate sector under discussion as well as a guide to the development process. This book therefore presents a comprehensive discussion of multifamily housing development, covering such topics as types of multifamily properties, market analysis, feasibility analysis, legal and regulatory issues, project financing, site planning, project design, marketing, leasing, operations and management, and trends.

Among the strengths of the book are its reliance on a variety of examples and real-world situations. The case study chapter documents 15 multifamily projects, including new construction, renovations, and conversions in urban and suburban areas. Other examples are discussed in the text or in the accompanying feature boxes.

Meeting the challenge of multifamily housing development requires expertise in all the disciplines that make up the development profession. Done effectively, a multifamily development should offer a pleasant and satisfying dwelling place that also is an attractive asset within its neighborhood and community. Creating such a property requires hard work and imagination; succeeding can pro-vide both financial and professional rewards. It is hoped that this book will help readers to better understand the multifamily housing development business, achieve success in applying its principles and best practices, and reap the rewards of that success.

Adrienne Schmitz
Project Director

Multifamily Housing Development Handbook

1. Introduction

Multifamily housing has not always gotten an easy ride in the United States. During the course of American history, multifamily housing has often been looked down on in our political system, our taxation system, and our neighborhoods. This reputation is undeserved, however; multifamily housing is actually a very important part of the American real estate industry. According to the U.S. Census Bureau, in 1999 building permits were issued for 351,100 housing units in multifamily buildings with five or more units.[1] Moreover, according to the National Multi Housing Council (NMHC), 272,000 people were employed in construction of multifamily housing in 1995, earning a payroll of almost $8 billion.[2] Multifamily housing provides a home for millions of Americans.

Multifamily housing can be found in all parts of America and in virtually every imaginable guise. It can range from luxury condominiums costing millions of dollars in New York City to affordable apartments that provide a home for the working poor in California. Although many different types of multifamily housing and a number of different forms of ownership are available, this book focuses on rental multifamily housing.

A great degree of innovation has occurred in the multifamily housing sector in recent years. Real estate investment trusts (REITs) have dramatically transformed the landscape of multifamily development, ownership, and management. The regulatory framework for multifamily housing has changed as well. More and more cities are taking steps to encourage multifamily housing as concerns about sprawl, traffic congestion, and environmental degradation grow. The design of multifamily housing is also becoming more innovative. Architects and designers are employing new materials and forms to create buildings with visual interest and character, and multifamily communities are providing more amenities and features than ever. Property management is employing increasingly sophisticated computer and communications technologies to provide improved levels of service to the residents of multifamily housing.

Despite the apparent preference of American households for owning a single-family dwelling, multifamily continues to be an essential housing form for a broad range of people. Apartments house the young and the old alike, whether they are aspiring homeowners or the ever-growing number of renters by choice—those who choose to rent apartments even though they could afford to buy a single-family house. Indeed, the residents of multifamily housing are as diverse as America itself, and there is no sound basis for stereotyping the people who live in apartments. To its residents, multifamily housing offers convenience, affordability, and flexibility. Multifamily housing even holds out hope for the revitalization of America's inner cities, as more and more communities, from Philadelphia to Dallas to San Diego, build multi-

Langham Court in Boston, Massachusetts, is an 84-unit mixed-income complex.

family housing in their downtown areas and find that people are eager to move in.

Multifamily housing is a mature part of the real estate business. People have been developing multifamily housing, both in this country and elsewhere, for centuries. Not surprisingly, the industry has risen and fallen with cyclical changes in the real estate market. For instance, in 1972 building permits were issued for more than 900,000 multifamily housing units in the United States, but by 1992 that figure had fallen to fewer than 139,000 units.[3] Developers of multifamily housing have been hit hard when they discovered, too late, that they had built more units than the market would absorb.

Since 1995, however, the multifamily sector has been doing very well. Most industry analysts agree that the sector is largely in equilibrium, apart from potential overbuilding in the luxury segment and in certain metropolitan markets. Investments in multifamily housing have provided solid, steady returns over the past few years, the credit quality of multifamily mortgages is high, and delinquency rates are near record lows.[4]

The multifamily business looks set for continued growth, and more of the innovation that has characterized the sector over the past few years will undoubtedly occur. Changes in lifestyles and changes in attitudes toward multifamily housing, to say nothing of the demographic trends that have always driven the housing market, point favorably in the direction of multifamily housing. Developers are discovering a number of niche markets where demand is unmet. Moreover, as the inventory of multifamily units ages, opportunities for rehabilitation and repositioning, along with improved property management, will grow. With skill, care, good analysis—and just a bit of luck—the multifamily industry will continue on its successful path.

What Is Multifamily Housing?

Based strictly on design, multifamily housing refers to a building that contains more than one dwelling unit. Multiple units can be stacked one on top of the other within the same building, or they can be side by side. The U.S. Census Bureau considers multifamily housing to be a structure with five or more dwelling units (the definition also used for this book). Multifamily housing includes more than high-rise apartment buildings. Moreover, all rental housing is not necessarily multifamily housing, and multifamily housing need not be for rent.

Forms of Ownership

Multifamily housing comes in a variety of ownership forms.[5] Most multifamily housing units are rented to residents. In 1990, according to the U.S. Census Bureau, of the occupied units in structures with five or more units, 14,253,445 units (90.3 percent) were occupied by renters, and 1,522,411 units (9.7 percent) were occupied by owners. And not all renters live in multifamily housing. One-third of the nation's rental housing units are in single-family detached dwellings.[6]

Multifamily housing may be owner-occupied, either as a condominium or a cooperative. A condominium is an arrangement whereby the household has individual ownership of its unit (defined as the space enclosed by the unit's interior walls) plus an undivided ownership interest in the property's common elements. Condominium ownership dates back to when the ancient Romans allowed individual citizens to own dwelling units in multiunit buildings. Only in 1961, however, was condominium ownership made legal in the United States, under Section 234 of the National Housing Act. Since then, the condominium has become an increasingly common form of ownership. Condominiums are very common throughout Florida and Hawaii, where resorts and senior housing communities abound.

In contrast, cooperative ownership arrangements arose in the United States in cities like New York, Chicago, and San Francisco in the years before Section 234 of the National Housing Act became law. Cooperatives were formed so that the households living in an apartment building could own, rather than rent, the homes they lived in. In a cooperative, the residents of the building form a nonprofit corporation and buy shares in the corporation, which uses those funds to purchase the building. The corporation actually holds the title to the building, and the residents lease their units from the corporation. Therefore, the residents do not technically own their units, but they do own shares in the corporation that

Multifamily housing is better designed than in the past. Bridgecourt in Emeryville, California, brings high style to a mixed-income community.

McLarand, Vasquez & Partners

Today's multifamily housing provides all the comfort, style, and amenities of single-family living, such as found in Jefferson Estates in Richardson, Texas.

Suburban garden apartments are the most common type of multifamily housing built today.

owns the building. Although complicated, cooperative ownership did succeed in the objective of giving residents ownership of their real estate. Since the passage of condominium legislation, however, cooperative forms of ownership are rarely used in multifamily housing.

Another special type of ownership of multifamily housing is timeshare ownership. It refers to the right to use, or the fee simple ownership of,[7] real estate for a specified period of time each year, usually in one-week increments. Timeshare ownership need not apply only to multifamily buildings. In fact, even space on cruise ships has been sold as timeshares. Still, many multifamily buildings in vacation destinations around the world use this form of ownership.

Product Types

Just as ownership of multifamily housing takes a variety of forms, so do product types that make up multifamily housing. One common way of differentiating multifamily products is according to their size and density. At one end of the spectrum are large single-family houses that have been subdivided into apartments. Such apartments were common early in the 20th century. At the other end of the spectrum are very-high-density high-rise apartment buildings, which may contain hundreds of units and sometimes even other uses, such as offices or stores. In between are low-rise multifamily buildings, commonly referred to as garden apartments.

Garden Apartments. Garden apartments are generally two to three stories, do not have an elevator, and can have interior hallways or allow direct access to the units from the outside. They usually have ten or more units in each structure. Site plans for garden apartment developments typically include landscaped common areas as well as surface parking. Increasingly, covered parking is provided, and some developers have begun to offer garden apartments that feature garages with direct access to their units. Such communities are often designed to resemble neighborhoods of large single-family houses, but they can still achieve densities of ten to 20 units per acre.

In this country, garden apartments began to be built in substantial numbers in suburban areas during the housing boom that followed World War II. Then as now, garden apartments appealed to a variety of markets, particularly households that could not afford a single-family house, such as singles, young couples, and the elderly.

Mid- and High-Rise Buildings. Mid- and high-rise apartments differ from garden apartments not just in terms of their size but also in how they are designed and built. As a rule, buildings with more than three to as many as eight stories are considered mid-rise, while buildings taller than eight stories are considered high rise. Nevertheless, these definitions may vary to some extent according to local conventions. For instance, in New York City a 12-story building might be considered mid-rise.

Perhaps the most important difference between mid- and high-rise buildings is found in their design and construction. Garden apartments are usually constructed of wood framing, while mid- and high-rise apartments, for structural reasons, must be built with steel frames or reinforced concrete. State and local building and fire codes help to determine how these structures will be built. For instance, buildings with more than three stories are usually required to install sprinkler systems. Mid- and high-rise buildings today are also generally required to have elevators.

Mid- and high-rise buildings can be virtually any form and height (above three stories) and therefore density, subject to the restrictions of local zoning codes. They can be constructed as rectangular slabs with single- or double-loaded corridors, or they can be towers with units opening from a central service core. Any number of combinations are possible. Depending on the location of the development, parking may be in surface lots surrounding the building, at grade but below the first floor of the building (which may sit on a podium), in a full-fledged parking structure, or in a below-grade parking garage. Both mid- and high-rise buildings have come to be designed with more articulated facades, employing a variety of building materials and other design features, such as gables, bays, and balconies.

The History of Multifamily Housing in the United States

Before the 19th century, multifamily housing did not exist in the sense that we understand it today. In colonial times, it was common for multiple households to live under the same roof, whether those people were family members or unrelated, or even if they were employees of the homeowner. These living arrangements in early towns and cities were usually born of economic necessity, reflecting the fact that in the late 1700s, most residents could ill afford a home of their own: only one in six inhabitants in the newly created United States owned any property.[8]

Beginning in New York City in the colonial era, landowners began to use ground leases. The owner of the land rented it to other parties for a specified number of years, with the lessee being encouraged, or even required, to build improvements on the land. Maintaining these improvements was the responsibility of the lessee, but when the lease expired the land and improvements generally reverted back to the landowner.[9] In many cases, these improvements were multifamily buildings.

Tenements and Apartments: Multifamily Housing in Nineteenth Century America

By the 19th century, America was industrializing rapidly as factories sprang up in and around the nation's towns and cities. Every year, the country's population grew as families formed and immigration continued. Industrialization encouraged people to move into cities, thereby creating the demand for affordable housing, which often meant higher-density multifamily housing. Many of the buildings constructed during this time came to be known as tenements, and although strictly defined as any building accommodating three or more households under a single roof, tenements quickly developed a sordid reputation.

For poor immigrants and migrants from the countryside, the tenements often proved to be the only viable form of housing in big cities like New York and Chicago. Tenements had the advantage of being within walking distance of work, and they at least provided some form of housing that these workers found comparatively affordable. But life in the tenement houses was difficult, to say the least. Most tenements were plagued by shoddy construction, with inadequate lighting and nonexistent plumbing. Overcrowding was rampant. These deplorable conditions made illness and disease a common feature of life in the tenements. Landlords often packed so many people into their tenements and spent so little on maintenance that these slum properties could actually be very profitable.[10] For the wealthier classes, a further benefit of the tenement slums was that they segregated and concentrated the poor, immigrants, and others deemed undesirable into ghettos where they would never have to tread.

By the middle to late 19th century, continuing economic growth and the introduction of new transportation technologies like the electric trolley began to allow better-off families to move to new homes in the suburbs. Left behind in the inner cities were the tenement slums that, in the face of continued immigration and poverty, became more crowded than ever. In fact, in 1893 a Board of Health census concluded that more than 1 million New Yorkers—70 percent of the population—lived in multiple-family dwellings, about 80 percent of which were tenements.[11]

Around that time a reform movement began that sought to improve the deplorable conditions in the tenements. In 1890, Jacob Riis, a journalist and social reformer in New York, published his landmark book, *How the Other Half Lives*, which documented with grim photographs the

High-rise residential buildings like Gables Peachtree in Atlanta (above) and Grand Gateway Garden in Shanghai are common throughout the world.

Tenement in New York's Lower East Side.

dreadful conditions to be found in the tenements. Similarly, in 1894 U.S. Commissioner of Labor Carroll Wright published an extensive and detailed inventory of just how bad things had gotten in the slums of Baltimore, Philadelphia, New York, and Chicago. Out of a sense of altruism —as well as a fear of what the tenement dwellers might do if conditions in the slums continued to deteriorate— reformers pressed for legislation to ameliorate the situation. New York pioneered tenement housing laws that provided minimum standards for new buildings. Along with model tenements, settlement houses, public health programs, and even slum clearance, these reforms slowly —very slowly—began to change life in the slums.

Not all multifamily dwellings in the 19th century were tenements though. Beginning in the 1850s, particularly as escalating land values in cities put detached houses out of the reach of all but the richest families, "respectable" multifamily buildings began to be developed. Termed "apartments," "apartment hotels," or "French flats" to distinguish them from the tenements, these multifamily buildings catered to the wealthy. These apartments alluded to the sophistication of European urban living, offering the latest amenities like electrical lighting and indoor plumbing in relatively spacious surroundings. The earliest of these projects, such as the Hotel Pelham in Boston (1855) and the Stuyvesant Flats in New York City designed by Richard Morris Hunt (1869), were wildly popular, maintaining waiting lists for units to become available. Investors and developers realized impressive returns on their investments, sometimes as high as 30 percent.[12]

Despite the early popularity of such projects, many Americans still felt an ambivalence toward multifamily living. Residents of the tenements were accused of living in, if not creating, hotbeds of criminality, prostitution, disease, and general depravity. The popular press also condemned the wealthier residents of apartments. Apartment living was thought to promote sexual promiscuity, which some felt would surely lead to the demise of the family. *The Ladies' Home Journal* was soon to declare the Bolshevik influence of apartments on women, and at the 1921 National Conference on Housing, James Ford, executive director of an organization called Better Homes in America, warned that "a child's sense of individuality, moral character, and intellectual efficiency could only develop in a private, detached dwelling."[13]

But the growing number of people who chose to make their homes in apartments largely ignored these criticisms. Moreover, the economics of real estate development in urban America continued to promote the construction of higher-density multifamily buildings. Improvements in construction technology such as the use of structural steel instead of load-bearing masonry walls and other innovations like electric elevators allowed multifamily buildings to become larger and more comfortable, as well as more attractive as real estate investments. It was becoming clear that multifamily buildings were to be a permanent part of the American landscape.

Multifamily Housing: A Way of Life for America's Cities
The census of 1920 confirmed that for the first time more Americans lived in urban areas than in rural areas. To satisfy the need for housing of this urbanizing population, a tremendous surge of apartment construction took place. Homeownership, particularly in urban neighborhoods, continued to be an unattainable dream for most Americans. Different forms of multifamily housing, whether duplexes and rowhouses, large old houses that had been subdivided into separate apartments, or mid- and high-rise apartment buildings, served to meet the needs of more people than ever before on a reasonably affordable basis. Luxury apartments were built in downtown areas close to business and entertainment centers, while more modest apartments were constructed along the transportation routes leading out of the city.

Many cities reported that more apartments than single-family detached houses were built within their boundaries during the 1920s. Nearly 40 percent of all the dwelling units built in the 1920s in the United States were multi-family units, and this construction boom continued until 1928. In all regions of the country, both the absolute number and the proportion of apartments rose throughout the decade.[14] Also during this decade, the use of standardized and mass-produced components increased in the construction of residential buildings. Pioneered by architects like Walter Gropius in Europe and developed later by the American Frank Lloyd Wright, standardization contributed to increased housing production while also exemplifying modern ideas about how homes should be built and how people should live.[15]

The Depression to World War II: Times of Change

The good fortunes of the multifamily industry were abruptly reversed with the stock market crash of 1929 and the ensuing depression. Unemployment was rampant, and financial markets imploded as banks collapsed and depositors lost millions of dollars. Real estate investment, development, and leasing actually hobbled through to 1931, but in the following year business ground to a halt as bankruptcy became a common state of affairs. Financing became completely unavailable and real estate values plummeted. New construction virtually stopped.

Before the Great Depression, it would have been inconceivable for the federal government to be involved in the production or financing of housing. The depth of this economic disaster, however, convinced Presidents Hoover and especially Roosevelt that governmental intervention was required. New institutions, including the Federal Home Loan Bank (FHLB) system and the Federal Housing Administration (FHA), were created to revive the housing industry and to stimulate the economy. The FHA and FHLB focused their attention mostly on single-family housing.

In an effort to help the public sector meet the demand for public housing, the federal government became in-

With urban living regaining its appeal, quality developments are being built in many cities. Langham Court in Boston's historic South End recalls architectural elements of its Victorian neighbors.

Government agencies at all levels have made commitments to provide affordable housing. Poco Way Renaissance in San Jose, California, consists of 66 rehabbed units and 64 newly constructed units; the project was the result of a partnership between the city of San Jose and the Santa Clara County housing authorities.

volved with multifamily housing as well. By entering this arena, the federal government took up the reformist cause begun in the 19th century. In 1934, the federal government established the Housing Division of the Public Works Authority and in 1937 the United States Housing Authority (USHA). These agencies were charged with the removal of the worst slum dwellings and their replacement with new, publicly owned rental housing. Under USHA regulations, local governments were to own the newly built housing, with the construction done by private contractors. Local governments paid for the housing by selling 40-year tax exempt bonds, while the federal government paid the interest and principal on the bonds through annual contributions. Operating costs were to be covered from the rents paid to the local governments by the tenants of the housing. Despite the fierce political debates that sometimes accompanied the legislation permitting publicly supported housing, the programs were successful. By the time World War II broke out, these programs had built more than 100,000 safe, sanitary, and affordable multifamily housing units.[16]

World War II and Beyond
During World War II, housing production declined dramatically except for housing directly related to the war effort. The lull in the industry did not last long, however. By 1945, as servicemen and -women returned home and as the economy moved back to a peacetime mode, it quickly became apparent that a massive shortage of housing existed in America. The homebuilding industry responded, and by 1950 housing starts had reached more than 1.5 million new homes, mostly in suburban areas.[17]

The postwar years were marked by a number of major changes in the way that cities were built in America. The FHA and the newly created Veterans Administration (VA) pioneered guarantees for home mortgages. Mass suburbanization began in earnest so that by 1950 many central cities began to lose population. The homebuilding

industry experienced incredible growth, and large-scale residential builders began to appear.

The fixed-rate, fixed-payment, long-term amortizing loan also played a role in the boom of homeownership. This type of loan, which still dominates the residential industry, took hold during the depression. Before the depression, lenders issued mostly short-term nonamortizing loans, often for only 40 to 50 percent of the property value. These lending requirements left the dream of homeownership out of the reach of many working people and led to high rates of foreclosure. Although the headline story of this period was the dramatic expansion in the construction of single-family detached homes, an astonishing number of multifamily units were being built as well.

Garden apartments were another innovation that became common in the years following the Great Depression. Although they initially emerged before the depression, the prototype garden apartment development was Sunnyside Gardens in Queens, New York, designed by architects Clarence Stein and Henry Wright in the mid-1920s. After the depression, Gustave Ring was one pioneer of the mass production of garden apartment communities. In Ring's view, garden apartments could offer residents all the conveniences of multifamily living without the problems normally associated with high-rise, high-density living. Ring's developments in the 1930s and 1940s included plentiful on-site landscaping and open space and a sense of peace and quiet as well as ample parking and accessibility to nearby shopping.[18] The buildings were designed as walk-up structures with one, two, or sometimes three stories, exterior entryways, and single-story floor plans for the units. Garden apartments have since proven to be a durable development model. Between 1960 and 1978, for example, almost 50 percent of the rental units built in the United States were garden apartments, and they are even more popular today.[19]

The federal government continued to play a major role in the evolving housing market after the depression.

Modern garden apartments still offer the advantages that they did in the 1930s but have added a level of luxury unimagined back then. At Village Green Cantera in Warrenville, Illinois, residents enjoy well-appointed common areas, private garages, and spacious, sun-filled units.

Creative approaches provide housing for those most in need. Step Up on Second in Santa Monica includes 36 units with on-site support services for homeless mentally disabled adults. By combining subsidies, tax credits, and rental income, the project maintains a positive cash flow.

The landmark Housing Act of 1949 promised "a decent home and suitable living environment for every American family," and to meet this goal, the government instituted a broad range of programs to intervene in the single-family and multifamily housing markets. These programs radically altered the shape of metropolitan areas in America. Subsidies for homebuyers and freeway construction achieved the laudable goal of allowing millions of people to own their own homes, often for the first time. But not all federal programs had such a beneficial effect. Perhaps the darkest legacy of federal housing policy during this period was the destruction left in the wake of the program begun in 1949 and reinforced by subsequent legislation that came to be known as urban renewal.

Ostensibly, the goals of urban renewal were to alleviate ingrained poverty in general and substandard housing conditions specifically. In cities around the country, this goal was to be accomplished by demolishing "slum" areas and redeveloping them with new homes, offices, or public facilities such as convention centers. In theory, urban renewal was to address the deplorable conditions to be found in the poorest sections of America's cities, but in practice, the result of urban renewal programs rarely improved conditions for the poor and more often made them worse. Little attention was paid to the impact of urban renewal schemes on existing community structures, businesses, or households. Too often, the renters who were displaced by urban renewal were given no compensation or any assistance with relocation. In fact, between 1949 and 1968, 425,000 housing units in low-income neighborhoods were razed for redevelopment, but they were replaced by only 125,000 units of new housing —and often those new units were luxury homes, unaffordable to the families that had been displaced.[20]

Public housing, which generally meant multifamily housing, was also a major component of the federal government's housing strategy. Perhaps ironically, public housing projects were built employing the latest in architectural and urban design theories, namely, modernism. America in the mid-20th century had already had some exposure to modernist design, an approach that advocated higher-density forms of housing, more open space, and efficient transportation flow while repudiating the vernacular in building design. Stuyvesant Town, developed in the late 1940s in New York's Lower East Side by the Metropolitan Life Insurance Company served as a prototype, with its repetition of high-rise residential towers in a park-like setting. Architects like renowned theorist Le Corbusier and Mies van der Rohe put these design principles into practice, often for high-profile clients in luxury projects. Unfortunately, American public housing projects built in the modernist style rarely achieved the level of design excellence that other, more luxurious, developments did. Instead, projects like Pruitt Igoe in St. Louis or the Robert Taylor Homes in Chicago became almost immediate failures, quickly serving to stigmatize both the concept of public housing and its residents. These disastrous public housing projects also served to reinforce the broader public's disdain for multifamily housing, particularly high-rise urban multifamily housing.

By the latter half of the 1950s, America's single-family housing binge was beginning to slow, and private multifamily housing began to be produced in greater quantities. A number of factors influenced this trend. Both land and construction costs were rising, favoring the development of multifamily housing. Multifamily products were also becoming an increasingly attractive investment option, with yields rising compared with office buildings and single-family homes. Not surprisingly, the federal government was also involved. In 1954, Congress passed new tax legislation allowing accelerated depreciation of multifamily dwellings. Further, the Section 608 program was created to insure mortgages for multifamily housing and thereby encourage its construction. The program was a success to the extent that it did spur the construction of multifamily housing, but a scandal erupted in

1954 when the government began to realize that builders were inflating their costs and fees to reap windfall profits at taxpayers' expense.

As the 1950s turned into the 1960s, the boom in the construction of multifamily buildings continued, although for somewhat different reasons. Baby boomers were beginning to enter the workforce, creating an increased demand for multifamily housing units as new households formed, while multifamily housing was also being constructed to serve the demand created by the substantial migration of people to the Sunbelt states like California, Florida, and Texas. In some cities in the United States in the mid-1960s, more multifamily units were built than single-family homes.[21] Federal policy continued to play a significant role in the boom. For instance, Section 202 subsidized the construction of rental housing for elderly people, and Section 221(d)(3) guaranteed below-market interest rates for affordable rental housing.

The multifamily industry also began to restructure during the 1960s and 1970s. Mergers and acquisitions between firms in the business were becoming more common, REITs began to transform the financial side of the business, and apartments and condominiums were becoming an increasingly common sight in suburban areas, where they were sometimes built as part of master-planned communities. Although condominiums were authorized for the first time only in 1961 under Section 234 of the National Housing Act, they quickly became popular.

The apartment industry also continued to adopt a variety of innovations in design during this period that allowed multifamily communities and homes to offer the same sorts of amenities that people could find in single-family neighborhoods: bigger and better-equipped kitchens and bathrooms, terraces and other outdoor areas, air conditioning and better soundproofing, community amenities like tennis courts and swimming pools —all in developments with a greater amount of open space than had ever been provided before.

The market welcomed all these changes with open arms. As the population grew, more and more people chose to live in multifamily buildings. In fact, it was more than just population growth that drove the increasing demand for multifamily units; new types of households were being formed that chose multifamily housing for a variety of reasons. The "traditional" household of a married couple with children was giving way to households headed by young and elderly singles, single-parent households, and other types of nontraditional households. In the five years leading up to 1972, housing starts of privately owned buildings with more than five units increased to levels never seen before or since, peaking in 1972 at more than 906,000 units. But the energy crisis of 1973, a steep rise in interest rates, and speculative overbuilding caused the number of multifamily starts to plummet through the remainder of the 1970s, bottoming out in 1975 at only 204,300 units started around the country.[22]

Throughout the 1970s, the federal government continued to support the multifamily housing market. The National Housing Act of 1968 created the Section 236 program, which subsidized the construction of privately owned affordable multifamily housing. Public housing units continued to be built at a rate of 60,000 to 100,000 units per year from 1969 to 1972.[23]

In 1973, however, the Nixon administration declared a moratorium on support for all federal housing assistance programs. Although the reasons for declaring the moratorium were complex and tied up with the politics of the day, it gave the administration and the Department of Housing and Urban Development (HUD) the opportunity to review all of the varied federal housing assistance programs. What emerged as a result of the ensuing deliberations was the Housing and Community Development Act of 1974. This piece of legislation had a major impact on the way the federal government financed affordable housing and community development. Section 8 was created as a way of turning federal assistance away from the direct provision of housing, intervening in the private market instead more indirectly. Similarly, community development block grants (CDBGs) consolidated a number of existing federal programs, aiming to provide greater flexibility in community development around the country. Both programs continue to play a major part in providing affordable housing in the United States.

In the late 1970s and the 1980s, the production of multifamily housing continued to fluctuate dramatically as conditions in the market—and the regulatory environment —changed. The Economic Recovery Tax Act of 1981 and

Located on Lake Michigan in Chicago, Montgomery Place is a 14-story rental apartment building designed for active seniors.

the deregulation of financial institutions in 1982 created substantial incentives for investment in real estate, and multifamily starts rose to nearly the levels of the early 1970s. By the late 1980s, circumstances began to change. The Tax Reform Act of 1986 removed many of the tax incentives for private multifamily housing, while the crisis in the savings and loan industry caused lenders to severely tighten their underwriting criteria.[24] Coupled with over-building and poor market conditions, multifamily housing starts as a percentage of total starts steadily fell until well into the 1990s. And conditions were no better in the world of assisted housing. Under the Reagan and Bush administrations, federal support for assisted housing fell drastically, and the construction of new public housing virtually ceased.

Recent Trends in Multifamily Housing

A number of important trends emerged during the 1990s that reveal the maturity and increasing sophistication of the multifamily industry. The developers of multifamily housing in recent years have found that they have been able to move into new markets, offer new types of products, and run their businesses with increasing professionalism. The dawn of the information age and the emergence of REITs provided the tools for a better understanding of market saturation and a more critical eye for underwriting, making the possibility of overbuilding less likely. All these trends bode well for the continued health of the apartment industry.

Low-income housing tax credits (LIHTCs) were created by the Tax Reform Act of 1986 in response to the loss of incentives for the creation of low-income housing and the growing crisis in affordable housing. Tax credits are granted to each state on a per capita basis and are administered competitively through the states' housing agencies. LIHTCs have been successful in creating incentives for private developers to construct low- and moderate-income housing, although their impact on the housing situation for people with very low incomes is debatable.

By the middle to late 1990s, the consensus was growing that many of the public housing initiatives of the past had failed. High-rise multifamily public housing units in urban areas were singled out as some of the worst failures. They were seen as unsafe, crime-ridden buildings that did little to lift the tenants out of the cycle of poverty. The Clinton administration responded by creating the Housing Opportunities for People Everywhere (HOPE VI) initiative. Under this program, many of the high-rise public housing structures were imploded and replaced with lower-density multifamily mixed-income neighborhoods that offered tenants the chance of one day owning the unit they lived in. Also during the Clinton administration, many project-based Section 8 contracts with multifamily property owners expired. The owners were given the option at that point of restructuring their debt through HUD and continuing as a Section 8 community or opting out of the program and becoming a market-

REITs became a major force in multifamily development and ownership during the 1990s. AvalonBay, which owns Toscana in Sunnyvale, California, is among the 20 largest multifamily REITs.

The resurging interest in urban living has created a market for adaptive use of industrial buildings. Such apartments offer large open spaces with high ceilings.

rate community. The program came to be known as the "Mark to Market" initiative.

Multifamily construction has increased in every major region of the country in every year since 1992.[25] As the children of the baby boomers began to form households and enter the multifamily market, they provided an important source of new demand. Moreover, interest in multifamily living has been growing among consumers—even when they could afford to buy a house. Both theorists and consumers are embracing new urbanism and the smart growth movement. These two philosophies of how to build better communities in the United States advocate multifamily development, and as they have continued to gain support, they have contributed to the rising interest in multifamily living.

Another big story in the multifamily industry in the 1990s was the resurgence of interest in downtowns. From New York to Denver to Seattle, American cities have been revitalizing their downtowns by adding new jobs,

new attractions, and—in a reversal of past trends—new residents. Today, these migrants to downtowns are finding homes in multifamily communities that are some of the most architecturally inventive and technologically advanced homes around. Conversions of distinctive warehouses or office buildings and new infill construction are helping to add to the vitality of urban neighborhoods while preserving some of our most treasured historic buildings. More and more cities—Phoenix is an example— are changing their planning and building codes to promote this type of development, and this trend is likely to continue.

Nevertheless, from 1994 to 1997 just over two-thirds of the rental units built in the United States were built outside central cities.[26] But whether they are in downtowns or suburbs, the multifamily communities developed in recent years all sport amenities that would have been unheard of in the past. It has become increasingly common for developers to offer residents the latest in high-capacity communications technologies and community Web sites. The 25- to 35-year-old demographic cohort has historically made up the largest group of multifamily residents. Today, this group is also the most technologically savvy, demanding access to the best and fastest communication technologies. Moreover, these improvements have not been just for the benefit of residents. Providing highly valued amenities helps to justify higher rents to residents for the services that they want.

"Service" has indeed become a more important word in the multifamily dictionary. New computer programs help property managers to better meet their residents' needs as well as enhance a property's financial performance. As in virtually every other aspect of life, the Internet has had an explosive impact on the multifamily industry. Web sites and Internet services now cater to every person in the multifamily business, dramatically changing the way that people find, evaluate, and move into their apartments.

More and more developers of multifamily housing have also begun to explore a variety of niche markets. As the baby boomers become senior citizens, the low maintenance and flexibility of multifamily housing become more attractive. Many in this active group will likely prefer leisure activities to spending time in the upkeep of a single-family home. Other markets such as student housing or corporate apartments with their prospects for substantial returns have also begun to capture the attention of developers. Niche markets by definition offer limited opportunities, but savvy developers will continue to explore and expand the realm of possibilities for developing specialized multifamily products.

A number of challenges remain for the multifamily industry. Affordability continues to be an intractable problem, and in fact, the number of renters facing a crisis of affordability has expanded in recent years. At the same time, the multifamily industry needs to continue to try to overcome its image problem by addressing misconceptions about what multifamily housing is, the people who live there, and their impact on neighborhoods. If the industry continues to innovate changes and to provide a valued product that people want to call home, then multifamily housing will continue to be an important part of our cities and towns, just as it has always been.

Notes

1. U.S. Census Bureau Web site: www.census.gov/const/C40/Table1.

2. National Multi Housing Council, *Apartment Living in America* (Washington, D.C.: NMHC, 1996).

3. U.S. Census Bureau Web site.

4. Jun Han and Mark Gallagher, "Outlook for the New Millennium," *Urban Land,* January 2000, p. 42.

5. This section draws on Charles J. Jacobus, *Real Estate: An Introduction to the Profession,* 8th ed. (Englewood Cliffs, New Jersey: Prentice-Hall, 1998).

6. Joint Center for Housing Studies, Harvard University, *The State of the Nation's Housing, 1999* (Cambridge, Massachusetts: Joint Center for Housing Studies, 1999).

7. "Right to usc" and "fcc simple" are legal terms referring to the ownership of real estate. In the case of timeshares, a right to use gives the buyer the contractual right to occupy a unit at a timeshare property for one week per year for a specified period of years. Fee simple ownership means that the buyer owns the unit for one week per year in perpetuity, holds title to the unit, and so on. In either case, buyers may buy multiple weeks of ownership per year if they wish. Fee simple ownership is the most common form of ownership in the timeshare market.

8. Donald A. Krueckeberg, "The Grapes of Rent: A History of Renting in a Country of Owners," *Housing Policy Debate,* vol. 10, no. 1 (1999), pp. 9–30.

9. Elizabeth Blackmar, *Manhattan for Rent, 1785–1850* (Ithaca, New York: Cornell University Press, 1989).

10. Mike E. Miles, Gayle Berens, and Marc A. Weiss, *Real Estate Development: Principles and Process,* 3d ed. (Washington, D.C.: ULI–the Urban Land Institute, 2000).

11. Gwendolyn Wright, *Building the Dream: A Social History of Housing in America* (New York: Pantheon Books, 1981), p. 123.

12. Ibid., pp. 136–37.

13. Ibid., p. 150.

14. Miles, Berens, and Weiss, *Real Estate Development,* p. 135.

15. Peter G. Rowe, *Modernity and Housing* (Cambridge, Massachusetts: MIT Press, 1993).

16. Miles, Berens, and Weiss, *Real Estate Development,* p. 147.

17. Ibid., p. 151.

18. Gustave Ring, "Modern Trends in Garden Apartments," *Urban Land,* May 1948, p. 3.

19. Carl F. Horowitz, *The New Garden Apartment* (New Brunswick, New Jersey: Center for Urban Policy Research, Rutgers University, 1983).

20. Martin Mayer, *The Builders: Houses, People, Neighborhoods, Governments, Money* (New York: W.W. Norton, 1978), p. 120.

21. Wright, *Building the Dream,* p. 260.

22. U.S. Census Bureau, *Statistical Abstract of the United States, 1999* (Washington, D.C.: Government Printing Office, 1999).

23. R. Allen Hays, *The Federal Government and Urban Housing: Ideology and Change in Public Policy,* 2d ed. (Albany, New York: SUNY Press, 1995).

24. The 1986 act also created low-income housing tax credits, a complicated tool that nonetheless is used as a financing mechanism for most affordable housing projects today.

25. Joint Center for Housing Studies, *The State of the Nation's Housing, 1999.*

26. Ibid., p. 23.

2. Market Analysis

Due diligence is the analytical evaluation that precedes major real estate decisions, including buying a land parcel or beginning a development. It includes evaluating the environmental, financial, legal, and other aspects that relate to developing and marketing the property. The analyses that typically make up due diligence can be divided into four primary components: 1) market analysis, 2) site selection and engineering, 3) regulatory approvals, and 4) financial feasibility. This chapter looks at market analysis; Chapter 3 covers site selection, Chapter 4 the regulatory and legal context for multifamily housing, and Chapter 5 financial feasibility analysis.

The Purpose of Market Analysis

A well-conceived multifamily project must begin with a thorough understanding of the marketplace in which the proposed development will compete. Market feasibility is fundamental to a development's financial success. It is perhaps more crucial to the successful development of multifamily housing than single-family housing, because once the development concept is established, it is far more difficult to make changes. A market analysis also increases in importance when the product type and geographical

area are less familiar to the developer, as it serves as a tool to educate the developer.

Understanding the market involves defining classic factors of demand and supply. Analysis of demand includes demographic and economic characteristics of households in the determined market area. Analysis of supply examines trends in prices and absorption and—most important—surveys the potentially competitive projects that will likely be marketed during the same time as the proposed subject property. A market analysis should seek answers to several basic questions:

1. What is the appropriate target market and market position for this project?
2. What are the size and rate of growth of the target market, and what percentage of that market can be attracted to the subject project?
3. What are the opportunities, gaps, or specialized niches where a need exists in the marketplace?
4. What is the appropriate rent range for the market?
5. What types of units and unit sizes are suitable for the market?
6. What amenities and unit features should be provided to appeal to this market?
7. What are the indirect economic constraints? Or what are constraints to development not related to supply and demand, such as regulatory issues, the physical site, community opposition, or other difficulties affecting development?[1]

Jefferson Estates in Richardson, Texas.

Some locations offer a wide choice of multifamily communities. Projects in these areas need to find a way to set themselves apart with better amenities, design features, services, or value.

Real estate market analysis requires statistics and equations but does not operate as an exact science. Much of the analysis must rely on a qualitative understanding of the market and its dynamics. Both the product and the consumer must be understood in terms of choices people make, evolving lifestyles, personal tastes, and many other considerations that cannot be quantified. Further, housing does not act like other consumer goods, because it is limited to a very local market. Thus, the universe of potential consumers is relatively small compared with that for most consumer products. Highly sophisticated statistical methods that can be applied to large samples do not necessarily work on such limited populations.

Market studies serve two main purposes. The studies facilitate internal decision making, providing necessary data for developing the concept and for preparing a realistic cash flow analysis. And lenders and investors use the documentation in their decision making. A thoroughly researched report with rigorous methodology becomes an invaluable aid for gaining financing. Analytical lenders and equity sources scrutinize the market data in a good report.

A well-documented market analysis can help obtain the necessary municipal approvals. More innovative projects in particular might need the political support that can be fostered by a clearly presented market rationale. And market studies provide invaluable guidance for planners, architects, and engineers in their design process, answering the questions "who is this project for?" and "how will the project affect the community?" Further, investing in a detailed market analysis saves time and money in the long run because it provides most of the information required for constructing a development impact analysis. Localities increasingly require development impact studies for determining impact fees (see Chapter 4).

A market analysis can address a broad spectrum of concerns. Developers of multifamily housing use general market studies to survey local or regional markets when contemplating geographic expansion, gathering information about available land, and determining feasible locations from the standpoint of costs and regulatory constraints. Market analyses also point to where the dynamics of supply and demand match the characteristics of the proposed development.

Many observers disagree about whether a local firm's real estate market analysis is better than one conducted by a well-known national firm based elsewhere. Some market analysts argue that the methods are identical no matter who conducts the analysis. Others point out that a local firm is more likely to have its finger on the pulse of the local development community and to have readily available contacts, existing databases of local development activity, and a better understanding of the local market's nuances.

Regional Context

Market analysts generally begin by looking at the regional setting where the proposed development will occur, including population and household trends, recent or anticipated changes in the economic base, and employment patterns, then narrow the focus to the county or city for more specific information. They collect data about population, households, employment, housing needs and activity, regulatory issues, transportation patterns, local schools, and other services. From there, the subject property undergoes more detailed analysis about the market areas that will specifically affect the project's development program and ultimately its success in the market.

Identifying the Market Area

The market area is the geographic area from which the majority of consumers will be drawn and the region that contains most of the competitive projects. Because of a housing market's local nature, the market area usually centers on a major employment node, a transportation corridor, or a desirable locational amenity. Physical barriers, either natural or manmade, or political considerations, such as a county line, usually determine the borders. Market analysis should target identifiable regions where the infrastructure creates market sectors of geographic, demographic, and socioeconomic interdependence.

The size of the market area varies, depending on the project proposed and the community. For example, in a densely populated urban area, a market area for a typical medium-priced rental apartment might encompass only a few blocks. In a sparsely populated semirural community with few competitive projects, the market area most likely comprises the entire county or even several adjacent counties. Further, a distinctive project with little or no competition will draw from a larger market area than a more standard project with a large pool of similar competitive projects. Most projects have a market area of no more than a two- or three-mile radius.

Housing consumers usually prefer certain geographic locales but not precise locations within those broad areas. Consumers select a geographic area based on such factors as area-wide prices, short commutes to work, cultural amenities, neighborhood quality, and the reputation of schools or other services. Multifamily households in particular tend to focus on convenience and lifestyle, putting a high value on commuting patterns, nearness of shopping, low maintenance, and amenities. Renter households tend to be smaller than owner households and are less likely to include children; schools are often not a major factor. Nevertheless, the quality of a school district may impact the overall quality of a neighborhood and its demographics.

Some questions are key in defining the market area: Where will most residents come from? What properties surrounding the subject project would a typical renter consider living in? The housing search for employed consumers often centers on where the unit is relative to the place of work.

The market analysis defines two market areas: the demand side of the economic equation (or target market area) and the supply side (or competitive market area). In most cases, these market areas are identical, although competitive projects can exist outside the target market area. In some instances, the two market areas are regions apart, as in the case of second-home resort developments. Most market areas for primary shelter, however, are within a one-hour commute of major employment centers or other key destinations.

Target Market Area

Target market areas define the location where the majority of demand for a proposed multifamily housing project exists. Various factors are considered in delineating the target market area for a proposed development:

- Travel Time from Major Employment Centers—With traffic congestion a serious problem in most metropolitan areas, housing decisions are usually based on proximity to employment. By identifying major employment centers and making assumptions regarding "acceptable" commuting time, market analysts can define a target market area. A new wrinkle in weighting this factor is the growing number of telecommuters and other home-based workers, creating new opportunities for housing those who can live anywhere.

- Mass Transportation Facilities and Highway Links—Commuting patterns and times are based largely on ease of access; thus, the target market's geographic

Nathalie Salmon House in Chicago combines family and single resident apartments with apartments for the elderly, thus broadening the project's market.

Hedrich-Blessing/courtesy of Nagle Hartray Danker Kagan McKay

Addison Circle in Addison, Texas, has easy access to major transportation corridors and airports as well as employment centers. The development will ultimately accommodate 4,000 to 5,000 residents.

Paris Rutherford/RTKL

RTKL

size is influenced by the availability of mass transit, the location of transportation corridors, and the speed at which they operate during peak travel times. Convenience of transportation is an especially important consideration for multifamily development.

- Existing and Anticipated Patterns of Development— Most urban settings contain areas of both growth and decline. Growth areas might be distinguished by certain desirable attributes, such as proximity to employ-

ment, affordability of housing, physical attractiveness, and/or outstanding community facilities. Sometimes building a desirable attribute can improve an area's desirability. Examples include new on-site amenities or services such as concierges or retail stores.

- Socioeconomic Composition—An area's income, age, household characteristics, and other demographic characteristics influence housing choice and location and thus target market areas (but note that it is illegal in the United States to target market segments based on race, religion, or ethnicity).

- Physical Barriers—Natural features like rivers, bluffs, and parkland and manmade features like highways or intensive development can sometimes form a wall through which a market's boundaries do not penetrate.
- Political Subdivisions—Municipal boundaries can be especially important when adjoining jurisdictions differ markedly in political climate, tax policies, or status, or when different attitudes about growth exist. School district boundaries are important if households with school-age children represent a major market segment. For easier data collection, a target market area often must be manipulated somewhat to conform to a political jurisdiction, such as a county or planning district within a county or city.

With these and potentially more local factors in mind, analysts should define the target market area with the objective of gathering meaningful data about market characteristics and the existence of core consumers able to purchase or rent the proposed multifamily housing product. That core comprises not only households already existing in the market area but also those willing to relocate to the area. The existing location of this core group varies with the type and location of the proposed property.

Identifying the demand-based target market area brings the analyst halfway to fully understanding the project's market potential. Often, the more significant portion of a market study is the supply side of the equation—the competitive market area.

Competitive Market Area

Unmet demand or residual demand is the key element that a market study seeks to identify. *Residual Demand* equals *Total Demand* minus *Net Absorption by Competitive Products*. To distinguish these parts of the equation, the supply of competitive projects must be understood in terms of both quantity and quality.

The competitive market area encompasses projects that potential consumers would consider comparable to the proposed development. Usually, the competitive market area's boundaries are loosely drawn to include projects that might not quite fall within the geographic market area but might be comparable for other reasons such as similar amenities, unit sizes, or neighborhood quality. An analyst usually excludes projects within the designated geographic market area that do not compete in terms of price, quality, or product type.

The projects identified as competitive provide the data the analyst uses to measure the competition and ultimately estimate absorption and capture rates and rents for the proposed project. Competitive analyses usually include only recent construction, newly renovated projects, and proposed projects that will be leasing during the marketing period, because such projects are the most comparable to new development and most suitable for assessing absorption trends. For rental apartments, those built in the last ten years would most likely be considered com-

An attractively landscaped pool is a required amenity in most suburban locales.

petitive; older properties might not have contemporary designs, features, or amenities. Exceptions include a market area with a limited number of competitive newer projects from which to draw data. Counting the entire multifamily inventory allows the analyst to consider household growth trends. This scale of analysis can use the number of multifamily units published in the most recent census with additions from building permit data.

Competitive projects should reflect the product type proposed for the subject project. Ideally, the market area consists of sufficient comparable properties to allow the survey to exclude any others. If the proposed project is a high-rise rental apartment building, only other elevator rental buildings are included in the inventory. Similarly, a proposed walk-up condominium project relies only on this type of project for its competitive survey. Further, if the proposed development will charge market rents, then subsidized or low-income targeted projects are not included in the survey. On the other hand, in a market area with few competitive projects, the prospective consumer has limited choices and so does the market analyst. In such an area, it might be necessary to widen the definition of "competitive," possibly including *all* multifamily projects in a certain rent range.

Demand Factors

Once a market area has been identified, the analyst can study its demographic characteristics. Demographic trends and projections form the basis for determining the demand for housing. Four demographic factors are of primary importance in analyzing the market potential for a project: employment, population, households, and income.

- Employment usually drives population growth. If an area has an increasing employment base, new workers will likely take up residence in the local area.

- Households are the unit of measure most relevant for assessing the potential housing market, because it is households that buy or rent a unit of housing.
- Household income is key to determining the pricing structure for the proposed development.
- Other demographic statistics may be relevant for evaluating the project's potential. An area that appeals to families but containing few small households may not generate the appropriate number of households for multifamily units. A neighborhood with an aging population might be a good area for a rental retirement community. If affordability is an issue in a particular area, unmet demand for multifamily housing might be a factor.

Employment

Demographers use projections of employment growth as one of the bases for determining population growth. For the residential market analyst, however, employment data serve as background, providing supporting evidence of market potential.

Because employment throughout a region determines population growth, the statistics gathered should be regional. Some of the employment statistics to examine include historical growth trends, total employment projections, and comparisons of local unemployment figures with regional, state, and national unemployment rates. These figures give some indication of the area's general economic health. A survey of major employers in the area, including expansion plans, reductions in force, relocations, and any new employers entering the region should be part of the employment background data. A major new industry moving into an area will most likely affect housing demand. Other factors, such as the breakdown of employment by industry and occupational classifications, are sometimes included as part of a more comprehensive market study.

Employment data are available from federal, state, and local government agencies and chambers of commerce. Federal and state agencies keep up-to-date figures on at-place employment and unemployment rates for cities and regions. Local agencies usually can provide lists of major employers and future plans for existing and new businesses. Business journals and newspapers also provide information.

Population

Population and household projections provide the number and characteristics of current and future households and thus the forecast of demand for new housing in the market area. Analysis of in-migration and out-migration also offers insight into present and future demand for housing in the market area.

Increases in population estimates typically rely on two factors: more births than deaths in the market area, and more in-migrants than out-migrants in the market area. Although population growth has slowed nationally, many regions of the country are experiencing significant surges of population growth as a result of shifts in population from other parts of the United States and immigration. Population may also shift because of changes in lifestyle and cohort- or age-related reasons, such as retirement or changes in household structure resulting from marriage or divorce.

A population trends analysis should begin with the population count from at least the last decennial census. Next, the analyst looks at the population for the current year or sometimes the midpoint between the last census and the next, depending on the availability of data. The more important but unfortunately more elusive data are the population projections for the next ten to 20 years. Some larger city or county planning agencies release reliable demographic projections, but many do not. Many large developers hire staff to generate these projections or contract with one of the large number of private firms that specialize in demographic projections and analyses. Many analysts are left to make their own projections based on past growth and development activity.

Households

Of greater significance in determining housing demand and market potential is an analysis of the number and type of households that contain a given population. Growing populations signal a corresponding, but not proportional, increase in the number of households. In many areas of the country in recent years, increases in the number of households have been more a function of decreasing household size and immigration than of natural population growth.

Over the last few decades, national trends have pointed to smaller households. In 1950, the average household contained 3.37 persons. By 1970, it had declined to 3.14 persons, and in 1990, the average household contained only 2.63 persons.[2] Forty or 50 years ago, households consisted mainly of a married couple and their children. This type of household is rapidly becoming a minority, and it continues to shrink. Today's household mix includes a broad array of nontraditional family and nonfamily household formations: unmarried couples, single or divorced parents, childless couples, singles at all stages of life, unrelated roommates, and others. Each household type has specific housing needs, and all of these nontraditional segments make for increased opportunities in the multifamily housing market. Studying specific local trends in household size and type can help determine the overall design, including the mix of bedrooms, floor plans, and amenities.

Income

An analysis of household incomes in the target market area indicates the region's economic vitality and provides valuable insight into the scope and magnitude of the available purchasing power (not counting a household's equity and appreciation). This part of the analysis involves tracking historic changes and projections in median or average household income for the target market area, secondary market area, and region, including the rate at which incomes rise and the number of households in

The outstanding design and amenities of Tierra del Rey appeal to the high-income renters of the Marina del Rey market.

© Steve Hinds Photography

© Steve Hinds Photography

each income bracket. Such information is invaluable in determining rent ranges that a significant portion of the population can afford. Income alone, however, cannot be used as an exact indicator of housing affordability. Because the affordability of housing is tied to a household's wealth (that is, the household's income and assets) not just its income, it is not possible to construct precise predictors of affordability.

Data on employment, population, households, and income can be obtained from a local planning agency or office of economic development, or from a firm that prepares customized demographic reports on specified study areas. The U.S. Census Bureau maintains a Web site with all the most recent census data, including details on population and housing characteristics. Data service companies offer computer-modeled demographic statistics, usually based on the most recent census figures. Local building permit data can be a source for estimating recent household growth, because a dwelling unit represents a household. A factor for noncompletion should be worked into the estimate. The margin of error for any of these data increases when market area boundaries differ from census tracts, particularly when market areas are small and, more important, when the census data are several years old. An area's demographics can change dramatically during the ten-year period between census years.

Real estate is different from other consumer products in that it cannot be moved to the consumer: the consumer must move to the product. Location is real estate's primary characteristic. Most projects must be custom tailored to the local market and cannot be mass produced for all markets. Because housing markets are so localized, the demographic data must be for the local area. National and even statewide trends are of minimal value in determining the market potential for a specific project.

Market Segmentation

In today's competitive environment, understanding the local market and targeting specific segments can help to set a development apart from the competition. After defining the market segment, the analyst must be careful not to overgeneralize with regard to target customers' needs. Not all young families want a suburban backyard, and not all retirees want to play golf. Within age or income cohorts, markets can be quite diverse, and to reach potential consumers, their preferences must be understood. Techniques for learning about preferences include focus groups, surveys of local residents, and surveys of current apartment shoppers. Market research can yield a wealth of information on the potential residents of a new project. But market research can also be flawed if the wrong questions are posed or the data are not interpreted correctly. It is important to be aware of the potential for incorrect assumptions.

Supply Factors

The current and projected housing stock in the competitive market area forms the supply side of the market analysis equation. Supply factors include the total number

figure 2-1

Apartment Supply in Sacramento CMSA and Natomas

Unit Type	Unit Mix		Average Square Feet		Average Rent		Average Rent per Square Foot	
	Sacramento	Natomas	Sacramento	Natomas	Sacramento	Natomas	Sacramento	Natomas
Studio/Junior 1-Bedroom	3.3%	0.0%	476	–	$467	–	$0.98	–
1-Bedroom/1-Bath	35.7%	29.6%	690	685	$565	$678	$0.82	$0.99
2-Bedroom/1-Bath	28.5%	28.2%	858	805	$619	$645	$0.72	$0.80
2-Bedroom/2-Bath	25.6%	37.7%	963	972	$743	$839	$0.77	$0.86
3-Bedroom/2-Bath	4.0%	4.0%	1,189	1,193	$839	$963	$0.71	$0.81
Townhouse	2.9%	0.5%	1,157	1,042	$838	$955	$0.72	$0.92

Age of Inventory	Unit Mix		Total Units	
	Sacramento	Natomas	Sacramento	Natomas
1990–1998	7%	23%	2,487	823
1980–1989	41%	77%	14,568	2,756
1970–1979	38%	0%	13,502	0
1960–1969	13%	0%	4,619	0
Pre-1960	1%	0%	355	0
Total	100%	100%	35,531	3,579

Sources: RealFacts; Economics Research Associates.

of units by unit type, rent levels, and absorption. These factors enable analysts to translate data about employment, population, households, and income into estimates of potential demand for a specific new development. The present rental housing stock is determined through an extensive survey of comparable currently leasing multifamily projects in the competitive market area. The future housing market must be estimated by an analysis of the proposed projects, which can be identified through preliminary and final plan approvals and relevant rezonings.[3]

Analyzing the Competition

In most housing market studies, the analysis of existing competitive projects is the study's most detailed portion. The existing project inventory provides a wealth of information about successful and not so successful projects at the current time in the specific market area. The analysis of competitive inventory usually takes the form of a narrative supported by a series of tables showing the number of units leased and the number remaining on the market, rents, square footage, tabulations of rent per square foot, and unit mix. Tables might also summarize standard features, amenities, and available options.

To identify competitive projects, there is no substitute for getting out and visiting each project in the competitive area and talking with a manager or other representative from each project. It is the only way to determine whether a project will be truly competitive with the planned development. Discussions with those already operating in the market are the most effective way to learn who makes up the market, where renters come from, what they like (or do not like) about current offerings, and what the most desirable products are for this specific group of consumers.

Market area averages and totals indicate how specific projects compare with the average and show overall leasing pace, absorption, units remaining on the market, average rents, and average square footage. Data also show which projects are leasing better than the market average and allow analysis in terms of size and rent per square foot. The market area's average rents and average absorption rate can help gauge how quickly competitive products are leasing. Arranging the data in a table or plotting a regression reveals the gaps in the market that offer development opportunities and show where the market is saturated.

The simplest way to allow for variances in rent and unit size in a project is by computing the average rent per square foot for all units in the project, even though consumers do not think in such terms. Communities with the lowest average rents or the lowest average rents per square foot should report the highest absorption rates, assuming all other factors are equal. If the analyst finds that consumers are not responding consistently to value, then all things are *not* equal and other factors must be examined.

Compiling historical data about absorption and rents for projects leasing over a three- to five-year period pro-

© Mert Carpenter Photography

Older developments often lack the amenities to compete with newer projects. At Toscana in Sunnyvale, California, a well-appointed conference center and large, deluxe gym are among the amenities that draw residents.

vides insights into the relative strength of the area's market and short-term trends. To be most useful, trend data must be put into a larger context. Analysts must determine plausible reasons for abrupt rises or falls in absorption. For example, restrictive zoning could keep absorption levels low despite strong demand. Changes in infrastructure or land uses can affect average rents and leasing pace. Completion of a new highway opens up a region, making it more desirable and causing rents to rise. Opening a new prison might make an area less desirable and cause rents to decline. A regional or national economic recession triggers a decline in absorption and rents in most housing markets. Trend data are usually available through real estate brokerage firms, real estate data services, or sometimes local government agencies.

Vacancy rates at existing competitive projects give an indication of the market's strength. A high overall vacancy rate should be seen as a sign of limited potential in that market. A 5 percent or lower vacancy rate can

figure 2-2

Apartment Rents in Sacramento CMSA and Natomas

Unit Type	9/97	12/97	3/98	6/98	9/98	12/98	3/99	6/99	Average Annual Change
Sacramento									
Studio	$401	$398	$411	$413	$416	$419	$425	$433	4.0%
1-Bedroom/1-Bath	$513	$517	$526	$531	$543	$558	$556	$565	5.1%
2-Bedroom/1-Bath	$542	$549	$555	$560	$573	$587	$589	$599	5.3%
2-Bedroom/2-Bath	$670	$680	$689	$695	$712	$723	$730	$743	5.4%
3-Bedroom/2-Bath	$771	$784	$789	$800	$824	$826	$833	$839	4.4%
Townhouse (2-Bedroom)	$706	$713	$720	$725	$750	$759	$766	$788	5.8%
Natomas									
Studio	–	–	–	–	–	–	–	–	–
1-Bedroom/1-Bath	$616	$628	$632	$638	$657	$669	$671	–	5.1%
2-Bedroom/1-Bath	$585	$595	$599	$609	$622	$679	$637	–	5.1%
2-Bedroom/2-Bath	$746	$757	$758	$769	$802	$812	$827	–	6.2%
3-Bedroom/2-Bath	$875	$907	$909	$901	$918	$923	$935	–	3.9%
Townhouse (2-Bedroom)	$895	$895	$895	$905	$905	$955	$955	–	3.8%

Note: Rents shown net of concessions.

Sources: RealFacts; Economics Research Associates.

indicate a strong market for this type of product. It is also important to view vacancy rates qualitatively. Older buildings that lack modern amenities may skew the market's vacancy rate upward and not accurately capture demand for a new project. Moreover, projects in the initial lease-up phase should be separated before tabulating the vacancy rate for the market area, as they have an artificially high percentage of vacancies. These projects do need to be counted in the absorption analysis, however.

The narrative also evaluates nonquantifiable characteristics of competitive projects. Factors such as location, design, and management must be considered. The quality of amenities or site advantages sometimes makes the difference between a top performer and a less successful project. These intangibles can often be ascertained only through discussions with leasing agents or surveys of potential renters.

Gauging the Development Pipeline

Because it can be several years before a project finally enters the market, the competitive analysis includes not only existing projects but also those in the development pipeline that will be in the marketing phase at the same time as the proposed property. They include projects requesting rezoning for multifamily residential use and those requesting site plan approval or other municipal approvals. They also include projects that did not require approvals or that were approved but were put on hold. Such projects can be more daunting to track through local government agencies, often requiring that an

analyst maintain contacts with local lenders, architects, developers, or others directly involved in the development process.

Once the proposed projects have been identified, relevant data, similar to that for existing projects, should be provided: the project name, the developer or builder, location, number of units planned, and, if known, the type of units planned, estimates of rents, and completion dates. Some data may be unavailable for projects in the early planning stages. Occasionally, a developer may be unwilling to reveal plans for a proposed development. Some planned projects may never actually get off the ground. Although the inventory of proposed projects usually fails to identify some developments and includes others that never become reality, it does provide a good overall indication of future plans for local building activity.

The completion date of proposed projects should be estimated. Projects having final approvals usually are marketed within six months, projects with preliminary approval are often six to 12 months from entering the market, and those having conceptual approval are probably at least one year or more from completion. Any developments that are in litigation, going though rezoning, or zoned but without further approvals should be included in the inventory. The status of any vacant or redevelopable parcels in the market area should be noted. Contacting the owner of such properties is often the only way to learn whether development will occur. Once a project begins to be marketed, the leasing pace can be estimated by applying the leasing pace of current projects.

figure 2-3
Multifamily Residential Project Pipeline

	Project	Units	Status
Market Area			
Sacramento (N/N or 80)	Apartment Building A	89	Construction
Sacramento (N. Natomas)	Apartment Building B	296	Construction
Sacramento (N. Natomas)	Apartment Building C	280	Approved
Sacramento (N. Natomas)	Mixed-Use Building A	180	Preapproval
Sacramento (N. Natomas)	Apartment Building D	208	Approved
Sacramento (N. Natomas)	Apartment Building E	319	Pending
Sacramento (N. Natomas)	Apartment Building F	450	Pending
Sacramento (N. Natomas)	Apartment Building G	239	Pending
Sacramento (N. Natomas)	Apartment Building H	250	Pending
Other Sacramento			
Sacramento (Southwest)	Apartment Building I	170	Pending
Sacramento (Downtown)	Mixed-Use Building B	154	Pending
Sacramento (Downtown)	Mixed-Use Building C	72	Pending
Sacramento (Downtown)	Warehouse Lofts A	26	Pending
Sacramento (Downtown)	Apartment Building J	266	Pending
Sacramento (Downtown)	Apartment Building K	272	Approved
Sacramento (Downtown)	Warehouse Lofts B	87	Approved
Sacramento CMSA			
Woodland	Apartment Building L	136	Approved
Woodland	Apartment Building M	173	Approved
West Sacramento	Apartment Building N	218	Approved
West Sacramento	Apartment Building O	170	Approved
Roseville	Apartment Building P	236	Approved
Roseville	Apartment Building Q	161	Pending
Roseville	Apartment Building R	200	Pending
Area Totals			
Market Area			
Under Construction		385	
Approved		488	
Pending/Preapproval		1,438	
Total		2,311	
Sacramento (Market Area + Other)			
Under Construction		385	
Approved		847	
Pending/Preapproved		2,126	
Total		3,358	
Sacramento CMSA			
Under Construction		0	
Approved		933	
Pending/Preapproved		361	
Total		1,294	

Sources: Sacramento, Woodland, West Sacramento, and Roseville Planning Departments; Economics Research Associates.

A growing market segment for high-end apartments is empty nesters moving down from single-family houses. The Charleston at Boca Raton, Florida, strives to capture this market with luxury appointments.

Identifying Product Types and Niche Markets

Location, site, and market potential are the factors that determine the appropriate product to be developed. An urban locale demands a different type of residential development from a suburban one. The typically higher price of urban land requires higher densities. Greater automobile ownership in suburban communities necessitates more parking. A historic neighborhood might have specific height and architectural controls that dictate development for a particular site. A waterfront site with panoramic views is better used for luxury condominiums than for entry-level housing. If the site is part of a master-planned community, any number of specific limitations could prescribe the type of project to be developed.

The identified market segment should suggest a special type of development. If the research detects strong demand from young families with small children, then the project should be planned with this market segment in mind and the greatest percentage of units should be large enough for such households. If the target market is young, first-time renters, a moderately priced project with few amenities and maximized unit space for the dollar might fit the bill. A growing elderly population might suggest a need for a retirement community and elder care facilities. Amenities, features, design, and unit size should reflect residents' needs and should be determined through market research.

Although it is frequently easy to continue developing and marketing rental products that have leased well in the past, it can be rewarding, both financially and in terms of serving a public need, to develop a new type of product. Comparable residential projects might not currently exist in the immediate market area, but if the demand analysis shows a need, the analyst should explore the possibilities. In an overbuilt market, thinking in terms of less standard types of development may lead to better opportunities but will require looking beyond the immediate market area for examples of successful comparable projects.

Any successful project results from a combination of careful analysis and instinct. But the more unconventional the concept, the less one can rely on hard data and analysis to justify it. It becomes necessary to examine successful projects relevant to the proposed concept and to determine what their attraction is. What are the projects' specifics that make them better than their competitors: unit sizes and configurations, deluxe features or finishes, recreational facilities, or exceptional value? Community amenities are an increasingly important tool in marketing a project. Many multifamily developers are racing to come up with newer and better amenities than last year's model. In addition to the obligatory pool and fitness center, some new communities feature putting greens, daycare centers, concierge services, business centers, and planned social events for residents. Units compete with deluxe kitchens and baths, decorator packages, and garages. In markets where rents are high, consumers expect deluxe features and amenities.

Traditionally, the largest multifamily housing markets have been those at both ends of the housing cycle: young singles and couples, and empty nesters. In addition to these age-related cohorts, lifestyle niches provide further market potential. They include people at income and age brackets that traditionally would purchase a single-family home but for any number of reasons choose multifamily living instead. In many instances, they make up target markets for more innovative product types.

Sometimes a new product type can be appealing to a narrow but profitable market niche. A well-conceived adaptive use of a building, mixed uses in a single structure (living above the store), or co-housing might find enough of a market niche to succeed.

Calculating Capture and Absorption Rates

Data determined through the market analysis provide a wealth of information for sound decision making. The most valuable product of market analysis is the number of units of a particular type that a submarket can absorb over a given period (demand minus supply).

Housing demand includes newly formed households, households moving into the market, and households moving within the market. Housing supply includes newly constructed units and existing units. One way to view demand for a new project is to assume that existing households moving within the market *equal* the existing supply of occupied units, allowing the analyst to subtract out both halves of the equation, leaving only the increase in households and new and vacant units to consider. In high-value real estate markets, a factor for demolition of older, functionally obsolete units may be required.

Analysts must estimate shares of this total demand that major housing types will attract—single family versus multifamily and for-sale units versus rental units. These allocations should be based on historic trends in the local market and projected based on economic and demographic changes. For example, as an area becomes more urbanized, a larger percentage of its households tend to reside in multifamily housing. Census data provide breakdowns of households by unit type and tenure (renter versus owner).

Once these data are refined, analysts can identify all components of the basic equation for demand (total demand minus total absorption by competitive products equals residual demand). Total absorption is projected based on the absorption performance of existing communities as well as projections of the expected performance of proposed communities that will be competitive during the marketing period of the subject project. The residual demand yields the number of units that can be absorbed by additional projects, including the subject property.

Once residual demand is known, the analyst must determine what share of that demand the subject project is likely to capture. Determining this capture rate is highly subjective and must take into account all the project's advantages and disadvantages in relation to all others that will be on the market. Factors to consider include

Cypress Crossing in Orlando, Florida, offers popular features like private garages, shady porches, and traditional styling.

location, site, features, amenities, design appeal, and value. The capture rate should not be overestimated. Projects currently being marketed provide a reasonable model for the potential capture rate.

Developers frequently confuse current supply with demand, interpreting a product's strong sales pace as indicative of more demand for that same product—which often leads to overbuilding. It is more useful to examine current and future holes in the market than just to concentrate on what has been leasing well. The analyst should consider some specific issues:

- What geographic submarkets have the greatest need for multifamily housing?
- What product type is needed most?
- What are the characteristics of renters who have the greatest need for units in terms of age, income, and household size and type?
- What types of features, amenities, and services do residents expect?
- What product types attract multifamily consumers and why?

Although a market study is one of the first elements in the development process, market research does not end with a project's completion: it continues after the project is up and running. In a rental project, such research is part of an ongoing effort during leasing and

management to keep tabs on competitors' vacancies, rents, and incentive programs.

Notes

1. G. Vincent Barrett and John P. Blair, *How to Conduct and Analyze Real Estate Market Feasibility Studies* (New York: Van Nostrand Reinhold, 1982), pp. 28–30.
2. U.S. Census Bureau, Historical Time Series HH6, *Average Population per Household and Family: 1940 to Present,* December 1998.
3. Figures 2-1, 2-2, and 2-3 are examples of tables used to analyze the market for a multifamily housing development in Sacramento, California.

3. Site Selection

Practices and standards for assessing a site's physical, regulatory, and environmental constraints have improved in recent years, but the difficulty of locating buildable sites has increased markedly. Because of rapidly increasing land costs and the scarcity of prime sites, properties that previously were considered unbuildable have become candidates for development. Thus, careful analysis is more important than ever for determining a site's current potential for development.

Selecting a specific property depends on a number of factors, including type of development planned, anticipated development size, cost and general location, and the market. In general, the worst reason for developing a parcel is that "I already own it." In an ideal world, a developer would always determine a development concept based on thorough market analysis and then set out to find a site with the necessary characteristics for that concept. Purchasing a site before all regulatory approvals are in place can cause problems.

Given the scarcity of buildable land, however, particularly land suitable for multifamily projects, developers frequently do have to conceive a project around a site they already own. Often, a site becomes available to a developer and a concept must be tailored to that site. At other times, a developer purchases a site for a specific project, but because of outside forces such as a change

in market conditions or the inability to obtain jurisdictional approvals, the original concept is no longer viable. In such situations, the developer must sell the property or create a new concept for it. It is absolutely necessary for the success of any development project that the site and development concept be appropriate for each other.

Factors Affecting Location

Developers often say that site selection involves three factors: location, location, and location. Certainly a residential development's success, particularly a multifamily one, has a great deal to do with its location within a metropolitan area, the position of major transportation facilities, the development's access to them, and the character of existing and prospective growth. The saying may be less important than it once was, however, because some entrepreneurial builders have created demand in areas perceived as poor locations. Such locations are risky, however, and usually must be of considerable size. They also require significant vision and creativity to ensure success. Although location is very important in site selection, balancing factors are the land cost, its suitability for development, and the developer's vision.

Foreseeing changes in the urban fabric before others do is one of the hallmarks of the most successful developers. Whether their predictions are based on careful research, intuition, or a combination of both, successful developers understand the locational dynamics well

Entrance to Hismen Hin-Nu, an affordable housing development in Oakland, California.

enough to survive over the long term. Successful developers understand how much they depend on the community's physical and financial health.

Multifamily housing, in all its shapes and forms, lends itself to a wider range of community types than single family housing. Because of its higher density and more cost-effective use of land, it is particularly suited to areas where land is too expensive for less dense housing. A downtown urban core could not support single-family houses on quarter-acre lots, but it could be an ideal site for a high-rise apartment development. Mid-rise or garden apartment developments can work nicely in a neighborhood business district and a largely residential area. Low-rise multifamily complexes are often included in the mix for master-planned communities, sometimes serving as a buffer between commercial or office uses and single-family residential areas. Often, a jurisdiction zones land for multifamily use if it has certain detrimental factors, such as being adjacent to a highway or backing up to a shopping center, making it inappropriate for single-family housing. Much of the available multifamily land in today's marketplace comes with preexisting obstacles to be overcome by the developer.

Fighting tradition or creating demand in traditionally nonresidential areas or low-income areas may carry more risks for the developer than a site in a solid, well-established residential community. Because of the dynamic nature of cities and their economies, however, perceptions of a good address constantly change.

Easy access to public transportation is an asset for multifamily projects in any price range. Consumers of multifamily housing tend to consider convenience a major factor in housing decisions, and public transit ranks high on the list of desirable conveniences. Surveys have shown that concerns about saving time and convenience are among the foremost motivations of potential and actual apartment residents.[1] In projects geared toward low-income households, land cost and convenience to work, schools, and shopping are important considerations for developers. The availability of public transportation is especially crucial in a low-income project.

Economists speak of macro- and microeconomic factors. Locational considerations can be broken into macrolocational or regional and microlocational or site-specific considerations.

Macrolocational Factors

Past city growth trends should be carefully studied to determine the direction in which high-, medium-, and low-cost development has moved. Higher-priced residential areas usually show the same general direction of movement outward from the urban center over years. If expensive residential development began northwest from the center, for example, successive outward extensions of higher-cost units usually continue in the same direction. This trend holds true even when development takes place in suburban areas outside corporate city boundaries. It is usually unwise to ignore established trends in

On the site of a blighted parking lot, Cascade Court brings affordable housing to downtown Seattle.

Seattle Housing Resources Group

Located on a light-rail corridor, Villa Torino is part of a redevelopment of downtown San Jose, California.

Riverside in Atlanta has enhanced its location by adding office and retail uses in a pedestrian environment.

land development, especially when the project is a conventional one. It is much easier to satisfy demand than to create it.

Access should be considered as one of the site's major attributes. If access to the site is available only on congested routes or through unattractive, rundown areas, it may be unwise to consider the property for development. Congestion is relative, however, and a rundown area could offer rewarding potential for redevelopment if the project's economic parameters are favorable. In some instances, it may be possible to acquire additional land or obtain rights-of-way that will permit a new or improved approach, thereby avoiding the negative image of undesirable existing land uses. In advertising a project, developers often select the most attractive route to the project rather than the shortest.

The most desirable sites for new multifamily development are those convenient to established or emerging employment centers. Sites near major employment cen-

ters tend to be the most expensive, increasingly making short commutes a luxury item. Those who cannot afford more expensive housing must often make the tradeoff in longer commuting times. Affordable housing often must be located in areas necessitating commuting times of more than an hour.

Residential developments near commercial, recreational, and cultural services will be easier to market than those located in areas where such services do not exist. Developers will benefit by asking themselves the same questions a prospective tenant would ask: "How far must I travel to shop, play, and be entertained? How long must I sit in traffic?"

The availability of utilities and public services must be evaluated carefully. In many parts of the country, permission to develop a site depends on the availability of water and sewer lines, with the jurisdiction deciding the location and timing of installation of utility systems. In other areas, lack of capacity has resulted in moratoriums

The development team is composed primarily of individuals in interrelated disciplines who contribute critical expertise to a project's completion and success.

Project Architect

A talented project architect not only determines the overall function and look of the property but also produces a distinctive, well-thought-out, and aesthetically appealing apartment community. The architectural firm chosen should have considerable multifamily design experience and be familiar with local architectural styles and building codes. The architect is involved in the project from the very beginning of the design process to the end of construction and sometimes beyond; however, the main tasks include early conceptual work, schematic drawings, working drawings, and construction administration.

Civil Engineer

The civil engineer is responsible for the property's infrastructure—water and sewer lines, storm drainage, easements, surveying, grades, roads, fire lanes, and parking—and works with the city to ensure that the property is fully integrated into the local infrastructure. A local engineer experienced in multifamily development is critical. The civil engineer is responsible for topographic surveying, designing the parking lots and access roads, refining the master plan, conducting a tree survey, and completing preliminary engineering for water and sewer lines, paving, drainage, and earthwork.

Hiring a civil engineer who also is a land planner is helpful in addressing "human" concerns, such as saving existing trees or highlighting views.

Landscape Architect

The landscape architect should have extensive experience in multifamily residential design and a clear understanding of the importance of curb appeal, overall project design, site detailing, and maintenance in determining whether a potential resident chooses to live in a community.

The landscape architect is involved throughout the entire project as an integral member of the design team, assisting in the site planning process and coordinating and melding the various components of the development into a cohesive whole. The architect's understanding of site constraints, potential costly pitfalls, ever-changing government regulations, and budget requirements can save unnecessary expense and delay. The landscape architect provides a statement of the project's central concept and schematic design, and development and construction documents.

Interior Designer/Merchandiser

A skilled multifamily interior designer is not merely a decorator, but a professional who understands the importance of functional space and successful marketing in the multifamily industry. Interior designers/merchandisers coordinate material and color selections for the entire project, including carpets, counters, walls, cabinets, and all other surfaces in individual apartments and common areas. The interior designer/merchandiser chooses common area fixtures and furniture, determines the personality and full complement of furnishings for model apartments, and sometimes even chooses the exercise equipment and pool furniture.

General Contractor

The general contractor manages the construction phase of a multifamily housing development. Although it is tempting not to use a general contractor in order to save on fees, third-party contractors often are necessary to ensure the cost-effective completion of the project.

Marketing/Graphics Consultant

A marketing professional supplies the development team with accurate information on the target market and the competition. The consultant then works with the team to establish the style and character of the new community and its marketing theme.

Consultants and Engineers

In addition to the development team, many consultants and engineers will play a role in planning the development.

- The *foundation engineer* designs the building foundation on the basis of the soil types found on the site.

on residential construction until additional capacity can or will be provided. When a residential development has several phases, the *future* availability of utilities must be carefully assessed, even when hookups for *current* phases are available.

The location and quality of public schools are important considerations for families with children. The quality of the school district can prove an effective marketing tool in some market niches. But schools may not be a factor at all if the project is geared toward non-family households.

Every prospective residential site is located within the regulatory jurisdiction of a county or municipality that will be responsible for considering the eventual development proposal. Developers must therefore consider the agency's position on growth and development, particularly attitudes toward multifamily development. Agencies often resist higher-density development, and a developer would

- An experienced *acoustical consultant* recommends construction techniques and material selections that can maximize soundproofing between apartment walls and floors.
- A *structural engineer* takes the completed building designs to determine spans and load capacity and recommends types and sizes of materials needed to obtain a building permit.
- *Mechanical/electrical/plumbing engineers* can be either independent consultants or subcontractors who design these systems.
- *Environmental consultants* perform environmental site reviews and identify and work through the regulatory approvals needed. They can provide advice on stormwater management, waste disposal, urban forestry, and other environmental concerns.
- A *market analyst* studies the market potential of the project and offers advice on pricing and product niche.
- *Traffic consultants* study the amount of vehicular traffic on each roadway affected by the new development and the number of cars that will be added once the development is completed.
- A *technology consultant* offers consultation, design, installation, and administration of telecommunications technology in apartment communities, such as hosting of Internet or intranet Web pages, video teleconferencing, and cable TV and satellite dish integration.
- A *management company* ensures the property's success by leasing units quickly to qualified residents at market rates and by maintaining the property.
- *Legal consultants* anticipate development issues associated with land acquisition, land development, partnership formation, project financing, project management, and disposition.
- The *title company* issues a title insurance policy to the owner or lender.
- A *mentor* is the final important member of a development team. The help, advice, and encouragement of an experienced professional can be invaluable in contributing to the success of any project.

■

be wise to meet with staff to understand its future dealings with the public agency before committing to a site.

Political issues must be considered when public hearings are required for regulatory approval. Successful developers understand such considerations and take the time to build political support from local government agencies and neighborhood groups.

These regional location considerations do not form an exhaustive list, but they point to some of the most frequent issues that developers should consider before purchasing a site. Each site, locale, and intended housing product requires its own set of considerations. Prudent developers know what is important in their intended market and examine the site with respect to its locational advantages and disadvantages.

Access to employment centers is the primary consideration in site selection and development, but access to local and regional shopping, schools, churches, and recreational places is also important. During the past 20 years, many urban areas increased in population without a corresponding commitment to and funding of transportation improvements. Vehicular trips generated have actually exceeded population growth because of increased percentages of two-worker families, more nontraditional households, and more young drivers. Severely congested freeways, arterial highways, and local streets, and increases in commuting times have resulted. With transportation problems on everyone's minds, developers must examine a potential site in terms of its regional and local accessibility.

Accessibility takes several forms: regional, local, site-specific, vehicular, public transit, and pedestrian. In its broadest context, a site should be evaluated for its accessibility to major employment and commercial centers in the metropolitan area, which in the past meant a site's proximity and access to downtown. But increasingly, suburban commercial centers are the focus of jobs and commercial activity.

The emergence of suburban locations is an important consideration for site selection, increasing the number of potential locations for highly desirable multifamily sites. No longer is a downtown site necessarily superior to a suburban one in terms of access to jobs and services. A site with easy access to an existing or emerging suburban core is easier to market than a more remote site that lacks such access. Developers should evaluate the growth dynamics of the metropolitan area and then determine whether a proposed site offers good regional accessibility.

Microlocational Factors
At the site-specific or microlocational level, a property being considered for residential use must be accessible to streets and major roadways. The actual nature of the streets connecting the project with the larger community depends on the multifamily development planned. A downtown development, for example, does not need highway access so much as it requires good access to local streets, sidewalks, and public transit. Suburban apartment projects usually generate significant amounts of traffic; thus, locations adjacent to collector streets and highways are advantageous. A marketing factor includes a site's visibility. A certain amount of visibility is essential, but a property without much road frontage has a quieter, more secluded feel. Secluded sites often require a larger budget for advertising and promotion.

If a property has poor or no access, a developer must be prepared to invest in roadway improvements. A difficult left turn across traffic into the project may require

Many suburban locations that were once remote bedroom communities, such as AMLI at Oakhurst North in Aurora, Illinois, are now edge cities with nearby jobs and services.

a traffic light. Any evaluation of a site must include a cost and feasibility analysis of providing access, and a determination of who will pay for it. If the project's access points conform to the jurisdiction's future land use and transportation plans, the city might aid the developer in funding certain improvements. More often, the jurisdiction looks for funding from the developer to advance its planned improvements. Alternatively, an improvement district can sometimes be created to fund improvements for a group of developments, in which all properties in the "benefit area" are assessed their share of costs and the jurisdiction picks up the public's share.

The developer should be aware of any off-site road construction scheduled to take place during the project's leasing phase. Such construction could make it difficult for potential tenants to visit the project or could aesthetically deter prospects and damage marketing efforts.

Property Tax Considerations

One commonly overlooked but extremely important item during the due diligence stage or when choosing between two or more sites is the millage rate, or tax assessment on the property. In one instance, a developer sold a property that had a cumulative millage rate—which included city, county, and school district taxes—of $2.29 per $100 of assessed valuation. Other properties in the market were closer to $2.90. When this figure was computed in the income statement on the expense side and then capitalized upon sale of the property, the seller made approximately $4,000 per unit in additional profit simply because of the lower tax rate. The following example shows how important tax rates can be.

Property A (200 Units)

Gross income	$2,400,000
Less: variable expenses	(570,000)
Less: property taxes @ $2.29	(430,000)
Net income	$1,400,000
Sale @ 8.75% cap rate	$16,000,000
Project cost	$13,500,000
Profit per unit	$12,500

Property B (200 Units)

Gross income	$2,400,000
Less: variable expenses	(570,000)
Less: property taxes @ $2.90	(500,000)
Net income	$1,330,000
Sale @ 8.75% cap rate	$15,200,000
Project cost	$13,500,000
Profit per unit	$8,500

The title company is one source of tax information; it can easily obtain the tax certificates or bills from previous years. Another good source is a tax consultant, who can fully investigate any taxing authorities, municipal utility districts, tax increment financing zones, and other tax scenarios that might apply to the property. The tax rate should be a major factor in any decision to purchase a property. It can have a tremendous effect on the bottom line as the stabilized property is operated and when the property is sold.

Although reliance on private automobiles for all transportation has been the norm for suburban areas since the 1950s, worsening traffic and longer commuting distances contribute to the increased use of transit in many metropolitan areas, especially for commuting to work. Development sites near transit stops and bus routes offer a good opportunity for multifamily development and for lower-income residents, who normally have lower rates of vehicle ownership. Unfortunately, the population most in need of convenient transit is the least able to afford the well-located housing that can provide it.

Convenience for pedestrians is an important consideration. Urban communities generally have a well-developed sidewalk system, but suburban communities have not consistently provided access for pedestrians. Sometimes suburban sidewalks are more ornamental than functional, with no links to other properties. Master-planned communities usually provide an integrated pedestrian system with trails or sidewalks linking residential, commercial, recreational, and public uses. Public streets, private trails, park areas, abandoned rights-of-way, and easements across private property should all be considered as opportunities to accommodate pedestrians, but public access must be balanced with tenants' privacy. Accommodating handicapped residents also is necessary. Wheelchair accessibility must be provided for any pedestrian byways, in accordance with the Americans with Disabilities Act of 1990.

Land Use

Existing, proposed, and historical land use patterns on and adjacent to a potential development site should be studied carefully to determine whether a potential conflict exists. Well-documented land use studies can reduce a developer's liability against potential lawsuits filed by future residents and eliminate difficulties in marketing caused by incompatible adjacent uses. A complete land use analysis includes several subjects: historical uses, current use, surrounding uses, and possible conflicting uses.

Historical Uses

Because some of the best multifamily locations lie in or near an urban area, many sites with the most suitable attributes are those that have had previous lives. A property's past, particularly if that past included any industrial uses, could significantly affect its potential for development. Federal legislation regarding cleanup and reuse of contaminated sites has opened new possibilities for land that was once abandoned as useless. The Environmental Protection Agency (EPA) defines such sites, sometimes called *brownfields*, as "site[s], or portion[s] thereof, that [have] actual or perceived contamination and an active potential for redevelopment or reuse."[2]

In 1995, in an attempt to expedite the cleanup of industrial waste sites, the EPA enacted the Brownfields Economic Redevelopment Initiative and Action Agenda. Provisions included funding pilot projects and research,

Providing safe and attractive pedestrian access is increasingly important, even in suburban communities. At Addison Circle in Addison, Texas, the ability to walk to shopping and services is an asset.

clarifying liability issues, entering into partnerships, conducting outreach activities, addressing environmental litigation concerns, and developing job training programs. Related action also has occurred at the state and local levels. One of the major effects of the brownfields initiative was an easing of previous requirements to restore a contaminated site to "pristine" conditions, making possible the cleanup and reuse of some sites once thought beyond repair.

The EPA also has issued new guidelines on limiting prospective purchasers', lenders', and property owners' liabilities. Several key issues regarding liability were addressed:

- Owners of uncontaminated property with groundwater that has been contaminated by a neighboring property will not be held liable for that contamination if the owner did not contribute to the contamination.
- Criteria are established for exempting from liability lenders or government entities that acquire a site through foreclosure, which should encourage lenders to be more willing to finance brownfield redevelopment projects.
- Guidelines for screening soil help decision makers determine those portions of a site that require further study but pose little risk to human health and therefore may be ready for development without extensive cleanup. This provision should streamline the evaluation of brownfields.
- Limitations are established for obligations of parties involved in properties where underground storage tanks containing petroleum are located.

The costs associated with surveys of historical use must be in proportion to the level of risk. A site that has been used only for agriculture may require only a cursory examination, while a site with a history of industrial activities may require both research and field tests to determine the likelihood of contamination. Prudent developers undertake the appropriate levels of analysis and then document their findings as protection against future legal action.

Some developers have begun to realize the potential of brownfields with only minor contamination. Many such sites are in excellent urban locations with ready access to transportation and infrastructure. Because environmental laws are constantly being revised, it is essential that the developer of a potentially contaminated site be thoroughly educated on the most current federal, state, and local legislation. Potential funding sources and tax incentives for brownfield redevelopment should also be fully investigated. The EPA's Comprehensive Environmental Response, Compensation, and Liability Inventory System (CERCLIS) is the federal data repository for brownfields, including information on site assessment and remediation and an up-to-date list of identified sites eligible for federal assistance with cleanup.

Not all historical uses pose development obstacles; some can be assets. Many times developers have capitalized on existing historical structures on a property by incorporating them into the development plan. The jurisdiction may require the developer to preserve and/or rehabilitate any historically significant properties on a site. Historic houses, barns, and other buildings have been successfully adapted for use as community centers or other focal points. Properly treated, such structures can lend a theme to the design and help to set the development apart from its competition. But incorporating historical

features into a new development implies additional costs that must be weighed against probable benefits.

Current Uses

Developers also need to be aware of a site's current use. Nonconflicting uses that generate income, such as farming or grazing, or even certain recreational uses, can help carry the land economically during predevelopment and development phases. Other uses—those that generate waste or damage the site's aesthetic quality—are less advantageous. The concept and purpose of a proposed project influence a developer's willingness to accept the difficulty of site assembly, removal of existing structures and physical constraints, and other limitations.

In valuable urban locations, and in some more desirable suburban locations, it is often economically justifiable to assemble multiple parcels with existing structures, clear the site, and provide a different, more intensive use, such as higher-density or more upscale apartments. This economic reality has led to the loss of housing for low- and moderate-income households in many inner cities. As a result, many municipalities offer incentives for developers to include affordable housing in new developments and often require them to do so.

Costs incurred in purchasing and improving a site derive from several factors:

- Carrying Costs—When property is acquired, expenses begin to accrue for site acquisition, taxes, and inter-

Bridgecourt in Emeryville, California, is built on a site that had been a major industrial, freight, and rail center.

McLarand, Vasquez & Partners

A landmark Beaux Arts hotel in Atlanta was rehabilitated as the Georgian Terrace, with 294 luxury apartments. A 19-story addition complements the original architecture.

est. During the time it takes to clear the site and to develop and market the project, the developer incurs substantial costs without any return.

- Demolition—Better methods of demolition—heavy equipment to bulldoze small frame buildings and dynamite to remove large masonry buildings—have greatly reduced the expense of site clearance; sometimes, the expense is reduced further by the sale of salvaged materials. A small or awkwardly configured site, however, can necessitate more expensive and time-consuming demolition methods.

- Assembly—Site assembly is most complex in urban locations where property has been subdivided many times. Government renewal and housing assistance programs in many cities can aid in the complex task of land assembly by acquiring blighted properties through condemning and clearing them and making the sites available for use at less than cost.

AvalonBay Communities

Avalon Cove is a luxury mid-rise apartment development on one of the last parcels on the Jersey City waterfront. The highly desirable site has outstanding views and is convenient to work, shopping, recreation, and services.

Surrounding Uses

The character of adjacent areas in large measure determines the use for an undeveloped parcel. If adjoining areas are compatible, they can enhance the desirability of a proposed multifamily project. When they are deleterious or conflicting, developers should proceed very cautiously.

Most desirable for multifamily development are sites adjacent to open space and community facilities like parks, museums, or libraries. Such facilities provide an attractive setting and frequently impart prestige. Because most sites are not blessed with these kinds of neighbors, however, on-site recreational facilities have become a standard in most new multifamily projects. These amenities can include improved open space, tennis courts, pools, trails, and greenbelts. In large developments, the recreational facilities and design features that can be included are almost unlimited.

Existing residential areas, either multifamily or mixed density, are a desirable setting for new multifamily de-

velopment. A site may be a previously undeveloped parcel or an underdeveloped tract in the path of suburban expansion or a bypassed parcel in the midst of a built-up residential neighborhood. If a shift to a higher density is proposed for an infill site, problems are likely to arise with regard to site planning, access and other physical factors, and the local government's and residents' perceptions of what the changes in density will mean to the neighborhood. Fortunately, multifamily development fits in well with a wider range of neighboring uses than single-family development. Other than noxious industrial or other aesthetically unattractive uses, a multifamily product can be adapted to most neighboring uses.

The municipality's comprehensive plan and zoning regulations provide an excellent perspective of the public's position about appropriate uses for any property under consideration. Nevertheless, an appealing new concept should not necessarily be rejected because it does not fit the locality's current notions of appropriate uses. Sometimes the jurisdiction may be enticed to rework its regulations to accommodate an innovative new approach to land use.

For many years, it has been common practice to place higher-density residential areas closest to commercial and industrial districts. Doing so serves to buffer single-family areas and to allow the multifamily residential areas to benefit from proximity to the higher-capacity street system and more extensive commercial and employment districts required for heavier population densities. In turn, cluster and attached housing is often located as a buffer between multifamily and lower-density, single-family development.

More recently, however, these planning practices have come into question. Local governments increasingly are willing to view development proposals in terms of integrating rather than separating different uses, a point illustrated by the increasing flexibility of land use controls through the widespread acceptance of mixed-use zoning, new urbanist concepts, and new towns. These kinds of development plans permit the mixed development of uses previously separated into exclusive districts, provided they are properly designed. The result is often a more livable, efficient, and attractive development.

The concept of synergy—that the whole is greater than the sum of its parts—is usually applied to commercial or mixed-use projects but is also applicable to multifamily sites. A good site for multifamily development is one that has positive synergy with surrounding land uses. For example, a multifamily site in an established or emerging suburban business core offers residents the convenience of employment and commercial services within easy driving or possibly even walking distances. A site in an area with several other successful apartment projects also has a kind of synergy and is more desirable than one that lacks such neighboring development. The best locations are naturally more costly than those with detrimental surroundings but are usually worth the expense, particularly for a high-end development. When selecting sites for multifamily uses, developers should look for sites with positive synergy with surrounding uses and avoid those where uses are likely to be incompatible.

Conflicting Uses

When an area's preconceived image has been created by uses incompatible with residential development, the probability of establishing a successful new development diminishes. Primary among the uses likely to pose problems for new residential development are power lines, railroad tracks, rundown commercial development, noxious industrial uses, shoddy and poorly planned existing residential development, and noise generators such as airports or congested highways.

In considering compatibility, developers should be aware of potential liabilities that could be incurred from building residential units too close to conflicting uses.

Proximity to large storage tanks of gas, oil, and other flammable materials should be avoided. Fire protection must be considered in heavily wooded or fire-prone areas, and flood damage could be an issue in flood-prone areas. Generally, protecting the public from such hazards rests with the municipality through its police powers (including zoning), but developers also need to protect themselves against possible liability by examining the potential conflicting uses near a given site.

Minimizing the adverse effects of through traffic is important. Whenever possible, neighborhoods split by existing or potential major thoroughfares should be avoided. If it is impossible to plan around a proposed highway, the developer should work with the local planning and highway departments to have the proposed road alignments as compatible as possible with the planned project. Any land that a developer might be required to dedicate to the highway department can pay big dividends in terms of better marketability for

The apartments at Phillips Place benefit from the synergies of the companion land uses; high-end retail stores, restaurants, and a cinema enhance residents' lifestyles.

the project. To avoid interference with daily life in the residential project, noise abatement measures, including walls, berms, landscaping, building setbacks, and increased window and wall soundproofing, might be required in buildings abutting heavily traveled thoroughfares.

Airports present a special case of potential adverse impacts because of recent rapid expansion of air transportation. The possible adverse effects noise has on a resi-dential neighborhood make it imperative for a developer to investigate fully a site within 15 miles of an airport to determine whether the site falls within a designated or proposed flight path. Because airports generate business and have become employment centers, nearby residential development has been spurred despite the noise. If a multifamily development is under consideration for a site near an airport, noise attenuation measures must be factored into the project's design and costs.

Al Ghurair Centre

Located in the heart of Dubai's downtown core in the United Arab Emirates, Al Ghurair Centre is undergoing a major $380 million renovation and expansion that will encompass 2.5 million square feet of mixed uses. The project incorporates the Middle East's first enclosed shopping center, originally built in 1980, and includes public and civic spaces, entertainment facilities, offices, luxury and short-term apartments, and parking.

More than 500 new and renovated luxury two- and three-bedroom apartments form the main residential compo-nent of the center. One hundred fifty new apartments will be constructed on top of a parking structure, and 365 apartments in towers above a three-level base of re-tail space will be renovated.

The 200 full-service, short-term apartment units will rival a hotel in their accommodations, services, and facilities. To take advantage of the increase in tourism in the area, the serviced apartments will provide one- to four-bedroom units to accommodate families on vacation as well as business travelers.

All units will be redesigned to include maid's quarters, storage, deluxe kitchens and baths, and new mechanical systems. Interior public spaces, including lobbies, corri-dors, and elevators, will be renovated using stone, wood, and tile finishes. The exterior will be completely reclad, incorporating traditional Arabic motifs in the design. Existing entrance and elevator towers will be topped with dramatically illuminated crowns designed to become landmarks of the cityscape.

Amenities will include a rooftop deck with an Olympic-sized pool, lush, oasis-like landscaping, children's play areas, a sports court, and a putting green. An intercon-nected network of overhead bridges and public areas will promote pedestrian traffic between the malls, apart-ments, and entertainment areas.

Al Ghurair Centre is a city within a city. Renovations will expand the complex to 2.5 million square feet of retail, office, entertainment, and residential uses.

As undeveloped suburban sites become more scarce, developers are turning to urban areas for redevelopment opportunities. Auburn Court in Cambridge, Massachusetts, is an infill project of mixed-income rental housing.

The Site

A tract of land has numerous characteristics that affect its suitability for development. Some characteristics are related to the natural geography of the land such as slope, drainage, vegetation, and soil types, while others are manmade, including boundaries, legal restrictions, and utilities.

Size and Shape

The best size for a development depends on local market conditions such as absorption rates, acceptable unit densities, and preferred amenity packages. For example, a developer seeking to rent a new project within 12 months of its completion needs to estimate the number of leases expected per month. If 15 units can be leased per month, then the developer can plan a project of 180 units. If zoning permits an average density of 24 units per acre, then the ideal site for this project would be 7.5 acres of buildable land. A larger site would accommodate more units and would require a longer lease-up period under this scenario. But because of taxes and carrying costs, the developer should not carry more land than is financially manageable. Many developers have gone bankrupt doing just that. Whenever possible, a developer should make future expansion possible through long-term options rather than outright purchase.

The site's size also influences property management. Although the optimum number of units varies by project, many developers consider 150 or 200 units the minimum number necessary to support a full-time maintenance and leasing staff. They look for sites that are large enough to accommodate that many units.

Design options increase as the site's size increases. A site that is too narrow prevents some more efficient designs, such as double-loaded parking that allows twice the parking spaces per drive area, or back-to-back units, where a shared wall accommodates utilities and units are more efficiently heated and cooled. A site that is too

deep may require a costly loop road or turnaround for emergency vehicles. A developer should always have a preliminary site plan drawn before proceeding with a contract to anticipate any development difficulties caused by physical constraints.

A project's amenities, such as pools, tennis courts, tot lots, and community centers, take additional land and require a certain number of units to be economically justified. A project with lavish and expensive amenities needs to be large enough to spread the costs of constructing and operating the facilities over enough units.

The process of land assembly is a business in itself, offering its own risks and rewards. Beginning developers should look for individual tracts that are large enough to accommodate the product they really want to build rather than trying to assemble several parcels under different ownership. Assembling tracts could involve numerous problems: multiple closings with corresponding legal fees, multiple lenders, and the possibility that key parcels cannot be acquired. Incomplete assembly carries costly penalties for developers who may have to pay exorbitant prices for outparcels or redesign a project to fit an inadequate site or give up the project altogether because of a single reluctant seller.

A skilled land planner can quickly prepare conceptual land plans showing alternative layouts for the desired product that emerged from the market analysis. Successful developers always take a market-based approach to land planning and product selection. Environmental and regulatory constraints also play a role in land planning. Although zoning determines the project's maximum densities, this maximum may not be attainable. Only after deducting acreage for streets, parks, proffered sites, environmental features, buffers, and other unbuildable areas can a planner determine a site's true yield in dwelling units.

Natural Characteristics

The parcel's natural features have a considerable impact on its suitability for development and its value. Slope,

soil conditions, geology, and hydrology all must be considered. Climate is sometimes viewed as part of the site's natural character, and solar orientation, wind, and fog conditions should be considered. Investigation of a site's development potential includes a study of natural features, usually by a civil engineer specializing in such studies.

Topography, Geology, and Soil. A site's topography influences the nature of the project and development costs. Moderately sloping sites, between 1 and 10 percent slope, are preferable to either steep or flat land. Gentle slopes create opportunities for more interesting site planning, allow for better drainage, and can reduce the amount of excavation required to provide structured parking. Flat land can present drainage problems that raise development costs. A site with steep slopes, greater than 15 percent, presents challenges that increase development costs. Some jurisdictions prohibit development or decrease allowed densities on steep slopes. On any site, however, a certain amount of grading will be necessary.

A site's geology must be considered, particularly if it lies in an earthquake-prone region. Unstable land is likely to be unsuitable for development. An understanding of the site's soil conditions is also important. Soil acts as an engineering variable not only in construction but also in waste disposal systems and water supply maintenance. The best soils are deep and moderately pervious. Heavy clay soils tend to expand and contract with water, causing foundations to crack. Impervious soils saturate quickly and cause problems with runoff. If rock is located close to the surface, excavation costs may escalate dramatically.

Radon, a radioactive gas found mainly in rocks and soil in certain geological areas of the northern United States, can exist in localized pockets anywhere. Radon gas enters buildings through foundations and moves through the building as air circulates. The greatest danger from radon exists immediately after it is released into the air. It has therefore been thought that taller buildings provide some protection. Some ongoing studies, however, indicate that air circulating through a building might transfer radon quickly enough to pose a potential hazard throughout the building. The EPA has issued a series of recommendations on reducing the risk of exposure to radon. Developers of multifamily properties should be aware of current standards and potential liability regarding radon.

Hydrology. Water is another consideration in the selection of a site. Surface water is that water exposed in lakes or streams; subsurface water occupies cracks and rifts in the soil or bedrock. Both surface and subsurface water can affect a development's feasibility. Surface water can be both a resource and a nuisance. Although people enjoy living in sight of water features and will pay a premium for views or for the privilege of direct access to water, the existence of water on or near a site can complicate the development process and add to costs. If a site contains or borders on a stream or other body of water, a floodplain study must be conducted. Some portion of the site will almost certainly be unbuildable. A developer

With careful site planning, a natural setting can be developed without destroying its assets.

One of the greatest challenges facing multifamily developers is simply finding a good site to build on. It is not just a matter of finding undeveloped land in desirable areas; it also involves finding prime sites and overcoming potential opposition that may arise while trying to acquire it, zone it, entitle it, and permit it. The bottom line is that to build successfully in any community, developers must first prove their integrity and their ability to produce quality work using designs and materials that will stand the test of time. This approach will earn the trust and acceptance of future neighbors.

Finding those neighbors is an important goal of the site search. Look for areas that are not already flush with multifamily properties. Investors look for special deals with barriers to future competition. A great location in an area with many other available multifamily sites may present too great a risk if future competition from other developers is a possibility. But if land can be secured in a good community with varied housing types and amenities and, if necessary, the target area can be rezoned from another use to multifamily housing, greater success is likely in raising development capital.

To supplement one's own skills in spotting good sites, it is often best to work with a professional land broker who knows the market area and understands the general parameters for development. When the land broker locates a property that fits the parameters for the type of community intended, whether luxury, market-rate, or affordable housing, a letter of intent expresses interest to the owner. A letter of intent is typically a nonbinding agreement that lays out the general parameters of the purchase. Consult an attorney who specializes in real estate purchases to assist with the specifics that should be included. The letter of intent, which is usually accompanied by an earnest money deposit, provides a period of time (usually three to six or even 12 months) for the developer to conduct due diligence on the site to determine its feasibility. The deposit is typically not at risk for an initial period, so it can be withdrawn at any time and for any reason. This period is essentially a "free look." Although the earnest money may not be at risk, it is possible to invest a great deal during the due diligence period

in market studies, engineering reports, architectural drawings, and legal fees for contract negotiations.

At the end of the free-look period, if due diligence proves the project's viability (it may be necessary to purchase additional time), the owner should be informed that the developer is prepared to proceed with the transaction. Estimate the time it will take to close the deal—anywhere from three to nine months. The letter of intent will then be replaced with a binding purchase contract that should be structured in a manner that gives the developer the time necessary to close the deal. The contract at this stage must include confirmation from the seller that there are no site improvements required by the municipality that have not yet been made. If the seller has made any previous commitments for on-site or off-site improvements, the new property owner assumes those obligations.

Criteria for Site Selection
Land:
- Zoning and restrictions
- Availability of utilities
- Topography and subsurface
- Environmental investigations
- Title reports and boundary surveys
- Property taxes

Location:
- Existing competition
- Potential barriers to entry
- Employment base and growth
- Access and visibility
- Adjacent property uses
- Neighborhood retail stores and services
- Education and recreation

■

should obtain a rough approximation of how much land lies within the floodplain before going ahead with a contract. Inland and coastal wetlands play a role in natural stormwater management and are vital for certain vegetation, fish, and wildlife. Because of these important ecological functions, development in wetlands is now strictly regulated.

Subsurface water must also be protected from pollution related to development. Groundwater can become

tainted from sewer lines, which commonly leak, and from polluted storm runoff.

Flood Control. A developer must be aware of any floodplains that affect the property. The potential for flooding increases when development reduces the natural floodplain or adds to runoff. Federal and state policy on flood damage control has shifted from an emphasis on structured controls such as dams and levees that often just relocate flooding, to regulatory controls like floodplain

Water access and views are popular amenities. At Glen Lakes in Dallas, residents enjoy a lakefront setting.

Mature trees are a prized amenity that should be preserved whenever possible. At Bellaire Ranch in Fort Worth, Texas, every effort was made to preserve the 100-year-old oak, elm, and cedar trees.

zoning codes, building codes, and open space programs that prohibit encroaching on the floodplain. If the site includes a flood hazard area, this land area will likely be removed from the tabulation of buildable acreage but can be used for open space and certain recreational amenities.

Vegetation and Wildlife. Selective clearing enables efficient building while maintaining some natural areas. Special efforts should be made to preserve ma-

ture trees, especially around sensitive environmental features such as streams or slopes, despite the temporary inconvenience during construction. Preservation efforts are rewarded with increased value and marketability for the project. Mature trees provide more than aesthetic appeal; they also help with erosion and sound control and improve energy efficiency. Moreover, they consistently rank high among consumers as a desirable amenity.

The developer must select a company to conduct a title search and prepare a title insurance policy. This information details the property's previous owners, deed concerns and restrictions, and the kinds of utility and other easements that may be involved. The title company also provides copies of all related survey documents—whatever agreements might exist that enable or have enabled others to use the property.

A boundary survey—a comprehensive drawing of the land that is necessary for determining placement of the project, integration of new utilities, and potential access points to existing roadways—also will pick up easements, building lines, misplaced fences, and any other pertinent information.

The seller of the property customarily provides the boundary survey, which can be addressed in either the letter of intent or the actual purchase contract. Typically, contract dates are determined by the purchaser's receipt of both the title work and an acceptable boundary survey. For example, if a 90-day free look was negotiated through a letter of intent, that period may not start when the agreement is signed but when the seller delivers the title work and the boundary survey. These documents are critical and must be thoroughly reviewed early in the due diligence process.

Large trees face considerable stress during construction. Heavy foot or vehicular traffic around the roots packs the soil hard and may kill trees. Trees often die as a result of exposure to chemicals. Even if trees survive construction, they often die later because their root systems have been disturbed or because the amount of water or sunlight they receive has changed. All of these factors can be avoided through use of a careful tree saving plan that should be an integral part of the early design process; in fact, the jurisdiction may require such a plan. Mature trees are a valuable asset to any development and often cost no more to preserve than replacement with new saplings would.

Although trees are the most obvious form of vegetation to consider in development, other forms of vegetation may require special handling. Grasslands, particularly in coastal areas, are a crucial component of erosion control. Many kinds of grasses, vines, shrubs, and wildflowers provide wildlife habitats or are included on endangered species lists, and their preservation becomes a legal issue.

Most jurisdictions require an environmental impact study as part of the approval process to assess the impact of a project on an area's natural features—including water quality, wildlife habitat, and ambient noise levels—and on the built environment—including public services, traffic conditions, and historic sites.

Easements and Covenants
An easement is the right of one party to use another's property for a specific purpose, such as running a utility line or gaining access to a landlocked parcel. Unless an easement is created with a specific termination date, it survives indefinitely, regardless of the property's ownership. Only the beneficiary, or the party benefiting from the easement, can terminate it, usually at some cost to the property owner. Utility easements usually grant access for making repairs, and new development cannot interfere with that access. For example, if pavement or a building is constructed over an easement, the utility company has the right to make utility repairs with no obligation to restore any damage done to the property owner's improvements. Utility easements commonly prohibit any placement of structures, surface improvements, or large landscape materials within the easement right-of-way.

Easements have other purposes. Scenic easements have been developed as a mechanism to preserve undeveloped rural areas with great aesthetic value. Such easements are used to protect important views in the natural landscape. Conservation easements are applied to preserve areas of ecological, historic, or scientific significance. Air rights grant permission to develop in the air space over a property, as, for example, when a railroad allows construction of an office building over a railroad station.

Covenants, also called deed restrictions, are private restrictions that remain in force for all future property owners, usually restricting the activities or uses permitted on the property. Covenants typically extend beyond regulations enforceable by public authority, but they cannot supersede public regulations or be illegal under any existing laws. A property owner may create deed restrictions at any time. Once created, however, they remain in force unless all parties subject to the covenants agree to remove them. A title survey is the only reliable document for investigating easements and covenants; they do not show up on plats. Developers must carefully review any easements and deed restrictions to ensure that none exist that will affect development.

Utilities and Public Services
Water, sanitary and storm sewers, electricity, gas, cable television, and telephone service are critical factors in site selection. Before purchasing a site, a developer should always confirm the proximity of services and whether they are available to the site. For example, a water line adjacent to the site may be unavailable to that property because the line's capacity is already committed or because the jurisdiction restricts development by limiting access to utilities. A developer should never simply take

One of the first steps in determining what utilities are available to serve a multifamily housing site is to write to local service providers. Letters should specify the location, site size, and approximate number of apartment units to be built, and include a detailed schedule for the first utility connections. A letter should go to the water department to verify water and sanitary sewer capacity, and it should request information on the size of the lines in the area, their proximity to the site, any access charges or connection fees that might apply, and any other pertinent information. Similar letters should be sent to the stormwater engineering department, the electrical utility, and the cable television franchise if applicable. The developer should obtain a letter from each provider indicating what services currently are available to the site. Investors and lenders will want copies of these letters as proof that the development will be properly served.

It is also necessary to determine whether the city or county government will assess impact fees on new multifamily construction to cover infrastructure improvements for a new development—including sewer lines and roadwork. These fees may range from $1,000 to more than $5,000 per apartment unit.

the word of the property seller but should verify availability with each utility company. Developers should ask the following questions before putting an option on the site:

• How long will it take to obtain service?
• How much will it cost?
• When is payment due?
• When must application for service be made?

Pritzker Apartments at King Farm is a mix of 402 high- and low-density units in a new urbanist community in Rockville, Maryland. Buildings fronting the streets form traditional streetscapes, while rear alleyways provide access to individual garages.

Torti Gallas and Partners-CHK, Inc.

• Are public hearings involved? (Public hearings may cause delays and increase political risk.)
• Is the provision of service subject to any potential moratoriums?
• Are easements needed from any other property owners before service can be obtained?
• Is the service capacity adequate?

Water and Sewerage. Ideally, developers want to tap into an existing suitably sized public water main on or near the site because it costs less. Thus, a developer should determine whether it is possible to connect the proposed project with an existing system and where that connection can be made. This connection could affect the planning and staging of development. If such a connection is possible, available capacity should be ascertained.

Whether an existing water main will be sufficient to serve a proposed project depends on the development's size and nature and the main's size and water pressure. The developer may be required to provide funds for upgrading the water distribution system if the existing water main proves inadequate.

The availability of water has become a critical issue in some arid western states. In the early part of the 20th century, the development boom in southern California was possible largely because water was imported from northern California and the Colorado River. Toward the end of the century, however, limitations were imposed on importing water supplies because of supplying communities' economic and ecological concerns.

Municipalities with scarce water have responded by imposing high water hookup fees on residential building permits. Others have imposed strict requirements for conserving water, including flow-restricting devices on plumbing fixtures, installation of drought-tolerant landscaping, and, in extreme circumstances, partial or total moratoriums on development until new water supplies are available. Developers should check the availabil-

Stormwater can be managed in ways that are aesthetically pleasing and environmentally sound. At Jefferson Estates in Richardson, Texas, a stormwater retention pond was carefully integrated into the landscape design.

ity of water at a site and, if it appears that supplies are limited, understand fully what will be required before a supply can be hooked up to the site.

If connection to a municipal sewer system is not immediately available, a developer should investigate the possibility of extending lines from the sewer main. Some localities maintain a policy against such expansion as a means of controlling development. Others, anxious to see urban growth, may assist developers in financing and negotiating sewer consortiums with other property owners to develop new sewer lines.

Stormwater. In the past, stormwater runoff has been handled by the most convenient method possible: the rapid disposal of surface water through closed man-made systems. Stormwater runoff has often been mismanaged under this philosophy, aggravating the velocity and volume of runoff problems downstream and increasing pollution of local streams. Potential legal

LakePointe in Kenmore, Washington, is a mixed-use project that includes 600 apartments, 200 condominiums, 400 seniors' units, and retail, entertainment, and office space in an exciting lakefront environment.

issues concerning the effects of stormwater management on adjacent properties during and after construction have led many jurisdictions to adopt stormwater management standards restricting the runoff's quantity and velocity after development to no more than predevelopment levels. Many areas also require filtration of stormwater before its release.

The preparation of a functional and aesthetic stormwater runoff plan requires coordination among the project's engineers, planners, and landscape architects. Much runoff can be handled through passive design elements, including proper grading and landscaping materials, rather than engineering systems. Such considerations need to be part of the early design plan. Recent trends in stormwater management encourage eliminating large stormwater ponds in favor of smaller "rain gardens" located throughout the development. Local stormwater management regulations may vary by jurisdiction.

Energy and Communication Utilities. Utility companies design, install, and maintain gas, electric, telephone, and cable TV lines according to their own specifications. Developers should ascertain each utility's capacity to serve the development and its policies about extending and financing the services. Utilities may be provided at no expense to the developer, or the developer may be charged the costs of extending service to the property. Relocating existing utilities may be the developer's responsibility or the utility company's obligation.

Solid Waste. The developer should determine what agency or private company is responsible for picking up solid waste, what fees are involved, and the magnitude of any potential problems with solid waste disposal to ensure that building permits are not delayed. Generally, trash pickup will not impose a constraint on development, but it will entail a tax or assessment that will be passed on to future residents.

Emergency Services. Emergency services include primarily police and fire protection, which the local jurisdiction almost always provides. Many municipalities have found it difficult to maintain emergency services during cutbacks in funding and rapid growth, however, and developers of large projects may be required to provide funds or land for new facilities in exchange for certain development rights. When evaluating a site's suitability for development, developers should consider the potential for such unexpected costs. When examining fire protection services, developers should consider the site's distance from the nearest fire station and the expected response time. Adequate access to public water supplies and adequate water pressure for fire protection should be available to the site. If the property will be gated, arrangements must be made with the relevant agencies to permit emergency access to the site.

Schools. For some multifamily developments, particularly those targeted toward nonfamily households, schools are not a major concern. But if the market analysis indicates that a project's residents will be families with school-age children, the developer must be especially concerned about the location, quality, and capacity of nearby schools. In some areas, schools are the single most important element in determining where a family decides to locate.

In an effort to create buffers for single-family areas, multifamily sites are often located adjacent to schools, making the project particularly appealing to families with school-age children. Developers of large projects, especially those targeted toward families with school-age children that would increase enrollments in schools, may be required to contribute fees or dedicate land for new schools.

Parks and Recreation. Facilities and open space for recreation are of great importance in site selection. A site adjacent to a park or recreation center comes with amenities already established, saving the developer the considerable costs of land, development, and operations. The amount and type of recreation needed vary with residents' anticipated lifestyles. Young families require play areas, young adults look for active recreational facilities, and retirees often want community centers and golf courses.

The developer's obligation to provide parks and recreation increases with the project's size. A small, 30-unit building may require nothing of the developer, but a 1,000-unit complex demands considerable recreational facilities, on site or off site. The municipality may require that the developer provide public recreational facilities in exchange for development rights. The extent of recreational facilities a developer must provide depends on the size and number of units proposed, availability of existing parks and recreation near the proposed site, and the municipality's regulatory requirements.

Notes

1. National Multi Housing Council and National Apartment Association, *The Future of the Apartment Industry* (Washington, D.C.: Coates & Jarratt, 1995), p. 33.

2. U.S. Environmental Protection Agency, "Brownfields Economic Redevelopment Initiative Fact Sheet," No. 500-F-97-092 (Washington, D.C.: U.S. Environmental Protection Agency, 1997).

4. The Regulatory and Legal Context for Multifamily Housing

Municipal, state, and federal agencies all impose stringent regulations on residential projects. These regulations have evolved over many years, and they have often been the result of efforts to reduce the presence of discrimination, unsafe conditions, or the negative impacts of development on neighborhoods and the environment. Today, the approvals process can be one of the longest and most onerous parts of the overall development process. The increase in regulatory examination means that developers have to spend more time studying the development site to ensure that the contemplated development concept is actually feasible. It also means that it is incumbent on developers and builders to understand the relevant legislation governing residential development and to do their best to comply with the rules.

Fair Housing, Accessibility, and Opportunity

The Civil Rights Act of 1968 gave the federal government the primary role of ensuring equal opportunity in and access to housing. Since the passage of the 1968 legislation, the role of HUD, the federal agency vested with jurisdiction over fair housing, has been expanded greatly. From a passive recipient of complaints by those whose

Bridgecourt in Emeryville, California, uses traditional stucco in new ways.

rights under the fair housing law had allegedly been violated, HUD was transformed into an active investigative agency, initiating its own research into the presence and scope of discrimination and other violations of fair housing practices.

Other federal agencies participate in guaranteeing equal housing opportunity and access to protected classes of citizens. The U.S. Department of Veterans Affairs has become an advocate for access to housing for the many disabled American veterans since the enactment of the Americans with Disabilities Act in 1990. The U.S. Department of Justice takes an active role in fair housing; the Attorney General may file suit in federal district court if there is reason to believe that a systematic pattern of housing discrimination exists.

The Fair Housing Act of 1968 and the Fair Housing and Fair Housing Enforcement Act of 1988

The Fair Housing Act (Title VIII of the Civil Rights Act of 1968) prohibits discrimination in housing based on race, color, religion, sex, national origin, handicap, or familial status (including individuals or families with children under 18 years of age and pregnant women). Although these groups are generally referred to as the "protected" classes and are the most likely to face discrimination in the housing market, the law protects all potential homebuyers and renters, not just those explicitly mentioned in the act.

The Fair Housing and Fair Housing Enforcement Act (Title VIII of the Fair Housing Amendments Act of 1988)

Handicapped access can easily be built into the design of a project without creating an institutional feel. At Villa Torino in San Jose, California, a ramp provides wheelchair access.

superseded the 1968 law; it emphasizes an individual's right to decent housing rather than addresses all civil rights. The 1988 act put some teeth in the 1968 legislation. Under the new law, the secretary of HUD has the authority for administering the act. The secretary's increased powers include conducting studies of suspected discriminatory housing practices in representative communities throughout the United States; publishing and disseminating reports, recommendations, and information derived from the studies, including an annual report to Congress; assisting other federal, state, and local public and private agencies to detect and eliminate discriminatory housing practices; and reporting annually to congress about the race, color, national origin, religion, sex, handicap, and family status of beneficiaries of and applicants to HUD programs. HUD receives complaints of unfair housing practices, investigates the complaints, and adjudicates them unless the aggrieved party opts to take the case to the appropriate U.S. district court.

Despite the many important enforcement mechanisms provided under the 1988 act and the new enforcement powers granted the secretary of HUD, the thrust of the new legislation remained unchanged. That is, discrimination in housing on the basis of race, color, religion, sex, age, national origin, disability, or familial status will not be tolerated under federal law. Many state and local governments have fair housing laws that are even more restrictive than their federal counterparts, and the act does not override those laws.

The law prohibits discrimination in residential real estate transactions, such as real estate sales and rentals, and makes it illegal to coerce, intimidate, threaten, or interfere with people exercising their rights under the act. It is also illegal for landlords to deny requests from disabled tenants to make reasonable modifications to housing, at their own expense, if the changes are necessary for the tenants to fully enjoy the unit. In some cases, the landlord may permit the changes only if the renter agrees to restore the property to its original condition before moving out. Landlords also are required to make reasonable accommodations in their rules, policies, practices, and services to provide an equal opportunity to people with disabilities to use and enjoy their homes. For example, a building with a "no pets" policy must allow a visually impaired tenant to keep a guide dog.

The Fair Housing and Fair Housing Enforcement Act of 1988 mandates that developers and builders of all residential structures containing four or more units designed for first occupancy after March 13, 1991, must be accessible to individuals with physical disabilities. In walkup buildings, only ground-floor units must be accessible; in high-rise buildings, all units must be accessible. (Two-story townhouses are exempt from the requirements.)

According to the National Association of Home Builders, accessibility includes an accessible building entrance; an accessible route into and through the unit; accessible public and common use areas; doors wide enough to allow passage by a person in a wheelchair; light switches, electrical outlets, thermostats, and environmental controls in accessible locations; reinforced walls in bathrooms so that grab bars can be installed if necessary; and accessible kitchens and bathrooms.[1] The law covers most newly constructed types of single-family and multifamily housing.

Detecting Violations of Fair Housing Laws

Many parties to the development process might unknowingly deny individuals access to decent, affordable housing on fair terms. These parties include architects, developers/builders, sales and rental agents, and mortgage lenders. Discrimination against prospective renters or homebuyers by any or all of these parties is unlawful. The Community Reinvestment Act of 1977 prohibits construction and permanent lenders from "redlining," that is, drawing boundaries around neighborhoods usually characterized by heavy concentrations of minority residents or low- or moderate-income households where the lender will not provide financing.

A developer or builder of multifamily housing must exercise extreme caution during several steps in the development process so as not to violate the Fair Housing Act. The first is in the design and construction of individual residences. HUD's Office of Fair Housing and Equal Opportunity issues guidelines for architects and builders to ensure access to the protected classes. The office assists developers and builders with project plans to ensure compliance with fair housing guidelines before the project begins rather than after construction has started—or, even worse, when a potential homebuyer or renter calls for an investigation.

Builders and developers of multifamily housing must also be careful with regard to the *marketing* and *advertising* used for their residential projects. Section 804(c) of the Fair Housing Act of 1988 states that "it is unlawful to make, print, or publish, or cause to be made, printed, or published, any notice, statement, or advertisement, with respect to the sale or rental of a dwelling that indicates any preference, limitation, or discrimination based on race, color, religion, sex, handicap, familial status, or national origin or an intention to make any such preference, limitation, or discrimination." For example, developers may face charges of discrimination if their advertising for one development uses racially mixed models while advertising for other developments does not.

Developers could also be liable for an advertising campaign that targets only certain geographic areas and is designed to reach a particular segment of a community. A developer's or builder's selective use of the equal opportunity slogan or logo can also constitute discrimination if, for example, the slogan or logo is used to advertise some properties but not others.

Developers and builders of multifamily housing must also be careful not to violate fair housing laws when renting units. Rental agents can prevent access to housing using many methods, ranging from the subtlest discrimination to the most blatant. For example, they can treat renters in the protected classes differently from those that are not according to how courteous they are or the extent of services they provide. The differences might include the amount of information required from prospective renters about income, assets, employment history, or credit history, the availability of certain kinds of housing, and the terms and conditions of the rental (rent, security deposit, and so forth).

"Steering" is a method of discrimination in which an agent uses favorable or unfavorable comments about an advertised apartment, its neighborhood, and schools and other public services in the area to direct prospective renters toward or away from a particular neighborhood. Although steering applies more to independent real estate agents than to a developer's in-house staff or local real estate agents with whom the developer has contracted to market the units, developers and builders must ensure that their agents do not engage in any of these discriminatory practices. Such behavior could at a minimum damage the developer's reputation and eliminate goodwill in the community but, more tangibly, expose the developer or builder to civil and criminal penalties.

Although noncompliance in design and construction is fairly obvious, noncompliance in rentals and marketing is much less so. In 1977, HUD pioneered an audit technique to measure discrimination in sales, finance, and rental transactions. Generally, an audit is conducted by teams comprising a person from a protected class and one from the corresponding nonprotected class (for

An existing property can be retrofitted for handicapped access, adding, for example, a gently sloped path where there are steps.

example, minority and nonminority). The team members are alike in all other ways. Each team member approaches a rental agent and compares treatment given the members, using various measures to uncover any discrimination. Federal, state, and local government agencies have used this method extensively to assess discrimination in rental transactions.[2] Some real estate agencies use this technique to train their agents in compliance with the law. In many instances, proper training can prevent future discrimination.

The Costs of Fair Housing Compliance

The Fair Housing Act's requirements for design and construction does add to the cost of each unit. Although cost estimates vary widely, a HUD report found that compliance with fair housing guidelines for accessibility would increase the project cost only slightly. Additional costs for compliance may require higher rents to make the project feasible, which could be particularly onerous for

One way to enable low-income households to expand their resources is to provide space for home-based businesses. At Hismen Hin-Nu Terrace in Oakland, California, housing is built above a market hall for small startup vendors.

developers trying to build affordable housing for low- and moderate-income households.

Although the costs of complying with fair housing legislation can be moderate if incorporated into the original design for the development, costs of retrofitting units can be quite formidable, even exceeding the property value. Moreover, the courts have no test of "reasonableness" that takes into account the organizational size and available resources for the modifications to make the property compliant, as it is presumed that developers were already aware of the law. As a consequence, developers cannot rely solely on local building officials to make them aware of necessary design modifications before construction. Although many developers have complained that local building officials did not apprise them of shortcomings in design before construction, both HUD and the U.S. Department of Justice have reaffirmed their stance that ignorance of the law is no defense.[3]

The cost of compliance may be high, but noncompliance can cost even more. Developers and builders can be denied federal, state, and local subsidies or have them rescinded by failing to observe the guidelines set forth in the Fair Housing Amendments Act of 1988 or the even more restrictive guidelines set by state and local authorities. Developers found guilty of one instance of noncompliance will be subject to more scrutiny on later projects.

Moreover, huge fines can be levied against builders, developers, and other parties who do not comply with the 1988 act. A prospective renter who believes that he or she has been discriminated against can file a complaint with HUD within a year after the alleged discrimination occurred. The aggrieved person may also file suit in a federal court whether or not a complaint has been filed with HUD. In addition to suits brought by private individuals, the U.S. Attorney General may also file suit in federal district court if there is reasonable cause to believe that a pattern or practice of discrimination is occurring.

Americans with Disabilities Act of 1990

The Americans with Disabilities Act (ADA) guarantees access to 12 categories of "public accommodation" and prohibits discrimination in employment and telecommunications for handicapped individuals. The ADA has very limited jurisdiction over discriminatory practices in housing.

The design and construction of a model apartment if it contains the rental office is one instance. Such models are considered public accommodation; without access to the rental office, persons with disabilities would effectively be denied housing. Models containing rental offices must be made accessible to persons with disabilities *if it is not too costly or difficult to do so.* All areas of the model used for marketing purposes, including parking (if provided), the building entrance, and internal areas, should be accessible. If it would be too costly to make the rental office accessible to handicapped individuals, however, then the law allows the meeting between the agent and the prospective tenant to take place in an accessible loca-

All public areas, including model apartments, should be designed for handicapped accessibility.

tion, such as the customer's home, another office, or any other mutually agreeable location.

Developers and builders are required to provide auxiliary aids and services for visually impaired, hearing-impaired, and speech-impaired individuals in models containing rental offices if they do not inflict "undue burden" on the builder. An auxiliary aid could be as simple as reading a sales brochure to a blind individual.

Equal Opportunity in HUD-Assisted Programs

Title VI, Section 504 of the ADA, and Section 109 of the Age Discrimination Act ensure equal opportunity to all individuals to participate in and benefit from HUD-funded activities without regard to race, color, national origin, age, or disability (or religion or sex in the CDBG program). Therefore, if developers receive federal assistance under any HUD program, including programs that insure mortgage loans, they are required to comply with all provisions of the Fair Housing Act.[4] Regardless of whether or not the developer or builder receives federal assistance, the Fair Housing Act of 1988 protects the rights of individuals that fall into the protected classes.

Environmental Laws

Perhaps the most complex legal issues are those relating to environmental concerns. Environmental issues for developers fall into two major categories: the site's predevel-

opment state, and the environmental impacts of development on the site and its surroundings. Both issues must be addressed to fully assess a site's potential for development. An undeveloped site might include environmentally sensitive areas, endangered or protected species, or other natural features that demand preservation. Or in the case of redevelopment of a brownfield, the site might contain hazardous waste that must be identified and dealt with.

Moreover, established owners and managers of multifamily property must be educated about numerous environmental issues to maintain health and safety for residents and employees, and to limit their own liability.

Environmental Issues for Developers

Developers often bring in consultants during site selection to conduct environmental studies. Environmental concerns can affect development costs, so understanding these issues before committing to a site makes economic sense. In the case of raw land development, the focus should be on environmental protection. Brownfields require investigation as to whether the site contains hazardous materials and, if so, the extent of the hazard. In addition to providing the developer with useful data, such studies are generally mandated by federal, state, and local environmental laws.

A thorough environmental study before the site is purchased can determine the potential costs and liability for protection and mitigation, but the study should not be so lengthy that the buyer loses the property to another

The Yards at Union Station is part of Portland, Oregon's, transformation of a riverfront industrial area to a thriving and diverse neighborhood.

buyer. Moreover, an overly expensive survey is not usually necessary at this point. On the other hand, if contamination is indicated, the property owner must ensure that proper studies are completed. The owner's liability for environmental cleanup or from the effect of environmental hazards can be far-reaching and expensive. If an environmental hazard is discovered at any time after the property is purchased, the owner must deal with the consequences.

Federal Environmental Laws

In the late 1960s, various federal agencies began imposing regulations on the environmental impact of development activities. Generally, any development activity with federal involvement is affected, including projects with federally backed mortgages. The National Environmental Policy Act of 1969 (NEPA) had the greatest impact, but other federal legislation has influenced land development as well: the National Flood Insurance Act of 1968, the Clean Water Act of 1972, the Comprehensive Environmental Response, Compensation, and Liability Act of 1980 (CERCLA), and the Superfund Amendments and Reauthorization Act of 1986 (SARA). Because laws are constantly evolving, this section provides only a general overview of some of the major laws that concern developers of multifamily housing.[5]

The National Environmental Policy Act. NEPA was enacted to promote environmental restoration and maintenance. The first national environmental policy, the act established the requirement for conducting environmental impact statements and assessments for developments with federal involvement.

NEPA involves a three-step process. First it is determined whether the development is subject to review. If so, an assessment determines whether the development poses a significant environmental impact. If not, a finding of no significant impact (FONSI) is issued. If, however, the potential for significant environmental impact exists, an environmental impact statement (EIS) is prepared identifying the environmental consequences of a proposed action, exposing any adverse environmental effects, and suggesting alternatives to the proposed action. If a project is expected to cause substantial environmental damage, a full environmental impact report (EIR) may be required under local or state law. Some communities that are particularly sensitive to environmental concerns may always require EIRs.

Cross-Cutting Environmental Laws. A number of additional environmental laws address the protection and con-

The National Historic Preservation Act of 1960 was a catalyst for thousands of restoration projects. Georgian Terrace began life in 1911 as an Atlanta hotel. In 1992, it was reborn as rental apartments.

servation of special resources. The EPA refers to these laws as "cross-cutters" because the requirements cut across all federal programs. The evaluation conducted under cross-cutters is usually integrated into other statutory reviews, such as the environmental review carried out under NEPA. The following cross-cutter laws are most likely to affect the development business:

- Endangered Species Act—Property owners can be liable for any actions that may directly or indirectly harm plant or animal species listed as "threatened" or "endangered" by the Fish and Wildlife Service, or cause destruction or degradation of its habitat.
- National Historic Preservation Act—This 1960 act was created to prevent the loss of irreplaceable historic buildings, structures, sites, or other objects that are eligible for listing in the National Register of Historic Places. It requires any undertakings that may affect a property on the National Register to be reported to the appropriate state historic preservation officer. It also establishes requirements for identifying and evaluating historic properties.
- Archeological and Historic Preservation Act—This act furthers the policies of the Historic Sites Act of 1935 and provides for the preservation of significant scientific, prehistoric, historic, or archeological cultural resources.
- The Wild and Scenic Rivers Act—This act preserves the free-flowing state of rivers listed in the national wild and scenic rivers system that have outstanding scenic and recreational qualities or that serve as habitats for fish and wildlife. The act prohibits any federal loans, grants, or licensing of a project that would affect the characteristics of these rivers.
- Executive Order 11990—This executive order addressing the protection of wetlands minimizes the destruction, loss, or degradation of wetlands and preserves and enhances the natural and beneficial value of wetlands. The order requires that a wetlands assessment be prepared for affected wetland areas describing alternatives considered. Procedures include a requirement for public review.
- Clean Water Act of 1977—This act, which was amended in 1987, was designed to "restore and maintain the chemical, physical, and biological integrity of the nation's waters." Protection of wetlands is the primary goal. Section 404 of the act deals specifically with wetlands, designating the U.S. Army Corps of Engineers the agency responsible for issuing permits for development of wetlands. Additionally, state regulators generally require a developer to minimize a project's adverse effects on wetlands and to compensate for any loss of wetlands by restoring or creating wetlands on or off site.

Comprehensive Environmental Response, Compensation, and Liability Act and Amendments. CERCLA was enacted largely to identify hazardous waste sites, to assess liability for their cleanup, and to create funding

Brighton Place Neighborhood Reclamation

Brighton Place is a multiphase housing project that involved the rehabilitation of 19th and early 20th century historic structures scattered throughout a badly deteriorated and crime-ridden district encompassing about five acres on Pittsburgh's North Side. The project, in 19 formerly vacant buildings, includes 34 apartment and single-family rental units, a self-service laundry, and management offices. Developed, owned, and managed by Northside Tenants Reorganization, a low-income tenant cooperative, the project used historic preservation tax credits and a mix of public and private financing from city and state agencies and several private foundations. By providing housing to needy families and rehabilitating historic structures, Brighton Place took the first step in reclaiming a badly deteriorated neighborhood. ■

Brighton Place was a piece of the renewal of Pittsburgh's North Side.

for cleanup of major areas of hazardous waste. Major hazardous waste sites were identified and placed on the National Priorities List. Liability was defined as "strict, joint, and several" and "retroactive," meaning that parties are held responsible regardless of intent or negligence, that each party involved can be held liable for the entire cleanup, and that parties are responsible for any contamination that exists, even if it occurred before CERCLA was enacted.

Auburn Court in Cambridge, Massachusetts, was built on a former industrial site. Contaminated soil was buried at legally accepted depths under parking areas or removed where necessary.

CERCLA, also called the Superfund Law, was amended in 1986 in the Superfund Amendments and Reauthorization Act. SARA increased funding for hazardous waste cleanup to $8.5 billion and more specifically defined the liability for environmental contamination. In 1996, EPA's Brownfields Economic Redevelopment Initiative established limits to liability to encourage redevelopment of previously used sites by eliminating the fear of unknown liabilities for purchasers, owners, and lenders. In sum:

At the end of the San Francisco Bay Bridge, a former industrial, freight, and rail center has been reclaimed for residential and retail uses. Bridgecourt, the residential component, includes 220 units, 91 of which are reserved for moderate-income residents.

- Landowners with no prior knowledge of contamination are no longer held liable for that contamination if they can prove that environmental due diligence was part of the process.
- If, however, an environmental assessment reveals contamination, the landowner can be held liable for cleanup without having been at fault or negligent, whether or not contamination occurred before ownership and whether or not contamination was legal at the time of its occurrence.

Environmental due diligence is the key to limiting liability for prior contamination. A property owner must therefore perform adequate environmental studies to protect against such liability.

The Environmental Assessment. For a landowner to claim no prior knowledge, under SARA it is essential that an appropriate environmental assessment be performed. An environmental assessment generally consists of three phases, each consisting of several steps:

I. Research into past uses to determine whether any potentially hazardous activities took place. Phase I research includes the following:
    • a historic chain of title search, documenting about 50 years, to reveal past owners involved in potentially hazardous activities
    • aerial photographs of large sites to locate any areas of visible environmental concern
    • a search of federal and state databases for known areas of contamination
    • interviews with local information sources regarding the site
    • a site visit to observe such concerns as storage tanks, drums, soil disturbance or discolorations.

II. Environmental sampling to reveal general hazardous waste areas, including
    • soil and groundwater testing in areas determined from Phase I activity to be likely sites of contamination

- verification of underground storage tanks
- a determination as to whether additional assessments should be performed.

III. A detailed assessment of any discovered contamination and a determination of options and costs of remediation, including
- thorough soil and groundwater testing in contaminated areas
- examination of underground storage tanks
- an assessment of the extent and nature of spillage and
- determination of options for remediation and their costs. Remediation costs, particularly if high, must be weighed against the project's continued economic feasibility.

Performing all three phases is not always necessary. Developers should use their best judgment to determine the appropriate level of assessment for the type of property studied. For example, if the first and second phase do not disclose any potential for concern, the third phase may be eliminated. If a site has very little potential for contamination, the second phase may also be eliminated. If contamination is discovered later, however, the landowner will be held liable.

Given that these assessments can be quite costly, the environmental analysis should be appropriately structured to the site. For example, if a site has been used as farmland for generations and shows no evidence of contamination, a cursory Phase I analysis is probably sufficient. On the other hand, a site with indications of buried waste should be more thoroughly investigated. CERCLA and SARA regulations are most pertinent to redevelopment of urban infill sites (see also Chapter 3).

National Flood Insurance Act. The National Flood Insurance Act of 1968 was established to provide property owners in flood-prone areas with reasonably priced flood insurance to relieve the federal government's fi-

Due Diligence on Potentially Contaminated Sites

Most knowledgeable developers and lenders routinely perform a site contamination due diligence test before closing on a real estate deal. Such a test, known as a Phase I audit, typically involves a review of government records for signs of likely chemical contamination (such as the presence of leaking underground gasoline storage tanks), a site visit, and interviews with current owners and operators. A quicker, less rigorous process for gathering information, called a *transactions screen,* often is conducted for smaller properties where contamination is unlikely. The transactions screen consists primarily of a review of government records.

The review of government records for either a Phase I audit or a transactions screen has been made simple, quick, and relatively inexpensive by the advent of sophisticated environmental databases that can provide the exact location and profile of all known U.S. sites contaminated with hazardous wastes; facilities that generate, store, treat, or dispose of hazardous wastes; underground storage tanks (leaking or not); and garbage dumps. Online access to these databases allows users to screen one or a portfolio of properties from their desks.

Operated by private companies, the databases contain information compiled primarily from state and federal government sources, particularly the U.S. Environmental Protection Agency. In addition, the Sanborn Map Company in Pelham, New York, has, since the 1870s, produced maps that are used by insurance companies to locate properties that store or produce hazardous (flammable) materials. Sanborn maps show previous uses of the property, including the location of fuel or chemical storage tanks and where potentially toxic substances were stored.

Given only an address, the firms that operate databases of environmental conditions can provide an environmental risk report that identifies potential environmental threats located on the property and in the general vicinity. They typically provide a report listing all potential problem areas and a map showing the locations of contaminated sites, underground storage tanks, and so forth within a one-mile radius of the property. The maps are designed to meet the American Society for Testing and Materials standard for the records search of a Phase I audit and the transactions screen.

Three large players in this very competitive market are Environmental Data Resources, Environmental Risk Information & Imaging Services (ERIIS), and VISTA Information Solutions. The kinds of services these companies and others like them offer include the delivery of maps and reports in only two to three days, online access to lists of suspect sites located near a client's target site, maps plotting the location of earthquake faults, and environmental profiles of individual companies or facilities.

Source: Adapted from David Salvesen, "Due Diligence Screens Made Easy," *Urban Land,* June 1994, pp. 8–9.

■

nancial responsibility for flood disaster relief. The act's second objective was to reduce damage in flood-prone areas through land use controls. By requiring localities to adopt floodplain management measures, including development restrictions in areas encroaching on floodplains, the effects of flooding can be minimized. Although the first objective has not been fully realized, flood control through responsible land use has become reality in many flood-prone communities across the United States.

Under the program, the Federal Emergency Management Agency has mapped and delineated floodplains and their potential flood hazards in jurisdictions throughout most of the country. The maps are available to guide government agencies and developers in making responsible land use decisions. Typically, local jurisdictions comply by restricting most development to areas outside the 100-year floodplain. In multifamily developments, floodplains are usually suitable for certain parking structures, landscaped areas, and passive recreational areas. Often, undevelopable floodplains can serve to meet a project's requirements for open space.

Environmental Issues during Redevelopment and Management of Multifamily Properties

Almost all redevelopment of structures built before the mid-1970s requires some environmental remediation (the removal or management of contaminants). The most frequently encountered contaminants in older buildings are asbestos in tiles and pipe coatings, lead-based paint, and polychlorinated biphenyls (PCBs), most commonly found in insulation for electrical products. Projects on previously used sites often must factor in toxic waste cleanup in their development costs. A competent environmental engineer or analyst should be consulted before undertaking such a project.

But environmental concerns do not end when a project is completed. Managers of multifamily properties must also be aware of a number of environmental issues.

Asbestos. Asbestos is a fibrous mineral that was once valued for its insulating and fireproofing qualities. Asbestos-based flooring, roofing, ceiling tiles, insulation, and other building components were used extensively until 1981, when the majority of asbestos-containing building materials were largely eliminated. The use of asbestos in building materials has not been banned outright, however, complicating the issue for developers of new projects and managers of existing projects. In the mid-1970s, it was determined that exposure to asbestos fibers posed a risk of lung cancer and other lung diseases. Remediation does not always mean removal. In many cases, simply leaving the material undisturbed is safer than removing it. Containment may be preferable. When asbestos is discovered in a building, a plan should be formulated for remediation based on the specific situation. If removal is indicated, experienced asbestos professionals must perform the job.

Amendments to the Occupational Safety and Health Administration's Construction Industry Standard made effective in 1995 place responsibility on the owner or manager of multifamily properties for making an inventory of materials presumed to contain asbestos and requiring certain measures to protect all workers from asbestos-related risk. The National Emission Standards for Hazardous Air Pollutants regulate removal of asbestos during renovation, demolition, or construction. Property owners and managers are subject to liability for anyone injured as a result of negligence in dealing with asbestos.

Lead. Most lead poisoning is caused by ingestion or inhalation of lead dust or fumes from lead-based paint, contaminated soil, and lead dust. Children under the age of six are most at risk for lead poisoning. Although it is commonly believed that children acquire lead poisoning from eating paint chips, this situation is not typical. Because dust from lead paint falls to the floor and eventually spreads around the home, children are usually exposed through inhalation and hand-to-mouth contact of lead dust.

Lead-based paint was banned for residential use in 1978 and is no longer available for general use. But it still exists in buildings constructed before that time, and managers of older properties should be aware of the potential hazard. Several testing methods are available, including sending paint samples to a laboratory for analysis, chemical testing of painted surfaces, and X-ray fluorescence, in which painted surfaces are exposed to a radioactive source to determine lead content. Once lead contamination has been established, several methods of remediation are possible:

- Replacing old painted doors, windows, and woodwork with new non-lead-painted components. This approach is often easier than removing paint from surfaces.
- Sealing lead-painted surfaces with nonlead coatings.
- Chemically stripping woodwork off site. (Stripping paint on site could generate hazardous levels of lead dust and is usually not recommended.)

Waste materials from removal of lead are considered hazardous waste in some states and must be treated accordingly. Every state has a lead control program. Property managers should contact the appropriate agencies to ensure compliance with state and local regulations. The U.S. EPA and HUD have jointly issued requirements for disclosure of lead-based paint hazards in housing. Lessors of most residential properties built before 1978 must disclose the presence of known lead-based paint; moreover, they must provide lessees with any available records or reports pertaining to the presence of lead-based paint and a federally approved pamphlet on the hazards of lead so that renters can make informed decisions.

Pesticides and Related Chemicals. Nearly every property manager will have to deal with pest control, including the elimination of termites, cockroaches, and mice, and chemicals used in landscape maintenance, such as herbicides and fertilizers. Property managers must obtain the most up-to-date information about the use, hazards, and regulation of chemicals. Qualified landscape and pest control contractors should provide material safety data sheets, prepared by chemical manufacturers in ac-

Protecting wetlands was among the environmental concerns in designing West Park Village near Tampa, Florida.

RTKL

cordance with federal regulations, for any chemical used on the property.

Indoor Air Quality. Although residential properties generally have sufficient ventilation to maintain adequate air quality, it is worth noting the most common sources of indoor air pollution. Improperly maintained heating, ventilation, and air-conditioning (HVAC) systems may be breeding grounds for microscopic organisms that could cause illness. An inadequate system might also allow smoke or odors from units to circulate to other units, leading to dissatisfied residents. Many construction materials contain formaldehyde or other chemicals that could be emitted, causing "sick building syndrome." People who are particularly sensitive or allergic to these compounds are at greatest risk.

CFCs. Chlorofluorocarbons (CFCs), which have been used as refrigerants in air-conditioning systems, have been implicated in damaging the atmosphere's ozone layer. As a consequence, the use of CFCs has been severely restricted. Procedures have been mandated for the storage, handling, and disposal of CFCs, and alternative refrigerants, retrofitted parts, and new equipment can replace all refrigeration and air-conditioning equipment using CFCs. Property managers should substitute approved refrigerants as efficiently as possible.

Radon. Radon, a naturally occurring radioactive gas, seeps into buildings from underground soil, water, or with other natural gases. Buildings with little or no underground foundation are believed to have less of a problem with radon than those with basements. Exposure to radon is known to cause lung cancer. Good ventilation decreases the risks from radon in buildings. Inexpensive radon test kits can determine the presence of radon, but a professional should test large properties. If radon is found to be present, properly sealing foundations and improving ventilation can usually abate the radon.

Underground Storage Tanks. A property may contain underground storage tanks—either in current use for heating oil or still in existence from an old, no longer used heating system or a previous land use. Federal regulation of underground storage tanks is designed to ensure that tanks are structurally sound and resist leaks, spills, and corrosion. The vast majority of tanks likely to be found on multifamily residential properties—those used only to store heating oil used on the premises and any with a capacity of 1,100 gallons or less—are not covered by federal regulations. Septic tanks and systems for collecting stormwater and wastewater, flow-through process tanks, and emergency spill and overfill tanks are also exempt.

For tanks that are not exempt, EPA regulations require owners to notify state and local authorities of the tank's existence and location. Prompt action must be taken to investigate any suspected leaks and to clean up any confirmed spillage. Tanks built before 1988 were to be retrofitted to comply with protective measures for spills, corrosion, and leaks by December 1998, and failure to meet requirements can result in penalties and civil liability.

The states are responsible for much regulation of underground storage tanks, and some states have more stringent regulations than those mandated by the federal government.[6]

State and Local Laws

Zoning and Subdivision Regulations. Zoning, nuisance lawsuits, and restrictive covenants are the three primary legal tools used for regulating land use. Zoning refers to land use control deriving from decisions by public legislative bodies and embodied in ordinances or statutes.[7] The common law of nuisance, simply put, prevents an owner from using property in ways that injure a neighbor's property. A restrictive covenant is a private agreement between parties; developers usually include a comprehensive set of private restrictions applying to a subdivision's land use.

Zoning divides communities into districts where specific land uses are dictated (for example, residential, commercial, light industrial). The forerunner of this type of

Euclidian zoning laws shaped the low-density character of suburban development that is prevalent throughout most of the United States today.

zoning was "use districts," first enacted in New York City in the early part of the 20th century, to prevent unregulated mixing of conflicting land uses. Upheld in numerous court cases, most notably *Village of Euclid, Ohio* v. *Ambler Realty Co.* decided by the U.S. Supreme Court, conventional—or Euclidian zoning as it became known—has evolved from preventing nuisances to a means for rationalizing controls over land use.[8]

Zoning is prospective rather than retroactive; that is, one cannot rely on it to correct existing conditions. But zoning effectively maintains the character of existing built-up areas.

Zoning usually is a municipal function. A municipality's authority to enact a zoning ordinance comes from enabling legislation,[9] which lists specific purposes for zoning, the first being to promote citizens' health, safety, morals, or the general welfare. In addition, the enabling act specifies a zoning ordinance's purpose as lessening congestion in the streets, securing safety from fire, panic, and other dangers, providing adequate light and air, preventing overcrowding of the land, avoiding undue concentrations of population, and facilitating adequate transportation, water, sewerage, schools, parks, and other public requirements. The zoning power stems from the police power of government to protect its citizens. States delegate this power to municipalities. With prevention of congestion one of zoning's prime purposes, planners in the first half of the 20th century believed that directly restricting development densities could best advance this goal.

Since then, the sprawl caused by the abundance of low-density development spawned by the zoning ordinances has changed many planning officials' thinking. Planners are now able to see advantages of more compact development, particularly at transportation nodes where heavy capital investments in public transit systems rely on the concentration of population associated with high-density housing. Although the true economies and diseconomies of sprawl are arguable, sprawl undeniably reduces the effectiveness of public transportation systems as more

individuals depend on private automobiles.[10] The idea of compact development has spurred many jurisdictions to promulgate zoning ordinances that encourage both rental and for-sale multifamily housing. High-density housing as an alternative to sprawl benefits residential developers, who often prefer to develop multifamily housing, especially where land prices are relatively high.

In addition to reducing sprawl, zoning for multifamily housing has been widely used as a policy tool to increase an area's supply of affordable housing. Whether increased densities actually reduce rents is debatable. Some developers have found the cost savings from higher densities are often offset by the higher land values and construction costs. Moreover, whether zoning for higher-density housing is an effective policy to ensure affordable housing is questionable as well, because decreased housing affordability is largely attributable to lagging incomes rather than higher housing costs.

More effective housing policies aimed at reducing housing costs for lower-income residents may include more rental vouchers and certificates to prospective occupants and the provision of direct project-based subsidies to developers of housing so that savings reach economically disadvantaged tenants. But federal project-based subsidies for the construction and substantial rehabilitation of affordable housing have been curtailed dramatically, with some programs like Section 8 new construction and Section 8 substantial rehabilitation eliminated altogether.

Higher-density housing does not necessarily represent a compromise for homebuyers who cannot afford single-family dwellings or renters who have not yet achieved homeownership. The presumption that single-family detached units are the dwelling type of choice for all households is incorrect. A household's preferred type of housing is strongly correlated with its stage in the life cycle. For example, a young professional couple may prefer to purchase an apartment condominium, not just because of its affordability but also because of the lifestyle it offers. Other factors can also influence a household's preferences:

ethnic and cultural background, past experiences in different living environments, or tolerance for having neighbors living close by. Given that some people prefer multifamily living, it is incumbent upon local jurisdictions to make provisions for multifamily housing in their zoning and other land use codes.

During the 1970s and 1980s, residential zoning came under assault by housing organizations and civil rights activists for its sometimes exclusionary effects. Exclusionary zoning refers to ordinances that effectively exclude most low-income and many moderate-income households from an area without directly prohibiting low- and moderate-income households from occupying housing in the area so zoned. Because a strong correlation exists between low incomes and minority status, communities that substantially restrict multifamily housing tend to exclude minorities.

One of the most prevalent techniques of exclusionary zoning prohibits multifamily housing. By limiting development to single-family dwellings, a community can effectively eliminate the most realistic opportunity to house low- and moderate-income people. Multifamily housing generally represents such an opportunity, because higher densities usually mean lower costs per unit and federal subsidies to developers are often geared to this type of housing. Precise factual data as to the national incidence of zoning ordinances that totally or substantially exclude multifamily dwellings are lacking, but it is clear that such exclusionary ordinances are quite common.[11] Like the total prohibition of multifamily housing, the impact restricts construction of affordable housing.[12]

The legal backlash from these exclusionary zoning practices caused many municipalities to reevaluate their zoning ordinances and to provide for a greater range of housing. Many developers of multifamily housing now face fewer zoning obstacles than they did in the past in certain areas. Indeed, some communities have even gone so far as to adopt "inclusionary zoning" provisions—a mandatory setaside of a specified percentage of housing units for low- and moderate-income households within each new housing project. As an incentive to construct such affordable units, developers may be offered density bonuses or relief from other standard exactions or development fees. Residential developers, particularly multifamily residential developers, should become familiar with the zoning designation for each site under consideration to determine whether any inclusionary provisions exist and, if so, how they can best be met.

Although many jurisdictions have been trying in recent years to encourage the development of affordable housing, particularly rental apartments, a countertrend has occurred in some jurisdictions because of the abundance of high-density housing. Prince George's County, Maryland, for example, a suburban county in the Washington, D.C., metropolitan area, now discourages high-density housing development to reverse outcomes of previous planning policies and zoning that encouraged high-density housing there. Developers' requests for sewer and water connections are sometimes denied unless the proposed projects are for lower-density single-family detached subdivisions with large, amenity-rich homes.

Another recent trend in zoning is the increased involvement of the public in land use decisions, sometimes called the NIMBY (not in my backyard) movement. Residential developers have found it increasingly necessary and advantageous to begin working with neighborhood and citizens' groups early in the planning process to avoid controversial public hearings and potential major changes to a proposed development plan. This observation is particularly true for developers of multifamily housing, as residents of predominantly single-family developments are often opposed to allowing high-density housing nearby.

In most municipalities, citizens' groups exert tremendous influence over local decision making and discretionary matters such as development permits. Further, 21 states and the District of Columbia have constitutions that allow voters to effectively bypass the legislature by allowing voters to accept or reject lawmakers' decisions (by

High-density housing can be a lifestyle choice for those who prefer urban living. This luxury high rise includes penthouse units and rooftop terraces with a pool and meeting facilities.

Sometimes NIMBY factions can be appeased by designing an apartment community to resemble the single-family neighborhoods that surround it, such as at Stone Manor in Frisco, Texas.

referenda) and/or permitting voters to actually propose and act on proposed legislation (initiatives).[13] Because zoning is a legislative action in most states, it is legally open to such initiatives and referenda; the frequency of initiatives and referenda related to land use escalated during the 1980s (especially in California), largely because of citizens' concerns about growth, traffic congestion, and loss of open space.

Zoning by referendum or initiative has become a concern for the development community and others. Although initiatives and referenda cannot be used to promote racial discrimination, some have argued that in fact the end result of some of these procedures is racially discriminatory—that the racial composition of neighborhoods can be altered by those actions that limit housing types and land uses. But discriminatory intent is difficult to prove. Courts in some states have ruled that these procedures do not apply to zoning because they preempt statutory procedures for notices and hearings.[14]

Despite concerns over these procedures, zoning by referendum or initiative is a growing regulatory problem for many residential developers, especially for developers of rental multifamily and affordable housing projects. Developers should be aware that zoning by referendum is a real possibility and measure carefully the controversy a potential development project might generate. The direct involvement of citizens in making decisions can result in considerable costs, loss of time, and possibly the inability to gain entitlements to use.

Flexible Zoning

By the 1970s, growing dissatisfaction with the patterns traditional zoning dictated (sprawl, segregated land uses, unreasonably low densities) led to the creation of a number of new development concepts and techniques, which in turn inspired the development of new, more flexible, zoning techniques. This section summarizes some of these techniques.

Floating Zones. A municipality defines a floating zone for a particular land use before identifying specific sites for the zone. Flexible zoning recognizes that a specific land use may be appropriate at some locations in the municipality without having to identify exact locations in advance. Floating zones are sometimes used for multifamily and special-purpose housing but seldom for single-family residential development. The first major court decision upholding floating zones concerned a floating garden apartment district.[15] In that case, the court ruled in favor of both the apartment project and the use of a floating zone. Developers of multifamily residences applying for a floating zone should understand the considerable municipal discretion this technique implies. Applications for a floating zone are often mired in long review periods, and are subject to input and considerable resistance from citizens; moreover, projects approved are often subject to numerous conditions.

Performance Zones. Rather than specify absolute densities (for example, dwelling units per acre) or building types that are allowed in a certain zoning district, performance zones rely on a set of standards that a development must meet as a prerequisite for approval. In residential projects, the standard of density is widely used. Although the average density of the total site is held constant, density over portions of the site may vary. For example, if a developer has a 75-acre site on which he would like to build various products at various densities and the average density for the site is four dwelling units per acre, then one possibility is to divide the site into three 25-acre portions. On the first portion, the developer can build six units per acre, on the second four units per acre, and on the third two units per acre. This combination of densities averages out to four units per acre, the average density allowed over the entire site.

Planned Unit Developments. Regulations in traditional zoning ordinances establish minimum standards, for example, an insistence on at least eight-foot yards on each side of single-family detached homes. These rigid minimum standards constrained better urban design, however. Zoning for planned unit developments, or PUDs, represents a departure from these kinds of standards. A PUD is a flexible tool that permits development that may not strictly comply with traditional cookie-cutter standards; the flexibility usually generates a better-designed project and amenities than would be likely under a more traditional zoning ordinance. A residential PUD can provide for more products and densities. More important, flexibility allows the development to respond more quickly to changing housing markets and demographic conditions.[16]

Transfer of Development Rights. A transfer of development rights (TDR) offers a remedy to landowners who are unable to develop their property to the maximum extent normally permitted by law because, for example, of a need to preserve environmentally sensitive land or a historic structure on the site. In such cases, the landowner can sell those "unusable" development rights to other landowners, who may apply those rights to their own properties. Many municipalities have successfully used TDR programs to preserve acres of open space, historic districts, or prime agricultural land by transferring development to areas where more intensive development is seen as desirable. TDRs, however, are administratively cumbersome and may raise constitutional questions.[17] Therefore, residential developers considering developing a site subject to TDRs should work with a qualified land use attorney.

Typological Coding. With new urbanism on the rise, some communities are supplementing traditional zoning, or even abandoning it altogether, in favor of typological coding. Introduced to the planning profession in the early 1980s by architects Andres Duany and Elizabeth Plater-Zyberk, typological coding contrasts markedly with zoning in that land uses are not prescribed. Instead, coding defines a set of building, street, and open space "types" to be used as building blocks to design the community.

Avalon at Arlington Ridge is a new urbanist neighborhood in Arlington, Virginia. It replaces housing built in the 1950s with high-density mixed-income housing.

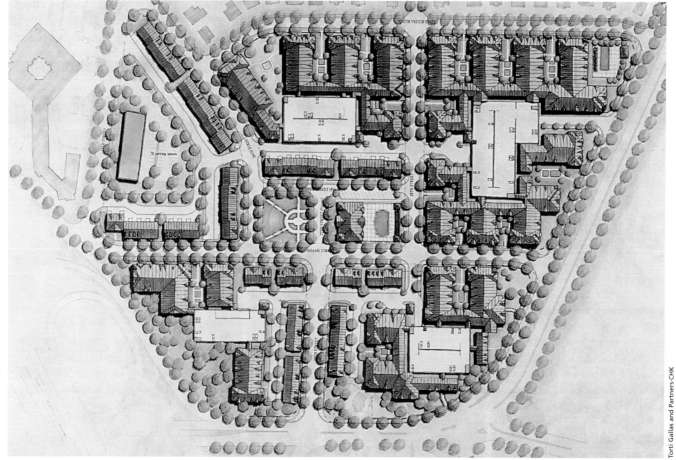

New urbanist coding produces a more urban character, as illustrated by Gables at Celebration in Florida. Front porches engage the street and allow for interaction between residents and pedestrians. Garages are located at the rear of the buildings.

A detailed regulating plan maps all streets, blocks, and lots, and assigns a building type or types to each lot. Other diagrams show how the building should sit on its lot.

Unlike zoning's "bubble diagrams," which dictate density and land use with little design control, the first priority of typological coding is to shape a community's public realm—its streets, squares, and parks—through the configuration of surrounding buildings. Drawings of proposed designs are fairly detailed, because critical elements are pinned down at the planning stage rather than hashed out during design review. Because the approach establishes so specific a plan initially, it enables the jurisdiction to eliminate the often contentious and arbitrary design review process and offers developers the assurance that if the project is in compliance with the code, it will be approved. Many regulating plans and codes are extremely short and to the point, with the full document as few as two or three poster-sized sheets.

Building and Fire Codes

Unlike the land development process, which is subject to a multitude of government regulations, construction of multifamily structures themselves is subject to only one significant public control—the building code.[18] Building codes follow one of three model codes. The most widely used model is the Uniform Building Code issued by the International Conference on Building Officials (ICBO) and used throughout the West and Midwest. In the Northeast, the predominant model is the National Building Code produced by Building Officials and Code Administrators International (BOCA). In the South, the Standard Building Code developed by the Southern Building Code Congress International (SBCCI) is most widely used. The organizations responsible for overseeing the model codes are also members of an umbrella organization, the Council of American Building Officials (CABO). CABO was formed in part to improve communications among the three organizations and to develop national standards for projects receiving federal funds.[19]

Some states have developed their own building codes —some drawn from a combination of the three model codes. When they do exist, comprehensive statewide building codes take three major forms: codes applicable only to buildings constructed with public funds, mandatory statewide codes, and codes available for optional adoption by municipalities. Nearly half of all states have no statewide code at all, giving the responsibility to individual jurisdictions.

The lack of standardized building codes creates problems that are exacerbated when new federal laws affecting residential structural design are passed. For example, a developer could be faced with having a project conform to several different codes in large metropolitan areas encompassing portions of several states, each with its own mandatory codes. Furthermore, some or all of the states within the multistate metropolitan area may set minimum standards and allow municipalities to amend them to meet local needs.

The movement toward standardized building codes is gaining momentum because of the difficulty of applying numerous and varied local codes to actual development projects. Indeed, building codes are becoming more standardized thanks to the International Code Council (ICC), an organization created in 1994 for that purpose. The ICC has already completed the International Plumbing Code (IPC), the International Private Sewage Disposal Code (IPSDC), and the International Mechanical Code (IMC). All have the support of the model organizations. Other model codes the ICC has worked on include the International Building Code (IBC), International Fire Protection Code (IFC), International Property Maintenance Code (IPMC), and International Zoning Code (IZC). As of 2000, all of them have been updated and published, and the ICC is now working toward getting the new codes officially adopted by jurisdictions around the country.

Building codes have been a major impediment to developers of rehabilitation projects; bringing old buildings up to current codes can be difficult and expensive. But in 1998, the state of New Jersey was the first to develop a separate code for rehab projects, recognizing that older buildings do not necessarily need to be brought up to the same standards as new construction to be safe and secure. New Jersey's rehabilitation code has served as a model for other states that are developing separate codes for building rehabilitation.

Have building codes achieved their goals? Building codes are created to guarantee homebuyers, renters, mortgage lenders, and others with a financial stake in housing a universally accepted level of safety and quality.[20] In fact, numerous policy reports argue that today's housing problem is mainly one of affordability and not one of poor quality or substandard construction. It can be argued that the decline in the incidence of inadequate housing has resulted more from the growth of the total stock, with building codes enforced on the bulk of new additions, than it has from a reduction in inadequate units. Thus,

building codes appear to have contributed substantially to the improvement of the housing stock.

In addition to guaranteeing a certain level of safety to homeowners, tenants, mortgage lenders, and others with a financial stake in the property, building codes often influence the site design and designation of lots as they relate to such items as attached garages, building heights, required exits, and setbacks, especially for multifamily dwellings.

Exactions and Impact Fees

To recover what is perceived as the public cost of new development, local ordinances often require developers to dedicate land, improvements, or fees as a condition of approval. In the past, these dedications were primarily for the basic infrastructure necessary to serve the development site, such as on-site roads and utilities. Now, however, dedications or exactions are often required for off-site improvements above and beyond

Every aspect of a project's design must comply with local building codes.

the immediate infrastructure needed for a development site.

Today, exactions may be required for improvements to arterial streets, flood control facilities, sewage treatment plants, schools and parks, fire and police stations, open space, or almost any other public necessity.[21] Developers are required to share the costs of infrastructure needed by the proposed subdivisions even if the improvements are not situated directly on the new development site. Also known as *shared infrastructure costs,* they are an alternative to development exactions, impact fees, and growth fees. Despite many alternatives for financing capital improvements, including taxes, general obligation bonds, revenue bonds, tax increment financing, user charges, special assessments, and special districts, the trend has been toward more widespread use of exactions by local governments.[22]

Some local governments have adopted standards by which to measure exactions, while others determine exactions project by project, thereby complicating a developer's ability to predetermine a project's feasibility. When no standards exist to measure exactions, developers can use exactions levied on similar developments in the area to "price" exactions for a feasibility analysis and as a basis for negotiating "equity."

Using exactions to finance infrastructure improvements raises a host of legal questions. Is the exaction a tax or a regulation? Does the local government have the authority to adopt such taxes or regulations? Do exactions violate the basic constitutional guarantees of due process and equal treatment? The legality of exactions rests on their relationship to the needs generated by the proposed development. For exactions to be legal, they must be "reasonably related" to the need generated by the proposed development.[23] In land use law, such reasonableness is usually determined by the "rational nexus" test rather than the "reasonable relationship test" and the "specifically and uniquely attributable test."[24] The rational nexus test for reasonableness represents a mid-

way position between the extremes of the reasonable relationship test and the specifically and uniquely attributable test. The reasonable relationship test essentially says that as long as there is some relationship, no matter how general or how long term, between the needed improvements and the new development, exactions are valid. On the other hand, the specifically and uniquely attributable test gives validity only to exactions arising from a need specifically and uniquely caused by the new development.

Under rational nexus, the midway position, development is viewed as a legitimate business enterprise that must not be unduly hindered by exactions or allowed to escape the expenses it incurs. For example, requiring a developer to improve a flood control channel that will not benefit the proposed development is not allowed; however, if the subdivision will drain into the channel, an exaction can be imposed for the proportionate contribution to the needed improvements. Exactions that benefit the community only (but not the development) are not legal, but developers do not always dispute this issue because court challenges are protracted and expensive and can undermine a developer's ultimate right to build.

Even when local governments have the necessary authority, developers can challenge the constitutionality of exactions imposed on them. A shared infrastructure cost may be charged with due process violations if the exaction is believed to "extend beyond the authority of the police power because it is arbitrary and capricious, and lacking a rational basis."[25] Unequal discriminatory effects, such as when the benefits that will accrue to current residents differ from those that will accrue to residents of the proposed development, raise the constitutional question of the guarantee of equal protection under the law.

Developers can sometimes take an active role even before impact fees are determined, thereby eliminating the need to go to court at all. Often communities

Almaden Lake Apartments in San Jose, California, takes advantage of an adjacent regional park and shares amenities and infrastructure with an adjoining single-family development. Such efficiencies help to make this affordable housing possible.

The pool and clubhouse at Summit Plantation in Plantation, Florida, are enhanced by dramatic lighting.

trying to avoid protracted court cases seek state guidance in drafting exactions and impact fees. Builders and developers who are involved can raise their concerns at this stage. Early intervention and involvement by developers will help ensure the fairness and uniformity of fees.[26]

On balance, the trend seems to offer wide support for development exactions for almost unlimited purposes so long as the purpose reflects a problem created to some degree by the particular development, the amount of the exaction bears some rough proportionality to the share of the problem caused by the development, and the exaction will be used to alleviate the particular problem created.[27] Because of the many legal challenges developers and landowners can raise, local governments should exercise caution in determining appropriate impact fees and exactions.

Local governments often rely on computer models to assess the impact of proposed developments on the existing infrastructure.

- Will the increased number of school-age children overburden the current school system?
- Will new schools need to be constructed?
- Can major arterial roads near the community handle the increased volume of traffic?
- Do roads need to be widened or generally improved?
- Will certain intersections warrant a traffic signal after development?

Careful analysis of current capacity versus future needs will lead to exactions that more closely reflect the proposed development's contribution to potential problems.[28]

Development exactions manifest themselves as dedications of land, construction of public facilities, and cash payments. Dedications of land usually take the form of a fixed percentage of the total amount of land in the subdivision or a density formula in which a given amount of land is required per dwelling unit or lot. The latter

formula is particularly applicable to multifamily housing. Some communities may give developers credit for private facilities in the proposed subdivision that reduce the need for new facilities. For example, a developer that plans private recreation facilities in the proposed development may be required to dedicate less land (or pay a smaller in-lieu fee) for the addition or improvement of nearby public parks.

Improvements to streets and utilities are specified on the recorded plat or map and, if the facilities are to be dedicated to the municipality, must meet public design standards. Improvements built by the subdivider that will remain in private ownership are sometimes constructed at standards less than the community would normally require. For example, private streets may sometimes be built narrower than would be required for public streets. Rarely do subdivision regulations require a developer to actually build a school or park. Residents of more than a single subdivision, or condominium or apartment complex, generally use such facilities, and serious issues of equity would be raised if the developer of a single subdivision or condominium or apartment complex were required to pay for recreation facilities that would benefit residents of other subdivisions or complexes.

In small developments, which may characterize the lion's share of multifamily housing developments, it is more likely that exactions will be made through impact fees rather than dedication of land and infrastructure improvements. A requirement for dedication of parks, schools, and other public facilities would be too great a burden for a small site. Instead, fees are combined with those obtained from other small developments to provide the necessary public improvements at some off-site location.

To ensure that developers complete the necessary improvements in accordance with the plat of record, municipalities require that a security be posted. Several options are available. The subdivider may:

Pritzger Residential at Celebration, Florida, includes 726 apartments. Six different building typologies of regional architectural styles create a varied neighborhood.

- obtain a performance bond from a surety company;
- obtain an irrevocable letter of credit from a lender (often the lender who is providing construction financing);
- place cash in an escrow account held in trust by the local government or by a financial institution;
- escrow personal property (stocks, bonds, equipment) or mortgage or give a deed of trust on real property; or
- enter into a three-party subdivision improvement agreement with the subdivider's lender and the local government.

If one of these options is used, the bond may not be released, the letter of credit withdrawn, the account closed, or the contract completed until a representative of local government (engineer or public works director) has certified that the required improvements have been completed according to specifications.[29]

Given the choices, developers prefer to minimize their upfront cash outlays. Thus, letters of credit from the construction lender or other financial institution, if acceptable, are preferred to cash escrow accounts.

Development Fees. Development fees (also called impact fees, infrastructure fees, capital facility fees, and connection fees) are payments assessed on a development to recapture the proportional share of public capital costs required to accommodate that development with public necessities.[30] As mentioned, developers of smaller projects are generally required to pay fees rather than dedicating land or constructing and dedicating public facilities. The fees are then pooled with fees from other small developments to fund capital improvements to infrastructure, provide parks, build new schools, and so forth. Development fees are similar to development exactions, but they are generally not applied to improvements related to a site. Many communities use development impact fees as an alternative to more traditional sources of funding large-scale capital improvements (e.g., taxes, general obligation bonds, revenue bonds, and assessment districts).

Impact fees charged against a development for capital improvements include police and fire protection, im-

proved transportation, water and sewer systems, solid waste disposal, parks, drainage systems, public schools, libraries, and other public facilities. Fees vary widely but may exceed $10,000 or more per single-family detached housing unit. Figure 4-1 depicts a typical fee schedule by land use type. Research indicates that the fees are generally passed on to consumers in the form of higher prices or rents.

Although the fee levied per unit of single-family detached housing is often higher than the fee levied per apartment, impact fees nonetheless tend to be regressive. That is, impact fees are more burdensome for households that occupy apartments and, on average, have lower incomes and a lower ability to pay than households occupying single-family detached homes.[31]

Similar to development exactions, it is illegal to assess developers with impact fees used to provide benefits to residents of other developments. In addition, fees for new development may not legally be used to pay for capital improvements required for existing municipal needs. Rather, the fees must be used for capital improvements required to meet needs created because of the new development. In practice, it is often difficult to distinguish between needed preexisting and new development-related capital improvements.

Determining Impact Fees. Some localities have adopted standards for measuring contributions from developers while others determine contributions case by case, complicating the developer's ability to judge valid costs and project feasibility. In most jurisdictions, fiscal impact analysis has become a sophisticated and comprehensive assessment.

The most common method employed has been the per capita multiplier, in which service costs per unit of population or employee are derived and then applied to the anticipated population increases or employees to be generated by the development in question. These costs are then matched against growth-induced revenues to yield the net fiscal impact. Today, more refined methods often consider the effects of a development over time, including the build-out period. Another refinement is the more accurate gauging of the number and types of populations to be generated by specific housing products. For example, an apartment development generally generates fewer school children per unit than a single-family development.

A more sophisticated and accurate method is marginal cost case studies. Site-specific scenarios are generated to gauge the project's service and infrastructure costs based on existing capacity to serve the new development and then calculating the additional need for services and facilities.

Residential Rent Controls and Other Rent Restrictions

Residential rent controls represent a threat, albeit a diminishing one, to the continued development and construction of new multifamily housing.[32] By 1995, 31 state legislatures had passed laws prohibiting local governments from adopting residential rent controls. Even in the more than 200 communities in the United States that have some form of residential rent control, concentrated in four states and the District of Columbia, most local ordinances exempt buildings constructed after a certain date, generally the date of the passage of the legislation. Most new rental housing is largely unaffected by rent control, but the continued possibility of new or strengthened rent control laws justifies a reexamination of residential rent controls.

Rent control ordinances vary widely from locality to locality—from very strict controls that restrict rents to well below market levels to more temperate ones that allow reasonable rent increases over a period of time. The differences in the stringency of rent controls have important implications for the burdens inflicted on owners of multifamily rental housing.

More temperate rent control ordinances generally have several common characteristics.

1. They generally exempt new construction.
2. They generally allow owners to raise rents enough to *adequately* compensate for inflation-induced increases in operating and maintenance costs and any rise in the general level of prices.
3. They generally include provisions that allow owners to raise rents to market-determined levels once the initial tenant moves out.
4. They allow owners to pass the costs of building improvements on to tenants without tenants' prior approval, and they have a relatively short amortization period for recapturing the investment.
5. They define *hardship to the owner* liberally and consider financing terms in determining the allowable increase in rents to adequately compensate the owner for the hardship.
6. They are much more permissive about allowing owners of rent-controlled housing to remove their units from the rent-controlled stock by converting rental units to for-sale condominiums (pending the approval of only a small share of tenants and requiring owners to reimburse displaced tenants for only small shares of relocation expenses), by converting their buildings from residential to nonresidential uses, and by completely demolishing the multifamily rental housing.

figure 4-1

City of Long Beach, California, Development Fee Schedule

School Fee

Commercial: $0.31 per square foot

Residential: $1.93 per square foot

Sewer Capacity Fee

$59.52 per equivalent fixture unit per Sections 107 and Table 10-1 of the Uniform Plumbing Code

Commercial: Applicable to all added plumbing fixtures

Residential: Applicable to new units only

Park and Recreation Facilities Impact Fee

Commercial: No fee

Residential:

Single-Family Dwelling Unit: $2,680 per unit

Multiunit Development: $2,070 per unit

Mobile Home Dwelling Unit: $1,522 per pad

Secondary Housing Unit (granny flat): $1,522 per unit

Accessory Residential Unit (artist studio, caretakers unit, personage): $1,015 per unit

Transportation Improvement Fee

Commercial (citywide)

Industrial: $1.10 per square foot

Office: $2.00 per square foot

Retail: $3.00 per square foot

Hotel: $750 per guest room

Movie: $140 per seat

Commercial (downtown CBD)

Office: $3.00 per square foot

Retail: $4.50 per square foot

Hotel: $1,125 per guest room

Movie: $90 per seat

Residential

Residential: $1,125 per unit

Senior Citizen: $663.75 per unit

Source: City of Long Beach, Department of Planning and Building Web site: http://www.ci.long-beach.ca.us/plan/develop.htm.

Developers considering multifamily rental housing projects must consider the degree of rent control prevailing in the area and local politicians' general attitudes about rent controls. Rent control ordinances restrict potential developers' and investors' ability to obtain the rent required to make the project feasible. If rents are severely restricted, investors will likely abandon plans for new rental housing altogether, although exempting newly built units from such controls is intended to prevent this occurrence. A healthy skepticism on the part of developers about such exemptions is prudent. For example,

Located on a former industrial site in Santa Cruz, California, Sycamore Street Co-op provides housing for low-income residents. Each unit has an accessory unit that can be sublet or used for a small home-based business.

New York City has twice enacted such laws only later to place new units under controls.

Rent control can create unanticipated negative outcomes in the rental market. The supply of new units may be constrained by developers who are afraid of the long-term consequences of rent control or the possibility of future rent control. Developers may choose to develop in markets where rent control would be unlikely, leaving the rent-controlled market out of balance with more demand than supply and consequently even higher rents in the nonrestricted apartment units. Often a free and open market is more effective at keeping rents affordable.

The deterioration of existing multifamily housing also may be an outcome. If owners of the older stock of rental housing cannot raise rents sufficiently, many will forgo maintenance, accelerating the pace of deterioration.

The adoption of residential rent controls has been defended as necessary to insulate low-income households from rising housing costs, but often the intended beneficiaries do not benefit. Rather, a moderate- or even middle-income household moves into a unit, has a substantial increase in income, and remains in the unit, thereby locking out an intended beneficiary.

The federal government can also restrict rents on multifamily rental units built under many of its housing programs. Generally, the government requires that developers receiving federal subsidies set aside a certain percentage of units for households with incomes below certain percentages (30 and 50 percent) of HUD's metropolitan area median family income. The maximum allowable rent to the tenants on these set-aside units cannot exceed 30 percent of the tenant's income. For units receiving Section 8 rental assistance, HUD pays the difference between the maximum allowable rent and the fair-market rent for the area (as determined by HUD).

The production of rent-restricted low-income multifamily housing is generally not financially feasible because of the limited revenue stream. The federal government recognizes this reality by providing subsidies to providers of rent-restricted housing. State-administered LIHTC programs also address this problem by providing tax credits to compensate for the restricted rents. Rent control regulations make no such accommodation for loss of revenue and create financial imbalances for property owners.

Another major difference between rent restrictions brought about by federal programs and rent restrictions that are a result of rent control is the issue of choice. A developer can choose to accept or reject federal subsidies or tax credits and can budget for this choice in the pro forma. In the case of rent control, the developer has no choice in the decision: if the law is applicable to his or her units, the rents must be restricted, with no compensation for the loss of revenue.

Regulations Governing Conversion to Condominiums[33]

Rapidly rising housing prices coupled with regulations, including rent control, that restricted the profitability of rental housing during the 1970s ushered in changes to the legal ownership of many multifamily rental properties from single ownership by a landlord to multiple ownership, particularly condominium and cooperative ownership.[34] The ownership of approximately 366,000 rental units was changed to condominium or cooperative ownership between 1970 and 1979, with 70 percent of such conversions occurring between 1977 and 1979.[35]

Trends in the Conversion of Rental Housing to Condominiums and Cooperatives. The condominium conversions of the 1970s evoked growing concern that such conversions would erode the supply of affordable rental housing. The concentration of conversions in areas with the highest housing prices was perceived as a threat by many middle-income renters, who feared they would be displaced or, if unable to buy converted units themselves, be forced to pay higher rents to the purchasers (investors) of their units.

A 1980 study by HUD allayed the fear that the condominium conversion frenzy would seriously reduce the number of affordable housing units nationwide. It found that between 1970 and 1979 the nation's rental housing supply was reduced by only 10,000 units overall.[36] Moreover, the study found that developers were more likely to convert properties already out of reach of the nation's low-income households. Thus, the snowballing movement to restrict the conversion of rental housing to condominiums and cooperatives began to melt as the threat of the disappearance of the low-income housing stock faded.

Despite escalating home prices between 1980 and 1991, the number of condominium conversions abated somewhat as a result of several factors. The Economic Recovery Tax Act of 1981 (ERTA) restored favorable tax treatment for investment in new and existing multifamily rental housing. In addition, the decline in the use of rent control ordinances restored the profitability of rental housing. Moreover, among the localities with rent control ordinances, an increasing number adopted vacancy decontrol provisions, which allowed the rent-controlled units to return to market-rate housing (at least for a certain period of time) after the initial tenant moved out.

The exception to the slowing condominium conversion craze occurred in urban areas experiencing high and escalating home prices. Despite the favorable rental climate, the property value of condominiums was higher than the value of the same properties as rental housing. In Seattle, for example, soaring home prices caused a dramatic jump in the number of conversions. In the first five months of 1990, 38 apartment buildings containing 508 units were converted, compared with only five buildings containing 44 units converted in all of 1989.

The rate of condominium conversions picked up somewhat after passage of the Tax Reform Act of 1986 (TRA 1986). The many benefits accorded rental real estate under the real estate–related provisions of ERTA were either drastically reduced or eliminated altogether under the new law. TRA 1986, with its lower marginal tax rates on ordinary income, encouraged developers to build for-sale housing or convert rental units to condominiums or cooperatives. Despite renewed interest in condominium conversion during the 1990s, the pace never approached the levels reached in the late 1970s.

Regulations. The wave of condominium conversions during the 1970s evoked swift responses from state and local governments concerned about the eviction of renters, the loss of affordable rental housing, and the legal ramifications of this relatively new form of ownership. In many areas where soaring home prices accelerated the pace of condominium conversions to unprecedented levels, conversions of rental apartments to condominiums were banned completely.

Rather than banning conversions, many states passed laws and local ordinances that fall primarily into three categories: 1) protection of tenants, 2) protection of the rental stock, and 3) protection of buyers or consumers. Ordinances protecting tenants focus on preventing landlords and converters from evicting tenants of buildings slated for conversion without according them various pro-

tections, including the right of first refusal to purchase the units they reside in and allowing them sufficient time to relocate. In New Jersey, for example, a no-eviction bill passed in 1987 gave tenants occupying apartments slated for conversion three to four years to vacate their residences.[37]

Ordinances protecting rental stock focus on preventing the disappearance of the housing stock affordable to low- and moderate-income households. The 1980 HUD study dismissed this concern, but interest has been renewed in recent years as Section 8 contracts between private developers and the federal government expire. A possible outcome will be the additional loss of affordable housing as private owners convert their assisted housing to market rate.

Ordinances protecting consumers and buyers focus on protecting purchasers of converted units from defects in the units, similar to other consumer protection laws. All products, including condominiums, carry with them implied contracts between the seller (the developer or condominium converter in this case) and the purchaser that the products will indeed perform the services they were designed to provide without compromising the safety and security of the purchaser. If the courts determine that the product fails to do so, then the seller is liable for the damages incurred.

Ordinances regulating conversion of rental housing to condominiums and cooperatives often impose significant costs on owners of multifamily rental housing. Devel-

A courtyard affords space for children to play at Sycamore Street Co-op.

To Convert or Not to Convert

Condominium conversion is a very complex and very expensive process. Developers or owners of multifamily property should carefully weigh both current and projected local market conditions before undertaking conversion. The following summary of market demand factors should be considered before conversion is recommended.

- Strong Demand for Homeownership—Demand is particularly strong in periods when homeowners can gain substantial returns on their equity, in areas where demand is high for owned housing rather than rental housing, and where affordable single-family homes are in short supply. Demographic and employment shifts also play a role.
- Declining Profitability of Rental Property—Conversions represent an opportunity to dispose of unprofitable rental property when rising operating costs make it difficult for a multifamily rental building or complex to generate sufficient cash flow and a reasonable return on investment.
- Social and Demographic Factors—Increases in one- and two-person households combined with consumers' preferences for more carefree living arrangements and amenities favor homeownership in condominium or cooperative units. In rapidly growing metropolitan regions, in-migrants may be attracted to condominiums for similar reasons. Converted units may fill a large short-term niche in an area where production of single-family units cannot keep pace with the influx of population.

■

opers often have to obtain special permits to convert the units and meet other conditions of conversion. Therefore, owners of multifamily rental housing wishing to convert their units should be aware of the costs involved and weigh total conversion costs against expected benefits. Developers and owners must make sure that their planned units (after conversion) meet the specifications for condominiums, which are more stringent than those for rental apartments.

The courts have generally held that conversions from rental housing to condominiums and cooperatives constitute a change in land use rather than simply a change in ownership. The change from rental housing to condominiums and cooperatives is subject to zoning laws on land use (zoning variations, zoning amendments, and so forth). Converters must be aware of the implications for zoning that the new land use will have and the additional time required to get the zoning change required for the conversion.

Developers of condominiums (both new construction and conversions of rental housing) are subject to a host of regulations, even after the units are converted and sold. In addition to guaranteeing that the product delivers to the purchaser what was explicitly guaranteed or implied, developers may have certain fiduciary responsibilities to the unit owners, condominium association, and/or cooperative apartment corporation even after the sale of the units. This responsibility arises from contracts, including leases, that developers may enter into with the condominium association or cooperative housing corporation during the formation of these corporate entities when the developer had the controlling interest.

Because of the myriad complex laws governing the conversion and contracts entered into with the condominium association or cooperative apartment corporation, developers considering converting rental housing or building new units would be wise to consult an attorney. Moreover, developers applying for funds from the federal HOPE 6 program to convert privately owned, government-subsidized rental housing to units available for resident ownership are also subject to the program's regulations. Therefore, thorough knowledge of federal programs and program rules and regulations is imperative for developers obtaining funds from federal programs.

Notes

1. Rhonda L. Daniels, *Fair Housing Compliance Guide,* 2d ed. (Washington, D.C.: National Association of Home Builders of the United States, 1995).
2. See Mary Boehling Schwartz, An *Assessment of the Evidence Regarding Fair Housing Testing,* National Association of Realtors® Working Paper, October 1987, which examines four fair housing studies, including HUD's 1979 Housing Market Practices Survey, the Greater Dallas Housing Opportunity Center/HUD 1979 study, the City of Boston/Abt Associates 1981 study, and the University of Colorado–Denver 1982 study.
3. Robert J. Alberts, "1988 Fair Housing Amendments Force Expensive Retrofitting of Multifamily-Unit Developments," *The Lieder,* Spring 1996: www.liedinstitute.org/s961.htm.
4. U.S. Department of Housing and Urban Development, *1993 Programs of HUD* (Washington, D.C.: U.S. Department of HUD, September 1993).
5. For the most up-to-date information regarding federal environmental laws, see EPA's Web site: www.epa.gov/.
6. Property owners and managers should contact the appropriate state environmental or health department for information on state regulations.
7. Norman Williams, *American Land Planning Law* (Chicago: Callaghan & Company, 1988), p. 434.
8. *Village of Euclid, Ohio* v. *Ambler Realty Co.,* 272 U.S. 365 (1926).
9. U.S. Department of Commerce, Advisory Committee on Zoning, *A Standard State Zoning Enabling Act under Which Municipalities May Adopt Zoning Regulations,* rev. ed. (Washington, D.C.: U.S. Dept. of Commerce, 1926). This model act was first issued in 1924, but the 1926 revised edition serves as the model for most state statutes permitting zoning. An excellent overview of the zoning process is

Herbert H. Smith, *The Citizen's Guide to Zoning* (Chicago: American Planning Association, 1983).

10. See J. Thomas Black, "The Economics of Sprawl," *Urban Land,* March 1996, pp. 6, 52, for a stimulating discussion of the economics of sprawl and who actually pays for sprawl.

11. Daniel R. Mandelker and Roger A. Cunningham, *Planning and Control of Land Development: Cases and Materials* (Charlottesville, Virginia: Michie Company, 1985), pp. 304–5.

12. Stephen R. Seidel, *Housing Costs and Government Regulations* (New Brunswick, New Jersey: Center for Urban Policy Research, 1978), pp. 169–70.

13. Iver Petersen, "Land Use Decisions via the Ballot Box: The Public Is Deciding Some Tough Questions on Zoning and Growth," *Urban Land,* August 1988, p. 33. Reprinted with permission from *The New York Times.*

14. Daniel R. Mandelker, *Land Use Law,* 2d ed. (Charlottesville, Virginia: Michie Company, 1988), pp. 273–79.

15. *Rogers* v. *Village of Tarrytown,* 96 N.E.2d 731 (N.Y. 1957). See also Mandelker, *Land Use Law,* pp. 260–62.

16. For additional information on planned unit developments, see Colleen Grogan Moore, *PUDs in Practice* (Washington, D.C.: ULI–the Urban Land Institute, 1985); and ULI–the Urban Land Institute, *Trends and Innovations in Master-Planned Communities* (Washington, D.C.: ULI–the Urban Land Institute, 1998).

17. Mandelker, *Land Use Law,* pp. 443–45. For an overview of programs and practices related to TDRs, see Richard J. Roddewig and Cheryl A. Inghram, "Transferable Development Rights Programs: TDRs and the Real Estate Marketplace," Planning Advisory Service Report No. 401 (Chicago: American Planning Association, 1987).

18. Stephen R. Seidel, *Housing Costs and Government Regulations* (New Brunswick, New Jersey: Center for Urban Policy Research, 1978), pp. 71–72. Seidel notes that "in addition to the building code, which principally is concerned with the shell of the structure, local building departments also commonly administer plumbing and electrical codes."

19. Steve Carlson, "Model Code Primer," *Journal of Light Construction,* January 1989, pp. 41–43.

20. Ibid, p. 72.

21. For an excellent discussion of exactions, see James E. Frank and Robert M. Rhodes, eds., *Development Exactions* (Washington, D.C., and Chicago: Planners Press and American Planning Association, 1987).

22. For a good overview of alternatives for financing infrastructure improvements, see Robert W. Burchell, David Listokin, et al., *Development Impact Assessment Handbook* (Washington, D.C.: ULI–the Urban Land Institute, 1994).

23. Mandelker, *Land Use Law,* p. 372.

24. Some recent court decisions have turned their backs on the rational nexus test of reasonableness in favor of the reasonable relationship test, which justifies exactions under less restrictive conditions and thus requires developers to "pay" for more new development-related needs. In many cases, however, the U.S. Supreme Court has overturned the decisions of lower courts relying on this less restrictive test for reasonableness. Thus, local government planners and regulators need to exercise greater caution in imposing exactions, impact fees, and conditions on development approvals.

25. James B. Duncan, Terry D. Morgan, and Norman R. Standerfer, *Simplifying and Understanding the Art and Practice of Impact Fees* (Austin, Texas: City of Austin, 1986).

26. Andrea LaFreniere, "Special Assessments: Soaring School Fees Present New Test for Builders," *Professional Builder,* August 1994, pp. 12–13.

27. Fred P. Bosselman and Nancy Stroud, "Legal Aspects of Development Exactions," in Frank and Rhodes, *Development Exactions,* p. 103.

28. See Burchell, Listokin, et al., *Development Impact Assessment Handbook,* pp. 163–74, for a discussion of the history of exactions, legal, policy, and substantive issues raised by exactions, and the development of a computer model that simulates the impact of a proposed development.

29. Frank S. So and Judith Getzel, eds., *The Practice of Local Government Planning,* 2d ed. (Washington, D.C.: International City Management Association, 1988), pp. 234–35.

30. James C. Nicholas, *Planning a Justifiable System* (Gainesville, Florida: Holland Law Center, 1987), p. 1. For a detailed discussion of development fees, see Arthur C. Nelson, ed., *Development Impact Fees: Policy, Rationale, Practice, Theory, and Issues* (Washington, D.C., and Chicago: Planners Press and American Planning Association, 1988); and Thomas P. Snyder and Michael A. Stegman, *Paying for Growth: Using Development Fees to Finance Infrastructure* (Washington, D.C.: ULI–the Urban Land Institute, 1986).

31. James C. Nicholas, "On the Progression of Impact Fees," *APA Journal,* Autumn 1992, pp. 517–24.

32. This section draws almost exclusively on Anthony Downs, *"A Reevaluation of Residential Rent Controls,"* a paper submitted to the National Multi Housing Council, April 1996.

33. This section draws heavily on *The Housing Ladder: A Steeper Climb for American Households* (Washington, D.C.: National Association of Realtors®, November 1990), pp. 39–67.

34. Condominium ownership involves the sole possession of a structure, land, or air space together with an undivided interest in common areas. Cooperative ownership involves the purchase of shares in a nonprofit housing corporation that entitles the owner-occupant to live in a particular unit in a multifamily building and use its common areas.

35. U.S. Department of Housing and Urban Development, *The Conversion of Rental Housing to Condominiums and Cooperatives* (Washington, D.C.: U.S. Government Printing Office, 1980), p. i.

36. Ibid., pp. i–ix.

37. Jeffrey Hoff, "Bill against Condo-Conversions Debated," *New York Times,* June 17, 1990.

5. Financial Feasibility Analysis

The next important step in completing a feasibility analysis for a multifamily development is to evaluate its financial feasibility. In essence, this analysis is the one lenders will want to see to make sure the project will live up to its performance expectations. How one analyzes the financial feasibility of apartments is similar to the process used for all income property. The steps of financial analysis begin with a simple back-of-the-envelope capitalization and end with direct equity, joint venture, or syndication analysis.

Analysis of any income property involves five stages:

- Stage 1—The pro forma statement: simple capitalization of pro forma net operating income (NOI);
- Stage 2—Discounted cash flow (DCF) analysis of annual cash flows during the operating period's stabilized cash flows;
- Stage 3—Combined analysis of the development and operating periods;
- Stage 4—Monthly cash flows during the development period;
- Stage 5—Discounted cash flow analysis for investors.

This chapter concentrates on Stages 1 and 2 and a before-tax version of Stage 5. Of all the stages of analysis, Stage 2 is the most important. It is known by various names, including DCF analysis and justified investment

Addison Circle brings an urban lifestyle to an edge city, Addison, Texas.

price analysis. Appraisers do a form of Stage 2 analysis when they compute the unleveraged returns on a building from the time of stabilized occupancy to final sale in seven or ten years.[1]

As part of the general framework, it is helpful to distinguish the development period from the operating period (Figure 5-1). The development period runs from the time the developer purchases the land through lease-up of the property. Although the operating period begins when the property is put into service, appraisers and lenders typically evaluate the property from the time it reaches stabilized occupancy (normally 95 percent)—the time when the permanent mortgage is funded—through final sale. Stage 2 analysis is used to evaluate this period (although in some cases the permanent mortgage may be funded in stages).

Stage 2 analysis is the developer's version of the architect's sketch pad. The developer goes through many iterations of Stage 2 analysis. For the first iteration, rents, expenses, costs, and other assumptions are crude estimates based on cursory evaluation. By the time developers are ready to commit to the earnest money contract (remove any contingencies that may allow them to get back the full purchase deposit on the land), they should have the best information possible about the property's expected performance. This information forms the basis for computing the expected returns to the developer and investors, assuming the property is purchased at the given price. If it is a to-be-built property, then the total estimated project

figure 5-1
Development and Operating Periods

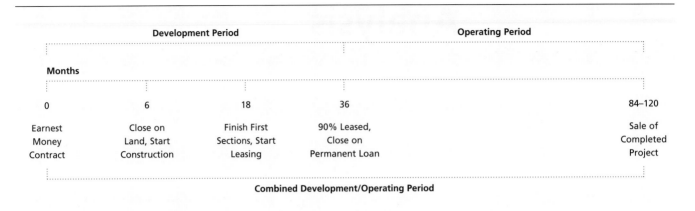

cost from inception to stabilized occupancy is used instead of the purchase price.

The stages of analysis correspond to major hurdles in the course of financing a project. Stage 1 is the developer's first cursory analysis based on simple pro forma income and cost estimates. Stage 2 justifies the overall value of the investment as an operating real estate venture and is given to mortgage brokers and lenders who will provide permanent financing. Stage 3 gives the de-

figure 5-2
Underlying Assumptions for a New 158-Unit Apartment Complex in Dallas, Texas

Total Project Cost	$7,834,355
Operating Reserve	$389,676
Total Capital Cost	$7,444,679
Net Present Value Discount Rate	20%
Years for Analysis	7
Mortgage Parameters	
Equity	$1,406,331
Principal	$6,428,024
Interest Rate	8.5%
Term (years)	25
Monthly Payment	$51,760
Annual Payment	$621,122
Depreciation	
Building Basis	$6,841,330
Life (years)	27.5
Factor	1.0
Straight-Line Depreciation	$248,776
Capitalization Rate at Sale	9.5%
Commission on Sale	4%

veloper a picture of the overall development, from inception through final sale. Stage 4 is given to the construction lender in support of the estimated construction loan required and interest reserves during construction and lease-up. Stage 5 is given to potential investors in support of the returns they will receive if they invest in the property given a specific deal structure.

The following case study illustrates the stages of analysis for a new 158-unit apartment complex, Shady Hollow, in Dallas, Texas. The complex has one-, two-, and three-bedroom units averaging 844 square feet that rent for an average of $698 per month. Estimated development costs total $7,832,000. Figure 5-2 lists the underlying assumptions for the property.

Stage 1—The Pro Forma Statement

The first step is to create a pro forma statement that estimates rents and expenses for the stabilized project. Inputs include the type and size of apartments to be built and market rents for the apartments (see Figure 5-3). The other needed inputs are estimated vacancy rate and operating expenses. Both the income and expense estimates should reflect local conditions and any specific features of the project. Income and expenses should reflect conditions as they will be at the time that leasing begins; for example, if the project is expected to require a year to design and build, rents and expenses should be projected as of a year from now. For Shady Hollow, the pro forma indicates total income of $1,298,190 and NOI of $872,375 (see Figure 5-4).

Calculating the Maximum Loan Balance

The project's pro forma NOI is the basis for determining the size of the loan for the project. Lenders use two common criteria—debt coverage ratio (DCR) and loan-to-value (LTV) ratio—to determine the maximum loan amount.

The debt coverage ratio is a tool used to measure the financial risk of an investment. It is calculated by divid-

figure 5-3
Rent Summary

Unit Type	Number of Units	Square Feet per Unit	Rent per Square Foot	Rent per Month per Unit	Total Square Feet	Total Annual Rent for Unit Type
1-Bedroom/1-Bath	36	590	$0.88	$517	21,240	$223,275
1-Bedroom + Den/1-Bath	20	741	$0.85	$631	14,820	151,520
2-Bedroom/2-Bath	24	832	$0.84	$699	19,968	201,277
2-Bedroom/2-Bath	46	952	$0.83	$788	43,792	435,117
3-Bedroom/2-Bath	32	1,050	$0.82	$857	33,600	329,011
Total	158				133,420	$1,340,200
Average		844	$0.84	$698		

Note: Mathematical discrepancies are the result of rounding.

ing NOI by the debt service for the project. A DCR of 1.0 means that NOI equals the debt service for the project. For income-producing properties, most lenders require a DCR of at least 1.2.

DCR can be applied directly to NOI to determine the maximum payment that can be assumed for the loan. Given the lender's requirements for amortization and interest, it is then possible to calculate the maximum loan that could be serviced by the project's income, less the required coverage. In this case, a DCR of 1.25 would allow monthly payments of $58,158. Assuming an interest rate of 8.5 percent and 25-year amortization, $7,222,598 is the maximum loan a lender would allow (the present value of the monthly payment divided by 1.25 for the given rate of interest and term).

To establish the maximum loan available using an LTV ratio, it is necessary to first determine the project's value. The value can be calculated by applying a capitalization rate to the pro forma NOI. The capitalization rate is determined by the market and by what similar properties have sold for. It reflects the relationship between a property's income and its value. The lender ultimately requires an appraisal to verify the income and assumptions about the capitalization rate used to establish the value. The value is then multiplied by the LTV ratio to determine the maximum loan amount. In this case, a capitalization rate of 9.5 percent yields a value of $9,182,895. With an assumed maximum LTV ratio of .7, the most that the lender will lend is $6,428,024.

Lenders typically look at both criteria when underwriting a loan and use the more restrictive one. When interest rates are low, LTV tends to be more restrictive, and when interest rates are high, DCR tends to be more restrictive. In this example, LTV is the more restrictive, so the maximum loan on the property would be $6,428,024 (see Figure 5-5).

Development Costs
Development costs are the other part of the equation needed to evaluate a project's feasibility. An overall static

figure 5-4
Pro Forma NOI

	Annual Revenue/Cost
Income	
Gross Potential Rent	$1,340,200
Less: Vacancy and Collection Loss (5%)	(67,010)
Plus: Other Income	25,000
Effective Gross Income	**$1,298,190**
	($9.73 per square foot)
Expenses	
Payroll	
Manager	$24,000
Assistant Manager/Bookkeeper	15,600
Maintenance	24,000
Porter for Grounds	14,400
Subtotal	$78,000
Payroll Taxes and Insurance (20% of payroll)	15,600
Advertising and Promotion	24,016
Maintenance Supplies (5% of effective gross income)	64,041
Administration, Management, Telephone (5% of effective gross income)	64,041
Utilities for Common Area (5% of effective gross income)	64,041
Real Estate Taxes	77,384
Insurance	38,692
Total Expenses	**$425,815**
	($3.19 per square foot)
Net Operating Income	**$872,375**
	($6.54 per square foot)

The Promenade at Aventura reflects the Spanish-style architecture of southern Florida.

STB Architects & Planners, Inc.

figure 5-5
Maximum Debt Calculation

Pro Forma NOI and Value	
Pro Forma NOI (from Figure 5-4)	$872,375
Capitalization Rate	9.5%
Value (NOI ÷ capitalization rate)	$9,182,895

Loan Terms	
Interest Rate	8.5%
Amortization (years)	25

Using Loan-to-Value Ratio	
Maximum LTV	70%
Maximum Loan Based on LTV	$6,428,024

Using Debt Coverage Ratio	
Maximum DCR	1.25
Maximum Monthly Payment (NOI ÷ DCR ÷ 12)	$58,158
Maximum Loan Based on DCR	$7,222,598

Maximum Loan (Lesser of LTV or DCR)	
Maximum Principal	$6,428,024
Monthly Payment	$51,760
Annual Debt Service	$621,122

cost estimate for the project must be calculated. The estimate should include the cost of acquiring the site, construction costs, and soft costs such as legal and accounting fees, architectural and engineering fees, and contingencies. The costs should also include the developer's overhead and costs associated with the initial marketing and lease-up of the project. As an initial rough estimate, interest costs can be approximated by assuming an average draw and length of the loan. The operating reserve during lease-up can be approximated by assuming a lease-up period and computing the rent lost from vacancies during that time. Figure 5-6 shows total development costs for Shady Hollow before interest and lease-up of $7,158,008. With estimated construction interest of $337,471 and an operating reserve of $336,761, project costs total $7,832,240.

Stage 1 analysis is sometimes called a back-of-the-envelope analysis because the simple returns can literally be computed on the back of an envelope. Still, the overall return (NOI divided by total project cost) and cash-on-cash return (cash flow after debt service divided by equity) are the two most commonly cited measures of return in the industry. For an apartment project, returns in excess of 10 percent are desirable. As inflation picks up, the initial cash-on-cash return may go down to 6 to 8 percent as developers look to the future for higher cash flows and profit from sale of the complex. For Shady Hollow, the overall return is 11.14 percent ($872,375 ÷ $7,832,240). The cash-on-cash return is 17.89 percent

figure 5-6
Development Costs

Development Costs		
Land ($2.70 per square foot for 5.13 acres)		$603,350
Land Carry (12% for 3 months)[1]		18,100
Approval Fees		42,000
Soft Costs		
Architecture		42,000
Engineering		24,000
Professional Fees		6,000
Marketing		54,000
Construction ($42 per square foot)		5,603,640
Furnishings		12,000
Taxes and Insurance during Construction		60,855
Developer's Overhead (5% of soft costs, construction, and furnishings)		287,082
Loan Origination Costs		224,981
Contingencies		180,000
Total Development Cost, Excluding Interest and Lease-up Costs		**$7,158,008**
Estimate of Construction Interest[2]		
Permanent Loan	$6,428,024	
Construction Interest	10.5%	
Construction Period (months)	12	
Average Draw	50%	
Estimated Interest Cost		337,471
Total Capital Cost		**$7,495,479**
Estimate of Operating Reserve[3]		
Gross Potential Rent per Month	$111,683	
Lease-up Period (months to reach stabilized occupancy)[4]	10.53	
Average Occupancy during Lease-up	50%	
Estimated Lost Rent during Lease-up		$588,013
Less: Pro Forma Cash Flow after Debt Service		(251,252)
First Year Operating Reserve Required[5]		336,761
Total Project Cost		**$7,832,240**

[1] "Land carry" refers to interest paid to the land seller as part of the land purchase contract.

[2] This calculation is a preliminary estimate of construction interest. A more accurate estimate is made as part of Stage 4 analysis.

[3] Operating reserve during lease-up represents the subsidy that will be required to cover operating costs and debt service before the project reaches break-even occupancy.

[4] Based on market studies, the project is expected to lease at a rate of 15 apartments per month. The project will then take 10.53 months to be fully leased (158 units ÷ 15 = 10.53).

[5] The operating reserve includes funds needed to cover operating costs and debt service during lease-up.

($251,253 ÷ $1,404,216). Both figures compare favorably with other deals.

Total Project Cost (Figure 5-6)	$7,832,240
Less: Mortgage (Figure 5-5)	(6,428,024)
Equity	$1,404,216
NOI (Figure 5-5)	$872,375
Less : Debt Service (Figure 5-5)	(621,122)
Cash Flow after Debt Service	$251,253

Stage 2—Discounted Cash Flow Analysis

The project is typically held for a period of time after construction and lease-up. To calculate the operating cash flows, the pro forma NOI is extended over time, usually ten years, showing growth in both rents and expenses. The growth rates for each could be adjusted separately, but in this example both rents and expenses are assumed to increase at a rate of 3 percent per year.

Appraisers and some lenders focus on the unleveraged before-tax returns because those numbers give the "pure real estate value" of the property (without financing or income tax considerations). Both leveraged and unleveraged analysis can be done on the same spreadsheet simply by changing the assumptions about the mortgage and income taxes.

Developers use Stage 2 analysis to determine whether the proposed building offers an attractive rate of return. The DCF analysis is performed many times as more detailed and accurate information becomes available about design, development costs, and anticipated rents. The initial runs of Stage 2 analysis may focus on the unleveraged returns for the project—the internal rate of return (IRR) on total project cost. The IRR represents the relationship between the present value of the cash flow and the capital invested. This return should range from about

Summit Properties, Inc., is a Charlotte, North Carolina–based REIT that owns and manages more than 60 communities, including the 530-unit Summit Fair Lakes in Fairfax, Virginia.

© Rick Alexander & Associates

12 to 15 percent, depending on the type of property, its location, and interest and inflation rates. (The higher the inflation rate, the higher the overall return.) The unleveraged rate of return is computed on NOI for each year of ownership, *starting from the time the building is fully occupied* and ending with the sale of the project. The unleveraged (before-tax) return for Shady Hollow is 14.9 percent. Note that in the example, Stage 2 analysis begins *after* the building reaches stabilized occupancy. All of the interest subsidies during lease-up are included in the total investment cost. In this case, we assume that the building is fully leased even though it is not yet built. Alternatively, we could assume that Years 1 and 2 are the lease-up years and that the project does not reach stabilized income for a full year until Year 3. Such an assumption lowers the apparent returns but more accurately reflects what happens in a new development where the building must be constructed and leased from scratch. These nuances are considered in the more detailed analysis of Stage 3 and discussed later in this chapter.

Appraisers calculate the present value of the future cash flow stream at a discount rate determined by the market (usually 11 to 13 percent). The concept of present value represents the reverse of future value. Just as one dollar will likely be worth more in the future, one dollar in the future is worth less than one dollar today. The discount rate is used to discount future values to present value. It also represents the investor's required rate of return. The resulting present value represents the value of the building once it is fully leased. The difference between the discounted value and the development cost is the developer's profit, also known as the net present value (NPV). Using the NPV method of DCF analysis, a prospective investment must show a positive NPV to justify the investment. The unleveraged net present value at 12 percent is $1,151,000.[2] This amount is the development profit for Shady Hollow.

The unleveraged IRR in Figure 5-7 is 14.9 percent, which is in line with the recommended unleveraged IRR of 15 percent for a project yet to be developed. Although an existing, occupied apartment project should produce an unleveraged IRR around 12 percent, new development projects should produce returns on the order of 15 percent to compensate for the added risks.

Although the unleveraged IRR is important, developers are primarily interested in the return on equity (ROE). The return on equity also is expressed as an IRR and takes into account the financing (leverage) and personal income taxes of the owner/developer. Stage 2 analysis focuses on the returns on the project as a single, undivided investment where one individual (100 percent owner/developer) puts up all the equity and receives all the cash flow.

Figure 5-7 shows the leveraged analysis of the project with mortgage financing. Developers focus on the leveraged before-tax and after-tax returns on equity because investment in the project must compete with returns available from other investments, such as stocks and bonds. Shady Hollow's before-tax IRR is 33.28 percent, the after-tax IRR 27.34 percent.

Selling the Development Proposal

For a developer new to the business of multifamily development, one of the biggest challenges may be establishing credibility with sources of capital. Establishing credibility is particularly important in seeking lenders and equity investors to fund the project. But regardless of a developer's experience, lenders and investors will not part with a dime unless they have complete confidence in the developer, the development team, and the viability of the project itself. One of the best ways to allay their fears and prove the viability of the project is to present a well-prepared and comprehensive development proposal or package. This presentation should bring the objectives of the whole property together, showing its goals in the best light and proving that the homework has been done properly.

Think of the lender as a strategic investor. He has received clear directions from his organization to find a certain type of transaction in certain markets. For a developer in search of capital, it makes sense to find out first the answers to several questions instead of going about the process almost blindly:

- Who has money? Which lenders and investment groups are currently in the market looking for transactions?
- Of the groups that do have money available, which one matches the developer's strategy? Whether the project is to be built to sell or to hold over the long term, who funds similar transactions?
- Of the groups that provide capital for similar development projects, what specifically are they looking for in terms of geographic market, transaction size, and other key points?
- Who makes the decision? Who pulls the trigger? Is it an individual or a committee or even a series of committees? What is the actual decision process?
- What are their biases or prejudices? What do the last five transactions they have completed look like? Exactly what caused them to reject deals in the past?
- What does their current portfolio look like compared with the parameters they are trying to achieve? Where are the holes in that portfolio that can be filled?

Answers to these questions will eliminate a lot of problems in trying to complete a transaction in today's very competitive capital markets.

■

figure 5-7

Stage 2 Analysis—Discounted Cash Flow

Project Costs	
Total Project Cost	$7,832,240
Capital Cost	$7,495,479
Land Cost	$603,350

Financing Assumptions	
Equity	$1,404,216
Mortgage Principal	$6,428,024
Interest Rate	8.5%
Amortization Period (years)	25
Annual Debt Service	$621,122

Depreciation Assumptions	
Building Basis	$6,892,130
Life (years)	27.5
Factor	1
Straight-Line Depreciation[1]	$250,623

Mortgage Calculation	Year 1	Year 2	Year 3	Year 4	Year 5	Year 6	Year 7	Year 8
Beginning Balance[2]	$6,428,024	$6,350,302	$6,265,710	$6,173,641	$6,073,435	$5,964,370	$5,845,666	$5,716,469
Ending Balance	6,350,302	6,265,710	6,173,641	6,073,435	5,964,370	5,845,666	5,716,469	5,575,852
Amortization of Principal	77,722	84,592	92,069	100,207	109,064	118,705	129,197	140,617
Interest	543,400	536,531	529,053	520,915	512,058	502,418	491,925	480,505

Depreciation								
Beginning Balance[3]	$6,892,130	$6,641,507	$6,390,884	$6,140,261	$5,889,638	$5,639,015	$5,388,392	$5,137,769
Less: Annual Depreciation	(250,623)	(250,623)	(250,623)	(250,623)	(250,623)	(250,623)	(250,623)	(250,623)
Ending Balance	$6,641,507	$6,390,884	$6,140,261	$5,889,638	$5,639,015	$5,388,392	$5,137,769	$4,887,146
Cumulative Depreciation Taken	250,623	501,246	751,869	1,002,492	1,253,114	1,503,737	1,754,360	2,004,983
Recapture	0	0	0	0	0	0	0	0
Remaining Book Value	$7,244,856	$6,994,233	$6,743,610	$6,492,988	$6,242,365	$5,991,742	$5,741,119	$5,490,496

Annual Cash Flows								
Gross Rent[4]	$1,340,201	$1,373,706	$1,408,048	$1,443,249	$1,479,331	$1,516,314	$1,554,222	$1,593,077
Vacancy Loss and Collection	(67,010)	(68,685)	(70,402)	(72,162)	(73,967)	(75,816)	(77,711)	(79,654)
Adjusted Gross Income	$1,273,190	$1,305,020	$1,337,646	$1,371,087	$1,405,364	$1,440,498	$1,476,511	$1,513,423
Other Income[5]	25,000	25,625	26,266	26,922	27,595	28,285	28,992	29,717
Effective Gross Income	$1,298,190	$1,330,645	$1,363,911	$1,398,009	$1,432,959	$1,468,783	$1,505,503	$1,543,141
Operating Expenses[6]	$425,816	$436,461	$447,373	$458,557	$470,021	$481,771	$493,816	$506,161
Total Expenses	$425,816	$436,461	$447,373	$458,557	$470,021	$481,771	$493,816	$506,161
Net Operating Income	$872,375	$894,184	$916,539	$939,452	$962,938	$987,012	$1,011,687	$1,036,979
Annual Debt Service	(621,122)	(621,122)	(621,122)	(621,122)	(621,122)	(621,122)	(621,122)	(621,122)
Before-Tax Operating Cash Flow	$251,252	$273,062	$295,416	$318,330	$341,816	$365,890	$390,565	$415,857

	Year 1	Year 2	Year 3	Year 4	Year 5	Year 6	Year 7	Year 8
Tax Calculation								
Net Operating Income	$872,375	$894,184	$916,539	$939,452	$962,938	$987,012	$1,011,687	$1,036,979
Interest	(543,400)	(536,531)	(529,053)	(520,915)	(512,058)	(502,418)	(491,925)	(480,505)
Depreciation	(250,623)	(250,623)	(250,623)	(250,623)	(250,623)	(250,623)	(250,623)	(250,623)
Taxable Income (loss)	$78,351	$107,031	$136,862	$167,914	$200,258	$233,971	$269,139	$305,851
Passive Loss Offset	0	0	0	0	0	0	0	0
Taxable Income	$78,351	$107,031	$136,862	$167,914	$200,258	$233,971	$269,139	$305,851
Passive Loss Carryforward	0	0	0	0	0	0	0	0
Taxes (28%)	$21,938	$29,969	$38,321	$47,016	$56,072	$65,512	$75,359	$85,638
After-Tax Cash Flow								
Before-Tax Operating Cash Flow	$251,252	$273,062	$295,416	$318,330	$341,816	$365,890	$390,565	$415,857
Taxes	(21,938)	(29,969)	(38,321)	(47,016)	(56,072)	(65,512)	(75,359)	(85,638)
After-Tax Operating Cash Flow	$229,314	$243,093	$257,095	$271,314	$285,744	$300,378	$315,206	$330,219

Calculation of Sale Price							Year 7	
Before-Tax Cash Flow from Sale								
Sale Price (capitalization rate 9.5%, using Year 9 NOI)								$10,915,572
Commission (4%)							(436,623)	
Adjusted Sale Price							$10,478,949	
Remaining Mortgage Balance							(5,716,469)	
Before-Tax Cash Flow from Sale							$4,762,481	
Taxes								
Adjusted Sale Price							$10,478,949	
Remaining Book Value							(5,741,119)	
Total Taxable Gain							$4,737,830	
Passive Loss Carryover							0	
Capital Gain							$4,737,830	
Tax on Capital Gain (28%)							$1,326,593	
After-Tax Cash Flow from Sale								
Before-Tax Cash Flow from Sale							$4,762,481	
Tax							(1,326,593)	
After-Tax Cash Flow from Sale							$3,435,888	

continued

figure 5-7
Stage 2 Analysis—Discounted Cash Flow *continued*

Return Measures	Investment	Year 1	Year 2	Year 3	Year 4	Year 5	Year 6	Year 7
Unleveraged IRR								
Project Cost	($7,834,355)							
Net Operating Income		$872,375	$894,184	$916,539	$939,452	$962,938	$987,012	$1,011,687
Adjusted Sale Price								10,478,949
Total Before-Tax Cash Flow	($7,834,355)	$872,375	$894,184	$916,539	$939,452	$962,938	$987,012	$11,490,637
Unleveraged IRR	14.9%							
Net Present Value @ 12%[7]	$1,151,030							
Before-Tax IRR								
Equity	($1,404,216)							
Before-Tax Operating Cash Flow		$251,252	$273,062	$295,416	$318,330	$341,816	$365,890	$390,565
Before-Tax Cash Flow from Sale								4,762,481
Total Before-Tax Cash Flow	($1,404,216)	$251,252	$273,062	$295,416	$318,330	$341,816	$365,890	$5,153,046
Before-Tax IRR	33.28%							
Net Present Value @ 15%	$1,662,334							
After-Tax IRR								
Equity	($1,404,216)							
After-Tax Operating Cash Flow		$229,314	$243,093	$257,095	$271,314	$285,744	$300,378	$315,206
After-Tax Cash Flow from Sale								3,435,888
Total After-Tax Cash Flow	($1,404,216)	$229,314	$243,093	$257,095	$271,314	$285,744	$300,378	$3,751,094
After-Tax IRR	27.34%							
Simple Return Measures								
NOI/Project Cost		11.14%	11.41%	11.70%	11.99%	12.29%	12.60%	12.91%
Before Tax Cash Flow/Equity		17.89%	19.45%	21.04%	22.67%	24.34%	26.06%	27.81%
Tax Shelter/Equity		0.00%	0.00%	0.00%	0.00%	0.00%	0.00%	0.00%

[1] Different from final depreciation as a result of variance between estimated construction interest and actual interest.

[2] The permanent mortgage balance was determined based on value and cash flow. During the development period, only interest will be paid on the construction loan. Amortization begins upon funding of the permanent loan, after stabilization.

[3] The depreciable basis is the total project cost, excluding land costs and operating losses during the lease-up period. The remaining book value includes the land cost.

[4] Gross rent escalates 2.5 percent per year.

[5] Other income escalates (or inflates) 2.5 percent per year. (Other income is usually tied to adjusted gross income, as vending machine fees and parking fees are tied to occupancy.)

[6] Operating expenses escalate 2.5 percent per year.

[7] Net present value equals the present value of future cash flows, less the initial investment. Unleveraged net present value represents the development profit.

Two bridges connect Harbour Place on Harbour Island to downtown Tampa, Florida, making it possible for residents to commute easily from the island to downtown.

Stage 3—Combined Analysis of the Development and Operating Periods

Some time before the developer makes a firm commitment on the earnest money, it is important to compute a more refined estimate of cash flows during the development period and operating period.[3] This stage of analysis provides measures of return for the entire life of the proposed project. Stage 3 is more accurate than Stage 2, which assumes that equity is invested at the time of stabilized occupancy whereas, in fact, it must be invested before construction begins. Because the time frame is extended one to two years before Stage 2 analysis and the initial years produce little if any cash flow, the IRRs for Stage 3 are necessarily lower than for Stage 2. Nevertheless, they represent the most accurate picture of how the project will perform.

Stage 3 evaluates cash flows quarterly during the development period, taking into account the anticipated monthly lease-up rate. It also shows when equity and debt funds will be needed and how long they will be accruing interest before the project's cash flow can support the debt service. In this example, costs are projected on a quarter-by-quarter basis.

Stage 4—Monthly Cash Flows during the Development Period

Stage 4 analysis (not shown) focuses on just the development period and refines the quarterly projections into monthly projections to support the request for the construction loan. Figure 5-8 presents the quarterly cash flows during the development period, including construction and lease-up of the project. The schedule here assumes that the project will be built during the first four quarters and that the project will be leased up over the next four quarters.[4] The estimated lease-up time (10.53 months) was calculated from the anticipated absorption of apart-

ments based on the market study. The project reaches stabilized occupancy after the second year.

The construction loan is limited to the amount of the permanent loan. In today's lending environment, it is unlikely that anyone will lend 100 percent of the costs of the project. The developer will be required to contribute equity. A primary purpose of the quarterly analysis of the development phase is to estimate the amount of the loan that needs to be set aside to cover interest

Westlake Tower Apartments in downtown Seattle, Washington, is a 24-story, 368-unit building atop retail space and parking.

figure 5-8

Stage 3 Analysis (Part 1)—Cash Flows during Development Period, Including Initial Lease-Up

	Total	Time Zero	Year 1 Total	Year 2 Total	Development Period				Lease-Up Period			
					Quarter 1	Quarter 2	Quarter 3	Quarter 4	Quarter 5	Quarter 6	Quarter 7	Quarter 8
Development Costs												
Land	$603,350	$603,350	$0	$0								
Land Carry	18,100	18,100	0	0								
Approval Fees	42,000	42,000	0	0								
Soft Costs			0	0								
Architecture	42,000		42,000	0	$29,400	$4,200	$4,200	$4,200				
Engineering	24,000		24,000	0	24,000							
Professional Fees	6,000	6,000	0	0								
Marketing	54,000		18,000	36,000				18,000	$18,000	$18,000		
Construction	5,603,640		5,603,640	0	1,400,910	1,400,910	1,400,910	1,400,910				
Furnishings	12,000		12,000	0				12,000				
Taxes and Insurance during Construction	60,855		60,855	0	15,214	15,214	15,214	15,214				
Developer Overhead (5% of soft costs, construction, furnishings)	287,082	300	284,982	1,800	72,716	70,256	70,256	71,756	900	900	0	0
Loan Origination Costs	224,981	224,981	0	0								
Contingencies	180,000		180,000	0	45,000	45,000	45,000	45,000				
Total Development Cost, Excluding Interest	$7,158,008	$894,731	$6,225,477	$37,800	$1,587,239	$1,535,579	$1,535,579	$1,567,079	$18,900	$18,900	0	0
Operating Costs during Lease-Up												
Months to Reach Stabilized Occupancy (10.53)												
Number of Apartments Leased				351					23	68	113	147
Vacancy Rate during Lease-Up (percentage of gross potential)				44.46%					85.44%	56.96%	28.48%	6.96%
Stabilized Vacancy (percentage of gross potential)				2.78%					0.73%	2.15%	3.58%	4.65%
Overall Vacancy Rate				47.24%					86.17%	59.11%	32.06%	11.61%
Gross Potential Rent (from pro forma NOI)	$1,340,201			$1,340,201					$335,050	$335,050	$335,050	$335,050

	Total	Time Zero	Year 1 Total	Year 2 Total	Development Period				Lease-Up Period			
					Quarter 1	Quarter 2	Quarter 3	Quarter 4	Quarter 5	Quarter 6	Quarter 7	Quarter 8
Vacancy Loss ($)	($633,096)			($633,096)					($288,716)	($198,061)	($107,407)	($38,912)
Adjusted Gross Rent	707,104			707,104					46,334	136,989	227,643	296,138
Other Income	13,884			13,884					910	2,690	4,470	5,815
Total Revenue	$720,989			$720,989					$47,244	$139,679	$232,113	$301,953
Operating Expenses	425,815			425,816					106,454	106,454	106,454	106,454
Net Operating Income	$295,173			$295,173					($59,210)	$33,225	$125,659	$195,499
Combined Cash Flow during Development Period	($6,862,835)	($894,731)	($6,225,477)	$257,373	($1,587,239)	($1,535,579)	($1,535,579)	($1,567,079)	($78,110)	$14,325	$125,659	$195,499
Construction Loan Balance and Interest Calculation												
Maximum Loan Balance (from financing calculation)	$6,428,024											
Equity (total project cost, less construction loan)	$1,406,331	$894,731	$511,600	0	$511,600	0	0	0	0	0	0	0
Construction Loan Account												
Beginning Balance				$6,000,548	0	$1,089,757	$2,674,096	$4,300,025	$6,000,548	$6,236,420	$6,386,049	$6,428,024
Loan Draw												
Construction Draw	$5,751,677		$5,713,877	37,800	1,075,639	1,535,579	1,535,579	1,567,079	18,900	18,900	0	0
Operating Deficit	59,210		0	59,210	0	0	0	0	59,210	0	0	0
Interest (10.5%)	944,757		286,671	658,086	14,118	48,761	90,350	133,444	157,762	163,954	167,634	168,736
Interest Accrued during Construction Period	286,671		286,671	0	14,118	48,761	90,350	133,444				
Interest Accrued during Operating Period	330,466			330,466	0	0	0	0	157,762	130,729	41,975	0
Interest Paid from Operations	327,620			327,620	0	0	0	0	0	33,225	125,659	168,736
Ending Balance	$6,428,024		$6,000,548	$6,428,024	$1,089,757	$2,674,096	$4,300,025	$6,000,548	$6,236,420	$6,386,049	$6,428,024	$6,428,024

figure 5-9
Final Development Cost Summary

Capital Costs	
Total Development Cost, Excluding Interest	$7,158,008
Interest Accrued during Construction	286,671
Total Capitalized Costs	$7,444,679
Depreciable Basis	
Land Cost	603,350
Depreciable Basis (capital cost minus land)	$6,841,330
Operating Reserve	
Operating Loss during Lease-up	$59,210
Interest Accrued during Operating Period	330,466
Total Operating Reserve during Lease-Up	$389,676
Total Project Cost (capital costs plus operating reserve)	$7,834,355

expenses and operating losses during the construction and startup phase. In this case, the total project cost is estimated at $7,832,240. Because the maximum loan is $6,428,024, the developer is required to come up with $1,404,216 in equity. The amount of equity must be expended before the lender starts funding the loan.

Figure 5-9 summarizes project costs and identifies separately the capitalized costs from the first-year operating loss. Both are project costs that need to be funded but are treated differently when calculating income taxes.

Figure 5-10 shows the operating period cash flows for Stage 3. The quarterly figures from Figure 5-8 are summed to obtain annual numbers and brought forward to Figure 5-10. This analysis resembles Stage 2 analysis except that the construction and lease-up years (1 and 2) are included, whereas Stage 2 analysis assumed that the

first year had stabilized occupancy. Note that the cash flow for Year 1 is zero because all the equity is invested before Year 1 and all costs are covered by construction draws. The before-tax IRR is 26 percent, the after-tax IRR 22.42 percent.

Stage 5—Discounted Cash Flow Analysis for Investors

The final step in the analysis is to divide cash flows for the whole project into the investor's and developer's shares. Stage 5 is the joint venture/syndication analysis. It is used to structure the deal between the developer and the equity investor. Although the final version of Stage 5 for the offering package is usually prepared by an accountant on an after-tax basis, the developer's analysis typically focuses on *before*-tax cash flows and IRRs to the investor. The project's viability hinges on attracting sufficient equity capital, so the investor's IRR is one of the key measures of return.

Stage 5 analysis should be done before one makes a firm commitment for the earnest money for the land. If the investor's IRR is below 15 percent (and higher if inflation exceeds 3 to 4 percent or the deal is unusually risky), then the land price or purchase price is too high. Alternatively, the investor can be given a greater share of the profits, but if too little money is left over for the developer, the deal is not worth doing.

Figure 5-11 shows the before-tax Stage 5 analysis for Shady Hollow. The investor who puts up the equity typically requires a preferred return. The preferred return is most often cumulative, which is to say that if funds are not sufficient to pay the preferred return, the deferred return is added to the equity balance and accrues interest. In this case, the investor receives an 8 percent cumulative preferred return and takes 80 percent of the remaining cash flow as paydown of the equity. The other 20 percent is split evenly between the developer and the investor. When

The Meridian at State Thomas is a luxury multifamily development in a historic Dallas neighborhood.

The Park at Greenway in Houston, Texas, is an infill development that provides high-end units clustered in landscaped courtyards.

the property is sold, the first distribution goes to pay down any remaining equity and unpaid preferred return. The balance is split 50-50. Under this structure, the developer receives some cash flow throughout the operating period. The investor's before-tax IRR is 17.1 percent.

Some investors may insist on receiving all the cash flow until they receive back their initial equity investment and preferred return. There is no "typical" deal structure. It is up to the developer to devise a structure that will attract the necessary equity.

When a single large investor is involved, the deal is negotiated directly between the developer and the investor. Institutional equity investors typically require 75 to 80 percent of the profits. Developers can often raise money more cheaply from private individuals. A common structure with private individuals during the 1980s was a 6 to 10 percent preferred return and a 50-50 split of the profits after return on equity. As money for real estate became scarce in the late 1980s and early 1990s, investors required as much as 80 to 90 percent of the profits. "Lookback IRRs" of 20 to 25 percent were also common; in essence, the investor had to achieve a 20 to 25 percent IRR before the developer received a share of the profits. These returns are difficult to achieve except when properties are purchased at deep discounts or perform especially well. They require getting in and out of the deal in a short time—two or three years at most.

As money became more available in the mid-1990s, terms of deals with investors became less stringent. Still, many investors lost money in the 1980s, especially in nonresidential property. It will be harder for developers to obtain the traditional 50-50 deal with investors for some time.

What to Look Out For

Financial analysis is a necessary but often misused tool. Experienced developers sometimes scoff at the latest

DCF and IRR techniques because the old rules of thumb (capitalized value should exceed cost by a comfortable margin, say 10 to 15 percent, or cash-on-cash return should be 10 to 11 percent) work just as well when a project is obviously a good investment. Stage 2 analysis can easily be misused to overestimate a project's returns. One should be aware of the major pitfalls:

- underestimating costs
- overestimating rents
- underestimating operating expenses, especially after five years
- underestimating or omitting a reserve for replacements
- underestimating or omitting tenant turnover expenses for repainting, carpets, draperies, and appliances
- overestimating rent escalation
- assuming too low a sale-year capitalization rate (which increases sale value)
- not allowing a sufficient interest reserve during lease-up or assuming an insufficient lease-up time.

The errors in analysis are compounded by developers' natural optimism—the predilection to make several optimistic or "aggressive" assumptions simultaneously. Making one optimistic assumption, such as too short a lease-up period, may not alter the results too much, but when two or three such assumptions are made, the resulting returns may represent a *very* optimistic and unrealistic case. For example, if three assumptions that each are likely to occur only 25 percent of the time are used together, the resulting case has only a 1.5 percent likelihood of occurring (0.25 x 0.25 x 0.25). Thus, one must be very careful about selecting assumptions for the variables that represent *average* or *most likely* values.

The other common mistake is going into too much detail too early in the analysis. It is inappropriate to analyze the cash flows on a monthly basis when one is first looking at a project because the data for costs and rents are so crude that the extra detail does not help.

figure 5-10

Stage 3 Analysis (Part 2)—Annual Before- and After-Tax Cash Flows during Development and Operating Periods

Mortgage Calculation	Initial Investment	Development Period		Operating Period						
		Year 1	Year 2	Year 3	Year 4	Year 5	Year 6	Year 7	Year 8	Year 9
Beginning Balance[1]	$6,428,024			$6,428,024	$6,350,302	$6,265,710	$6,173,641	$6,073,435	$5,964,370	$5,845,666
Ending Balance	$6,428,024			$6,350,302	$6,265,710	$6,173,641	$6,073,435	$5,964,370	$5,845,666	$5,716,469
Amortization of Principal				77,722	84,592	92,069	100,207	109,064	118,705	129,197
Interest				543,400	536,531	529,053	520,915	512,058	502,418	491,925
Depreciation										
Beginning Balance[2]			$6,841,330	$6,592,554	$6,343,779	$6,095,003	$5,846,227	$5,597,452	$5,348,676	$5,099,900
Less: Annual Depreciation			(248,776)	(248,776)	(248,776)	(248,776)	(248,776)	(248,776)	(248,776)	(248,776)
Ending Balance			$6,592,554	$6,343,779	$6,095,003	$5,846,227	$5,597,452	$5,348,676	$5,099,900	$4,851,125
Cumulative Depreciation Taken			248,776	497,551	746,327	995,103	1,243,878	1,492,654	1,741,429	1,990,205
Cumulative Straight-Line Depreciation			248,776	497,551	746,327	995,103	1,243,878	1,492,654	1,741,429	1,990,205
Recapture			(0)	(0)	(0)	(0)	(0)	(0)	(0)	(0)
Remaining Book Value			$7,195,904	$6,947,128	$6,698,352	$6,449,577	$6,200,801	$5,952,026	$5,703,250	$5,454,474
Annual Cash Flows										
Gross Rent[3]			$1,340,201	$1,373,706	$1,479,331	$1,516,314	$1,554,222	$1,593,077	$1,632,904	$1,673,727
Vacancy Rate			47.24%	5.00%	5.00%	5.00%	5.00%	5.00%	5.00%	5.00%
Vacancy ($)			633,096	68,685	73,967	75,816	77,711	79,654	81,645	83,686
Adjusted Gross Income			707,104	1,305,020	1,405,364	1,440,498	1,476,511	1,513,423	1,551,259	1,590,040
Other Income (2.5%)[4]			13,884	25,625	26,922	27,595	28,285	28,992	29,717	30,460
Total Revenue			$720,989	$1,330,645	$1,432,286	$1,468,093	$1,504,796	$1,542,416	$1,580,976	$1,620,501
Operating Expenses (2.5%)[5]			$425,815	$436,461	$470,021	$481,771	$493,816	$506,161	$518,815	$531,786
Other Expenses			0	0	0	0	0	0	0	0
Total Expenses			$425,816	$436,461	$470,021	$481,771	$493,816	$506,161	$518,815	$531,786
Net Operating Income			$295,173	$894,184	$962,265	$986,322	$1,010,980	$1,036,255	$1,062,161	$1,088,715
Less: Annual Debt Service			(658,086)	(621,122)	(621,122)	(621,122)	(621,122)	(621,122)	(621,122)	(621,122)
Plus: Operating Reserve Funded by Construction Loan[6]			389,676							
Before-Tax Cash Flow			$26,763	$273,062	$341,143	$365,200	$389,858	$415,132	$441,039	$467,593
Tax Calculation										
Net Operating Income			$295,173	$894,184	$962,265	$986,322	$1,010,980	$1,036,255	$1,062,161	$1,088,715
Interest			(658,086)	(543,400)	(536,531)	(529,053)	(520,915)	(512,058)	(502,418)	(491,925)
Depreciation			(248,776)	(248,776)	(248,776)	(248,776)	(248,776)	(248,776)	(248,776)	(248,776)
Taxable Income (loss)			$(611,689)	$102,008	$176,959	$208,493	$241,289	$275,421	$310,968	$348,014
Less: Passive Loss Offset			0	(102,008)	(176,959)	(208,493)	(124,228)	0	0	0
Taxable Income			0	0	0	0	$117,061	$275,421	$310,968	$348,014
Passive Loss Carryover			(611,689)	(509,681)	(332,721)	(124,228)	0	0	0	0
Taxes (28%)				0	0	0	32,777	77,118	87,071	97,444

	Initial Investment	Development Period		Operating Period						
After-Tax Cash Flow from Operations		Year 1	Year 2	Year 3	Year 4	Year 5	Year 6	Year 7	Year 8	Year 9
Before-Tax Cash Flow			$26,763	$273,062	$341,143	$365,200	$389,858	$415,132	$441,039	$467,593
Taxes			0	0	0	0	(32,777)	(77,118)	(87,071)	(97,444)
After-Tax Cash Flow			$26,763	$273,062	$341,143	$365,200	$357,081	$338,014	$353,968	$370,149
Sale Price Calculation										
Sale Price (end of Year 9, based on Year 10 NOI)										$11,746,661
Less: Commission (4%)										(469,866)
Adjusted Sale Price										$11,276,795
Less: Remaining Balance on Mortgage										(5,716,469)
Cash from Sale before Tax										$5,560,326
Taxes										
Adjusted Sale Price										$11,276,795
Less: Remaining Book Value										(5,454,474)
Total Taxable Gain										$5,822,320
Less: Passive Loss Carryover										0
Capital Gain										$5,822,320
Tax on Capital Gain (28%)										$1,630,250
Total Tax from Sale										1,630,250
Cash from Sale before Tax										$5,560,326
Less: Tax										(1,630,250)
Cash from Sale after Tax										$3,930,077
Return Analysis										
Equity (–)	($1,406,331)									
Before-Tax Cash Flows from Operations		0	$26,763	$273,062	$341,143	$365,200	$389,858	$415,132	$441,039	$467,593
Cash Flow from Sale before Tax										5,560,326
Total Before-Tax Cash Flow	($1,406,331)	0	$26,763	$273,062	$341,143	$365,200	$389,858	$415,132	$441,039	$6,027,919
Before-Tax IRR	26%									
After-Tax Cash Flows from Operations	0	0	26,763	273,062	341,143	365,200	357,081	338,014	353,968	370,149
Cash Flow from Sale after Tax										3,930,077
Total After-Tax Cash Flow	($1,406,331)	0	$26,763	$273,062	$341,143	$365,200	$357,081	$338,014	$353,968	$4,300,225
After-Tax IRR	22.42%									

[1] The permanent mortgage balance was determined based on value and cash flow. During the development period, only interest will be paid on the construction loan. Amortization begins upon funding of the permanent loan, after stabilization.

[2] The depreciable basis is the total project cost, excluding land costs and operating losses during the lease-up period. The remaining book value includes the land cost.

[3] Gross rent escalates 2.5 percent per year.

[4] Other income escalates (or inflates) 2.5 percent per year. (Other income is usually tied to adjusted gross income, as vending machine fees and parking fees are tied to occupancy.)

[5] Operating expenses escalate 2.5 percent per year.

[6] Net present value equals the present value of future cash flows, less the initial investment. Unleveraged net present value represents the development profit.

figure 5-11

Stage 5 Analysis—Returns to Investors

Initial Equity	$1,406,331
Cumulative Preferred Return	8%
Priority Payback of Equity	80%
Investors' Share of Remaining Cash Flow	50%

	Initial Investment	Development Period		Operating Period							
		Year 1	Year 2	Year 3	Year 4	Year 5	Year 6	Year 7	Year 8	Year 9	Year 10
Before-Tax Cash Flow	($1,406,331)	$0	$0	$26,763	$273,062	$341,143	$365,200	$389,858	$415,132	$441,039	$6,027,919
Preferred Return											
Beginning Equity Account Balance			1,406,331	1,406,331	1,406,331	1,406,331	1,253,578	1,041,647	796,426	515,292	195,440
Preferred Return Earned			112,507	112,507	112,507	112,507	100,286	83,332	63,714	41,223	15,635
Preferred Return Paid Currently			$0	$26,763	$112,507	$112,507	$100,286	$83,332	$63,714	$41,223	$15,635
Unpaid Return Account											
Beginning Balance			0	112,507	198,250	37,695	0	0	0	0	0
Deferred Preferred Return			112,507	85,744	0	0	0	0	0	0	0
Deferred Preferred Return Paid			0	0	160,555	37,695	0	0	0	0	0
Ending Balance			$112,507	$198,250	$37,695	$0	$0	$0	$0	$0	$0
Equity Account Balance											
Beginning Equity Account Balance			1,406,331	1,406,331	1,406,331	1,406,331	1,253,578	1,041,647	796,426	515,292	195,440
Equity Payback			0	0	0	152,753	211,931	245,221	281,135	319,852	195,440
Ending Balance			$1,406,331	$1,406,331	$1,406,331	$1,253,578	$1,041,647	$796,426	$515,292	$195,440	$0
Equity Payments Recap											
Preferred Return Paid Currently			0	26,763	112,507	112,507	100,286	83,332	63,714	41,223	15,635
Deferred Preferred Return Paid			0	0	160,555	37,695	0	0	0	0	0
Equity Payback			0	0	0	152,753	211,931	245,221	281,135	319,852	195,440
Total Payments on Equity			$0	$26,763	$273,062	$302,955	$312,217	$328,553	$344,849	$361,076	$211,075
Remaining Cash Flow											
Before Tax Cash flow			0	26,763	273,062	341,143	365,200	389,858	415,132	441,039	6,027,919
Total Payments on Equity			0	26,763	273,062	302,955	312,217	328,553	344,849	361,076	211,075
Remaining Cash Flow			$0	$0	$0	$38,188	$52,983	$61,305	$70,284	$79,963	$5,816,844
Investors' Share of Remaining Cash Flow			0	0	0	19,094	26,491	30,653	35,142	39,982	2,908,422
Investors' Cash Flow Recap											
Investment	1,406,331										
Total Payments on Equity			0	26,763	273,062	302,955	312,217	328,553	344,849	361,076	211,075
Investors' Share of Remaining Cash Flow			0	0	0	19,094	26,491	30,653	35,142	39,982	2,908,422
Before-Tax Investors' Cash Flow	($1,406,331)	$0	$0	$26,763	$273,062	$322,049	$338,708	$359,205	$379,990	$401,057	$3,119,497
Investors' Before-Tax IRR	17.1%										
Net Present Value at 15%	$461,987										
Developer's Cash Flows											
Before-Tax Cash Flow to Developer	$0	$0	$0	$0	$0	$19,094	$26,491	$30,653	$35,142	$39,982	$2,908,422
Net Present Value at 15%	$890,376										

Homan Square in Chicago is a 54-acre master-planned development of 600 rental and for-sale residential units. The project was intended to stabilize and revitalize the community through innovative affordable housing.

In fact, it may make it harder to see what is going on. A basic rule of financial analysis is that the level of detail should be no greater than the accuracy of the information analyzed. Therefore, Stage 4 monthly cash flow analysis is appropriate only after considerable time and money have been spent collecting the best possible information about operations and development costs. Until that point, it is a waste of time.

Last, one should always use common sense. The various measures of return should correlate with standard rules of thumb. Good projects typically meet the following measures of return, although they vary according to the degree of risk:

Measure of Return	Existing New Development	Stabilized Property
Cash-on-cash return		
(cash throwoff/equity)	8–10%	8–10%
Overall return (NOI/total cost)	10–11%	9–10%
Unleveraged IRR	15%	11–12%
Before-tax leveraged IRR	20–25%	15–20%
After-tax leveraged IRR	15–20%	12–15%
Investor's before-tax IRR	16–20%	14–18%

These rules of thumb are rough guidelines. Returns may be higher or lower depending on the risks associated with a particular deal and the general economic environment and geographic location.

One should remember that financial analysis is an iterative process. Stage 2 analysis is necessary many times during the course of collecting better and better information about a deal. Fortunately, once the model is set up, it is a five-minute exercise to introduce better information and rerun it. But care must be taken to double check that the assumptions and results make sense. Simple measures of return for cash-on-cash returns and capitalization rates still apply. One should avoid the trap of creating so complicated a spreadsheet that key numbers become lost in the pages and pages of analysis.

Notes

1. Stage 2 analysis is standard throughout the real estate industry and is taught in most real estate graduate schools and executive training courses. A more detailed discussion of the five stages of analysis is found in Richard Peiser and Dean Schwanke, *Professional Real Estate Development: The ULI Guide to the Business* (Washington, D.C.: ULI–the Urban Land Institute, 1992). Most real estate finance textbooks describe DCF in detail; see, for example, William Brueggeman and Jeffrey Fisher, *Real Estate Finance* (Homewood, Illinois: Richard D. Irwin, Inc., 1996).

2. Unleveraged discount rates are published for pension fund investors and life insurance companies. Institutional investors were looking for unleveraged returns of 11 to 12.5 percent on "stabilized" apartment projects in 2000.

3. The developer's deposit money for the land is usually nonrefundable.

4. One typically considers Time Zero to be the time when the developer closes on the land. When closing occurs a long time before start of construction, it is simpler to assign Time Zero as the start of construction and to include land carry, design, and other interim costs as "costs to date." "Number of apartments leased" in Figure 5-8 is the average for the quarter (46 units leased each quarter).

6. Site Planning and Product Design

The developer's approach to design should be driven largely by the market. The multifamily residential market is segmented into many submarkets, with each niche demanding specific elements. A project will not succeed unless the design, including its architecture, features, amenities, and pricing, fits the target market's requirements. A resident willing to pay rents in the upper ranges will not be satisfied with a basic unit lacking style and luxury features, while a renter on a budget will be unable to pay for expensive extras. Still, with a creative approach, even a low-budget project can be an attractively designed asset to the community and provide a satisfying living environment for its residents.

The developer establishes the guidelines within which the architects and planners work. The developer should choose the design team with care, selecting professionals experienced with the particular product type the developer seeks to build. The designers should not be allowed to dictate amenities, or the sizes and mix of units. These decisions should be made jointly and based on the results of the market analysis for the proposed project. And every decision about design should take cost and ease of maintenance into consideration. Although the architect's mission is to design the project, the developer should be somewhat familiar with design to give the architect the required guidance and to be able

Community center, the Villas at Cityplace, Dallas, Texas.

to visualize what an architect's floor plans and elevations portray.

One of the most important and rewarding tasks for a developer is working out all the plan's details during the design stage. Everything from the site plan to the layouts for the units should be thoroughly examined and critiqued at this stage to avoid costly mistakes later in the process. The developer should mentally drive through the site, use the facilities, walk through every unit type, look out every window, and imagine living in each unit. The developer should try to answer the following questions while looking at the plans:

- What does a prospective resident see when driving up to the project?
- When he enters the leasing office?
- What do the balconies look like from the street?
- What does the street look like from the balconies?
- Do the bedrooms offer privacy?
- Is the kitchen functional?
- How does the design improve on other competitive projects?

Fixing a design flaw is easier on the drawing board than it is in the field or, worse, after the project is built.

Multifamily residential developments are among the most complex projects to design. Design of multifamily projects includes both subjective and formula components and must accommodate all the functional needs

Bold colors and forms spell exciting curb appeal at Tierra del Rey in Marina del Rey, California.

of a large number of people at a relatively high density, while protecting individuals' and households' privacy. At the same time, multifamily buildings must also provide a sense of ownership and community among a diverse and sometimes transitory population. Multifamily residential design often results from a series of compromises between notions of ideal living conditions (derived from concepts of single-family housing) and the economic realities of higher-density dwelling.

Differences in design among regions should be respected and included as part of the project's concept. Market demand drives many regional trends in design. Elements that are appealing in some regions are just as likely to be viewed as unsatisfactory or outdated in others. Although a project need not conform to a narrow interpretation of the appropriate design, disregarding regional variations in building configurations, architectural style, and type of units is a mistake.

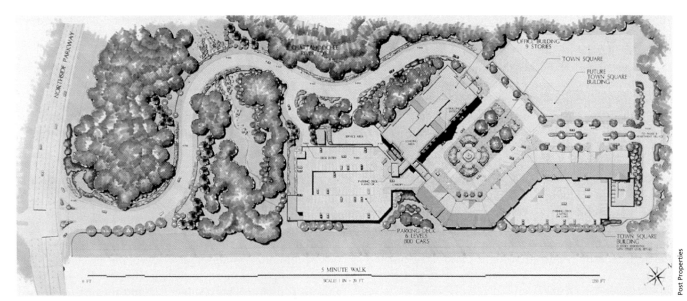

The site plan for Riverside in Atlanta preserves natural features and amenities in a pedestrian-oriented mixed-use development.

Site Planning

Any good site plan respects the natural characteristics of the site and its surroundings. Beyond that, the primary determinants of the site plan are the desired and permitted density, the parking layout, and requirements for emergency access. The density of the project is, in turn, a compromise determined by market factors and zoning requirements.

Multifamily residential development has evolved into a few specific forms, each yielding certain levels of density. Garden apartments, at densities of 20 to 30 units per acre, historically were two- or three-story walkups with open or enclosed stairwells and corridors. Buildings looked "commercial" or "institutional" and had little architectural interest. Affordability was nearly always the key factor in design. Mid-rise buildings of four to eight stories provided densities of 30 to 40 dwelling units per acre. Again, affordability influenced design. High-rise buildings of more than eight stories provided densities of more than 40 dwelling units per acre. Their design often resembled office buildings or hotels.

Today, a renaissance in architectural design is taking place, and it has been perhaps more apparent in the design of multifamily housing than in any other form of development. Creative architects and developers are inventing new forms of housing that better suit a more diverse and discerning public and make for improved urban and suburban landscapes. Many of the ideas and innovations that originated in upper-income multifamily residences are filtering into designs for lower-priced multifamily projects. Projects designed to resemble single-family homes rather than office buildings or hotels led the design trend in the 1990s. At the turn of the millennium, urban loft-like projects are popular.

Multifamily projects can take many forms, from multilevel units randomly stacked in small clusters to sculptured high rises with classical residential architectural elements that create a distinctive project identity. No

Poco Way Renaissance skillfully blends affordable housing into an existing neighborhood in San Jose, California.

longer is "multifamily" synonymous only with "affordable." Although affordable products remain a driving force of multifamily development, those who rent by choice make up an increasing market segment. They are higher-income households that choose a multifamily unit for its lifestyle, including ease of maintenance, desirable location, smaller financial investment, and less responsibility than owner-occupied single-family homes. Residents of higher-end multifamily housing often take a role in the design of their units, customizing finishes to suit their own tastes.

New urbanist community plans are shaping some new apartment projects. In master-planned projects developed in the style of the new urbanism, apartments are designed as small buildings, located close to the street, and integrated into old-style "city" blocks with other forms of housing and commercial activity. Live/work units and residential units above street retail shops often are part of new urbanist plans.

The quality and variety of multifamily architecture has reached new heights, exemplified by Bridgecourt in Emeryville, California (left), and the Villas at Cityplace in Dallas.

Traditional forms of multifamily housing have yielded to new configurations, making for greater flexibility for both residents and developers. New forms appeal to renters from diverse market segments, many of whom perceive multifamily housing as the optimal lifestyle.

Townhouse Forms—Stacked, Mews, Piggyback

Buildings with townhouse-like exteriors can contain multiple types of units, including a mix of stacked flats and two- or three-level units, each with private outdoor spaces. Achievable densities are greater than those of traditional townhouses. Communal or individual garages underneath the buildings decrease the acreage dedicated to parking, allowing for better, more attractive site design.

Mews with buildings back to back or facing can be clustered tighter than traditional townhouses. Piggyback units—for example, a flat on the first level facing front and a two-story unit above it facing rear—also allow increased densities. Such designs work well on small infill parcels and introduce the possibility of multiple unit types in a single structure.

Six-, Eight-, or Ten-Plexes—"The Big House"

New garden apartments often consist of small buildings designed to look like a large single-family house, each containing six to ten flats. Elevations incorporate stylish residential design elements, and site plans resemble those of single-family subdivisions. Surface parking

At Stone Manor in Frisco, Texas, garden apartments are designed to look like large single-family houses.

© Steve Hinds Photography/courtesy of Humphreys & Partners Architects

Affordable housing need not be bland and cheap. Across the country, outstanding designs abound for those of lesser means. Many cities are deconcentrating affordable housing. Rather than isolating massive subsidized projects from middle-income developments, many cities are developing scaled-down, neighborhood-friendly housing integrated into communities of varied income levels. The federal low-income housing tax credit program (also known as Section 42) has also led to development of projects that mix tax credit units in projects with market-rent units. While providing a more community-oriented environment, the scaled-down projects face less opposition from the existing community.

Parking

The land area designated for parking often amounts to more than the building area. The dimensions, arrangement, and location all require study. Zoning regulations is minimized by the use of integrated garages, and the outdoor parking that remains is in landscape-screened groups of three or four spaces—not the concrete sea found at earlier garden apartments. Such projects successfully overcome difficulties in rezoning because of their single-family look.

Courtyard Buildings

Buildings oriented around courtyards provide desirable private outdoor space and views for residents, away from the noise and traffic of urban surroundings. Courtyards and buildings erected over structured parking allow more efficient use of expensive land.

Infill Buildings

Infill lots can present great challenges—as well as great potential. Once overlooked, they are often the best-located properties in an area. Configurations designed to take advantage of these sometimes difficult sites require creatively fitting new shapes into tight spaces and integrating them into an existing community's fabric. Local residents typically provide a built-in market for such projects.

Scattered-Site Low-Income Housing

The size, shape, and location of low-income housing is changing. Massive, old-style public housing projects isolated from the larger community are turning into human-scale projects integrated into mixed-income neighborhoods. Local housing authorities are involved in projects that scatter low-income housing on small—usually infill—sites throughout the community. Some public and private developers have combined low-income units with market-rent units in the same project.

Mid-Rises—The Big House Gets Even Bigger

Buildings of four to eight stories may provide the density that an expensive urban site requires. Mid-rises are following the trend toward more home-like appearances using traditional architectural elements such as multi-gabled roofs, chimneys, porches, and materials that evoke home, such as red brick. Buildings are more articulated, allowing for a greater number of corner units, which take advantage of more light, better views, and cross-ventilation. Parking is usually structured, at grade or below.

David Allison

One Columbus Place in New York (right) is a mixed-use project that includes offices, retail space, and 729 rental units, of which 20 percent are low- and moderate-income units.

High Rises

High rises are also taking on a more home-like appearance today through architectural elements and traditional building materials. Like mid-rise buildings, high rises are more varied in height and shape, allowing for more corner units, private terraces, and more diverse streetscapes. In the largest cities, high-rise apartments are viewed as the most desirable housing because of their security and on-site services. Responding to a very discriminating market, new buildings imitate the graciousness of pre–World War II luxury high rises with their high ceilings, large, well-defined rooms, and quality finishes.

◼

usually determine the number of spaces. Typically, 1.75 spaces per unit is the standard, but requirements could be higher if there is a high ratio of large units or lower if a project has access to public transportation or limited land. The market study helps to decide whether the number of spaces should be greater than required by zoning.

Because parking occupies so much land and design of the lot is fairly regulated, it becomes a critical element of design. The design is further complicated by the neces-

sity to locate it near building entrances while screening it from view as much as possible. Breaking parking areas into small clusters of spaces with landscaped buffers is aesthetically preferable to massing all parking in one large area.

Increasingly, however, parking means enclosed garages. Enclosed parking used to be a strictly urban amenity, with suburban apartments relying solely on surface parking. In recent years, however, developers of suburban proper-

Parking

The ultimate density of the property is typically controlled more by the design and efficiency of parking arrangements than by building structures. Local codes determine how many parking spaces are required for the property, but the developer has to decide where they go and how they are configured. Many options are available. Arrangements for parking lots can include single-loaded, double-loaded, razor blade, parallel, perpendicular, and tandem schemes, as well as parking structures. The project can include detached garages and carports or, if the building style allows it, integrated attached, direct-access garages for each apartment.

Parking configuration is a key component in determining the overall characteristics of the community, yet parking areas are traditionally granted less attention than more exciting components like recreation centers, water features, landscape elements, and other open space features. As parking areas for the community are designed, the following questions should be considered.

- How can the perception of the development as a community or the feeling of being in a neighborhood be improved through parking and building configurations?
- How can the feeling of security and ownership be enhanced by making parking areas feel more like private space? How can spaces be dedicated to individual apartments without the use of restrictions or signs?
- How can outdoor spaces (including parking areas) be made as much fun as indoor amenities?
- How can parking be used as an opportunity to individualize homes?
- How can the basic design features of parking areas, such as form, layout, materials, proximity to buildings, size, lighting, landscaping, and drainage, be improved economically?
- What other uses could parking areas serve?
- What added features or qualities would residents be willing to pay an increased rent to enjoy?

■

ties have found individual or clustered garages that incur minimal construction costs to be highly profitable. Garages can require less land than the equivalent number of parking spaces, as garages are usually located under the structure. Garages add nothing to the building's footprint and little to its development cost, and provide added monthly income to the developer. Some projects charge a separate monthly rent for a garage; others include the cost in higher rents.

If garages are provided for residents, a certain number of surface spaces are set aside for additional vehicles, guest parking, and visitors to the leasing office. Ideally, pedestrian circulation should be kept separate from vehicular access, although walking distances between parking and units should be as short as possible.

Amenities

Selection of the project's amenities begins with the market analysis. A good market analysis answers several questions: What are comparable properties in the market area offering? Do projects with certain amenities have an edge in marketing, or do lower-priced projects with fewer amenities attract more residents? And perhaps most important, will residents pay for the amenities?

Amenities sell the product. What some communities consider standard and even essential, other communities view as luxurious. Generally, if amenities are wanted and used, residents will pay a reasonable price for them—unless of course operating costs do not correspond with residents' incomes. In highly competitive rental markets, a project usually must offer an amenity package comparable with other projects. In some markets, developers try to gain the edge by offering the most up-to-the-minute amenities, such as on-site business centers with computers, fax machines, and high-speed Internet access.

Usually a site plan contains both active and passive recreational facilities. Landscaped areas can serve as buffers, are visually attractive, add to the project's overall market appeal, and serve as passive recreational areas. A six-foot-wide walking trail surrounding the property can be used for walking, running, biking, or skating and costs little to construct and maintain. Integrating landscaped areas with active recreational facilities, such as pools and children's play areas, yields the most attractive site plan. Placing a lavishly landscaped pool within view of the leasing office often works as a marketing tool. Marketers strive to present the image of a resort-like lifestyle as a prospective resident enters the leasing office.

Pools are demanded in most areas and at most price levels. Although they serve as design features and recreational amenities, pools also bring up liability issues. Diving boards, once standard equipment, have vanished, along with the deep end. Pools are now shallow and used for wading or possibly lap swimming. They should be considered mainly a focal point for outdoor communal space. Attractive deck areas around the pool for sunning and socializing are also important.

Tennis courts have faded in appeal as a result of declining popularity of the sport and the costs and land involved. Market research should determine whether tennis courts and other ball courts should be included in the recreational package.

Creating play areas is essential if the project is targeted to families with children. Most projects should give some space to play areas even if the development is geared largely to a singles market, as some residents will likely be part-time parents. Play areas should be attractively designed and integrated into the overall project aes-

Private garages are an increasingly popular option. At Gables Celebration, garages are accessed by rear alleys.

thetics. Moreover, play areas must meet the most current safety standards.

Indoor Recreation and Other Project Amenities. Party rooms, exercise rooms, racquetball courts, libraries, and meeting rooms might all be considered as part of the amenity package if the market shows interest in such facilities. Indoor basketball courts have been very successful in more northern climates, as they provide an opportunity for year-round recreation.

Business Centers. Demand is growing in many markets for on-site business services, including the use of computers and printers, fax and copy machines, mailing and shipping services, and even secretaries and meeting space. Most new high-end apartment communities provide a business center with some or all of these services, and many residents take advantage of the facilities for personal and business tasks. With greater numbers of people telecommuting at least part of the time, business services are expanding.

The business center at Bozzuto Management Company's Harbor Park in Reston, Virginia, contains computers, printers, fax and copy machines, a mailing center, and workstations with telephones. About 20 residents pay $50.00 per quarter for unlimited use, and other residents can use the center on a limited basis for a small charge. Based on the success of this facility, Bozzuto is incorporating larger business centers in its newer projects.[1]

Needs for home-based business services are likely to change as telecommunications equipment evolves. As more and more households have their own computer equipment, residents want expensive equipment that becomes quickly obsolete such as high-quality color printers, scanners, and layout and graphics programs. But when certain amenities fade in popularity, the developer should have a profitable backup plan for the obsolete space. Avalon Properties, for example, designs its business centers to be convertible to other uses, such as libraries, when the centers become outmoded.

The meeting space afforded by business centers can be a draw. Jeffrey Roberts, president of Village Green Development and Construction in Farmington Hills, Michigan, finds that residents with home-based businesses have their own PCs and other equipment but use business centers to conduct meetings with clients in a professional atmosphere.

Home-based workers are not the only users of business centers. Architect Mark Humphreys has found computer

Today's amenities often include well-appointed business and conference facilities like those at Tierra del Rey.

A drainage pond becomes an amenity with naturalized landscaping and a pedestrian bridge.

rooms to be a highly desirable amenity for low-income apartment communities. School-age residents whose parents cannot afford computers can do their homework assignments there, for example.

Amenities typically are located in a building apart from the units, often called the clubhouse. For some time, it has been common for the clubhouse (or community center) to house the leasing office. Some recent plans separate the leasing office from the clubhouse so that the business of running the development does not infringe on the sense of community provided for residents. In some larger properties, developers even separate the marketing function from resident services for existing tenants.

Landscaping

Zoning requirements usually stipulate open landscaped space. Such space is also a marketing tool, creating first impressions of the development for a prospective resident. Landscaping should set the tone for the development; it should be professionally designed and impeccably maintained. Open space should be considered an integral part of overall site planning and design. Walkways, recreational facilities, stormwater management, erosion and sedimentation control, and utility easements can be provided in a project's open space system.

Landscape design must consider the climate, terrain, and cultural influences of the region where the project is located. A desert climate will not, and should not be made to, support an English country garden. The best

landscape designers effectively use hardy indigenous plants that provide interest during all seasons. Easier maintenance is possible through careful planning.

Xeriscaping, a method of landscaping that relies on the proper plant selection and planning to conserve water, minimizes the use of chemicals and reduces the amount of labor-intensive maintenance by carefully considering a site's climate, soil, existing vegetation, and topography. Such methods can be applied to any kind of climate or site.

Product Design

Building configurations must conform to market demands, zoning, and limitations of the site. Market demands are shaped by the demographic characteristics of the target market and by local trends in residential product design. It cannot be emphasized enough that respect for local design trends is an important element of good residential design. What is appealing to a New Englander can be entirely inappropriate for a south Florida resident.

Exterior Architecture

Exterior materials and architectural design closely relate to marketing the project and the target market's preferences. A project directed at a high-end market must reflect that level of quality in its exterior appearance; moreover, the surrounding area's character should also be considered. The style and materials of a new project should be compatible with existing development. A project in a newly developing area should aspire to set the tone for future development.

Regional traditions and climate play very important roles in an apartment building's exterior design. Brick and Early American styling are common throughout the Southeast and along the East Coast. Spanish-influenced stucco architecture defines the Southwest and Florida, and wood siding commonly dots the northern regions. Tastes always change, however, and new materials and building methods often deliver new styles.

Rooflines, in addition to shedding rain and snow, help to establish a residential character. A shallow or flat roof in a northern climate can spell disaster under the weight of a heavy snowfall. The silhouettes of various rooflines can create a residential village-like impression. Like the rest of the building's design, the roof design and materials are determined partly by regional traditions and styles. In Florida and the western states where Spanish styling is popular, a roof might be made of real or synthetic clay tiles. In the Northeast, slate shingles or standing seam aluminum roofing can be handsome choices.

Balconies are an attractive design feature for new buildings. The most functional balconies are architecturally integrated porches, nestled into building niches for privacy. A balcony's size is important in its usability. Balconies

Balconies must be large enough to be usable.

smaller than six feet deep cannot serve as comfortable living areas. Balconies deeper than six feet may excessively shade the unit or the one below.

Economies of scale can be achieved by repeating building types: the fewer the number of building types, the greater the potential for minimizing design and construction costs. Wall segments, foundation cables, and roof struts can be manufactured in groups, decreasing labor costs as more work is done by semiskilled workers. At the same time, however, marketability may require consider-

Classic colonial architecture lends southern appeal to the clubhouse at the Charleston at Boca Raton, Florida.

Determining Unit Mix, Sizes, and Interior Spaces

Market research yields an appropriate number of apartments for the community based on vacancies and overall demand, and it is then possible to determine how many of each floor plan and size would be most desirable. If the target market includes many small families, more two- and three-bedroom apartments will likely be necessary than studios and one bedrooms; if the market is predominantly singles and young couples, the opposite is true. The architect and other key members of the development team can help determine how each apartment style will be equipped—how kitchens and baths will vary and how windows, doors, cabinetry, and utility areas will be placed, for example.

The architect first creates rough sketches of the floor plans for each type of apartment in the mix. From there, the developer works closely with the property management staff and the interior design team to revise and finalize the initial plans before the architect proceeds with schematic drawings. Pay close attention to concerns like natural light, closet size, wall space, and properly sized spaces for furniture.

The way a room is visually measured helps in placing walls and determining unit sizes. A person's eyes automatically go to the corners of a space when standing in it, particularly toward the less obscured ceiling. The height of the ceiling and the apparent corner-to-corner dimensions give a quick impression of the size of the space. Placing the entry to a space on its diagonal axis makes the space feel much larger than an entrance from the center of a wall. This principle of "view diagonal" can make interior spaces more dramatic and more livable. The placement of windows and mirrors can have the same enlarging effect on interior spaces. A glass patio

door placed in the corner of a room rather than in the middle invites views to the outside and expands the feeling of room size. Similarly, a bathroom vanity mirror that spans the entire length of the vanity can have the effect of erasing the corners of the bathroom and expanding the space. Focus on view diagonals with the placement of corner windows and doors when planning interior spaces. It will not affect the cost of construction, but it can increase the sense of area significantly.

It is also important to look at connections between apartments to assess any acoustical concerns early in the design process. Sound deadening is an important issue in the design of all multifamily units. Changes in these areas are best made early, because the expense of altering designs increases exponentially as the project advances. Once the architect has the developer's approval of the conceptual designs, he or she assembles the floor plans into overall building footprints and then integrates the buildings into the developing site plan. As the pieces start coming together, the architect begins working on building elevations, and the character of the community begins to take shape.

able variety in the complex's appearance. The institutional look fostered by long, unbroken walls and rooflines is a thing of the past.

Interiors

Unit Mix. The mix of units by size and type must be based on results of the market study. Which competitors have the most vacancies? What unit types are vacant? Does pent-up demand exist for a unit type in short supply? Unit types most often range from studio apartments through two- or three-bedroom units with two baths; some include extras such as sunrooms, dens, and lofts. Some luxury units in New York City have as many as five bedrooms with private baths for each. In many markets, apartment developers are seeing increased demand for larger units designed to serve families. In projects designed for lower incomes, family-sized units should predominate. If the target market is young singles just starting out, demand will be for a mix of two-

master-bedroom units and one-bedroom units. In very-high-rent urban locales, studio units are popular, but in more distant suburban areas, demand is nonexistent for such small units.

Nationally, unit sizes have increased in recent years. In 1999, the median size of a new multifamily unit was 1,105 square feet, compared with a median of 955 square feet in 1990 and only 882 square feet in 1985. Further, the percentage of new units constructed with three or more bedrooms has increased continually. In 1985, three-bedroom units accounted for only 7 percent of new multifamily units. In 1990, that figure increased to 11 percent, and by 1999, three-bedroom units accounted for 19 percent of new multifamily units, nearly three times the percentage only 15 years earlier.[2] Much of the increase is attributable to the demand for home offices. Certain niche markets also play a role in determining unit types. For example, apartments housing students require special floor plans, because typically more students share a unit.

Multifamily units are getting larger: average unit size grew from 882 square feet in 1985 to 1,105 square feet in 1999.

Unit Design. A chief objective of designing an attractive apartment unit is to make a relatively small space seem larger than it is. Large windows and open floor plans are the best tools for expanding the feel of the living space. L-shaped units offer greater design opportunities than rectangular units. High ceilings can be an especially effective means of increasing the impression of space for only a marginal increase in cost. The traditional eight-foot ceiling height is being replaced, and nine feet is the current standard, especially in high-end units. High, vaulted, or coffered ceilings are commonly used on top levels of buildings.

Adequate kitchen and storage areas make apartments more livable. The kitchen should provide a minimum of 16 linear feet of counter space, including room for appliances. Each bedroom should offer a minimum of 12 linear feet of closet space, and guest and linen closets should provide another four linear feet of storage. These standards can be met in a one-bedroom floor plan of 600 square feet and a two-bedroom unit of 850 square feet. In smaller units, however, some compromises may be necessary. Creative use of apartment space for closets and storage makes the project more marketable.

Most markets today demand laundry facilities in the unit, and fully equipped kitchens with dishwashers, disposals, wood cabinetry, and built-in microwave ovens. Consumers demand more and better-appointed baths. In most markets, two-bedroom units should have two baths. In higher-priced developments, master baths must compete with those in new single-family homes. Amenities include large soaking tubs, separate showers, and double vanities. Quality at the lower end has risen correspondingly.

The apartment's finish materials should be chosen not only for durability and ease of maintenance but also to reflect the latest styles. Vinyl flooring has been commonly used in kitchens and baths, but ceramic tile or marble may be demanded in higher-end apartments. Ceramic has gained favor in lower-end units, where developers cite durability as a prime criterion. Carpeting of an appropriate quality is popular in most markets for living areas. Some developers use name-brand carpeting as a marketing tool. Some features, such as uniform window treatments, should be standard in all units, because they improve the overall look and therefore the value of the project.

Certain optional features can add value to the unit in terms of additional monthly rents. Depending on the market, such features might include fireplaces, individual security systems, and garages. To recover costs for added features, a rule of thumb is that the developer should be able to increase an apartment's monthly rent by at least 1 percent of the construction cost of the feature. For example, a unit with a $1,000 fireplace should be able to command rents at least $10 per month higher than those without a fireplace. Otherwise, the feature is not cost-effective. Many markets are experimenting with custom features. Prospective residents pay for the upgraded features and leave them in place when they vacate the unit, creating an upgraded apartment. After the resident leaves, the owner can charge more rent for the unit or remove the features if styles change.

Tradeoffs between construction costs and operating costs are a common issue. For example, exterior wood siding may save construction costs, but because such siding requires maintenance and tends to leak, maintenance costs will be high. High-maintenance materials also depress a project's resale value, because an operating expense statement shows replacement reserves and maintenance expenses reducing net operating income. Good design and effective use of materials can help to reduce costs by diminishing labor expenses. For example, janitorial costs can be reduced by minimizing interior public spaces.

Mechanical Systems

Renters' preference for flexibility has made individually controlled and metered HVAC systems standard—and cost-effective. Further, separate HVAC systems facilitate any future conversion to condominiums. Mechanical systems can be contained in the walls, ceilings, or roof spaces of the unit, but they require an outside compressor. The compressor can be located on the roof, where it must be screened and integrated with the roof design, or on the ground outside the unit, where it still must be screened but also placed to minimize noise. Another approach is to locate all mechanical rooms off a hallway

separate from units. This placement removes the noise from the units and facilitates repairs because a maintenance person does not need to enter the unit.

Units should be prewired for cable television, security systems, Internet connections, and multiple telephone lines, with outlets in all rooms. Some developers report the need for as many as eight separate telephone lines per unit. With technological advances in communications and increasing numbers of workers telecommuting from home, up-to-date wiring systems are essential. Retrofitting wiring in a completed building is very expensive and difficult. More and more developers see the wisdom of building "smart buildings," with all systems integrated and controlled by computer. Such technology is essential in luxury apartments, and before long it will be an expected feature in lower-end projects as well.

Utility meters and trash bins, always potentially unsightly, should not be overlooked during the design phase. A bank of meters, for example, can be quite obtrusive. Utility companies prefer that meters be grouped together and often have a say in their placement. Now that electricity and gas have been deregulated in some areas, negotiations with competitive companies could facilitate the placement of meters. Submetering also allows for optimal placement of meters away from visible areas.

Privacy and Security

Layouts of buildings and individual units need to provide privacy, regardless of the project's density. Many of

Today's apartment units often feature fireplaces, built-in shelving, and designer moldings.

the techniques employed in the design of the site, building exteriors, and units are devices for creating visual separation. Sometimes building codes provide useful criteria. For example, a code might stipulate that a wall with windows be separated from a facing wall with windows by at least 30 feet, that a wall with windows be separated from a facing wall without windows by at least 20 feet, and that two outside walls without windows be separated by at least ten feet. Vertical and horizontal projections such as walls and balconies should be used to ensure that units cannot be seen from other apartments or from common areas. Privacy for individual apartments is increased by fences, walls, and well-placed landscaping.

Design elements can be used to create a sense of ownership. Studies of successful subsidized housing projects have shown that residents take better care of their units when a transition area of "semiprivate space" is provided between the outdoor public space and the interior. The semiprivate space may range from an inset doorway to a fenced-in front patio or yard. Inside space should include an entrance foyer or at least some kind of separation (for example, different flooring material) from the living area.

Security has become an increasingly important issue, not only in urban areas but also in suburban communities. A plan that minimizes the number of entries into a project provides greater traffic control and therefore better security. Entries to units should not be hidden from view, and walkways and breezeways should be visi-

At Addison Circle in Addison, Texas, interior courtyards provide quiet outdoor space for residents.

ble from several points. Exterior lighting can greatly improve the perception of security as well as actual security. At the same time, exterior lighting must be properly designed so that light does not shine directly into units or cause glare for motorists or adjoining properties. The property should not be overly lit, detracting from its residential character. Lighting and landscaping designs should be coordinated so that trees and shrubs do not interfere with lighting as they grow, creating dark areas.

Architecture can enhance security and privacy without turning its back to its surroundings. At the Meridian in San Antonio, Texas, the entrance opens into a brick-paved parking and pedestrian plaza and pool area.

Electronic security systems for each unit as well as at the project entrance are an increasingly common item in some parts of the country, most notably in California, Florida, and Texas, where they are becoming standard. They are still the exception in the Midwest and the Northeast. Gated community entrances are a growing and highly controversial trend. Although a gate lends an air of prestige to some communities, research thus far indicates that secured communities give an improved *perception* of safety without indicating that crime rates are actually lower in gated projects. Data do not support the perception that renters prefer a gated project, that higher rents can be charged, or that the property value will be more stable. Some experts believe that the trend toward gated communities is largely driven by developers rather than the market. The costs involved are considerable, particularly in a gated community with a guard, and a developer should be able to determine what will be gained from the expense.

Gated apartments in some communities project a negative image for marketing. Prospective renters—and the community at large—sometimes view the gates with suspicion. Gates respond to a perception that an area has a high crime rate and that the overall community is dangerous, needing to be isolated from the outside.

Some police officers believe that the walls surrounding gated communities offer protection for criminals, who cannot be seen from the outside and are believed to belong inside once they are there. And gates cannot protect residents from the criminals living among them. Some gated communities report that most criminal activity is minor vandalism by youth who live there (which is typical of criminal activity in all communities, gated or not).

Although some renters and developers believe that gates can effectively lock out crime, in reality they may be exacerbating crime-related social ills. Secured developments may be turning their backs on the greater community, possibly creating new problems of isolation and actually increasing crime over the long term.

The Planning Process

Planning a multifamily development entails comprehending and synthesizing the market's demands, the developer's needs, and the concerns of the public and governmental agencies, and creating a development concept that will satisfy each entity.

Site planning involves designing a project and obtaining the necessary government approvals to begin construction. It begins at the conceptual level with a study of alternative sites and becomes more formalized and specific after a site has been selected. When used as a tool in decision making, site planning minimizes the developer's risks and maximizes the project's long-term benefits.

Once a general concept has been established for a development, the next steps include preparing detailed plans, providing internal direction, and meeting regulatory specifications. Preparing and processing plans for residential development projects can be complicated and time-consuming, often requiring several years of revisions until the plans meet the requirements of all parties. As projects have grown in scale and complexity, so has the regulatory environment. Effective developers have adapted to the increased public scrutiny with heightened sensitivity to the issues that must be addressed.

Site planning proceeds through three general stages: concept planning, preliminary planning, and final planning. Each stage involves the collection and analysis of information and the identification and evaluation of alternatives. The preliminary and final stages usually require public review. These activities are highly interdependent and are normally undertaken in several cycles during each stage. Developers typically go through preliminary and final planning for each phase of a multiphase project.

The developer and project planning team undertake site planning in consultation with representatives of public agencies. The developer also invites local citizens to participate. During the entire design process, lines of communication should be kept open between the development team and government officials, planning staff, and affected citizens. Cooperation and understanding can facilitate the process, often eliminating the need to rework a plan that does not meet jurisdictional requirements. Early in the planning stages, the developer should plan to meet with local officials to brief them about the proposed project and to gain insights about their concerns.

Setting a realistic work program and schedule to guide site planning is essential. The work program and the schedule must state specific requirements for submitting materials and review periods necessary for the project's approval. Once the required approvals have been identified, a realistic schedule for completing the approval process can be prepared. As new requirements are identified during planning, the work program and schedule will need to be revised. The time required for a project to receive all of the approvals necessary for construction to begin varies widely among jurisdictions, from a few months to several years. And a large, complex project usually takes longer than a smaller, simpler one.

Concept Plans

Concept planning for a project deals with site-related issues at the broadest possible level. Often the process is conducted before the developer commits to a specific site so that opportunities for and constraints on development can be explored. During this stage, the developer evaluates alternative land use arrangements—building configurations, sizes, general amenities, locations for open space, and placement of major roads. The product of concept planning is a diagram of the site depicting generalized land use areas and major road alignments. During this stage, developers should attempt to obtain a clear

Phoenix Urban Housing is a 400,000-square-foot mixed-use project containing 415 residential units as well as retail space.

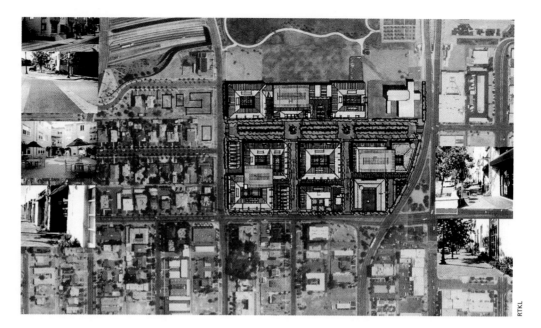

RTKL

RTKL

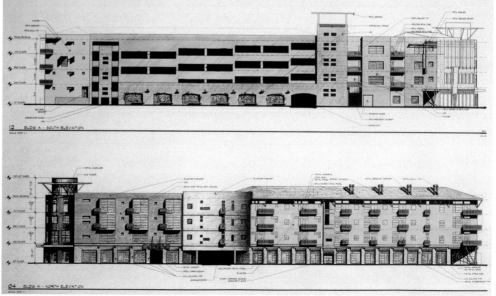

RTKL

The combination of water, landscaping, and a path system creates an intimate natural courtyard environment.

understanding from local authorities of the amount of contributions ("proffers" or exactions) the developer is expected to make for roads, infrastructure, and other public facilities. This information is integral to evaluating a project's economic feasibility.

Base Maps. To initiate site planning, a base map is necessary showing site boundaries and existing features. Generally, two base maps should be prepared: a site map and a context map. The site map should cover an area extending slightly beyond the site's boundaries, allowing for consideration of adjacent uses and physical features. Because the site map is to be used for recording site-specific information and for site planning, its scale and size should conform to any local requirements for a site plan submission. These requirements vary widely. The site's boundaries, topographic contours, water features, and existing adjacent roads should be included on the site map.

The context map, which should be prepared on a relatively small scale, is used to orient the site in its location, to configure the site, and to record relevant off-site information, such as the site's boundaries, existing roads, local boundaries, and landmarks.

Regulatory Analysis. The regulatory analysis involves identifying all applicable local, state, and federal regulations and their particular requirements for submissions and reviews. These regulations directly affect the project's schedule, and they can often be an important consideration in evaluating alternative plans. The developer should prepare a plan of action for meeting the conditions of approval for every level of government.

Local requirements for approving similar projects can vary considerably from one jurisdiction to another, and requirements for different types of projects can vary within the same jurisdiction. Local land use regulations for residential projects traditionally are contained in zoning and subdivision ordinances. Consultations with staff are important for gaining a clear understanding of the regulations and how the jurisdiction interprets them. Most

states have some type of enabling legislation for local regulations, which often provides a foundation for interpreting the intent and validity of a particular municipality's regulations. Depending on the project's nature and applicable regulations, a proposed residential development can be processed under conventional, planned unit development, or flexible zoning standards (see also Chapter 4).

Site Analysis. Much site data should have been collected during the feasibility study and site selection. This preliminary information is cursory, however, because it was intended for use in comparing the merits of potential sites rather than for making detailed development decisions. The development team must add to the preliminary database, collecting information from various public and private sources to complete the process.

The project team should first inventory the data already collected, then check with local sources for the availability of additional data. Very often, information from local agencies can be obtained free of charge or at nominal cost. A check with municipal agencies and planning departments, state highway and public works departments, utility companies, and local engineering firms will identify existing data. Existing data to use include topographic maps, soil surveys, soil borings, percolation tests, and environmental assessments for other projects in the area, and any earlier studies done on the subject property. Tax assessment records and recorded deeds are sources of information regarding easements, rights-of-way, and covenants that may exist on the property. An initial inventory of locally available information determines the scope of material that still must be obtained.

As valuable as maps and data are, nothing can replace personal knowledge. The developer should compile notes and photographs or even a videotape to gain a clear idea of important features for future reference, paying special attention to vegetation, slopes, rock outcroppings, vistas, wildlife, wet or potentially wet areas, easements, rights-of-way, and existing structures. Such a survey helps determine what features may be important to preserve and whether construction equipment can move easily about the site.

The most effective site analysis comes from systematically collected information. Relevant information should be collected and mapped for all elements of the site's environment, including physiography (the lay of the land), geology, soils, groundwater, surface water, vegetation, wildlife, past and present landownership, land use, existing circulation, and infrastructure. It is important to ascertain whether any state or local projects are on the books that would affect the property. Once data have been collected, the planning team can analyze the information to establish a basis for the identification and evaluation of development alternatives.

One method for determining the suitability for development of specific locations on the site is an environmental approach. Maps that identify various site characteristics are overlaid to show where sensitive areas coincide. After slopes, geologic features, floodplains, and other environmental considerations are charted on the map, land parcels are classified according to suitability for various types and intensities of land use, from those requiring protection and maintenance to those that can accommodate extensive modification and intensive development. The final map that results from this synthesis provides an ecological description of the site and its natural processes that will enable the development team to understand and test the consequences of various alternatives for planning and design.

A second method of analyzing information about the site is to identify opportunities for and constraints on development. Opportunities are features that make the site attractive for residential development—views, well-drained soils, gently sloping terrain—whereas constraints are features that make the site unattractive for development—floodplains, steep terrain, shallow soils. Most sites contain both opportunities and constraints, and creative designers can take advantage of the opportunities while turning constraints into assets. The site plan showing opportunities and constraints also identifies potential design strategies for further consideration during subsequent and more specific site planning. Some of these strategies might include landscaping to screen or improve unsightly areas, creating water features to contain stormwater runoff, providing pedestrian walkways along watercourses prone to periodic flooding, and orienting development to take advantage of scenic areas.

Definition of the Program. Concept planning is the first opportunity to test a specific development program for the site under consideration. During concept planning, the development team should articulate the optimum development program for the site based on the developer's understanding of the local market, regulatory constraints and requirements, the project's feasibility, and the site's characteristics. In particular, the program

At the Promenade at Aventura, traditional Florida architectural features blend with native plantings.

Eastbridge in Dallas, Texas, is designed to blend with the surrounding community with its use of traditional craftsman styling and materials, including stone, stucco, and wood shingles.

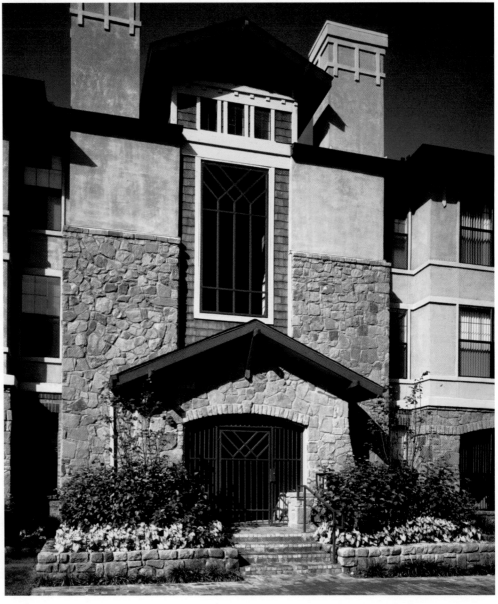

Village Green at Cantera in Warrenville, Illinois, includes 343 units in a pastoral lake-side setting. About 40 percent of the units have direct-access garages.

© Bloodgood Sharp Buster/Jess Smith

© Bloodgood Sharp Buster/Jess Smith

should specify a minimum number of dwelling units. Information about the type of amenities, the character of the project, any nonresidential uses to be accommodated on the site, and functional relationships among the various land uses envisioned for the site should also be specified as part of the development program.

Study of Alternatives. The results of the regulatory analysis, site analysis, and program definition provide the basis for the study of alternative concepts. From the regulatory analysis, it is possible to determine what types of development local authorities are willing to permit on the site. The site analysis indicates which portions of the site are developable and what opportunities and constraints exist for developable parcels. The development program identifies the developer's objectives and expectations.

Preliminary Plans

During preliminary planning, the concept plan is refined through the identification and evaluation of alternative locations for buildings, streets, parking, pedestrian circulation, and landscaped areas. One of the most informative products that can be prepared during preliminary planning is an illustrative site plan or artist's interpretation that schematically depicts how the site might appear after development. Such plans should not be considered final plans but working drawings. By the end of preliminary planning, the local government and the developer often make commitments concerning such issues as the total number of units, building types, roadway configuration, and the amount of open space and exactions.

Preliminary planning requires more detailed data than concept planning. Once the concept plan has been

The 193-unit Carillon Point in Kirkland, Washington, is a mixed-use project on a wooded slope.

wetlands, soil types, and the vegetative cover, including the location, size, and species of trees. Many jurisdictions have completed comprehensive topographic maps that are available to the public. If topographic maps are not available, an aerial survey is a fast and economical way to produce a current and accurate map.

A boundary survey should be at a scale of one inch equals 100 feet for parcels of 100 acres or smaller, and at one inch equals 200 feet for larger parcels. It should include bearings, distances, curves, and angles of all outside boundaries, and the boundaries of all blocks and individual parcels. In addition, it should accurately locate existing streets, easements, boundary markers, and official benchmarks. The survey shows names of adjoining property owners, the area of all parcels making up the property in square feet or acres, and the precise location of the site in terms of latitude and longitude.

Utility surveys should identify all easements; the existence of underground water, gas, electricity, and steam mains; and the location, size, and elevation of sanitary sewers, storm drains, and any other utility-related facilities existing on or under the site. If the amount of data necessitates it, separate maps should be drawn for each utility.

Site Evaluation. The site evaluation for preliminary planning is a refinement of the site analysis for concept planning. Detailed information about the environment is used to refine the analysis of opportunities and constraints and the investigation of the site's suitability for development. Where necessary, these analyses are supplemented by site-specific field investigations and studies.

The site evaluation provides a basis for assessing the potential environmental impacts of alternative plans considered during preliminary planning. The environmental impact assessment is useful in evaluating alternative plans and serves as the basis for the formal environmental impact assessment that may be required as part of the submission for the preliminary plan.

established, the project planning team will be in a position to identify additional information that must be collected and analyzed. At a minimum, topographic, boundary, and utility surveys of the site are necessary.

Topographic, Boundary, and Utility Surveys. For all but the simplest of projects, a careful field topographic survey should be undertaken. In addition to showing the precise contours of the property, it should also indicate topographic features, water features, marshes and

Today's garden apartments are often configured like residential neighborhoods rather than buildings surrounded by parking lots, such as at the Promenade at Aventura in Florida.

STB Architects & Planners

Refining the Program. As new information about the site becomes available and as alternative preliminary plans are evaluated, the development program that was defined during concept planning also needs to be refined. By this stage, the project planning team should be able to identify prototypical footprints for proposed buildings. These building footprints may also need to be refined as the study of alternative preliminary plans proceeds.

As in concept planning, studying alternative preliminary plans is an iterative process. Typically, land planners prepare multiple alternative plans for the development team's review and critique. The team identifies advantages and disadvantages of each alternative and prepares a new set of revised, combined, or redefined alternatives for further evaluation. On the basis of this evaluation, the developer selects a preferred plan for refinement. The process of preparing and evaluating alternative plans can be shortened if a thorough analysis was prepared during concept planning and if the preapplication conference was successful in identifying public and private objectives of development.

Preparation of the Preliminary Plan. The developer normally initiates preparation of the preliminary plan by submitting a formal application. Requirements for submission vary, but they often include written documents as well as site plans and other graphic information. The list of required documents may include, but is not limited to, the following items:

- legal description of the site, including ownership
- statement of planning objectives
- construction schedule
- quantitative information, including the number of units proposed, unit mix, proposed lot coverage, densities, amenities, and any nonresidential construction
- market feasibility study or other studies required by the reviewing body
- phasing plans
- contact information for adjacent property owners
- deeds of ownership
- zoning of subject and adjacent parcels.

Required graphic materials may include:

- site plans showing existing site conditions
- maps showing the location and size of all existing and proposed structures and improvements
- maps showing locations and sizes of all areas to be reserved as common open space, developed as recreational facilities, or conveyed as public parks, school sites, or other uses
- existing and proposed utility systems
- general landscape plan, including any buffer areas
- any additional information regarding adjacent areas that might assist in the evaluation of the proposed project's impact.

In addition, information about the design and construction of residential units and buildings, in-

Storyboarding

One of the best ways to give the architect an idea of objectives for the property is through the use of storyboards. A storyboard is a visual representation of the ideas and vision for a property. Storyboarding can also be an effective presentation tool. It enables the audience to "see" the developer's vision in an organized and logical progression. It is a flexible technique that is adaptable to a variety of concepts, from defining the target market to describing architectural style.

An effective storyboard includes collages of images that best convey the architectural style, characteristics, and feelings the developer is trying to achieve. They could include pictures clipped from magazines of people representing the type of residents that make up the target market, landscaping, chairs, kitchens, architectural themes, exterior spaces, works of art, books, or anything that relates to the vision of the community and its residents. The storyboards can include images that relate to the movies the target market would enjoy, the food it likes, the cars it drives, or even the clothes it wears. The architect does not copy or directly emulate elements of the collage, but the images will get his or her creative energies flowing in the right direction as the themes emerge. Architects are extremely visual people, and communicating with them in this manner is often easier than trying to articulate the vision because the developer might not even be able to do that.

The storyboards and project program give the architect the information he or she needs to begin to create the apartment neighborhood envisioned. In their early meetings, the developer and the architect spend time going over these items as well as many others, such as the topographic survey maps and the tree survey. Throw ideas back and forth and ask each other a lot of questions. The architect prepares some early sketches and begins to develop his or her conceptual ideas.

■

cluding typical floor plans and building elevations, may be required. In most cases, however, this specific level of building information is not required until final site plans or applications for building permits are submitted. If possible, developers should avoid submitting detailed building information before it is required, because doing so limits one's flexibility to change plans and features in response to changing market conditions.

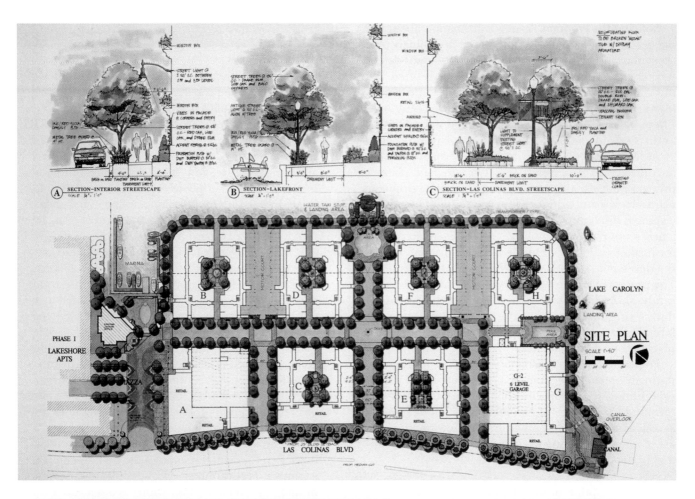

Columbus Shore is a waterfront town center with 503 apartments that is part of Las Colinas, a major master-planned community in Irving, Texas.

A developer should not invest too much time and money on preliminary plans in case, as frequently happens, the project does not proceed. At the same time, however, sufficient care should be taken that the plans satisfy government agencies and financial backers.

Final Plans/Construction Drawings

During final planning, the preliminary plan is further refined. The major difference between the preliminary and final plans is the level of detail required. Drawings that might have been presented schematically for the preliminary submission must be engineered for the final one. Site plans must be sufficiently detailed for legal recording, and any other graphic information, such as landscape plans, must also be submitted in final form. Project team members must be sure to dot all I's and cross all T's.

Most ordinances require the planning staff or commission to certify that the final plan substantially complies with the approved preliminary plan. Whether or not the municipality required certain changes to the plan during preliminary approval, the final plan typically varies somewhat from the preliminary plan submitted. The appropriate regulations and the reviewing authority usually take into account the need for minor variations, perhaps specifying the parameters for such changes.

Up to this point, all work on the project has been on paper. Usually no actual site work can begin without obtaining approvals from the local governing body. Careful work during the planning stage, including preliminary meetings with government officials and local citizens groups, ensures a relatively smooth approval process.

Preliminary Plan Review. The planning staff normally reviews the preliminary plan submitted, often under a time limit imposed by the ordinance. During this period, staff members may confer with the development team to clarify information included in the submission or to request additional materials. The staff might also advise the developer to make minor changes that could contribute to a favorable review. Some planning departments also distribute copies to appropriate local, state, and federal agencies for review and comment. These agencies could include the public school system, which might be responsible for determining whether existing school facilities are adequate for meeting the demands of a new development. Other reviewing agencies might include the fire department, which would review the plan for emergency access, the county arborist, who would evaluate the development's plan to save trees, and others with a specific interest in the development. State agencies may include state highway departments. Federal review may be required for specific environmental issues.

The planning staff then incorporates any comments received into its report of findings and recommendations, which is then transmitted to the planning commission. The developer has an opportunity to make a formal presentation about the project at a public hearing before the planning commission. As part of the hearing, the public is given the opportunity to make comments, both pro and con, about the project. Increasingly, overcoming public opposition has become a major part of the developer's efforts during the approval process. Developers should anticipate any community opposition and work proactively with local groups to gain their confidence and acceptance of the project early in the planning process.

The commission may pose some detailed questions about the proposal during the hearing; it can render its decision immediately after the hearing or within some specified period. The commission may approve, approve with conditions, or deny the application. More often than not, conditional approval is given requiring the applicant to modify some aspect of the proposal before final approval is granted. All conditions should be put in writing, in language acceptable to both the commission and the applicant. If an application is denied, the applicant normally has the right to appeal the decision.

After the preliminary development plan is approved, the applicant has a set time period in which to submit a final development plan. If a final plan is not submitted within that period, preliminary approval is usually revoked. This provision discourages speculation. Often, extensions to the approval period are granted to account for specific economic or regulatory conditions.

If a development is to be phased, a preliminary development plan should be submitted for the first phase only. The developer should work in increments that can be geared to actual marketing of the development. This approach allows the developer flexibility in

Ten Ways to Expedite Project Review and Approval

1. Know what approvals you will need.
2. Know the agency's procedures.
3. Inform yourself about local issues.
4. Make sure every application is as final and complete as possible before it is submitted.
5. Make your presentation as comprehensible as possible without compromising technical accuracy.
6. Whenever possible, use graphics to make your points.
7. Disarm mistrust by cultivating a reputation for openness.
8. Consider the regulator's point of view.
9. Before making any formal submission, speak informally with those involved in the review.
10. Get whatever expert help you need.

Source: Peter Salwen, "Shepherding Large Projects through Reviews," *Urban Land,* July 1988, p. 13.

Paseo Colorado is a mixed-use urban development in Pasadena, California. The project includes 392 residential units above nearly 500,000 square feet of retail, entertainment, and office space.

later phases in terms of timing and scale to best meet current market conditions. It is good policy, however, to submit the bare essentials of the remaining phases, even though the reviewing authority will not approve them at this stage. Doing so helps to keep surprises to a minimum.

Final Plan. The final development plan is normally submitted to the planning staff, which may or may not issue another staff report documenting compliance with the preliminary plan and with any conditions of preliminary approval. The city council or other local legislative body is often responsible for granting the final approval because it entails some legislative action, such as accepting dedicated properties, or accepting and recording site plans. If so, or if major changes have been made to the preliminary submission, a second public hearing may be required during review of the final development plan. Following approval of the final plan, other necessary administrative approvals can be obtained, building permits issued, and construction begun. Failure to begin construction within an allotted period normally results in revocation of the approval. It is not unheard of for plans to proceed thus far and then collapse because of a developer's inability to obtain financing, changes in the market, the developer's bankruptcy, or other difficulties.

Developers should keep in mind that the approval process can take a considerable amount of time, ranging from a few months to several years. It is necessary that the first phase of development be scaled to meet the projected market conditions at the time construction can proceed. The longer the processing time, the more difficult it is to anticipate market conditions and achieve this objective.

Amendments. Further changes in the final development plan often become necessary. Most minor changes will not affect the overall integrity of the development and are easily administered. Major changes, however, may force developers back through the preliminary plan approval process. In some cases, the limits of permitted

deviations from the plan are specified; in others, they are left to the discretion of public officials.

Changes to the final plan most often involve changing the product type or unit mix to better respond to the market. For example, after opening the first phase, a developer may find that one unit type rents better than another. Changing building footprints is usually not a problem for the jurisdiction, but more drastic changes in the product type, such as number or size of units, may send the developer back for new discretionary approvals. Developers need to be aware of the locality's limits for allowing the final plan to be amended and, unless absolutely necessary, stay within those limits.

Notes

1. Maryann Haggerty, "The Business of Setting Up Shop: Apartment Complexes Offer Tenants Tools of the Trade and Workplace Space," *Washington Post,* August 17, 1996.

2. U.S. Census Bureau Web site: www.census.gov/const/C22/Table 8.

7. Financing and Investment

Ultimately, every development project comes down to a simple matter of money. The truth is development takes a great deal of money, and very few developers have sufficient resources to fund a development project on their own. So where does a developer get the capital for a new development project? Although there are numerous possibilities, the best source of capital and how to get it vary from project to project.

Risk and Reward

Developers need to be aware of the pivotal role that risk and reward play in the financing process. The greater the risk involved in an investment, the greater the potential reward required to induce the investment. A key component of risk is uncertainty. The more uncertain an investor's expected return, the higher the potential return needed for investment.

Any number of variables, including the project's type and size, the stage of development, and the developer's financial strength and experience, affect the project's risk profile. Some of these variables may be, at least to some degree, under the developer's control, while others are simply inherent to real estate development. The project's risk profile has a profound impact on the availability and cost of financing.

The Georgian Terrace in Atlanta is an adaptive use of a historic hotel built in 1911.

It is critically important that the developer learn to identify and assess risks and potential rewards of a development project when seeking financing. Tolerance for risk and expectations for returns vary widely among financing sources. In the end, financing a multifamily housing development becomes a matter of matching the project's risks and rewards with potential financing sources' investment criteria.

This chapter is not intended to answer every question a developer might have about financing a multifamily project. It provides a framework for understanding the financing process and serves as a guide to the sources and means of obtaining funds for multifamily development projects. Throughout this chapter, the focus is on the effects of risk and reward on the financing process. The chapter starts with a discussion of the various types and sources of financing available for multifamily development, then looks at the variables that affect the availability and cost of financing, and ends with a discussion of the process and analysis required to procure financing for a multifamily development project.

Types of Financing

Equity

Financing comes in two forms—equity and debt. Equity is money invested in a development project. It represents ownership and carries with it all the attributes of ownership. It shares in the profits and losses of the project and, most important, shares in the risks as well. Because equity investors get everything that is left after all the project's expenses, debts, and liabilities have been paid, they have the potential to reap the greatest reward when the project goes well. But they also have the greatest risk of loss. For when things go poorly, the equity investors can lose not only the return on their investment but also their entire investment. In fact, equity investors' losses may not be limited to their initial investment; in some cases, in-

The Mortgage Package

The mortgage package should be 75 to 125 pages and filled with concise, relevant, and comprehensive information, photographs and easily digestible charts, and lots of white space. Tell the story of the development logically and in an enjoyable manner. The package should not be a cure for the reader's insomnia. Most important, each package must be customized to address the individual needs and objectives of the target lender or investor. Adapt the package to the types of programs and investment strategies the lender or investor has in place. If the object is a short-term equity investor, focus on the market potential and projected final sale price of the property. If the object is a long-term holder, focus more attention on debt coverage ratios, the longevity and durability of construction materials and designs, operating skills, and the strength of the management company. It is not necessary to start over every time for a new package, but the information will have to be restructured, possibly even reordered, to emphasize or deemphasize different elements of the development.

Remember also that the package has to sell the deal on the developer's behalf, because chances are the developer and the person who makes the final decision will never actually sit across the table from each other. Whether the meeting is with a junior loan officer or the president of the bank, a loan committee always makes the final decision to approve or reject the request. Convince the primary contact of the project's worth and he will become an advocate, but he needs to have the proper tools to convince his own bosses or committees to approve the project. To provide these tools, the development proposal must be complete. The mortgage package should include seven sections: an executive summary, descriptions of the location, project, and market, the development team, financial information, and appendices.

■

vestors may be personally liable for the project's debts and liabilities—which could, in effect, place the investors' entire net worth at risk.

Equity investors in real estate can receive their return in the form of cash, tax benefits, or both. Cash returns may come from the cash flow generated by operation of a property and from the profit realized on the sale of a property that has increased in value. Tax benefits may be in the form of deductions that can be used to offset taxable income from other sources or in the form of tax credits that can be used to directly offset tax liability. The availability of these forms of return and their relative importance vary from project to project and from investor to investor, depending on the type of project, the source of financing, and the investor's objectives. For example, an equity investor interested in tax benefits is more likely to invest in a low-income housing project that will provide tax credits to the investor than in a project that will produce taxable income. On the other hand, a tax-exempt investor such as a pension fund is more likely to invest in a project that produces a reliable cash flow than in one that generates tax benefits the tax-exempt investor cannot use.

The key characteristic of equity is that no promise exists that equity investors will receive a return on their investment or that they will even recoup their investment. Because of this risk, equity investors generally expect higher returns than debt holders.

The decision to seek equity investors is frequently a matter of necessity. The developer simply does not have either the cash or the ability to borrow sufficient funds to finance the proposed project. At other times, the decision to seek equity investors is a matter of choice. In the absence of equity investors, the developer alone bears all the risk associated with the project. By bringing in equity investors, developers can reduce their personal exposure by sharing the risk of the project. As discussed in "Leverage" below, bringing equity investors into the project affects the potential return to the developer. The decision to seek equity investors and how much equity investment to accept requires developers to balance their ability to complete the project without an infusion of capital and their desire to reduce exposure to the project's risk with sharing the project's potential profits with equity investors.

An equity investment can be structured as an investment in the project, an investment in a development entity created solely for the proposed project, or as an investment in the developer itself. How the investment is structured influences the arrangement for distribution of the project's profits between the investor and the developer. The developer is generally entitled to a set development fee or a priority return before the equity investors begin to share in the project's profits. When the equity investment is made in a specially created development entity, sometimes referred to as a *special-purpose entity,* or in the developer itself, the priority return to the developer may be greatly reduced or eliminated.

An equity investment's terms and conditions are a matter of negotiation and can profoundly affect the proj-

Prairie Court is located near
Frank Lloyd Wright's home,
Oak Park, Illinois, and takes
its design cues from the master. The 125 units are focused
around an entry courtyard,
with common facilities located
on the first level.

Located in Cambridge, Massachusetts, Auburn Court is an affordable mixed-income community that strives for racial and economic integration. Seed money from private lenders and charitable organizations paid for development costs before the start of construction.

Goody, Clancy & Associates

Final Loan Negotiations

Once the developer and the lender agree on the basic terms of the loan, the negotiations begin on other, seemingly less critical, issues. The basic terms included in most commitment quotes or loan applications are loan amount, interest rate, loan maturity, guaranty requirements, prepayment options (or penalties), and funding requirements.

Each of these issues may appear to be quite simple, yet a complete document that addresses all these matters comprehensively can contain more than 100 pages. As the loan application or commitment document is negotiated, remember that almost nothing is standardized in this industry and that almost nothing in your documents should be considered boilerplate. Moreover, very few issues are "small." Almost everything in the loan documentation can have huge ramifications on the performance of the investment. Treat the process with great care. Understand fully every question the attorney asks before answering. And understand fully the ramifications and risks involved in each clause of the document before agreeing to it. These cautions sound obvious, but developers have lost fortunes by not thoroughly understanding the full ramifications of the commitments they were asked to make. Whether basic partnership documents, a preliminary loan commitment, or a final equity agreement is involved, there is no fine print in this business. Understand every word.

ect's success. Therefore, the developer must fully understand the potential ramifications of the terms and conditions of equity investment. It is therefore advisable that experienced counsel assist in negotiating the terms and conditions of an equity investment.

Debt

Debt is money loaned to a developer. The distinguishing attribute of debt is a promise by the borrower that the lender will receive repayment for the loan plus a specified return. Debt has a claim on the development project superior to that of equity investors. Both during the operation of the property and when it is sold, available cash pays expenses first, then required debt payments, and finally equity investors with whatever remains. Equity investors receive returns only after the lender has been paid. The promise of a specified return combined with the priority position of the claim against the project's assets make the return on a loan much more certain than on an equity investment. Because of this reduced risk, the expected return on a debt investment is generally less than an equity investor would expect. How much less depends on the strength of the promise to repay the loan. Two factors affecting the strength of the promise of repayment are whether the equity investors are personally liable for the loan and whether a specific pledge of assets exists to secure the loan.

Debt can be recourse or nonrecourse. Recourse means the borrower is personally liable for repayment of the loan. In the event of default on a recourse loan, the lender can look not only to the project's assets for repayment but also to the borrower's personal assets. In a nonrecourse loan, only the project's assets secure the loan. In the event of default on a nonrecourse loan, the lender's only remedy is to seize the project's assets through foreclosure. The lender's recovery is limited to the value of the project's assets. The borrower is not responsible for any deficiency if the project's assets are not sufficient to repay the loan. Because the project's assets and the bor-

Almaden Lake Apartments in San Jose, California, is a mixed-income apartment development consisting of 144 units built in conjunction with 84 single-family homes. The development received unsecured financing from private investors for energy efficiency.

rower's assets back a recourse loan, it is perceived as being safer than a nonrecourse loan.

Debt can be secured or unsecured. A secured loan, such as a mortgage, is backed by a specific pledge of assets. The assets securing a loan may be the entire project or a specified group of assets. A secured loan may also be recourse or nonrecourse. Secured debt has a claim against the pledged assets that is superior to the equity investors and to any unsecured debt. An unsecured loan does not have a specific asset pledged as collateral. Thus, the likelihood of repayment favors the secured loan over the unsecured loan.

Although debt is generally safer than equity, a certain degree of risk is still involved. In the event of a failed development project, the chance that loan principal will be lost depends on the amount of equity invested, whether the loan is recourse or nonrecourse and secured or unsecured, and the project's value on sale. Although the

Jefferson at NorthEnd in Dallas was developed by JPI, one of the largest private multifamily developers in the country.

lender generally experiences loss only after all the equity in the project and all the other assets backing the loan have been exhausted, the lender still bears some risk of loss.

In addition to recourse and security, the prospective developer should be familiar with a few other concepts related to debt. Debt can carry a variable or fixed rate of interest. In a variable-rate loan, the interest rate for the loan is tied to a specified index of short-term interest rates. The actual interest rate charged is the sum of the specified index, referred to as the base rate, plus some specified amount. The amount added to the base rate to determine the interest rate on the loan is referred to as the *spread*. The prime rate, the interest rate at which commercial banks lend money to their most creditworthy borrowers, and the London interbank offered rate (LIBOR) are the most frequently used indices for setting the base rate of variable-rate loans.

The spread charged on a variable-rate loan varies according to the particular lender, the use of the loan proceeds, and market conditions at the time the loan is made. The spread does not change during the life of the loan, but the actual interest rate charged on the loan is adjusted to reflect changes in the specified index. Generally, the rate charged is adjusted at certain prespecified times—monthly, quarterly, annually, or any other period specified in the loan agreement.

Like a variable-rate loan, the interest rate charged on a fixed-rate loan is established by adding a spread to a specified index or base rate. The index or base rate used to set the rate charged on a fixed-rate loan is often the rate of U.S. Treasury notes with a term the same length as that of the loan. Sometimes the index used to establish the rate charged for a fixed-rate loan is a specified corporate bond index, such as Moody's AAA bond index. Unlike a variable-rate loan, the rate charged on a fixed-rate loan does not change during the term of the loan.

The establishment of a loan's rate is referred to as *locking in the rate;* the date when a rate for a loan can be locked in varies from lender to lender. Some lenders lock in the rate when the loan application is filled, others when a commitment to make the loan is issued, and still others only when the loan is actually funded. Once the loan rate has been locked in, there is generally a specified time during which the loan must be funded or the specified rate will be subject to change. Some lenders may be willing to lock in the rate early or lengthen the period during which the loan can be closed at the specified rate in exchange for a *rate lock fee.* The exact amount varies, but it is typically a fee equal to approximately 1 to 3 percent of the loan amount. If the loan fails to close, the rate lock fee is forfeited. Part or all of the entire rate lock fee may be refunded when the loan is successfully funded.

Most loans for real estate development and ownership are for a fixed term that can be as short as a year or as long as 30 or 40 years. Virtually all real estate loans have provisions making them immediately due in full if the borrower fails to meet certain covenants and conditions contained in the loan agreement.

Repaying a loan before its maturity date is referred to as *prepayment.* As a general rule, debt that carries a variable rate of interest can be prepaid at any time without restrictions or penalties. Conversely, most fixed-rate debt has restrictions against prepayment, which may actually prohibit prepayment or may allow prepayment with a penalty. The two most common forms of prepayment penalty for real estate loans are fixed penalty and yield maintenance. A fixed penalty is often a specified percentage of the balance outstanding at the time of prepayment. The specified percentage often varies depending on the remaining loan term. A partial prohibition against prepayment is frequently combined with a penalty. For example, a loan with a ten-year term may have a prohibition against prepayment for the loan's first five years. The loan would then have a declining penalty of 5 percent of the outstanding balance in the sixth year, 4 percent in the seventh year, 3 percent in the eighth year, 2 per-

cent in the ninth year, and 1 percent in the tenth and final year.

An alternative to the fixed penalty is the yield maintenance penalty, which attempts to ensure that in the event of prepayment the lender will receive the income that it would have received under a full-term loan. In short, a yield maintenance provision sets out the basic method for determining the penalty due by comparing the income the lender would have received under the loan with the amount it can earn by reinvesting the prepayment amount at current interest rates and then adjusting for present value. Adjustments for present value allow the lender to be compensated for all future income now rather than as a stream of payments.

Hybrid Financing

Some financing combines attributes of equity and debt and is referred to as *hybrid financing.* Hybrid financing can involve an equity investment that, while ultimately dependent on the project's success for its return, includes a provision for a preferred or priority return under which the equity investor will receive a certain return before the developer shares in the profits of the project. Another form of hybrid financing involves a loan that, in addition to its required interest payments, has a clause that allows the lender to participate in a share of the profits.

The principal advantage of hybrid financing is that it frequently reduces the overall cost of financing to levels that are more acceptable to the developer and may provide greater proceeds—in turn lowering risk. This reduction in uncertainty should result in the developer's being able to attract equity investors at a lower overall cost. This logic holds equally true with debt investors. A loan that entitles the lender to participate in the project's profit should have a lower interest rate than a loan in which the lender's return is limited to set interest payments.

Leverage

The use of borrowed money to finance a development project is commonly referred to as *leverage.* A key decision in any development project is how much leverage to use. Two competing precepts underlie this decision: 1) in general, the more equity invested in the project, the lower the risk and the lower the potential return; and 2) the use of borrowed money to finance a development project can greatly enhance the potential return to the equity investors while also increasing the risk.

Positive leverage occurs when the use of borrowed money results in an enhanced return to the equity investors. Figure 7-1 illustrates the effect of positive leverage when the property is sold. In this example, the return to the equity investors increases dramatically as the level of leverage increases. In fact, assuming all other parameters of the project are the same, the more debt used, the greater the return. The problem is that while greater leverage increases the potential return, it also increases the risk of failure.

figure 7-1

The Effect of Positive Leverage

Assumptions			
Purchase Price	$10,000,000		
Sale Price	$11,500,000		
	All-Cash Investment	50 Percent Leverage	90 Percent Leverage
Equity	$10,000,000	$5,000,000	$1,000,000
Loan	–	5,000,000	9,000,000
Cost	$10,000,000	$10,000,000	$10,000,000
Sale Price	$11,500,000	$11,500,000	$11,500,000
Less Cost (including loan repayment)	(10,000,000)	(10,000,000)	(10,000,000)
Gross Profit	$1,500,000	$1,500,000	$1,500,000
Interest Expense	–	(500,000)	(900,000)
Net Profit	$1,500,000	$1,000,000	$600,000
Equity Invested	$10,000,000	$5,000,000	$1,000,000
Total Return	$11,500,000	$6,000,000	$1,600,000
Return on Equity	15%	20%	60%

The example in Figure 7-2 illustrates the negative effects that leverage can have. In this example, the use of leverage combined with a modest reduction in sale price results in what would have been a profitable project's becoming a money-losing proposition if no leverage is used. This scenario is generally referred to as *negative leverage*. In addition to a reduction in sale price, negative leverage can result from cost overruns, delays that result in increased interest costs, and increasing interest rates. Any item that results in more expenses or a reduction in gross profits can lead to negative leverage. Using leverage makes a project much more sensitive to any failure to achieve its time schedule or projections.

Leverage can have a similar effect, positive and negative, during the operation of the property. Figure 7-3 illustrates the potential effect of leverage on operations. In this example, it is easy to see that appropriate leverage can greatly enhance the return on the equity invested in the property. When the property fails to meet its cash flow projections, however, leverage can greatly reduce the return on the investor's equity. Leverage makes a project much more sensitive to the risk of failure, for if the property's cash flow is insufficient to pay the mandatory debt service, the property may be lost through foreclosure.

Unfortunately, the question of how much leverage to use in any particular project has no definite answer. It is simply a matter of balancing the availability and cost of equity with the availability and cost of debt. Frequently,

the answer is more a matter of necessity than of preference. Because leverage increases the risk to both the equity investor and the lender, both the equity investor and the lender frequently impose limits on the amount of debt they will allow to be used to finance a development project.

Ownership Structures

A number of different ownership structures can be used for multifamily development (see Figure 7-4): direct ownership, general or limited partnerships, corporations (C corporation, subchapter S corporation, or REIT), and limited liability company (LLC).

Direct Ownership
Direct ownership is the simplest ownership structure. In this format, the developer holds the total equity interest, controls the project, and, if the project is successful, reaps all the reward. He also bears responsibility for the project. The developer alone is liable for all debts, liabilities, and risk associated with the project. Unless the developer has a substantial amount of equity available to commit to the project, he or she may find it difficult to obtain debt financing because of insufficient equity. The need for additional equity and the desire to share the project's risk with others generally lead a developer to seek additional equity investors. When the developer seeks

figure 7-2

The Effect of Negative Leverage

Assumptions			
Purchase Price	$10,000,000		
Sale Price	$10,500,000		
	All-Cash Investment	**50 Percent Leverage**	**90 Percent Leverage**
Equity	$10,000,000	$5,000,000	$1,000,000
Loan	–	5,000,000	9,000,000
Investment	$10,000,000	$10,000,000	$10,000,000
Sale Price	$10,500,000	$10,500,000	$10,500,000
Less Investment	(10,000,000)	(10,000,000)	(10,000,000)
Gross Profit	$500,000	$500,000	$500,000
Interest Expense	–	(500,000)	(900,000)
Net Profit	$500,000	0	($400,000)
Equity Invested	$10,000,000	$5,000,000	$1,000,000
Total Return	$10,500,000	$5,000,000	$600,000
Return on Equity	5%	0%	–40%

figure 7-3

The Effects of Leverage on Operating Results

Assumptions			
Property Purchase Price	$10,000,000		
Annual Cash Flow before Debt Service	$925,000		
Leverage Amount (80%)	$8,000,000		
Interest Rate	8%		
Term (years)	30		
Annual Debt Service	$704,414		
	All-Cash Investment	**80 Percent Leveraged Investment with Cash Flow at Projection**	**80 Percent Leveraged Investment with Cash Flow 10 Percent below Projection**
Annual Cash Flow before Debt Service	$925,000	$925,000	$832,500
Debt Service	–	(704,414)	(704,414)
Cash Flow after Debt Service	$925,000	$220,586	$128,086
Cash Invested	$10,000,000	$2,000,000	$2,000,000
Return on Equity	9.25%	11.03%	6.40%

Georgian Terrace, a luxury apartment community in Atlanta, Georgia, successfully integrates the rehabilitated 1911 Georgian Terrace Hotel and a new 19-story addition. The project was the result of a partnership between two developers.

additional equity investors, the other forms of ownership come into play. The developer has to carefully consider the ownership strategy most beneficial to all parties.

Partnerships

A partnership is an unincorporated legal entity formed by two or more persons or entities to pursue a common business undertaking. No limits are placed on the number of partners in a partnership; the partners may be individuals, corporations, or other partnerships. The partnership's activities and its relationships are controlled by the partnership agreement.

A partnership, although structured as a legal entity for business purposes, is not a taxable entity and does not pay taxes. A partnership operates as a pass-through entity, passing all its profits and losses through to its partners, who are individually responsible for their respective portion of the taxable income or individually benefit from their portion of any losses. Thus, unlike a standard C corporation (see below) where taxes are due on the project's profits from the corporation and the investors, a partnership is not subject to double taxation.

A partnership can also distribute losses to its partners. Although the use of partnership-generated losses by individual partners is somewhat limited, passing through losses offers great benefit to the partners. In addition, a partnership can allocate income, gain, losses, and tax credits to partners. In some cases, these special allocations may be the partners' primary reason for investing.

figure 7-4
Features of Selected Ownership Forms

Ownership Form	Ease of Formation	Ability to Raise Funds	Management
Individual	Simple and inexpensive	Limited	Flexible, independent, may lack expertise
Tenancy in Common	Simple and inexpensive	Limited but superior to individual ownership	Depends on owners, may be cumbersome
General Partnership	Moderately easy	Limited but superior to individual ownership	Generally by designated partner(s)
Limited Partnership	Moderately difficult and expensive	Limited but superior to general partnership	Good, by general partners or agents
Ordinary Corporation (C corporation)	Complex and expensive	No problem if closely held; if public, depends on investment	Continuous and centralized
S Corporation	Complex and expensive	Limited, unsuited for income property	Determined by relative share of ownership
Real Estate Investment Trust	Complex and expensive	Good	Centralized, by advisory group
Limited Liability Corporation	Moderately easy	Limited but superior to individual ownership	Generally by designated member(s)

Source : Adapted from James H. Boykin and Richard L. Haney, Jr., *Financing Real Estate,* 2d ed. (Englewood Cliffs, New Jersey: Prentice-Hall, 1993), p. 288.

Its status as a pass-through entity for tax purposes and its ability to make special allocations have made the partnership the most popular ownership structure for multifamily development.

Partnerships come in two basic forms: general and limited. The distinguishing characteristics between them include the number of classes of partners, control of the partnership's operations, and the level of liability assumed by the various partners.

General Partnership. General partners share in the partnership's management and share in its profits and losses. Most important, all general partners share full liability for the partnership's debts.

Limited Partnership. Within a limited partnership, two classes of partner can exist: general and limited. The general partner (or partners) controls the partnership's operations and is personally liable for the partnership's debts and actions. The limited partner (or partners) is a passive investor. Limited partners do not play an active role in the partnership's operation. As passive investors, they are not liable for the partnership's debts beyond the amount of their investment. Nevertheless, limited partners do exert a certain level of control, as they have the right to remove and replace the general partner under certain circumstances.

Joint Ventures

Development projects are frequently structured as joint ventures between two or more entities. Although it is in many ways similar to a partnership, a joint venture is not an ownership entity. In a joint venture, two or more entities agree to combine their resources to carry out a common business activity. The entities may be individuals, partnerships, or corporations. The activities of the joint venture and the relationship among the entities are defined by a contract among the entities. A joint venture is frequently used in development activities when the overall project is beyond the scope of knowledge, experience, resources, capabilities, or risk tolerance of a single entity. For example, a developer might jointly undertake a project with a landowner or a financial institution, or a multifamily developer and a retail developer might combine forces to create a mixed-use development project. The key distinction between a partnership and a joint venture is that the joint venture is not in and of itself a legal entity. It is merely a contractual agreement between the parties to jointly undertake a common business venture.

Corporations

A corporation is a legal entity chartered by a state or the federal government. The owners of a corporation are generally referred to as *shareholders*. Three types of corporations are commonly used for multifamily development: the C corporation, the Subchapter S corporation, and the REIT.

C Corporation. The C corporation is what most people think of when they hear the word *corporation*.

Personal Liability	Income Tax Treatment	Transfer of Ownership	Dissolution
Unlimited	Single	Simple and inexpensive	Excellent
Unlimited	Single	Potentially difficult	Potentially difficult
Unlimited	Single	Poor	Fairly simple
Limited for limited partnership; unlimited for general partner	Single	Poor for general partner; fair for limited partner	May be time-consuming and tie up invested capital
Limited	Double	Superior	Simple process but needs shareholders' approval
Limited	Single	Impeded by ceiling on number of shareholders	Simple process but needs shareholders' approval
Limited	Modified single	Superior	Complex
Limited	Single	Superior	Simple process but needs members' approval

Villa Torino Apartments in San Jose, California, was funded by a private corporation.

Virtually all companies that trade on the public stock exchanges are C corporations. Although some C corporations are small and owned by just a few shareholders, there is no limit on the number of shareholders. The day-to-day operations of a C corporation are controlled by the company's management, which reports to a board of directors elected by the shareholders. Shareholders do not generally have a say in the operations of a C corporation other than their ability to elect the company's directors and to vote on certain major matters, such as a merger of the corporation with another company.

Individual shareholders of a C corporation are not liable for corporate debts and liabilities beyond the amount of their investment. Individual shareholders can easily transfer their interest in the company to someone else through the sale of their stock, and the stock transfer from one owner to another does not affect the operations or legal status of the corporation. C corporations are fully taxable entities, however. As a result, the shareholders of a C corporation are subject to double taxation. The corporation must first pay taxes on all its earnings, and the shareholders must pay taxes on any earnings distributed to them as dividends. A C corporation cannot pass tax losses on to its shareholders.

Subchapter S Corporation. A Subchapter S corporation combines features of a corporation and a partnership. The shareholders of a Subchapter S corporation are not individually liable for the corporation's liabilities or subject to double taxation. A Subchapter S corporation, limited to 75 shareholders, is not a taxable entity. It does not pay taxes itself on its earnings like a C corporation but instead passes its income and losses through to its shareholders. A Subchapter S corporation cannot make special allocations of income or losses like those made by a partnership, but it can pass through certain tax preference items to its shareholders.

Real Estate Investment Trust. A REIT is a C corporation that has elected to operate under a special set of rules and regulations in exchange for certain treatment under the tax code. A REIT may be public or private, but it must have at least 100 shareholders. Three basic types of REIT are equity, mortgage, and hybrid. Equity REITs own real estate, mortgage REITs lend money to real estate owners, and hybrid REITs do both.

A REIT's shareholders are passive investors, and the REIT's management makes all management decisions. Investors have limited liability and are not liable for the REIT's debts and obligations beyond their investment. Investors can reduce or increase their investment in the REIT simply by buying or selling shares.

REITs do not pay corporate income tax. Instead, taxable income is passed through to shareholders—but not without a price. To qualify as a REIT, a company must comply with an exceedingly complex set of rules governing virtually every aspect of corporate structure, governance, and operations. REITs cannot pass through losses or make special allocations of income or loss.

In recent years, many REITs have structured themselves as UpREITs or DownREITs. Both structures involve creating a partnership within the REIT's corporate structure. In an UpREIT, a single operating partnership holds all the corporation's assets and conducts all its operations. The corporation is the general partner of the operating partnership. A DownREIT, in contrast, may have multiple partnerships, each with its own assets and operations, and the corporation acts as the general partner for each partnership. Both these structures allow the REIT to have both limited partners and corporate shareholders. The limited partners enjoy the benefits of partner status, primarily the ability to contribute property in exchange for an interest in the REIT's partnership without incurring current liability.

Limited Liability Company. A limited liability company is a legal entity very similar to a Subchapter S corporation. Like a Subchapter S corporation, an LLC offers investors limited liability, single taxation, and the ability to be actively involved in management. But unlike a Subchapter S corporation, no limits are placed on the number of investors.

Investors in an LLC are referred to as members. Managers, who may be members, control the operations of the LLC. An LLC has no restrictions on a member's involvement in management. In general, the members and managers of an LLC are not personally liable for the LLC's debts and obligations; their liability is limited to the amount of their investment. For tax purposes, an LLC is a pass-through entity. It passes all income and loss on to its members and thus avoids double taxation. Unlike a Subchapter S corporation, an LLC can make special allocations of income and loss.

Syndication. The word *syndication* is sometimes used to describe a group of investors formed to invest in a development project, but a syndication is not a legal ownership entity. When correctly used, syndication refers to the process of forming a legal entity and finding investors to provide equity funding for the acquisition or development of a project. The most frequently used ownership structures associated with syndication are partnerships, joint ventures, and limited liability companies.

Choosing an Ownership Structure

Because the ownership structure defines the rights and relationships of the equity owners, choosing an ownership structure for a particular development project is frequently dictated by the source of the equity for the project. The choice of ownership structure is also important to the equity holders, because certain structures are better able to convey the full benefits of ownership, especially tax benefits, to the equity holders.

Each ownership structure has characteristics that may or may not make it suitable for a particular development project. In selecting an ownership structure, the developer must consider the:

- amount of equity needed,
- difficulty and cost of forming the entity,

Developed by Columbus Realty Trust, a REIT, Columbus Square is a luxury, mixed-use multifamily community in uptown Dallas. It features live/work lofts and living spaces above ground-floor retail stores.

- amount of involvement the equity holders will have in the management of the project,
- amount of liability the equity holders are willing to assume,
- equity holders' ability to increase or decrease their investment in the project,
- tax ramifications, and
- importance of tax benefits to the equity holders.

Avalon Gardens in Nanuet, New York, was developed by AvalonBay, one of the largest multifamily REITs in the country.

© Bill Horsman

Choosing an ownership structure balances the attributes of the various ownership structures with the project's needs and the equity investors' desires. Because they offer the best blend of cost, tax benefits, and flexibility, the partnership, Subchapter S corporation, and limited liability company tend to be the best structures for multifamily development. Direct ownership, while certainly the easiest to form, generally does not provide sufficient equity to finance but the smallest development projects. Corporations and REITs, on the other hand, offer the potential to raise the most equity but are costly and difficult to form and administer. These structures are generally not the best choice for a developer seeking to raise equity for a multifamily development unless extremely large amounts are required or the developer is already organized as a C corporation or a REIT.

Financial Analysis

Matching the risks and potential rewards with potential funding sources' investment criteria is key to financing multifamily housing development. The developer must identify and, to the extent possible, quantify the risks and rewards of a particular project. This process is generally referred to as the feasibility study (see Chapters 2 through 5).

The financial analysis portion of the feasibility study is the primary information that potential equity investors and lenders use to base their decision on whether to fund the project. Although most tests used in the financial analysis are quantitative and relatively easy to calculate, simply meeting the required standards does not guarantee that a particular project will be funded. At best, the various formulas and tests serve as benchmarks in determining the project's viability.

Ultimately, the decision to invest in or lend money for a particular project is a subjective judgment based on an overall review of information contained in the feasibility study and the financial analysis. When preparing the feasibility study and financial analysis, it is important to provide accurate and detailed information so that potential equity investors or lenders can become as familiar and as comfortable with the situation as possible. The developer should anticipate potential investors' and lenders' questions and concerns and address them openly and honestly.

The feasibility study and financial analysis should be as accurate and reasonable as possible. They are based on a number of assumptions—assumptions that can have a dramatic impact on the conclusions to be drawn from the study. If the assumptions are too conservative, a deserving project will not be built. If the assumptions are too aggressive, a project that is doomed to failure may be funded. The best approach is to make every effort to use reasonable assumptions and include a variance analysis.

Too often a developer tries to manage the information included in the feasibility study and financial analysis to match its choice of investor or lender. The better course is to develop a thorough feasibility study and financial analysis using reasonable assumptions that, to the maximum extent possible, accurately represent the situation and then match the investors and lenders to the project. The project's ultimate success or failure is judged on the basis of whether the project met or exceeded the expectations created by the feasibility study and the financial analysis.

Equity Investors' Analyses
In addition to the feasibility study prepared by the developer, potential equity investors prepare their own analyses. These analyses focus on the investment's potential return and the potential risk. The two most important studies for a potential equity investor are a discounted cash flow analysis, which measures the potential return, and a sensitivity analysis, which attempts to measure the risk. (Such analyses are discussed at length in Chapter 5.)

Lenders' Analyses

In addition to the general feasibility analysis, all potential lenders conduct their own economic analyses. Figure 7-5 shows an example of the type of analysis a lender undertakes. This analysis focuses on two key calculations: the debt service coverage ratio (or debt coverage ratio) and the loan-to-value ratio. In making these calculations, the lender relies on the pro forma financial statements provided by the developer in its financial analysis.

Debt Coverage Ratio. The DCR is perhaps the single most important calculation for a lender. Lenders use the ratio to determine the maximum loan amount they will make for a particular project. The debt coverage ratio is calculated by dividing the property's net operating income by the annual debt service.

$$\text{Debt Coverage Ratio} = \frac{\text{Net Operating Income}}{\text{Annual Debt Service}}$$

Net operating income is revenue minus all expenses, excluding debt service, for one year. NOI represents the cash that will be available to pay the debt service and the return to equity investors. For development projects, the revenue figure used in this calculation is a projection based on anticipated market rental rates for properties similar to the proposed project, adjusted for anticipated occupancy. The expense number used in this calculation is the total of all projected cash expenses, excluding debt service, and certain adjustments required by the lender

for noncash expenses. In calculating NOI, most lenders require that projected expenses include an estimated property management fee, even if the owner intends to manage the property itself, and a reserve for maintenance and replacement of the asset. These adjustments vary from lender to lender according to the lender's underwriting guidelines.

Annual debt service is the total of the payments on the proposed loan, including interest and principal, required to be made during one year. A number of financial calculators and simple computer programs are available that will calculate annual debt service. Another way to calculate annual debt service is to multiply the amount of the proposed loan by the mortgage constant for the proposed loan. The mortgage constant ratio is calculated by dividing the annual debt service for a loan by the loan amount.

$$\text{Mortgage Constant Ratio} = \frac{\begin{array}{c}\text{Annual Debt Service}\\ \text{(Interest + Principal)}\end{array}}{\text{Loan Amount}}$$

Figure 7-6 provides the mortgage constant for a number of loans and demonstrates how the mortgage constant is calculated. To determine the annual debt service for a particular loan, simply multiply the mortgage constant from the table by the proposed loan amount.

The DCR is one of two measures lenders use to set the maximum loan amount. All lenders have a proscribed minimum DCR to make a loan. This ratio varies from

The Charleston at Boca Raton, Florida, is a high-end project that caters to empty nesters.

figure 7-5
Lender's Analysis

Debt Coverage Ratio		
Assumptions		
Number of Units in Property	200	
Estimated Cost of Construction per Unit	$47,500	
Estimated Total Cost	$9,500,000	
Estimated Market Rental Rate per Month	$710	
Estimated Vacancy	5%	
Estimated Annual Property Operations Expenses per Unit	$2,875	
Estimated Property Management Fee	4%	
Annual Reserve for Maintenance and Replacement per Unit	$250	
Net Operating Income		
Gross Potential Rent (number of units x estimated market rate x 12)	$1,704,000	
Less Vacancy Adjustment	(85,200)	
Revenue		$1,618,800
Expenses		
Property Opertions	(575,000)	
Management Fee	(64,752)	
Reserves	(50,000)	
Total Expenses		(689,752)
Projected Net Operating Income		$929,048
Estimated Property Value		
Projected Net Opertating Income	$929,048	
Assumed Capitalization Rate	9.25%	
Estimated Property Value		$10,043,762
Annual Debt Service		
Loan Amount (80% of value)	$8,000,000	
Interest Rate	8%	
Amortization Schedule	30 years	
Annual Debt Service		$704,414
Debt Coverage Ratio		
Net Operating Income ÷ Annual Debt Service		1.32
Loan-to-Value Ratio		
Loan Amount ÷ Property Value		79.7%
Maximum Permanent Loan Amount		
The lesser of:		
• the Maximum Loan Amount at a Minimum Coverage Ratio of	1.25	$8,440,927
or		
• the Maximum Loan-to-Value of	80%	$8,035,010
Maximum Permanent Loan		$8,035,010
Maximum Construction Loan		
The lesser of:		
• the Maximum Loan Amount at a Loan-to-Cost Ratio of	90%	$8,550,000
or		
• the Maximum Permanent Loan of		$8,035,010
Maximum Construction Loan		$8,035,010

figure 7-6

Mortgage Constant and Annual Debt Service

Interest Rate	Amortization Period (Years)								
	0	5	10	15	20	25	30	35	40
12.0%	12.00%	26.69%	17.22%	14.40%	13.21%	12.64%	12.34%	12.19%	12.10%
11.5%	11.50%	26.39%	16.87%	14.02%	12.80%	12.20%	11.88%	11.71%	11.62%
11.0%	11.00%	26.09%	16.53%	13.64%	12.39%	11.76%	11.43%	11.24%	11.14%
10.5%	10.50%	25.79%	16.19%	13.26%	11.98%	11.33%	10.98%	10.78%	10.66%
10.0%	10.00%	25.50%	15.86%	12.00%	11.58%	10.90%	**10.53%**	10.32%	10.19%
9.5%	9.50%	25.20%	15.53%	12.53%	11.19%	10.48%	10.09%	9.86%	9.72%
9.0%	9.00%	24.91%	15.20%	12.17%	10.80%	10.07%	9.66%	9.41%	9.26%
8.5%	8.50%	24.62%	14.88%	11.82%	10.41%	9.66%	9.23%	8.96%	8.80%
8.0%	8.00%	24.33%	14.56%	11.47%	10.04%	9.26%	8.81%	8.52%	8.34%
7.5%	7.50%	24.05%	14.24%	11.12%	9.67%	8.87%	8.39%	8.09%	7.90%
7.0%	7.00%	23.76%	13.93%	10.79%	9.30%	8.48%	7.98%	7.67%	7.46%

Mortgage Constant

To determine the mortgage constant for a loan, first locate the column for the amortization period for the loan. Then find the appropriate interest rate for the loan at the left of the table. The mortgage constant for the loan expressed as a percentage is located at the intersection of the amortization period and the appropriate interest rate. For example, the mortgage constant for a loan with a 30-year amortization period and a 10 percent interest rate is 10.53 percent.

Annual Debt Service

To determine annual debt service for a loan, multiply the amount of the loan by the mortgage constant. For example, the annual debt service for a $1 million loan for 30 years at 10 percent interest is $1,000,000 x 10.53% = **$105,300.**

project to project based on the type and stage of development. In recent years, minimum debt coverage ratios accepted by lenders have ranged from as low as 1.15 to 1.00 to as high as 1.50 to 1.00.

Debt coverage ratio is a good measure of the risk associated with the loan. The lower the DCR, the more likely a default will occur if the project fails to achieve its projected cash flow. Each lender sets its own required debt service ratio based on its understanding of and tolerance for the risk of the project.

Once the lender's required debt service ratio has been established, the maximum loan amount can be calculated using the proposed project's net operating income, mortgage constant, and debt coverage ratio (see Figure 7-5). First, the proposed project's net operating income is derived from the information contained in the feasibility study and the developer's pro forma financial statements. Then the cash available for debt service is determined by dividing the net operating income by the required debt coverage ratio. Finally, the maximum loan amount is determined by dividing the cash available for debt service by the mortgage constant.

Loan-to-Value Ratio. The loan-to-value ratio is the second measure lenders use to determine the maximum loan for a proposed project. The loan-to-value ratio is calculated by dividing the loan amount by the property value.

$$\text{Loan-to-Value Ratio} = \frac{\text{Loan Amount}}{\text{Property Value}}$$

All lenders have specified maximum loan-to-value ratios for various project types. Like the debt coverage ratio, the loan-to-value ratio is a default risk measure. The more equity invested in the project, the less likely that a failure to achieve pro forma financial results would lead to default. And the more equity invested in the project, the less likely that a drop in value would result in the lender's failure to recoup its principal on the property's sale, either on the open market or as a result of foreclosure.

To estimate the property value used in the calculation of the loan-to-value ratio, the lender looks at the cost of construction and an estimate of the completed project's market value. Generally, market value is calculated using a direct capitalization rate and a discounted cash flow analysis.

The *capitalization rate,* generally referred to as the *cap rate,* is the ratio of the property's net operating income to its value.

$$\text{Cap Rate} = \frac{\text{NOI}}{\text{Property Value}}$$

Thus, if a property's NOI is $925,000 per year and its fair market value is $10 million, the cap rate for the property is 9.25 percent.

$$\text{Cap Rate} = \frac{\$925,000}{\$10,000,000} = 9.25\%$$

The property's cap rate is simply an expression of the relationship between the property's operating income and its value at a particular moment in time.

Direct capitalization is an estimate of the property's value made by comparing the property's anticipated income stream with that of other comparable properties. This method of estimating value assumes that properties with similar characteristics and income streams have similar values. To estimate the property value, divide the anticipated NOI by an assumed cap rate.

$$\text{Estimated Property Value} = \frac{\text{Projected NOI}}{\text{Assumed Cap Rate}}$$

The number used for NOI in this calculation is the NOI projected to be available in the first year following purchase or completion; it is based on the financial pro forma provided by the developer. Lenders generally require that the NOI projection include a provision for vacancy, a management fee, and replacement reserves. The exact amounts vary from lender to lender.

The lender or lender's appraiser specifies the assumed cap rate used in the calculation, which is generally based on cap rates for recent sales of similar properties. Selecting an appropriate cap rate for use in the calculation of direct capitalization is highly subjective. In theory, the assumed cap rate should reflect the cap rate of similar properties, but the determination of what is a similar prop-

erty can be quite difficult. Any number of factors, including the property's age, its exact location, its market appeal, and the economic outlook for the property's submarket, can have a marked effect on the value and cap rate.

The process of estimating value by means of direct capitalization is not an exact science. The calculation's accuracy depends totally on the quality and accuracy of the projected NOI and assumed cap rate used. A slight variation in either of these numbers can dramatically affect the property's estimated value.

An alternate means of estimating a property's value is the *discounted cash flow* method. Unlike direct capitalization, which considers only the property's NOI in the first year, the discounted cash flow method allows for consideration of a varying stream of income over a specified holding period and determines the present value of an investment with a similar income stream. Figure 7-7 illustrates a discounted cash flow analysis. This simplified model assumes that the property's NOI increases at an annual rate of 3 percent, but the discounted cash flow method could just as easily account for a more varied income stream.

To calculate the estimated value by this method, the proceeds available from the sale of the property at the end of the holding period must be estimated using direct capitalization. Generally, the cap rate assumed in this calculation is slightly higher (to reflect the property's age) than that used in the calculation of current value using direct capitalization. In the model illustrated in Figure 7-7, the cap rate assumed upon sale at the end of Year 5 is 9.5 percent, compared with 9.25 percent used in the calculation of current value in Figure 7-5. The final step in the calculation of discounted cash flow assumes a discount rate, that is, a yield that would be expected from an investment similar to the subject property. In the model, the assumed discount rate is 10 percent. The estimated property value determined by this method represents the amount an investor would need to invest to receive the indicated cash flow, including proceeds of a

Amortization versus Interest Only

A loan may be amortizing or interest only. In an amortizing loan, a portion of each payment is allocated to repayment of principal; with each payment, the principal amount of the outstanding loan is reduced. The amount of each payment allocated to repayment of principal is determined by the length of the amortization period. The shorter the amortization period, the higher the portion of each payment allocated to repayment of principal. Conversely, the longer the amortization period, the lower the portion of each monthly payment allocated to repayment of principal.

Although repaying borrowed funds as quickly as possible is a worthwhile goal, in real estate investment it may work against the developer, because the required payments of amortizing loans include both principal and interest.

The payments are generally larger than the payments required on an interest-only loan. As a result, amortizing loans make a bigger demand on the project's cash flow than an interest-only loan. Second, although interest payments are fully deductible in determining the taxable income from a property, principal payments are not tax deductible. Therefore, when owners place an amortizing loan on a property, they will increase their equity in the property by reducing the outstanding debt with each payment, but they will also reduce current cash flow while increasing taxable income and tax liability. In cases where operating cash flow might be somewhat limited—often the case in the early years of a new development project —it may be better for the developer to use an interest-only loan and minimize the demands on the project's current cash flow. ∎

figure 7-7

Discounted Cash Flow Analysis

Assumptions					
Discount Rate		10%			
NOI		Increasing at 3% per Year			
Cap Rate at Sale		9.5%			

Estimated NOI					Estimated
Year 1	Year 2	Year 3	Year 4	Year 5	Proceeds of Sale
$929,048	$956,919	$985,627	$1,015,196	$1,045,652	$11,337,066*

Present Value = $10,758,034

*Proceeds of sale estimated using direct capitalization of projected NOI for Year 6:

Year 6 NOI	$1,077,021
Cap Rate at Sale	9.5%
Estimated Proceeds of Sale	$11,337,066

sale at the assumed discount rate. This value may be more or less than the value determined by the direct capitalization method.

Once the lender has estimated the property's value, the maximum loan amount can easily be calculated by multiplying the property value by the specified loan-to-value ratio. The maximum loan amount provided by calculating loan to value is then compared with the amount provided by calculating the debt coverage ratio. Ultimately, the maximum loan the lender will make is limited to the lesser of these amounts.

When calculating the maximum loan amount for a short-term loan, the lender generally analyzes the property as though the lender is being asked to make a long-term loan. Although the project's completion triggers the long-term financing, the property's feasibility analysis for long-term financing is extremely important and, in most cases, controls whether or not the developer receives short-term financing, such as a construction loan. The permanent financing is extremely important to the short-term lender, because it provides the *takeout*, that is, the funds to pay off the construction loan. Thus, virtually all lenders analyze a project as though they were providing long-term financing. Having a permanent loan ready or committed to take out the short-term loan is extremely important.

Types of Debt Financing

Loans fall into two categories based on the length of the loan—short term and long term. The type of loan available varies with the project's stage of development at the time the loan is made. Generally, loans for the planning through construction stages are short term. In addition, any loan from completion until the property

is sold, in the case of a build-to-sell development, or until permanent long-term financing can be put in place, in the case of a build-to-own project, is a short-term loan. Only after completion and stabilization when the property is in the hands of the final owner/operator is long-term financing placed on the property.

Interim loans are short-term loans used to fund the project's development up to completion. Interim loans carry a variable interest rate, are full recourse, and have no scheduled interest or principal payments until maturity, when both the principal and all accrued interest are due. Interim loans generally include those used to fund predevelopment activities, land acquisition and development, and project construction. Interim financing also includes any "bridge" or "gap" financing during the period following the completion of construction but before the property sale or the placement of permanent financing. The interim loan generally is repaid with proceeds from sale of the property or with funds from a permanent loan placed on the completed property. Figure 7-8 displays the sources of debt financing.

Permanent loans are long-term loans that fund property ownership and operation after construction is completed. These loans can have a variable or fixed interest rate, are frequently nonrecourse, and have a required monthly payment that generally includes principal and interest. Figure 7-9 compares construction loans and permanent loans.

The development stage controls not only the type of loan being made but also the source of the loan. Although a particular lender may be willing to lend funds for the long term for a fully completed, operational apartment community, that same lender may be unwilling to make a loan for land acquisition or to finance construction. To a large extent, risk drives the decision. As the project moves through the stages of development, more and

The twin 39-story towers of West End Towers in New York City feature 1,000 rental apartments and retail and commercial space.

nent financing is put in place only after completion and stabilization of the property. At the very least, the permanent loan is not fully funded until certain conditions, such as minimum occupancy, have been achieved. As a result, the cost of a construction loan is generally higher than that of a permanent loan. Figure 7-10 describes the characteristics of different lenders.

Financing the Various Stages of Development

Planning/Predevelopment
A developer generally bears the cost of planning and predevelopment. Well-capitalized developers may be able to find a lender willing to make a full recourse loan backed by the developer's assets to fund planning and predevelopment, but nonrecourse, project-backed financing is generally not available because at this early stage, the project has no assets to secure the loan.

A developer may be able to find equity investors who are willing to help fund planning and predevelopment, but this equity is generally very expensive. An equity investment at this early stage is extremely risky. Many events can prevent the project from proceeding, and, because the project has no assets at this stage, failure usually means a total loss of investment.

Land Acquisition and Development
A number of options are available to developers seeking financing for land acquisition and development. But similar to the planning and predevelopment stage, only well-capitalized, well-established developers will be able to obtain a loan from an institutional lender for land acquisition. Again, it is a matter of perceived risk. Lenders look to the cash flow generated by the project and underlying value of the project's assets for repayment. At this stage, no cash flow exists and the land value may in fact be reduced once development begins. Thus, loans for

more money is invested until the project is completed. At the same time, the risk associated with the project increases, peaking during the construction stage. When the project is completed, its risk is reduced to purely operational issues. Thus, construction loans generally carry more risk than permanent loans. Any number of factors can adversely affect the repayment of a construction loan: delays in construction, cost overruns, or the failure to achieve the projected occupancy or lease rates. Perma-

figure 7-8
Sources of Debt Financing

Type of Financing	Commercial Banks	Savings & Loans	Insurance Companies	Pension Funds	Credit Companies	Securitized Lenders	Mortgage REITs	Government Agencies
Line of Credit	Y	Y	N	N	N	N	N	N
Letter of Credit	Y	N	N	N	N	N	N	Y
Planning/Predevelopment	Y	N	N	N	N	N	N	N
Land Acquisition	Y	Y	N	N	Y	N	N	N
Land Development	Y	Y	N	N	Y	N	N	N
Construction	Y	Y	Y	Y	Y	Y	N	Y
Bridge (Gap) Financing	Y	N	N	N	Y	Y	N	N
Takeout Commitment	Y	Y	Y	Y	Y	Y	N	Y
Standby Commitment	N	N	N	N	Y	N	N	N
Permanent Mortgage	Y	Y	Y	Y	Y	Y	Y	Y

figure 7-9
Comparison of Construction Loans and Permanent Loans

	Construction Loans	Permanent Loans
Term	Short term (18 to 36 months)	Long term (10 to 30 years)
Interest Rate	Floating	Fixed or floating
Funding	As construction or renovation is completed	Upon closing (except for required holdbacks)
Security	Secured by property	Secured by property and income from property
Liability	Borrower may assume personal liability	Nonrecourse to borrower
Repayment	From proceeds of permanent loan	From sale of property or assumption by buyer

figure 7-10

Characteristics of Lending Sources

	Short-Term Lenders	Long-Term Lenders	Floating-Rate Lenders	Fixed-Rate Lenders
Commercial Banks	●	●	●	●
Savings & Loans	●	●	●	●
Insurance Companies		●		●
Pension Funds		●		●
Credit Companies		●	●	●
Securitized Lenders		●	●	●
Mortgage REITs		●		●
Government Agencies		●		●

land acquisition will be made only as full recourse loans and only when the developer or the development group has significant equity or assets at risk. Because they are considered so risky, land acquisition and development loans are usually quite expensive.

To proceed with a project, the developer must have control of the land. But if a loan from an institutional investor is not a viable alternative, how does the developer gain control of the land? Fortunately, a number of ways can be used to acquire control of land that require little or no money from the developer.

Seller Financing. The selling landowner can provide financing by taking back what is commonly referred to as a *purchase-money mortgage*. In this situation, the seller transfers landownership to the developer in exchange for a loan secured by the property. Although sellers frequently require some downpayment, it is not uncommon for the loan to be for the full purchase price of the land. The loan is generally due in full upon sale of the completed project or, in cases when the developer intends to hold and operate the property, when the developer receives permanent financing. Depending on the loan agreement, interest payments may be required during the term of the loan, or the interest may accrue and be included in the payoff amount.

When the seller finances the loan, the seller must agree to subordinate its loan to any future construction loan, as all construction lenders will require that the construction loan be a first lien. If the seller has not agreed to allow the construction loan to take priority over the land loan, the developer will usually be unable to obtain construction financing.

Seller Contribution. Seller contribution is similar to seller financing except that instead of taking back a loan, the seller takes an equity interest in the project. The contribution may be structured as a joint venture, a partnership, or a limited liability company. A seller contribution offers several advantages to the developer. First, it does not require the developer's capital. Second, because it is considered equity invested in the project, it increases the developer's ability to obtain construction and permanent financing. Third, it does not raise the subordination issue created by seller financing.

Land Option. Another method for gaining control of the property without using much money is to obtain an option to acquire the land. In this approach, the developer pays the landowner for the exclusive right to buy the property for a predetermined price during a specified period of time. Although no standard amount is attached to a land option, it represents a modest amount—often

1 to 10 percent of the specified purchase price. The option payment may be made in one lump sum or in a series of payments over the life of the option. The option may include additional payments for extensions or the occurrence of certain events, such as the successful rezoning of the property. Once an option payment has been made, it is usually nonrefundable.

Land Lease. Land leases are rarely used in multifamily development, except for affordable or subsidized housing projects. Under the terms of a land lease, the developer rents the land from the owner for a specified period in exchange for a series of payments. Land leases are usually for substantial terms, frequently 50 or more years, and landownership never transfers to the developer. At the end of the lease, including any renewal options, all the improvements the developer has made to the land revert to the landowner. Although a land lease is a very low-cost way to gain control of the land, it represents only temporary control. Land leases can make it substantially more difficult to place permanent financing on the project or to sell the property.

Construction

Construction loans are short-term loans used to finance development; most have terms of fewer than three years. The loans are almost always full recourse and carry a variable interest rate. Generally, no interest or principal payments are due during the term of the loan. Instead, the interest is added to the principal, and the entire balance, principal plus accrued interest, is due when development is complete and the property is sold or obtains permanent financing. Construction loans are funded in a series of *draws* or payments made as the construction reaches certain specified levels of completion. Interest is charged only on the outstanding balance at any point in time.

From a lender's point of view, a construction loan is riskier than a permanent loan on a completed, oper-

Grand Venetian is a 514-unit luxury apartment project in Irving, Texas, developed by Palladium Group and financed by Malone Mortgage at a total development cost of $36 million.

ational property. Any number of factors—cost overruns, construction delays, changing market conditions, rising interest rates—can lead to a default. Because of the perceived risk, construction loans are more expensive than the permanent financing available after completion. Generally, the interest rate charged for a construction loan is a variable rate tied to a specified index of short-term interest rates plus some specified amount. The amount added to the base rate to determine the interest rate on the loan is referred to as the *spread*. Although spreads vary with market conditions at the time the loan is made, spreads of 0.5 to 2 percentage points above the prime rate are fairly common. The spread could be considerably higher, however, depending on general economic conditions and the lender's perception of risk.

In addition to the interest charged during the term of the loan, the lender usually charges a fee upfront, sometimes referred to as an *application* or *commitment fee*. This fee is generally expressed in units called *points*. One point represents an amount equal to 1 percentage point of the loan amount. The number of points a lender charges depends on market conditions and the lender's assessment of loan risk, but a 1- to 2-point charge is not unusual for a construction loan. The lender also holds the developer responsible for any costs associated with making the loan, such as the cost of a survey, an appraisal, or an environmental report, and the lender's legal fees. If a loan is extended, the lender generally charges the developer additional fees and expenses.

Commercial banks have been the primary source of construction loans, but the loans may also be available from credit companies and certain government agencies. Construction loans may even be available from lenders normally associated with permanent loans, such as pension funds and life insurance companies, but to secure a construction loan from these sources generally requires the developer to commit to placing the permanent loan on the property with the lender making the construction loan.

Postconstruction

Takeout Commitment. The construction loan is generally repaid using the proceeds from the sale of the development or, when the developer intends to hold and operate the property, from the funds made available by placing permanent long-term financing. The lender issuing the construction loan generally requires the developer to have a commitment from a buyer or permanent lender that it will be ready to take the property upon its completion, referred to as a *takeout commitment.*

In some cases, the construction lender may be willing to accept another lender's promise to issue a bridge or gap loan (discussed below) as a takeout commitment upon the project's completion. Virtually all sales contracts and commitments for permanent financing contain contingencies that, if not met, relieve the purchaser or new lender from its obligation to buy or finance the property. At the very least, the takeout lender is not obligated to fully fund the takeout loan until the property

Camden Property Trust owns and operates 158 multifamily properties with 55,935 units. Heron Pointe in Tampa, Florida, is one of its properties.

has met the occupancy and revenue standards specified in the takeout commitment. Construction lenders are very concerned about any such contingencies. From the construction lender's point of view, the fewer such contingencies, the stronger the commitment.

Standby Commitment. A variation of the takeout commitment is the *standby commitment*. Similar to the terms of a takeout commitment, a permanent lender has committed to provide permanent financing upon the project's completion; however, the developer does not expect to ever use the promised loan unless no other alternative is available. Instead, the developer intends to wait and explore the options. For example, a developer may have undertaken a project with the expectation of selling it but upon completion may find that he is unable to sell it because market conditions have changed. In such a case, a standby commitment provides a fallback position, allowing the developer to fulfill its obligation to pay off the construction loan. The real purpose of the standby commitment is to assure the construction lender that the developer will have the ability to pay off the construction loan when the project is completed.

Bridge Financing. Sometimes the construction loan matures before the property can be sold or long-term permanent financing can be obtained. In such cases, the developer needs a loan to "bridge" the period from maturity of the construction loan to sale or permanent financing. *Bridge loans* are usually one- to three-year, re-

course loans at a variable interest rate. A bridge loan is generally repaid with proceeds from sale of the property, in the case of built-for-sale properties, or from the proceeds of a permanent loan placed on the property by the developer.

Gap Financing. Occasionally, a developer is unable to obtain sufficient permanent financing to repay the construction loan in full when it matures. Perhaps the property has not yet achieved the performance standards required for full funding of the takeout commitment, or perhaps the property's performance does not yet support a new permanent loan in an amount sufficient to pay off the construction loan. In such a case, the developer needs a *gap loan*. A gap loan is usually a short-term, full recourse loan with a variable interest rate. Repayment of the loan comes from additional releases from the takeout loan as the property achieves the specified performance standards or as the property's performance improves to the level that allows for a permanent loan of sufficient size.

Permanent Financing

Permanent loans are long-term loans used to finance real estate ownership. They usually are for more than five years, sometimes as long as 40 years. At one time, a 30-year term was the norm, but the trend in recent years has been for permanent loans to have shorter terms.

Permanent loans may carry a fixed or variable interest rate. The interest rate is generally stated as a spread over a specified well-known index. In the case of fixed-rate loans, the rate is set at the time the loan is made and the index used is frequently U.S. Treasury bonds with a term equal to that of the loan term. The interest rate on a variable-rate loan changes over time as the underlying index moves. The timing of adjustments to the rate charged is specified in the loan agreement, but it generally does not occur more frequently than monthly or less frequently than annually. Any number of indices can be used as the basis for setting a variable interest rate, depending on the lender's preference.

Permanent loans may be interest only or amortizing. For an interest-only loan, monthly payments consist purely of interest. No principal is paid until the loan is paid in full at maturity. For an amortizing loan, monthly payments consist of interest and principal. The loan may be fully amortizing, sometimes referred to as *self-liquidating,* or may have a *balloon.* For fully amortizing loans, the amortization schedule matches the term of the loan, and, assuming all payments are made on schedule, the loan is paid in full with the final monthly payment. For a balloon loan, the amortization period is longer than the loan term. Thus, although the monthly payments of principal reduce the principal due when the loan matures, the regularly scheduled monthly payments do not pay the principal in full and a balloon payment equal to the remaining balance of the principal is due at maturity. A common example of a balloon loan is a loan with a 30-year amortization and a ten-year term.

Permanent loans are mostly nonrecourse, but they are secured by the property using a first mortgage (sometimes referred to as a *first deed of trust*). In case of default, the lender's only remedy is to foreclose and attempt to recover the outstanding debt through sale of the property.

The principal sources of permanent loans for multifamily properties have been life insurance companies, pension funds, and government programs. In recent years, Wall Street conduit programs and mortgage REITs have become increasingly important providers of multifamily permanent financing.

Sources of Financing

A number of variables influence the sources of both equity and debt financing for multifamily development projects, including a project's size, the type of property (garden/mid-rise/high rise), targeted income level of the project's residents, market conditions, the development stage, and the development entity.

Sources of Equity Financing

Equity financing comes from the developer, the land owner, individuals, and groups of investors and joint venture partners.

Developer. The starting point for the equity required to develop a multifamily property is the developer's own resources, which may include cash or other assets that can be borrowed against or pledged as additional collateral to help secure the loans required. By relying totally on his own resources for the necessary equity capital, the developer retains ownership and control of the project and is in the best position to maximize profits. Unfortunately, few developers have sufficient assets to provide the equity capital except for the smallest projects.

Landowner. The landowner from whom the developer is acquiring the land can contribute the land in exchange for an equity interest (see "Land Acquisition and Development" above). The value of the contributed land is considered equity invested in the project; it increases the developer's ability to obtain the balance of the financing required for the project. The contribution may be structured as a joint venture, a partnership, a limited liability company, or, if the developer is organized as an UpREIT, a contribution to the REIT's operating partnership.

Individuals. Virtually every developer has at one time or another, often early in his career, gone to relatives, friends, or business associates seeking funds for a development project. Most of us do not have acquaintances who can provide sufficient financing to fund any but the smallest projects. There are individuals, however, who will invest in multifamily projects. The difficulty is to find them. Fortunately, they tend to have cadres of professional advisers—attorneys, accountants, bankers, real estate brokers, business and investment advisers—who are generally the best source for locating private investors.

Investors. Groups of investors can be formed to invest equity capital in a development project. The process of

Addison Circle, developed as part of a public/private initiative, strives to create a sustainable, high-density, mixed-use neighborhood in Addison, Texas.

Cascade Court, an affordable housing development in Seattle, was constructed for $7.2 million, or $71,160 per unit.

A. General requirements for a loan submission package
1. Project information
   a. Project description—legal description of site, survey, photographs of site, renderings of building and any parking facilities, development strategy and timing
   b. Site and circulation plan, identification of any easements, availability of utilities, description of adjacent land uses, soil tests
   c. Plans for building improvements. Detailed list of amenities.
   d. Identification of architect, general contractor, principal subcontractors. Supporting financial data and past performance of parties. Copies of any agreements executed among parties. Description of construction and development procedures.
2. Market and financial data
   a. Full set of financial statements on the borrower and any other principal project sponsors, past development experience, list of previous project lenders
   b. Pro forma operating statement. Detail on proposed leasing terms to tenants, including base rent, escalations, expense stops, renewal options, common area expense allocation, overage (retail leases), finish-out allowances, other commitments.
   c. Detailed cost breakdowns including:
      • Any land acquisition costs
      • Any necessary land development costs
      • Any required demolition costs
      • Direct or hard costs with breakdowns for excavation, grading, foundation, masonry, steel work, drywall or plastering, HVAC, plumbing, electrical, elevator, and other mechanical, any special finish-out or fixtures
      • Indirect or soft costs, including architects, engineering fees, legal fees, property taxes, interest [during the] construction period, development fees, insurance and bonding fees, estimated contingency reserve, anticipated permanent loan fees

   d. Any executed lease commitments or letter of intent from tenants detailing all terms of leases
   e. Market study and appraisal, including all comparables and detached schedule of rents charged by competitors
   f. Loan request, terms, anticipated interest rate, amortization period, anticipated participation options
   g. Equity to be provided by developer and/or other sponsors (cash and/or land); anticipated financing of draws/repayment
3. Government and regulatory information
   a. Statement as to zoning status
   b. Ad valorem taxes, method of payment, reappraisal dates
   c. All necessary permits, evidence of approved zoning variances, etc.
4. Legal documentation
   a. Legal entity applying for loan (evidence of incorporation, partnership agreement)
   b. Statement of land costs or contract evidencing purchase
   c. Detail regarding deed restrictions, etc.
   d. Subordination agreements
   e. *Force majeur* provisions (events beyond the control of the developer such as an "act of God")

B. Additional information needed for interim loan package
1. A copy of the permanent or standby commitment from the permanent lender. Details on the amount, rate, term, fees, options relative to prepayment, calls, and participation. Details on contingencies that the developer must meet before the commitment is binding.
2. *Detailed* architectural plans and specifications
3. *Detailed* cost breakdown
4. All data relative to requirements list in Part A and *updated* as appropriate

Assuming that 1) upon review of all relevant materials in A and B, the interim lender makes a commitment and 2) the developer goes forward with the project, the next step [is] to close the interim loan.

forming the group and finding investors is referred to as *syndication.* Syndications are generally organized as partnerships or limited liability companies. They may be private, with a limited number of investors, or public, with hundreds of investors. A syndication's advantage is that it vastly increases the number of investors and the capital that can be raised. It is, however, generally quite an expensive process, and the developer generally must relinquish a major ownership interest to the investors.

An alternative to syndication is to find a joint venture partner who will put up the required capital. Possible joint venture partners include REITs, pension plans, and insurance companies.

Equity REITs, those that invest in real estate, generally focus on a particular type of property. It is not unusual to find an equity REIT that limits its investments to luxury garden-style apartments in suburban locations or to low-income mid-rise apartments in urban locations.

C. Interim lender closing requirements
 1. Project information: *final* drawings, cost estimates, site plan, etc.
 2. Market and financial information: statement that no adverse change in borrower's financial position has occurred since application date
 3. Government and regulatory information: all necessary permits, notification of any approved zoning variances, etc.
 4. Legal documentation
    a. Documentation indicating that the permanent lender has reviewed and approved all information in Part A and all updates in Part B
    b. All documentation relative to contracts for general contractors, architects, planners, subcontractors. Evidence of bonding, conditional assignment of all contracts to interim lender. Agreements of all contractors to perform for interim lender. Verification of property tax insurance contracts, etc.
    c. Inventory of all personal property that will serve as security for the interim loan . . .
    d. Any executed leases and approvals by permanent lender
    e. Copies of ground leases and verification of current payment status by the lessor/owner
    f. The interim lender will also insist on an assignment of all leases, rents, and other income in the event of default *and* a guarantee of loan payments by the borrower (personal liability). After review of all items indicated above, the interim lender will provide the borrower with a loan commitment detailing the terms of the loan, including amount, rate, term, fees, prepayment and call options, and any participations. However, the *permanent* lender may require certain agreements with the interim lender, including a buy-sell agreement or tri-party agreement.

D. Permanent lender closing requirements
 These requirements are necessary *if* the developer 1) completes construction and 2) satisfies all contingencies (including lease-up requirements) contained in the permanent loan commitment before the expiration date of the permanent commitment.
 1. Market and financial data
    a. Statement of no material changes in financial status of borrower, or
    b. A certified list of tenants, executed leases, and estoppel certificates indicating verification of rents currently being collected, any amounts owed, and any dispute relative to payments on finish-out costs agreement with the developer
 2. Project information
    a. Final appraisal of project value
    b. Final survey of building on site
 3. Government and regulatory information
    a. Updates on currency of property taxes
    b. Certificate of occupancy issued by building inspector
    c. Other permit requirements (fire, safety, health, etc.)
 4. Legal documentation
    a. Delivery of the construction loan mortgage (if assigned to the permanent lender)
    b. Architect's certificate of completion with detailed survey and final plans, etc.
    c. Endorsements of all casualty and hazard insurance policies indicating permanent lender as new loss payee
    d. Updated title insurance policy
    e. Updated verification on status of ground rents (if relevant)
    f. An exculpation agreement relieving the borrower of personal liability (if applicable)
    g. Lien releases from general subcontractors, verification of any payments outstanding, and proposed disposition

Source: William B. Brueggeman and Jeffrey Fisher, *Real Estate Finance and Investments*, 10th ed. (New York: Irwin/McGraw-Hill, 1996), pp. 486–87. Reproduced by permission.

■

They might also focus on a particular geographic region. Although some equity REITs restrict their investments to well-established operating properties, many do invest in development projects. An investment in a multifamily development project could involve a direct cash investment, a joint venture with the developer, or a takeout commitment in the form of an agreement to acquire the property after it is completed and has attained certain specified performance standards.

Most pension funds prefer equity investments in investment-grade properties. They may make such an investment for their own accounts or as a joint venture partner, or they may grant hybrid-type loans. Pension funds generally prefer seasoned, high-quality properties but occasionally invest in development projects.

Insurance companies frequently make equity investments in multifamily properties either for their own account or on behalf of accounts managed for real estate investors such as pension funds. Insurance companies may also be joint venture partners with an operator, developer, or other investor. Insurance companies are more likely to invest in existing properties but sometimes invest in development projects.

Sources of Debt Financing

The best source for a loan depends on a number of factors, including the type of project, stage of development, size of the loan required, and the experience and financial strength of the borrower. Potential borrowers must understand that lenders enter and leave the market continuously. A lender who may be willing to make a particular loan today may not make any multifamily development loans tomorrow. Some key factors influence a lender's willingness to lend funds for multifamily development: the general state of the nation's and the region's economies, their future economic health, the outlook for the multifamily housing industry, and the lender's

Mortgage Brokers

One way to get ahead of the learning curve is to work closely with a competent mortgage broker who knows multifamily housing in your area or in a nearby major financial center. Some specialize in HUD, Fannie Mae, or FHA programs, while others focus on conventional, market-rate programs through pension funds or insurance companies. A mortgage broker typically charges a fee of 0.5 to 1.5 percent of the project's total cost, but the expenditure can be well worth it. Mortgage brokers help to prepare the package and present the proposed development to a wide variety of potential lenders or investment groups. They can guide the developer through the many pluses and minuses of various programs and the advantages of working with one lender over another. They can also advise the developer on the different types of transactions that can minimize—or even eliminate in the case of a standby commitment, presale, or even an institutional joint venture—the equity required to complete the transaction.

If the project is in a dynamic market and is well conceived, a successful broker may show the package to ten possible lenders and come back with four or five statements of interest and the initial loan program terms. The developer then has worked through the many factors that determine what type of loan works best for his strategy—personal goals, overall business goals, whether the completed property is to hold on to or to sell quickly—and established his own criteria.

financial and business strategy. Even if a lender is in the market to make loans on multifamily projects, the terms and conditions of loans that are available at any particular time vary greatly. Thus, in planning a development, the developer should survey the market, determine which lenders are making which types of loans under what terms and conditions, and then decide the best source of debt financing for a particular project. Debt financing comes from commercial banks, savings and loan institutions (S&Ls), REITs, pension funds, insurance companies, credit companies, securitized lenders, government and quasi-government agencies such as FHA, Fannie Mae, and Freddie Mac, and tax credits such as those for low-income housing and historic properties.

Commercial Banks. Commercial banks are the principal source of multifamily construction loans and are a good source of permanent financing. Commercial banks may be a funding source for planning, predevelopment, land acquisition, and development, but loans for these purposes are available only to financially strong, experienced developers. When making loans for planning or predevelopment, the bank must totally rely on the developer's financial strength and experience. Loans for this purpose are in the form of personal loans to smaller developers or lines of credit. When making loans for land acquisition and development, the bank not only evaluates the developer's financial strength and experience but also requires the developer or the investors to make a substantial equity investment in the project. In addition, commercial banks can, for a fee, provide letters of credit for a developer who needs to enhance its creditworthiness to obtain financing from another source.

Savings Institutions. Savings and loan associations and other savings institutions provide a full range of real estate loans, from construction loans to permanent financing. In recent years, savings institutions have become more focused on loans for smaller projects in their local markets.

REITs. Mortgage REITs specialize in real estate loans, while hybrid REITs make both equity investments and loans. Either type of REIT is a possible source of both construction and permanent financing. Most REITs focus on a particular type of property, such as multifamily housing, but some offer loans for a wider variety of properties. As a rule, REITs prefer to make participating loans, which offer the REIT an additional contingent return such as a share of the cash flow or the project's profit, or convertible loans, which offer the REIT the opportunity to convert some or all of the loan to an equity position.

Pension Funds. Although pension funds generally make equity investments in existing properties, they also provide debt for real estate projects, primarily permanent financing. On occasion, pension funds may make construction loans. Pension fund loans may be structured as pure debt or as hybrid-type loans such as participating or convertible loans. As a rule, pension funds prefer *investment-grade* or *institutional-quality* properties.

■

Toscana in Sunnyvale, California, was developed by Avalon-Bay, a multifamily REIT that focuses on developing, redeveloping, acquiring, and managing apartment communities in high-barrier-to-entry markets.

Insurance Companies. Insurance companies are a major source of permanent financing for existing properties and takeout commitments on development projects. Some insurance companies provide construction loans but generally do not provide other types of interim financing. Insurance companies do not make loans generally for planning and predevelopment or for land acquisition and development.

As a rule, insurance companies are interested only in larger projects. They are not generally a good source for small projects.

Credit Companies. Many credit companies provide short-term real estate loans, including construction, bridge, and gap loans. They may even provide short-term loans for the acquisition of existing properties. As a rule, credit companies are much more flexible than banks and insurance companies and often make loans that could not be obtained from those sources. In exchange for flexibility, credit companies generally charge higher interest rates than banks or insurance companies. Loans from credit companies are often hybrid, with both a base interest rate and a participation interest rate. Such loans also frequently have a *look-back* provision; that is, the lender is entitled to receive a minimum rate of return over the life of the loan that is more than would be provided by the base interest rate. At maturity, the lender compares the total amount of base and participation interest paid over the life of the loan with the interest required for the lender to receive its minimum return. If both base and participation interest paid to date is more than the amount required for the lender to receive its minimum return, no additional interest is due. If the amount paid is not sufficient to provide the lender with its minimum return, the lender is entitled to a deficiency payment sufficient to bring the return up to the specified minimum.

Securitized Lenders. Securitized lenders service mortgage conduits. Securitization is the process of convert-

The Villas at Cityplace, an apartment community in the uptown section of Dallas, was financed by First American Bank of Dallas.

Consisting of 127 loft-style apartment units, Post Properties's Block 588™ in Dallas had a total buildout cost of $22 million and a funds-from-operation yield of 10 percent.

ing individual assets, such as commercial mortgages, into a new financial instrument or security that represents an undivided interest in a segregated pool of assets. The best examples of securitization involving real estate–related assets are commercial mortgage–backed securities (CMBSs). In a CMBS, a number of commercial mortgage loans are pooled, and then interests in the pool are sold to investors. A traditional portfolio lender, such as an insurance company or commercial bank, or a conduit (a special-purpose entity formed solely to originate mortgage loans to create CMBSs through securitization) can originate the mortgage loans in the pool.

Government Finance Programs. A number of government and quasi-government agencies offer support for the development of multifamily housing, either through direct loans or by using other mechanisms such as tax credits, low interest rates, or high loan-to-value ratios. These financing programs can be tremendously helpful

to developers, and in the case of affordable housing projects, using these sources of funds often makes the difference between a project that is viable and one that is not. The only downside from the developer's perspective is that a number of regulations and restrictions usually accompany these funds.

The federal government has a long history of involvement in the financing of multifamily development projects. Although the past two decades have seen dramatic reductions in the amount of direct federal spending on housing production (particularly with respect to affordable housing), a number of governmental and quasi-government agencies continue to play an important role in the financing of multifamily development. Moreover, state and local governments have also created their own programs to fill in the void left by federal cutbacks.

Low-Income Housing Tax Credits. Two types of tax credits are available for the construction of low-income housing,

Adversity Yields Opportunity: Commercial Mortgage–Backed Securities

In 1991, Congress established the Resolution Trust Corporation (RTC) to work through the tens of billions of dollars of loans from failed federally insured S&Ls. To efficiently handle the disposition of the commercial mortgages held by those institutions, the RTC issued the first publicly rated securities consisting of a pool of mortgages secured by commercial property—commercial mortgage–backed securities. Investors greeted CMBSs with enthusiasm. By the end of 1995, the RTC had issued $17 billion of these securities.

With its mandate fulfilled, the RTC ceased operation at the end of 1995. As its legacy, the RTC left a new way to finance commercial real estate through commercial mortgage securitization.

Conduits: The Legacy of the RTC

Conduits are organizations that make commercial mortgages with the intention of turning them into securities for investors. Conduits are not like banks, as they do not rely on a base of deposits to fund loans. Rather, they use short-term borrowings to fund loans that are held in inventory before securitization. Once the conduit has accumulated a portfolio of sufficient size, the loans are pooled and securitized and the resulting securities sold to investors.

Although banks and institutional lenders have returned to making commercial mortgages, the greatest growth in the mortgage finance industry has been in CMBSs. According to *Commercial Mortgage Alert*, CMBSs issued jumped from $17.5 billion in 1993 to $44 billion in 1997 to more than $78 billion in 1998. The rate was expected to slow by at least 25 percent in 1999.

Conduits' Value to Borrowers and Investors

Both fixed-income investors and commercial property borrowers recognize the value of loans from conduits. The securities, made up of conduit loans, are attractive to investors because they offer good risk-adjusted returns. For commercial real estate owners and investors, conduits have added liquidity and depth to the commercial mortgage market.

Tips for Seeking Loans through Conduits

Conduits can be excellent sources for borrowers seeking permanent financing for a real estate project. Several issues surrounding conduits should concern every potential conduit borrower, however.

- Because conduit loans are resold as a security, the underwriting standards and procedures for the loans must be strictly followed. If the loan is somewhat out of the ordinary and underwriting standards or procedures must be waived to make the loan, a conduit is not generally a very good source for the loan.
- All commercial property loans with conduits are subject to risk criteria established by the rating agencies in the CMBS markets; not every potential loan will fit those criteria.
- Fulfilling the entire due diligence requirements for a conduit loan can be quite expensive. It is important to get from the conduit a clear idea of the legal fees and other costs associated with the environmental, engineering, and appraisal reports that must be performed for most commercial mortgages.

Borrowers seeking commercial mortgages of less than $2 million should look for a conduit that has a streamlined program, including reduced fees for the required due diligence reports.

∎

one granted through a competitive process that provides a 9 percent rate on eligible project development costs and the other granted through a noncompetitive process that provides a 4 percent rate. Projects must meet one of the following income requirements: 40 percent of the units must serve persons with incomes of 60 percent of the area median income; or 20 percent of the units must serve those with incomes of 50 percent of the area median income or less, adjusted for household size. Once applications are received, scoring criteria are applied. Rents must be restricted for ten years.

Tax credits attract private investment for affordable apartment units. The benefit to investors is that tax credits shelter both passive and nonpassive income. Typically, credits from passive activities can be used only to offset income taxes on passive income. Individuals are limited to using tax credits against income taxes on the last $25,000 in income in any one year.

Internal Revenue Service/State Housing Finance Agencies
- Low-Income Housing Tax Credits.

Department of Housing and Urban Development
Cooperatives and Condominiums
- Mortgage insurance for cooperative units (Section 213): HUD retains authority for this program, but it is no longer in use.

Manufactured Housing
- Manufactured home parks (Section 207(m)): New commitments are no longer being made under this program.

Production
- Section 8 new construction/substantial rehabilitation: Program repealed in 1983; subsidy continues for the renewal of contracts.
- Section 8 loan management setaside: No new funds being issued; used only for the renewal of contracts.
- Property disposition setaside program.
- Mortgage insurance for rental housing (Section 207): HUD retains authority for this program, but it is no longer in use, except for refinancing.
- Mortgage insurance for rental and cooperative housing (Sections 221(d)(3) and (4)).
- Mortgage insurance for rental housing in urban areas (Section 220): Rarely used.
- Supplemental loan insurance for multifamily rental housing (Section 241(a)).
- Mortgage insurance for purchase or refinancing of existing multifamily housing projects (Section 223(f)).
- Flexible subsidy program.
- Two-year operating loss loans (Section 223(d)).
- Qualified participating entities risk-sharing pilot program (Section 542(b)): Commitment authorization expired at the end of FY 1996.
- Housing Finance Agency risk-sharing program (Section 542(c)): Commitment authorization expired at the end of FY 1996.
- Small projects mortgage insurance.

Preservation
- Portfolio reengineering demonstration program.

Special Needs
- Mortgage insurance for nursing homes and assisted-living facilities (Section 232).
- Supportive housing for the elderly (Section 202).
- Rental housing for the elderly (Section 231): Rarely used.
- Supportive housing for persons with disabilities/mainstream housing opportunities for persons with disabilities (Section 811).

- Mortgage insurance for single-room occupancy projects (Section 221(d)): Rarely used.

Supportive Services
- Multifamily housing drug elimination grants.
- Congregate housing services program: New applications are not being funded; funds available only for the renewal of expiring grants.
- Safe neighborhood grants.
- Neighborhood networks.
- Multifamily housing service coordinators.

Fannie Mae
- Conventional financing.
- Affordable housing financing.
- Equity investment.

Freddie Mac
- Conventional mortgage purchase program.
- Rate-reset mortgage.
- Negotiated transactions.
- Second mortgage.
- Bond credit enhancement.
- Senior housing and assisted-living pilot.

Ginnie Mae
- Multifamily mortgage-backed securities program.

National Park Service/Internal Revenue Service
- Historic preservation tax incentives.

U.S. Department of Agriculture: Rural Development, Rural Housing Services
- Rural rental housing guaranteed loan program.
- Rural rental housing program.

Sources:

IRS (LIHTCs): http://www.irs.ustreas.gov/prod/ bus_info/mssp/lihtc-1.html

HUD: http://www.hud.gov/progdesc/multindx.html

Fannie Mae: http://www.fanniemae.com/multifamily/index.html

Freddie Mac: http://www.freddiemac.com/multifamily/prod.html

Ginnie Mae: http://www.ginniemae.gov/multi/multifamily.html

National Park Service/IRS (historic preservation): http://www2.cr.nps.gov/ tps/tax/

U.S. Dept. of Agriculture (rural): http://www.rurdev.usda.gov/rhs/ Developer/dev_splash.html

Sedona Ranch, a 312-unit community in San Antonio, Texas, acquired permanent financing from Prudential Insurance Company.

The Financing Process

Once the development plan has been finalized and the project's cost is projected, the developer arranges financing. The goal is to find the proper blend of equity and debt from the available sources to raise sufficient funds to finance the project.

The standard procedure for financing a development project is first to obtain a commitment for permanent financing and then a development or construction loan. Frequently, the amount of equity capital needed is determined by the equity required by the lenders to grant the construction and permanent loans. In other words, the equity required is simply the difference between the cost of the project and the amount that can be borrowed. Once the amount of equity required is determined, the developer can start the search for equity investors.

The market for multifamily debt is constantly evolving. The exact terms and conditions that any particular lender offers at any given point vary depending on a great many factors, including current interest rates, projections of interest rates, the general economic outlook, terms and conditions offered by competitive lenders, and the lender's financial condition and business strategy. Not only do terms and conditions change; lenders change as well. Lenders enter and leave the market constantly, at times aggressively seeking new borrowers and at others not issuing new loans.

Developers must do a detailed survey of the market at the beginning phases of planning to determine possible sources of financing and likely terms and conditions. At this point, a mortgage broker can be helpful, especially for less experienced developers. A good mortgage broker has detailed knowledge of the market, the types of loans available, and the likely terms and conditions of available loans. Knowing which lenders are most likely to respond positively to a request for a loan can greatly reduce the time and expense required to obtain the required financing. A mortgage broker can also help with the loan application. "General Submission and Closing Requirements for Permanent and Interim Loans" (see pp. 154 and 155) lists the information normally required in a loan application. Preparing the application is no small task; many lenders have very specific requirements about its format and content.

8. Marketing the Project

The marketing team should be involved early in the development process to allow for establishment of a long-term mission, interaction with the design team during decision making, and general involvement in the project concept well before preleasing begins. A qualified marketing staff can help to ensure that each aspect of the project's design, including unit sizes and mix, is appropriate for the target market. The marketing staff makes certain that pricing reflects the specific market and that the product will be competitive in its market area. A marketing viewpoint is important in ensuring continuity of the project's theme and design, addressing functionality, and choosing a design and materials whose durability and requirements for maintenance make for long-term efficiency.

Marketing professionals should be involved in early architectural decisions. For example, a market analyst studies the interior specifications of apartment units that are leasing well in the competitive market to assess the proposed units for their practicality and stylishness. Marketing professionals advise developers about those features and finishes that are expected, optional, obsolete, or not in demand in the marketplace. The marketer can also estimate the rent a particular feature can command in the specific market so that the developer can determine whether a feature or design element will be cost-effective.

A solid, well-conceived marketing plan is an important component of the package presented to the mortgage lender. Marketing expertise can be an advantage when requesting a loan for a project. Having a team well versed in marketing could make the difference in competition with other teams showing less experience in marketing. Failure to prepare a strong marketing plan can jeopardize the loan's approval. The developer should involve the marketing team by the time a loan application is submitted. Further, the analytical aspects of marketing should begin before the project site is put under contract to confirm the developer's expectations regarding the site's suitability for the proposed project. Often, the developer does not realize the importance of bringing in the marketer at this early phase and assumes others will fill that role.

Three Basic Aspects of Marketing

More than just leasing the finished product, a marketing team has three major functions: analysis, strategic planning, and implementation. These three functions can be handled by separate entities whose efforts are coordinated or by one marketing firm that provides all services. All three functions should be integrated into the early planning stages.

Analysis

The main tasks involved in analysis are the market analysis and the marketing audit (see Chapter 2 for details about the market analysis). Analysis begins with compiling factual marketing information relating to the over-

Villa Torino in San Jose, California.

To meet the demands of the target market, styling, features, amenities, and unit types should be determined by the market study.

all apartment market, including competitive rent surveys that supply the critical data for due diligence. The market analyst also studies the entire primary and secondary markets to be able to recommend development strategies regarding sites, pricing, and product type.

Insufficient market research during predevelopment can result in a product that has not been designed to suit the target market. Focus groups can be used to assess a product's market appeal. If questions about design arise at later development stages, it may be necessary to determine the market segment the product does appeal to and then repackage it to attract that market.

Market analysis starts during predevelopment and continues throughout the project's life. To remain competitive throughout buildout and lease-up, ongoing market research fine-tunes prices and position. The competitive rent analysis should be performed on a regular basis throughout the lease-up period to supply up-to-date information about the project's performance compared with the competition. That is, similar unit types should be compared for value, with project and unit amenities adjusted accordingly. The competitive rent analysis enables management to revise rents to maximize absorption and income.

As construction proceeds but before the project reaches the leasing phase, a *marketing audit* is performed. A marketing audit surveys the competitors' ability to market their properties and determines the subject project's marketing strategy, plan, and budget.

The first step involves "shopping the competition": visiting each project and discussing marketing and management concerns, and gathering all the competitors' advertisements from apartment publications, newspapers, magazines, telephone directories, collateral pieces, and any other materials given to prospective residents. Radio advertisements should be taped and signs and billboards photographed.

The information collected should be arranged (mounted on poster board, for example) so as to note

each competitor's strengths and weaknesses. Every detail must be scrutinized. All the competitors' materials and marketing campaigns are critiqued to determine the most effective way to market a property, assigning the materials a quantitative rating to track performance over time. The most successful campaigns can then be improved on.

The marketing budget can be estimated by assessing competitors' budgets. The analyst first requests rates for advertising from all publications where competitors place ads. Based on those rates for size of ads and frequency of placement, the marketer can estimate advertising costs and compare them with the proposed budget for the new development. A marketing audit does not duplicate the advertising campaigns of a competitor but attempts to understand what amount should be spent for advertising to attract the market so that future decisions can be based on this information. An audit is especially valuable in an unfamiliar geographic area. After the marketing audit has been studied, the best attributes of the competitors' promotions can be used to set minimum standards for the new project's marketing campaign. The goal is to be a cut above the competition.

Strategic Planning

Strategic planning addresses quality of life and how the project can improve it for prospective residents. It does so by keeping abreast of long-term market trends and the details of marketing a property. The strategic marketer determines the elements of the product's concept—the project's theme, the product mix, finishes, and amenities. Strategic marketers understand the value of staying knowledgeable about every aspect of marketing a property— and that continuous time and effort are required. The strategic marketer understands the market as a whole and the details of the micromarket that will be used to make the property competitive. The depth of one's understanding of the market allows for valuable insights from the earliest stages of development. A strategic marketer

Selecting Community Amenities

The amenities selected for the property and the methods in which they are presented help determine not only the personality of the property but also its position in the market. Differentiating the property from the competition is imperative. In selecting and designing the apartment community's amenities, take the best ideas from the competition and look for ways to improve them.

A second function of the amenities offered at a property is generating premiums—for example, selected upgrades in views, security, comfort, or convenience. Many items or services that residents would normally purchase elsewhere can be integrated into the amenity package.

One challenge in selecting amenities is predicting residents' value judgments. Before selecting each amenity, the developer should ask the following questions:

• Am I selecting this amenity because of convention? Am I making this choice simply because everyone else in the market has it?
• Am I selecting this amenity because of necessity? Will residents require this amenity before they select an apartment in this community?
• Am I selecting this amenity because of desire? Is this an important amenity for the property simply because residents want it? Will the return on investment be justified?

Take the time necessary to select amenities wisely. Do not mistakenly assume that more features are better. Focus on expanding benefits rather than on just features. Look at the choices from the target market's viewpoint. Balance selections against their value and budgetary judgments. Create amenities that come to life as they define the property and the people who live there. Without this quality, the amenity package becomes a standard list of unimpressive bullet points in the marketing brochure.

■

The architecture and design elements at Columbus Shore in Irving, Texas, carry out a Venetian theme.

might also work as the representative of the property management team.

The strategic planner, using the due diligence report as a point of reference, prepares a marketing plan. The objectives are to best position the property to ensure rapid and successful lease-up and to achieve the asset's stability once lease-up has been accomplished. Marketing and lease-up can then proceed with only minor adjustments in response to changes in the market.

The marketing plan should begin as soon as the construction loan is approved. The plan should address quantitative and measurable goals: What tasks are to be accomplished? How much will each task cost to complete? What quantifiable results should be expected?

The developer then critically reviews marketing plans to determine their adequacy and appropriateness for the development and to rationalize costs. The marketer should answer the developer's questions with facts and

An attractive entrance sets the tone at Jefferson Estates in Richardson, Texas.

data to support the marketing plan. If an expensive advertisement in a particular magazine, for example, has been shown to bring in a large portion of a similar project's renters, then it may be well worth the expense.

Using a team with all disciplines represented throughout planning should be a given for each new project the developer undertakes. Because each apartment project has its own characteristics and markets change continually, a marketing plan formulated for an earlier project will not work for the new one. Anything that affects the way a prospective resident experiences the new rental community should interest the strategic marketer. Working with each member of the development team, the strategic marketer's job is to push for greater understanding of all the project's marketing aspects.

With the Developer. The strategic marketer is responsible for discovering and communicating the developer's vision for the project. Specifically, the strategic marketer helps to determine ingress to and egress from the devel-

opment, suggests alternate routes, and alerts the developer to road construction and other potential problems, all from the marketing perspective. An unattractive view from an entrance or difficult traffic pattern could negatively affect marketing the project and its ultimate success. The strategic marketer addresses questions about utilities and other infrastructure and their impact on the community's marketability. For example, placement of transformers and electric lines, choice of gas or electric utilities, and options for telephone and cable service all relate to the market's perceptions and preferences.

With the Land Planner. The feasibility study supplies preliminary recommendations about the unit mix, from which building footprints can be established. The strategic marketer works with the land planner to clarify issues regarding the footprints, such as the position of dumpsters, playgrounds, parking, and landscaped areas. It is not enough to fit everything required onto the available land. The result must meet the needs of prospec-

Why Are We Doing This?

When the marketing program recommends an approach or a solution, the developer should question the reasons behind it. If the reason is sound, based on previous experience or data, the developer can proceed confidently. For example, a marketer may suggest creating a two-page, four-color advertisement to run in various apartment marketing publications throughout lease-up. If the expense for such an advertisement is considerably higher than expected, the developer might challenge the wisdom of committing this amount of the budget. If the marketer's response to "why are we doing this?" relies on successful past experiences and this particular publication has been the primary source of traffic and rentals, the expense is justified.

On the other hand, if the marketer has used a media source that is not the first or at least the second source of traffic and rentals, the effort must be reexamined—from distribution of the publication to the ad itself. The ad may be poorly written, not reflective of the property or its target market, or positioned poorly in the publication.

For the ad to be visible and effective, it must not share the moment of attention—that short time when the consumer is looking at the message—with anyone else, especially a competitor. It is worth paying a premium to have the consumer's undivided attention.

■

During the early stages of planning, while building footprints are being established in a new community, the strategic marketer works with the land planner to establish priorities for the development's property lines. Far from being unimportant edges, property lines are the property's features experienced by outsiders, especially prospective residents. If a plan locates the development's most unattractive aspects along property lines, marketing can be seriously compromised. Therefore, a hierarchy of property lines should be established, reserving the best features for the most visible property lines.

Valuable elements to display along property lines include views of a golf course, water features, parks, or woodlands. Such features should be sited according to visibility from primary, secondary, and tertiary property lines. Paying attention to the relative priority of property lines can help to maximize the property's value.

Primary

The primary property line usually runs along the main thoroughfare that will bring customers to the property, but it is not necessarily at the front of the property. For example, an existing golf course or attractive body of water on the property line becomes the primary focus. A high-quality, distinctive feature almost always becomes the primary property line.

Failure to set priorities for property lines is unwise for a number of reasons that affect marketability, function, aesthetics, and residents' long-term satisfaction. In one instance, the land planner placed parking, trash compactors, and other unattractive community facilities along the main thoroughfare, which was the primary property line. What should have been the community's visual focus for prospective residents and drive-by traffic became a major drawback in leasing it. Moreover, the trash compactors were sited at each corner of the property, making the entire property unattractive from outside and inside. The property generated no curb appeal, and prospective tenants completely ignored attractive sites and desirable amenities located elsewhere in the complex.

Secondary

Designation of the secondary property line is based on the developer's sense of responsibility to surrounding property owners and surrounding properties' intended uses. In one case, a multifamily property with a slope adjoined an area of high-end houses, making the back of the multifamily property visible from the homes. The land planner pushed less attractive uses, such as parking, to the back along the area facing the homes. The strategic marketer pointed out the potential public relations crisis, and the land planner reworked the secondary property line and made the view more attractive. Exercising a sense of responsibility does not cost the careful devel-

Attention must be paid to all property lines, with the best features reserved for the most important edges.

oper more when issues are anticipated during planning. This kind of consideration can avert a major problem—as well as often enhancing the value of the project.

Tertiary

Locations of the remaining property lines should be considered in relation to adjoining properties and thoroughfares to minimize management issues and security risks such as loitering, and to maximize the property's usefulness and aesthetics. Assigning priorities to property lines affects how those on the outside view the community, which will in turn affect the project's value and performance.

tive residents for a certain quality of life as defined by the developer's vision and market requirements.

The goal of the strategic marketer's work with the land planner is to combine all these issues into a powerful statement that clearly conveys a sense of arrival for prospective residents. It cannot wait until the clubhouse opens. The marketer's eye can help to avoid such mistakes as an unattractive utility located in critical curb appeal areas.

Distribution of unit types within the building footprint is also an issue for the marketer's expertise. If, for example, all the larger, three-bedroom units are located along the property line, more people, cars, and activity will be concentrated at that visible edge, giving the appearance of an overly crowded development. Mixing unit types within one area during lease-up is advantageous, because a variety of units can be released for occupancy at one time, serving more needs and offering a variety of prices. The leasing agent then has the ability to capture the entire range of the project's market niche.

With the General Contractor. The general contractor works with the developer to decide the direction construction will take, including the route for construction traffic and the order and timing of when buildings will be completed and turned over to property management. The strategic marketer coordinates these activities based on the marketing plan.

This issue affects locations of model apartments. To avoid setting unrealistically high expectations for prospective residents, models are best placed in a less desir-

able location in the community. The construction route also determines which units come online during each phase. Marketers must plan for enough of each product type to be available during construction.

With the Architect. The strategic marketer usually works with the land planner and architect simultaneously to come up with a unit mix and a footprint appropriate for the project. If possible, clustering all of one unit type on one level or in one area of the community should be discouraged. Placing larger, family-oriented units above small units that will likely house a single person or couple also should be avoided. It is often the marketer's responsibility to point out the inherent problems of such configurations.

With the Landscape Architect. The strategic marketer works with the landscape architect on exterior lighting, water features, plant materials, and the irrigation system, and sets priorities for specific point-of-sale areas requiring attractive landscape design. Specifications for major signs, sidewalks, and plant materials establish the critical first image. Seasonal plants added for color are usually the property manager's responsibility.

With the Interior Designer. The strategic marketer and the interior designer consider the furnishings, wall coverings, carpeting, lighting, and accessories that contribute to the community's overall concept and emotional impact on prospective residents.

With the Property Manager. A representative of the property manager should be included from the begin-

Effective Marketing through Site Planning

Effective site planning can enhance a property's sense of community, can help to generate premium rental income, and can greatly enhance marketing. Consider the following techniques in designing the site plan for a property:

- Imply security or peace of mind, which does not mean large, imposing masonry walls topped with barbed wire. It does mean the proper placement of landscaping, berms, water features, or other features that suggest a sense of separation from the surrounding area. Lighting, gates, and fences also play a key role.
- Develop visual privacy. Do not allow ground-level homes near a well-traveled community entry to have an unobstructed view of this busy, public area. Use building orientation, screening, landscaping, and berming to shield these views along the entry drive. Prospective residents will question the privacy that a community can offer if they have open views into apartment homes from busy areas.
- Appeal to all the senses. Prospective residents use all their senses in forming an impression of a property. Use color, texture, and interesting form in buildings and landscape for visual excitement. Special paving through textured pavers or patterns at the entry pro-

vides sound and feel while announcing the arrival and slowing of traffic. Sound can also be provided with running water in the form of streams or fountains. Smell is addressed by using fragrant flowers or shrubbery, and taste can be satisfied by serving refreshments during the marketing presentation. Find creative ways to excite all the senses of prospective residents.

- Show quality conspicuously. From the front entry of the community through the entire marketing sequence, take advantage of every opportunity to showcase quality. Quality features can involve signage, light standards, street furniture, pavement textures and color, curbing, and select building facades lining the arrival path.
- Place infrastructure carefully. Coordinate locations with consultants for hydrants, transformers, meter boxes, utility and light poles, and street signs so that no "secondary items" end up in the wrong place. Refuse containers, utility motors, and mechanical equipment should be located away from public view and attractively screened without blocking easy access.

Exterior lighting, landscaping, and signage all create an image for marketing the Grand Venetian in Irving, Texas.

© Steve Hinds Photography

ning to take advantage of his or her operational experience in design of the project. Management's specific areas of expertise are likely to include security and safety, maintenance of chosen designs and materials, and prospective residents' needs and preferences. Property managers can also identify opportunities for additional income that need to be planned before construction. They examine the design concept to determine those features that will become assets or liabilities for the developer.

Property managers should be able to advise the developer about paving surfaces that are easiest to maintain and about particular materials or designs that have caused problems at other properties. They are often familiar with the maintenance requirements of various landscape elements, such as which trees and shrubs require a long season of leaf raking and those that drop their leaves all at once. Specifically, property managers will have experience with:

• Security and Safety—Safe design of terrace and balcony railings, playground equipment, keyless entries to recreational spaces, key control, video surveillance, front gates;
• Functionality—Parking in relation to unit entrances; sound control in walls, floors, and ceilings; adequate hot water and other utilities; quality and amount of lighting; traffic patterns; the effect of the project's design on the staff's workloads;

• Recreational Facilities—Which facilities attract renters, which will be used, which are economical to maintain.

The strategic marketer and the property manager should coordinate plans for many of these issues to ensure that the property operates soundly and is marketable. The property management team's experience in lease-up of new construction is an important resource for the project.

Implementation

Implementation includes running an advertising campaign, compiling traffic reports, and handling on-site marketing, including hiring and supervising marketing staff. Managing events, including ground-breaking ceremonies and the grand opening, falls under implementation. Although the property management team is usually responsible for much of the implementation, the strategic marketer can ensure that implementation heads down the right path. By using a carefully thought-out strategic marketing plan, plans will not have to be reworked throughout lease-up and the implementer will not have to shift focus and efforts.

The developer must build a team with expertise in all the aspects of strategic marketing and then stick with the plan. If the team is not skilled in strategic planning, efforts to implement the plan are wasted. If skilled analysis is lacking, strategic planning cannot be based on qual-

Model apartments should be furnished to reflect the tastes of the target market and to carry out the marketing theme, as shown at Champion Farm at Springhurst in Louisville, Kentucky.

ity information. And good analysis and planning will reach a dead end without skilled implementation.

Developing the Marketing Strategy and Plan

A marketing strategy is the philosophy the team supports and consistently follows throughout the life of the project. The strategy focuses on what is to be done, why, and the projected outcome. The cornerstone of any marketing strategy is target markets. Every aspect of the development, from its design to its advertising campaign, should focus on appealing to those market segments.

The property's advantages should be clearly defined. What makes the property different, better, more marketable than its competitors? In short, what makes it special *from the marketing point of view?* A project's distinctiveness may be its affordability, location, aesthetics, units, life-

style, or other characteristic that makes it outshine the competition.

Each building's release date is essential; the times when the project will be leased should be defined. Estimated building release dates should be reviewed with regard to which unit types and sizes will be released at each stage. Doing so will help the team understand what needs to be done at each point in the process to reach those dates. For example, if a large number of one-bedroom units is to come on line, marketing can be focused on promoting those units to the appropriate market segments. Determining unit types, number of each type, time of year when leasing will occur, and the next building release date will maximize the team's marketing effort.

The marketing plan ties into the established marketing strategy. The marketing plan can be thought of as a blueprint for the advertising campaign, public relations effort, and leasing activities, including hiring and managing the leasing staff and preparing budgets and schedules for each component.

The plan also specifies the design of all elements to create a coordinated image for the project. Based on the targeted market profile and the project's distinctive selling points, an overall theme is carried out in all community design elements, including its name, logo, signage, sales displays, interior design, brochures, and other print and media materials.

The Marketing and Leasing Budget

The marketing and leasing budget should cover all aspects of marketing. It should include appropriate amounts for exterior and interior marketing-related features, preleasing activities, general marketing, and promotional materials and events. A typical marketing budget includes:

- Exterior Marketing—Directional signs, identification signs, banners, flags;
- Interior Marketing—Model apartments, sales displays;
- Preleasing—Flyers, voice mail setup, staff, signs for construction and leasing, advertisements in appropriate publications, a Web site;
- Recognition Marketing—Advertising campaign, staff, promotion materials, public relations, press releases and other print media, community involvement in charitable events, memberships in community organizations;

- Other—Nominations for awards, move-in gifts, goodwill gestures to outside leasing agents and contractors.

Preleasing. Some companies advocate the use of sales trailers during preleasing; others believe that a trailer is an unnecessary cost. If no units will be ready for occupancy within 60 days, it is probably ill advised to set up such a trailer.

A better use of resources is to concentrate on completing the leasing information center and clubhouse as early as possible in the construction timetable. It should take approximately 60 days to construct, with the first residential construction ready for leasing two weeks later. The leasing center creates a sense of arrival and will do a better job of selling the product than a temporary trailer would at no additional expense. Meanwhile, all the necessary information about the project before leasing begins can be dispensed by voice mail, succinct printed pieces, or a Web site.

The voice message should be considered an advertisement; it should be a professional presentation detailing interior and exterior features and the price range for each unit size. It should request callers to leave a name and number and offer to mail additional information. The preleasing staff should handle responses immediately. Printed materials should provide extensive information, including the phone number for voice mail. A properly executed voice mail message usually garners a large number of deposits.

Walking paths are among the least expensive and most desired amenities.

© Steve Hinds Photography

Waiting List. A waiting list, begun 75 days before the first building release date, is an excellent leasing tool. To be most effective, the list should not assign specific apartment units to residents until 21 days before the project receives its certificate of occupancy. Unavoidable delays can spell public relations disasters. In one case, a property lost 40 percent of its deposits because disgruntled potential residents spread the word about their displeasure. The momentum created by a waiting list should enable the team to achieve 100 percent occupancy within 14 days of receiving the certificate of occupancy on each building. The focus should be on leasing the next building coming on line rather than on unavailable semifinished buildings. This approach generates the most income possible during lease-up.

The waiting list should include information about the apartment desired and the preferred move-in date for each prospective tenant, giving the leasing agents control over filling units as they become available. A small refundable deposit (about $50) ensures a serious prospect.

Each day, the leasing staff should review the waiting list, comparing it with units nearing completion, and contact the appropriate customers. Until a suitable unit becomes available, contact should be maintained with potential clients through a newsletter, note, or reminder that the next section is due to open. This kind of attention keeps interest high.

By being proactive, the staff will be able to work 60 to 75 days in the future based on its strong list of potential residents, realistic estimate of completions, and practice of never promising a building prematurely. By concentrating on the next section coming on line, agents prevent clients from requesting apartments whose availability is uncertain. If a client is adamant about leasing a specific apartment, the client should be bound to an agreement for occupancy no later than 14 days after the certificate of occupancy is received.

The fundamental idea of working the waiting list is to minimize the number of days an apartment stands vacant. Doing so increases income to the property by reducing or eliminating vacancy loss and replacing it with rental income.

Leasing Information Center. Leasing information centers exist to lease units. A leasing center should not also serve as an office, a clubhouse, or resident relations department. Ideally, no desks full of paperwork or office equipment should be visible, and no distracting telephones should be allowed in the area.

The leasing information center should contain tables where agents and clients can close deals and sign paperwork and displays that depict the lifestyle being sold. It should be a relaxing, attractive, and comfortable area that makes prospective residents want to linger. Lighting should be at a comfortable level and the sound system excellent. The center should be visible from many angles from other offices so that staff can immediately see a potential customer. It should have its own entrance so that prospective residents can immediately be in the sales environment.

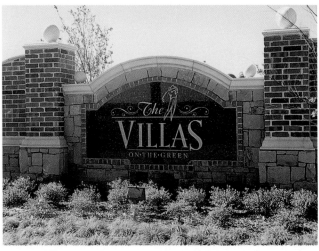

The marketing plan specifies design of signage, displays, advertising, and other elements.

Colors and furnishings should be consistent with the project's theme and chosen with the target market in mind. Light, airy pastels and warm, cozy reds and browns reflect different images and appeal to different market segments.

The resident services office should be at the other end of the building or next door. It should contain the necessary office equipment, including fax machines, computers, and copiers. All paperwork should be taken care of in the resident services offices.

Staffing the Leasing Center. Today's prospective residents are sophisticated home shoppers, and the leasing staff should be chosen accordingly. Staff should comprise well-trained professional sales personnel experienced in dealing with clients. And as professionals, staff should be paid accordingly, with rewards to motivate specific achievements. One arrangement for compensation that works well is to offer a base salary plus a bonus pool rather than individual bonuses. The bonus pool encourages teamwork. For example, a bonus could be offered to the sales team for each building occupied within 14 days of receiving the certificate of occupancy. If the building is 100 percent leased, the staff would receive the entire bonus, and it would get 93 percent of the bonus if it completes 93 percent of the leases. Additional bonuses could be offered as incentives for leasing particularly difficult specific units.

The old rule of thumb of one leasing agent for every 100 units in a new project is considered inadequate today. With staffing at that level, agents do not have the time to give prospective residents the service and attention they need. If the leasing center is understaffed, sales will be lost. Using additional personnel is cost-effective when compared with the cost of losing leases.

Because apartments turn over regularly, marketing is a continuous and long-term effort. Therefore, a well-trained, professional sales staff contributes a great deal to the project's marketability. Some developers use leasing companies that specialize in grand openings and initial lease-up. Others prefer to have the same team continue to manage the property once lease-up has been completed. If a leasing team does not have the project's long-term interests in mind, it might show a tendency to disregard applicants' creditworthiness to reach total occupancy quickly.

Advertising

Advertising motivates potential residents to visit the project, beginning with positioning the property in terms of pricing and target markets and then flooding the marketplace with the strong message of the property's selling proposition. Advertising should begin 75 days before the first building's release date. It can be very expensive, so a marketer should determine which advertising media are the most cost-effective. They are different for each market and product concept. Discussions with other local developers, property managers, and advertising agencies can help to identify the best media for advertising the project. Advertising agencies typically recommend that

© Steve Hinds Photography

STB Architects & Planners, Inc.

The leasing center should serve only one purpose—to lease units. It should not be cluttered with papers or office equipment.

When a project first opens, demand may be so strong for new development that leases are signed quite rapidly. Initially, the community's newness often outweighs any of its negatives. But eventually the most desirable units—those with the best locations, floor plans, and features—are leased, leaving only the less appealing units. Known as the *point of depletion,* this time usually occurs between the ninth and 12th months of a one-year lease-up program.

There are ways to prevent this event from occurring. At the beginning of lease-up, when demand and traffic are high, it is easier and faster for leasing agents to assign the most desirable apartments—the ones that sell themselves. But a conscious effort to lease the less desirable units will minimize the effects of depletion.

Emphasize less desirable apartments in marketing materials. Absorption statistics by unit type and floor level reveal a market's perception of which units are least desirable. These units are the ones requiring additional marketing effort.

- One of the less desirable (but not the worst) unit types should be used as a furnished model. It is imperative that nothing take away from the positive impressions that prospective residents receive, but expectations should not be raised beyond what can actually be delivered. Prospective residents always want the floor plans they can actually see and visualize as home. Therefore, a professionally decorated model is easier to lease than a unit depicted only on a floor plan. Two factors should be considered equally in choosing a unit for the model—the unit mix and how desirably a floor plan compares with others. For example, if there are more of a particular floor plan but it is not the most desirable plan, it should probably be used as a model. If the least desirable floor plan accounts for only a small percentage of the unit mix, however, it should probably not be featured as a model or in an advertisement.
- Model apartments should be in less than optimal locations. They should not be in the worst location, but they should definitely not be in the best to avoid raising customers' expectations unrealistically. For example, models should not be located adjacent to the community building or pool, because residents will be disappointed when they find their unit lacks this advantage. Showing the model will be less convenient, but it is smarter marketing.
- Highlight the less desirable and less functional floor plans in advertisements. Doing so attracts those who do find the unit appealing, resulting in a more equal absorption of floor plans in units that are still vacant.
- The best units, those with choice floor plans, great views, and ideal locations, will take care of themselves. If necessary, agents can always encourage clients to opt for the more desirable apartments.

Compensate for negative features. In every community, some floor plans or locations are less marketable than others. By being aware of these shortcomings, agents can compensate for the drawbacks.

- Compensate during design. Ideally, problems are apparent during design, before the community has been built. Steps can be taken at that point to offset an inferior design with an added amenity available only in those less appealing units. For example, adding built-in bookcases to offset an unattractive view or double sinks to offset a too-small bedroom makes the unit more appealing. A common way to make top-floor units desirable is to outfit them with vaulted ceilings, ceiling fans, and gas fireplaces, making the extra flight of stairs worth the climb.
- After the design stage, effective merchandising helps to turn negative features into positive ones. For example, bar stools around the kitchen bar demonstrate an alternate eating and entertaining arrangement, negating the impact of an overly small dining room. Prospective residents should be encouraged to imagine themselves in the apartment. Targeted floor plans should be featured in advertisements, giving the leasing staff more opportunities to show that unit and to sell it to clients who already have that unit in mind.
- A single floor plan should be depicted per page of a brochure or panel of a sales display, enabling the marketing of any given floor plan by itself. If floor plans compete for attention, potential residents compare them, and the agent loses the ability to control the focus. It is obviously impossible to prevent a client

the advertising budget equal about 1 percent of the development's hard costs. This amount is variable, however, depending on market conditions and the property's size, nature, and visibility.

Each weakness of a competitor uncovered during the marketing audit presents an opportunity for the marketing team. The team should always keep these weaknesses in mind when developing the marketing and leasing strategy, but mentioning a competitor by name should always

be avoided in advertisements, brochures, and even during conversations with potential residents.

Computers and the Internet are changing the way we do business, and the real estate industry is no exception. The numerous apartment rental services with Web sites are taking advantage of a very important way to advertise properties and attract tenants. Even if they do not intend to start an Internet rental service, those who develop or manage multifamily properties need to from looking at every page of a brochure or every panel of a display, but it can be more difficult to compare plans side by side. For example, floor plans can be mounted on a multisided kiosk in the leasing center.

- Floor plans should be named rather than identified by size or number of rooms, which might emphasize shortcomings. Referring to "the Rembrandt" instead of the two-bedroom, one-bath model means that the client will be less inclined to focus on the number of bathrooms. Unit types should be named carefully, avoiding any possible negative connotations.
- Advertising on the cover of a local apartment publication during crucial periods is an effective way to keep momentum strong. Reserve the cover page well in advance for the critical ninth through 12th months of leasing (for a one-year lease-up period).
- As a final effort, incentives can be offered to leasing agents or to renters who lease a hard-to-market unit. A prospective renter could be offered rent specials, decorating allowances, or free upgrades by selecting a certain model. The leasing staff could be motivated with a tiered bonus plan. For example, every one of a less appealing model could bring a bonus for the agent, with an additional bonus for every one that is also on the third floor.

Planning ahead, taking a strongly proactive marketing stance, and preparing the leasing staff to take positive action can minimize the point of depletion, greatly reduce vacancy loss, and maximize income from the beginning. Once lease-up is completed, similar strategies can be used to keep occupancy and satisfaction high throughout the project's life.

■

understand how these services work and what they have to offer.

It is important to know the difference between an Internet rental service and a Web site devoted to one company or rental property. Internet rental services are at one end of the spectrum of Web-based services. They allow visitors to the site to identify vacancies and to view floor plans and photographs of the unit and building or even to take a virtual tour of the units. These services aim

Prospective residents can imagine themselves living in a well-appointed model unit, such as this one at the Charleston at Boca Raton, Florida.

to help consumers with every aspect of their move, and the larger Internet rental services do everything from sell packing supplies and renters insurance to arrange movers and allow visitors to the site to compare cities on the basis of crime rates, the economy, and the quality of schools.

At the other end of the spectrum are Web sites devoted to a specific property management company or apartment building. Developers and managers of multifamily properties today are well aware of their residents' increasing use of computers and the Internet, and savvy property owners and managers are using their own Web sites to post information about the property's services and amenities or maintenance schedules. Such sites may serve as brochures for a property or simply announce current vacancies. Property-specific sites can also play a major role in helping property managers to provide better service to their residents, offering them a chance to submit their comments to management or to request service. Using the Internet in this way can help keep tenants satisfied and improve retention rates.

Other benefits come from having a presence on the Web. Perhaps the most important is that a good Web site can be an excellent way to advertise a property. The Internet allows people who are looking for an apartment to quickly and easily evaluate different properties, saving them the hassle of driving all over town to look at different units. Moreover, the interactivity of the Internet allows users to customize their searches to find, for example, only those vacant two-bedroom units with a pool on site. Although the evidence thus far suggests that most consumers want to be able to access information about apartments both in print and on line, on-line advertising clearly outperforms other advertising media on the basis of cost per lease.[1]

Property owners and managers need to develop a well-thought-out strategy when planning their Internet presence. Money spent on a Web site will not necessarily generate commensurate benefits. Successful developers and

AMLI at Oakhurst North in Aurora, Illinois, features a clubhouse that can be used for residents' events.

property managers should have good answers to the following questions: What do we want to achieve by going on line? How will an on-line presence add value to our property or company? What strategies will we use to achieve our goals? How will we measure success?

Whether one uses a Web site to advertise one property or many, the key to success is to attract a lot of traffic to the site. Like any kind of advertising, a Web site should put your message where customers will see it.

One of the easiest ways to achieve a high level of traffic is to sign up with one of the larger Internet rental services, two of the largest of which are SpringStreet and rent.net. Rent.net has agreements with some of the largest apartment REITs and fee-management companies in the United States; it lists vacancies in thousands of apartment communities with a total of several million units. More than 4.5 million users visit the rent.net Web site every month.

The marketing campaign for Northlake Farms in Gurnee, Illinois, a Section 42 (LIHTC) project planned for low- and moderate-income occupancy, focused on two areas. First, as with any rental project, the goal was to lease units as quickly and efficiently as possible. Second, it was necessary to allay the concerns of residents of the relatively upscale suburban town about having an affordable housing development in their midst. And because of the project's affordability, the marketing campaign had a very tight budget. There were no extra funds for billboard advertisements, a direct mail campaign, or radio or television ads. The marketing team considered it a challenge to replicate the success it often met with far larger budgets. The extremely successful lease-up and community relations campaign that resulted proved the strategies' effectiveness.

Positioning the Asset

Behind the concept of Northlake Farms Apartments lies the strong belief that *affordable* and *excellent* must not be mutually exclusive in multifamily housing. The goal of marketing has been the redefinition of affordable housing and the *communication* of that distinction. The project's target market is low- to moderate-income renters in Lake County, Illinois. Prospective residents must meet strict government requirements regarding income and household size.

Northlake Farms is located in a highly desirable northern Chicago suburb, in a region of equestrian farms. The development took the upscale horse farms as its theme, following through with rich colors, brass accents, lush landscaping, and architectural and decorative accents to establish the quality and stability of a genteel rural lifestyle. Despite careful attention to the project's image, however, neighbors in the Village of Gurnee strongly opposed the project. The marketing team found it would have to persuade the wider community that an affordable multifamily housing community was an asset, not a threat, to the community.

The first marketing tool produced was a preleasing flyer. It was distributed door to door to neighborhood businesses 90 days before the project's clubhouse was completed, before any portion of the development was available to show. The inexpensive but well-designed flyer contained a wealth of information, allowing the marketing team to begin to counter the widely held belief that *affordable* means subsidized housing full of crime and drugs.

Every employee became a walking, talking representative of Northlake Farms. Hiring individuals of obvious excellence, style, personality, and confidence was essential to the effort. These employees won over audiences by being well-informed ambassadors of the Northlake Farms de-velopment. When the time came to hire a property manager, a highly competent person from the local community was selected, furthering the public relations effort and demonstrating that Northlake Farms intended to be a participant in the local business community.

Putting Limited Marketing Dollars to Work

Because Northlake Farms is an affordable community and neighbors generally have major misconceptions about what that means, marketing resources were allocated to educate the public. The strategy was to blanket the businesses in the surrounding community and parts of Chicago, targeting major community leaders. As part of its corporate outreach, the marketing team attended every mayor's breakfast, every chamber of commerce meeting, and every major community event as a way of developing positive community relationships.

Internally, some of the marketing budget was used to create a sense of urgency for the leasing team. Rather than bonuses for individual performance, a bonus pool was offered to the entire team for successful performance. The bonus was based on the percentage of a building that was occupied by the 14th day after the certificate of occupancy was issued.

This strategy had the additional effect of encouraging the team to avoid assigning a specific address each time an apartment was leased. Instead, the leasing team proceeded systematically, one building at a time, assigning apartments from the waiting list as units became available. An effective, precisely executed strategy for the waiting list was vital to the success of leasing.

The Waiting List

Working from the waiting list allowed the leasing team to minimize the number of days a completed apartment stood vacant. Rather than immediately assigning a specific apartment in an unfinished building to a client, the leasing team noted the apartment and move-in date desired. This approach gave the leasing professionals control over leasing buildings as they became available and helped to minimize the problems that came with unavoidable construction delays. Effective use of the strategy allowed the leasing team to work 60 to 75 days in the future in assigning units.

To create a sense of urgency in prospective residents, buttons and signs that said "ask about our waiting list" were placed in the leasing center. This administrative decision was critical because of the volume of paperwork involved in processing a Section 42 application. Establishing a waiting list allowed staff to begin the paperwork immediately and prevented delays in moving in. The only downside of this strategy was the necessity of reverifying applications if 90 days had elapsed. Knowing the complications of reverification, the leasing team worked even harder to assign an available apartment and to move in those people who were approaching the 90-day limit. As a result, the team minimized the problem of not knowing when a specific apartment would be available and maximized the potential for filling a building completely within two weeks of its availability. The leasing team was thus able to concentrate its attention on clients.

Advertising Media

Based on their previous experience leasing other apartment projects, the marketers knew that apartment publications were their primary source of traffic. In January 1994, nine months before preleasing began, the team secured the front cover of an apartment publication and reserved space in both major Chicago apartment publications to ensure saturation. An ad in the Yellow Pages hit the streets on October 10, 1994, 20 days before preleasing began. No newspaper advertising was used.

Timeline

By May 1994, six months before the beginning of leasing, a logo was designed, and designs for the preleasing flyer and the permanent brochure were being prepared. The logo was based on an equestrian theme, in keeping with the tone of the Gurnee community. The choice improved the project's identification in the community and helped the neighbors to accept Northlake Farms.

By November 1994, the leasing team hit the streets, armed with preleasing flyers. The property manager was on board and had started personal, corporate, and community outreach. Efforts included meeting individually with local leaders and attending community events and meetings to increase the visibility of Northlake Farms while enhancing the property's image.

An elaborate, radio-style voice mail message was established to communicate all the details about the community to potential residents. Callers were invited to leave their names and addresses to receive a preleasing flyer. The voice mail telephone number appeared on signs.

In just 45 days, mail applications with application fees and security deposits began to arrive. At that point, no clubhouse or leasing center was finished to show prospective renters, but voice mail and community outreach paid off.

Suddenly severe weather hit the entire area on January 10, 1995. Completion of the first building was delayed until February 21. Although the situation was not ideal, it did not cause the problems it might have if units had been preassigned. Prospective residents from the waiting list were called to inform them of the delay. By keeping them informed, the staff retained their loyalty.

Grand Opening

The tight budget permitted only one promotional piece for a direct mail campaign. That one piece had to work especially hard. The grand opening, which was cosponsored by the local chamber of commerce, required an elegant invitation. The strategy was to invite not prospective residents, but influential community members and leaders. If they were impressed, they would make ideal promoters of Northlake Farms.

A great deal of effort was invested in the leasing center and sales displays. In every detail, from the approach to the building to displays and furnishings, the leasing center reflected the warmth, style, quality, and desirability of the community and depicted how well it would meet residents' needs. An entire room—without desks or telephones—was devoted to leasing. The welcoming atmosphere and abundant information mounted in an entertaining display on a central kiosk gave prospective residents everything they needed to make a decision.

February 15, 1995, arrived with more than 12 inches of snow on the ground and temperatures of five degrees below zero. Inside the white tent extending from the 3,000-square-foot clubhouse, 225 of the Chicago area's most influential people attended the event. Politicians, human relations managers, directors of departments, and city officials from Gurnee and the Chicago area gathered to welcome Northlake Apartments. The opening was a tremendous success in dispelling any negative views about the project.

Successfully Meeting the Objectives

Traffic is often used to measure the success of a residential marketing campaign. For Northlake Farms, however, that measure was not as useful as tracking the number of apartments in each completed building that achieved full occupancy by the 14th day after the certificate of occupancy was received. Ultimately, it did not matter how much traffic was generated or what percentage of units was closed, although both are important contributors to the project's success. The objective was to produce income on the asset as quickly and efficiently as possible. Achieving 100 percent occupancy by 14 days after a certificate of occupancy was received was considered on target for the project.

Public opinion about the development was less quantifiable, but it was clear that many community members' original negative viewpoints were reversed. The success of the comprehensive marketing effort to educate the public about the project's desirability was evident in the number of community leaders who showed their support of the project.

Ongoing Success

The leasing campaign's peak was February 1995, a deliberate strategy despite the lease-up period's not ending until December 31, 1995. The key to success was the proactive preleasing campaign, beginning 90 days before the clubhouse was completed to one month after. After that, print media and corporate outreach continued, but at a less intense level. The results: For 11 consecutive buildings out of a total of 14, 100 percent occupancy was achieved within 14 days after the certificate of occupancy was received, right on target. No rent concessions were offered at any time.

For all tax credit developments, placing buildings in service as quickly as possible is critical. This pressing need combined with an unusual number of construction delays resulted in three buildings put into service in December, right in the middle of the holiday season. Despite this unfortunate timing, the leasing team continued its efficient work with the waiting list of qualified clients. At the end of the coldest winter months, the final three buildings were at 50 percent, 72 percent, and 100 percent occupancy. In one year, marketing generated 1,000 prospects and leased 514 apartments.

Leases in the first two buildings, which expired March 30 and April 30, 1996, were renewed for all but two households. Those two apartment units were reassigned to new residents before the first leases' expiration dates. The aggressive and well-structured marketing campaign ensured that the project generated maximum income; the marketing team smoothed the way for low- and moderate-income residents to live in a desirable community.

The marketing strategy should emphasize what makes the property distinctive.

Although not all apartment property Web sites will be able to achieve such a high volume of traffic, smaller companies must work with these large services to attract attention to themselves. Individual companies can pay to have their properties linked to these larger services and listed on the Web. In this way, individual properties that might not be able to attract any attention on their own can piggy-back on the larger service to gain visibility in the Internet marketplace. Developers and property managers can also help to increase traffic to their Web sites by making the site as useful with as much content as possible—provide customers with the information they want, provide useful links, and make sure the information provided is up to date and accurate.[2]

Other benefits come from having a presence on the Web. For instance, sophisticated on-line services can assist in screening tenants. ChoiceDATA has a product called ReLEASE that offers tenant, credit, and landlord histories, verifies employment, and checks criminal records on line. Such services greatly accelerate screening. Moreover, experience shows that using these tools generates very solid leads. Automated screening helps to eliminate decisions colored by prejudice that used to occur during screening, and property managers can use the Web to reduce risks and costs.

But no matter how large an Internet rental service or how sophisticated a Web site, certain challenges are still associated with having an on-line presence for a multifamily property.[3] First, there is much more to having a Web site than making an initial investment and then sitting back to wait for customers to roll in. Web sites require ongoing maintenance to ensure that the information provided is up to date and that links to other sites are valid and useful. Second, Web sites and rental services should be thought of as extensions to rather than replacements of the leasing office. Property managers still have to retain quality staff to deal with customers when their phone calls eventually come. Third, no matter how attractively they are designed, it can be very dif-

Columbus Shore, a mixed-use development in Irving, Texas, leased at a rate of more than 50 units per month. The project brings activity and synergy to the area with its street-level shops, public spaces, and marina.

ficult to use a Web site to acquire a comparable amount of information about a potential tenant when compared with traditional leasing techniques.

Clearly, these problems are not insurmountable. Once a solid Internet strategy has been developed, apartment owners and managers should seriously consider how they can use the Web and Internet rental services to market their property, boost cash flow, and provide the best customer service possible.

Measuring the Marketing Plan's Success

Measuring success lies in the average number of new leases signed per week since the start of leasing. Known as the absorption rate, the number typically averages four to seven per week. A lower absorption rate calls for reassessment of the leasing plan to determine where the difficulties lie. Higher absorption could mean that there was pent-up demand for this rental product or that the product and marketing effort have been outstanding. Or rents could be low for the product (based on the competition), and increasing asking rents should be considered. An analysis of the most competitive current rents determines whether rents are appropriate for the market and product.

Another evaluation tool is cost per rental or monthly advertising dollars spent divided by total monthly rentals. If advertising dollars have been well spent, the cost per rental should be well within the amount budgeted. Otherwise, an examination of the advertising program is in order.

Assessing the success of the marketing plan can be as quick as calculating the percentage of units occupied on the 14th day after the certificate of occupancy is received. Occupied units finally generate income for the project and force attention on putting more product on the market quickly to fill demand for a declining supply. Achieving occupancy quickly also minimizes the loss resulting from vandalism that sometimes occurs in unoccupied buildings.

Marketing's ultimate goal is to meet the developer's objectives. The leasing staff should concentrate on raising rents in accord with market demand, exceeding the pro forma's estimated income, and managing consumers' expectations to minimize complaints.

Notes

1. Sandy Asirvatham, "Web of Confusion," *Multi-Housing News,* April/May 1996, pp. 16–22.

2. Joe Dysart, "Promoting Your Web Site," Tech Trends Supplement, *Urban Land,* October 1999, pp. 30–32.

3. See Neil Fjellestad and Carol Levey, "Web Leasing: Help or Hype?" *Journal of Property Management,* March/April 1999, pp. 66–72; and Laura Ochipinti Zaner, "Leasing in the Internet Age," *Multifamily Trends,* Winter 1999, pp. 30–32.

9. Management and Operations

Once built, rental apartments transform into a service business. The consensus of the multifamily housing industry is that property management plays a key role, as the quality of management makes the difference between strong performance and mediocre performance. Effective property management has as much, if not more, potential to add value to the property as its construction, financing, or marketing.

Today's top apartment owners and developers pay considerably more attention to management and operating issues than they did in the past. Companies with large apartment portfolios—REITs and private development companies—typically have their own management entities. Sometimes REITs do not have development companies or construction companies, but very few of them contract out the management of their apartment properties.

The recognition of this shift in importance is reflected in the hiring practices and compensation levels of property management professionals. The longstanding rule that an employee in a real estate company has to be on the development side of the business if he or she wants to make the best money is no longer true. And many developers have discovered that third-party fee management can be a profitable business to even out the ups and downs

of business cycles. A first-rate management company is vital to the property's operation and ultimately the bottom line.

The Importance of Good Management

Many players involved in apartment rehabilitation and repositioning describe how they have used good property management techniques to make a big difference in the bottom line. Weeding out poor property managers tops the list of opportunities in apartment rehabilitation. Acquisition managers and REITs thrive on finding instances of poor property management. No better opportunity exists than when a leasing manager will not take the time to talk to customers or models are not properly merchandised or the maintenance crew cannot find anything in the workshop. Bringing new people into the management office and treating residents as though they are glad to have them makes REITs more money than development and construction. Often mediocre management leaves substantial opportunities for raising revenue and saving expenses on the table. This "low-hanging fruit" can be easily harvested by an aggressive and effective property manager, producing immediate sustainable increases in income and therefore value.

One property investment firm reports that when acquiring property, its management company immediately puts in management controls. It installs its infor-

Site 17 in Seattle is a five-story wood frame structure over a three-level concrete base. Bold colors appeal to the project's young urban target market.

Improving management is as important as upgrading hard assets when acquiring underperforming properties.

mation systems and implements proper management procedures, including some stringent rent and qualification standards (rent due on the first of the month, late on the second, and notices delivered on the third; income at least four times rent). Collection losses are dramatically decreased just from implementing these simple procedures.

Adding to the bottom line is the whole point of good property management. Property management should not be a stepchild of the development group, and for many companies this is a cultural change. Running projects— that is, leasing them and generating the cash flow and the returns that will make the investors or the partners happy—is one of the most important parts of what apartment developers do.

Simply stated, the goal of management in a property's operations stage is to run the project to meet the investment owners' goals. Management's task is complicated by changing markets and competitive conditions over a project's life.

Expertise in property management should not be merely tacked to the end of the construction phase when operations begin. This expertise should be included in the project's planning and design. Operating concerns should be incorporated in design and marketing decisions from day one. The management staff should be involved actively in initial feasibility analysis and project design, and it should help underwrite the project's operating expense budget. The upfront involvement of ex-

perienced property managers can produce rewarding design ideas that will lower the long-term cost of operations. Some property management groups are called on to underwrite new development deals independent of the developer's numbers—a cultural change that the development partners sometimes find hard to accept.

Building and site design obviously play a role in the project's maintenance and operations costs. A developer should look at total projected operating expenses before starting construction. Materials and design decisions that factor in operating efficiencies, even if the initial costs are higher than some alternatives, can produce significant paybacks in the future. Making tradeoffs between initial lower construction costs and later higher maintenance costs, or vice versa, is a common practice. Using cheaper construction materials and techniques that entail higher maintenance costs in the operating phase can depress the project's value insofar as the maintenance expenses and replacement reserves on the statement of operating expenses reduce the property's net operating income.[1]

A key change in the business in recent years is the much greater emphasis on property management in all development phases. At one time, development companies may have spent $1,000 on initial planning for a development project. Today, once land is identified as promising, a full team is assembled to identify the project that will be developed. And the property manager plays a key role in the decisions on product and design—an approach that provides tremendous dividends down the road. Planning for a development project now costs more than $100,000.[2]

The developer should endeavor to have as much good information as possible on future operations and maintenance, including but not limited to costs, to make informed design decisions. Property managers can make many useful contributions to the design process and should be included in all design review meetings. The increasing importance of residents' personal and property security can be addressed in part by improving design. Property managers' perspectives, based on experience with defensible space, can be valuable in this effort. The following suggestions for successful multifamily residential design are based on issues related to operations and management:

- Plan ahead for trash disposal. Make containers easy to reach, easy to clean around, difficult to sense, and screened where possible.
- The Postal Service requires that mail boxes be grouped together. Place mail boxes near the manager's office so that the manager can see residents as they come and go. Design a clear and simple apartment numbering system.
- Make the leasing office visible from the street and easy to find, and provide reserved parking nearby.[3]

The developer of Cascade Court Apartments, a 100-unit affordable housing project in downtown Seattle,

Landscaping and architectural features can indicate separation of public and private spaces.

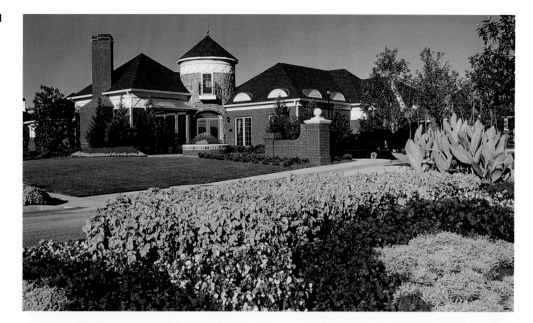

Cascade Court in Seattle is a 100-unit complex of affordable housing that accommodates families and individuals. An enclosed courtyard offers a safe place for children to play.

Seattle Housing Resources Group

learned from experience that the design of a project that attracts families with children should anticipate maintenance problems. For example, it is nearly impossible to keep the planters filled with bedding plants because the children consider them extensions of their play space.[4]

For developers, some experience in hands-on property management can be useful in implementing development projects. It gives them firsthand knowledge of residents' concerns, and there is no better way to learn the details that work best and those that should be modified.

Usually the most volatile element in net operating income is the turnover rate. Although turnover sometimes offers a good opportunity to raise rents, for units renting near the market rate, turnover can be costly in terms of the renovations and cleanup required to prepare an apartment to rent again and lost rent during

First impressions are key to a project's reputation and leasing success.

Camden Property Trust

Gables Residential

vacancies. In general, apartment managers need to try to limit the turnover rate.

Management's ability to affect turnover depends a great deal on the causes. Some reasons for turnover are beyond a property manager's control, but others can be easily fixed. Residents move out of a rental community for the following major reasons:

- Job Transfers and Layoffs—Ebbs and flows in the employment market are beyond the control of property managers, but managers can at least try to ensure that layoffs in one company or one industry will not affect too many residents' ability to pay rent at one time by screening for the range of occupations on residents' applications.
- Shift to Homeownership—Powerful psychological, cultural, and financial forces encourage American households to buy rather than rent if they are able to do so. Nevertheless, the apartment industry should

learn how to better promote renting as a permanent housing choice for a larger share of the market. Many well-positioned apartment complexes could stem the tide to homebuying and even lure back current home-owners.[5] Management could play a key role in promoting renting as a lifestyle choice determined by the kind and quality of services delivered, renters' access to time-saving conveniences, high-tech communications, and entertainment resources, and the availability and effectiveness of security services. Some programs, such as Equity Residential Properties's Rent with Equity program, allow residents to earn credits toward the eventual purchase of a home. Such programs can be effective marketing tools and can prolong tenancy as residents endeavor to maximize the credits.
- Dissatisfaction with the Unit, the Amenities, or the Management—Long tenancies are encouraged by physical design and excellent management. Handling maintenance needs expeditiously is one solution to

high turnover. A good idea when residents move into a unit is for the maintenance manager to send a welcoming letter asking for their comments and other feedback. This kind of attention pays off in renewals and rental rates that considerably improve NOI without making any significant changes in the product.

- Problems with Residents—Handling problem residents promptly also reduces turnover. Management needs to ensure that residents understand the community's rules and regulations when they move in. It can be helpful to have the rules in writing and have residents sign a statement indicating they have read and understand them. When noise or other behaviors irritate neighbors, the manager should try to reach an amicable solution with all parties involved. But if such a solution cannot be found and one party is at fault, the manager should enforce the rules quickly and firmly. Eviction may be the best solution.
- Competition—Current and anticipated market competition is closely related to residents' dissatisfaction. Managers must be keenly aware of competing apartment communities in the area and know the amenities offered and rents charged. Ensuring that rents are geared to square footage and services offered is an important management function, and management must also keep up with the competition or find ways to exceed competitors' services and amenities. Rents cannot be based on pro forma projections but must reflect current market conditions, especially the constantly changing balance of supply and demand by unit type. Because conditions can change quickly and a vacant unit can cost much more than a slight reduction in rent, pricing should be monitored weekly or even daily in some cases.[6]
- Inadequate Screening—Failure to screen applicants properly can cause problems in collecting rents and eventual loss—voluntary or forced—of the resident. Developers sometimes hire leasing companies specializing in the initial lease-up of new projects. If, as is usual,

they are compensated according to the number of leases generated and are not penalized for early lease terminations, they may not be very discriminating about the people to whom they lease units. The manager should be empowered to monitor the creditworthiness of prospective residents brought in by outside leasing agents. If the developer plans to sell the apartment project in the near future, it may be preferable to increase the short-term cash flow, which is generally the most important consideration for buyers, at the expense of long-term profitability. To increase occupancy immediately, the seller might be less selective about the residents. But if the sale falls through, the owner may have to clean out unreliable or troublesome residents.[7]

The Management Team

Operating an apartment project of any size efficiently requires people with a variety of skills. Management tasks range widely, including everything from establishing budgets to repairing mechanical systems to surveying residents. Apartment property managers are responsible for the following functions:

- initial marketing and lease-up (often assigned to an outside source);
- ongoing marketing and leasing;
- collecting rents, handling accounts, and keeping records;
- making ongoing reports to owners;
- maintaining and repairing units, and readying them for new tenants;
- maintaining and repairing systems and common areas, housekeeping;
- maintaining landscaping and grounds;
- operating recreational and other supplemental facilities provided for residents or overseeing their proper operation;

Large properties offer greater opportunities for operating efficiencies. Ventana Apartment Homes in San Antonio, Texas, includes 390 units.

Embrey Partners

- hiring and training staff;
- keeping residents informed about apartment policies and operating activities of interest to them;
- surveying residents' likes and dislikes;
- initiating services for residents;
- dealing with residents' complaints about physical problems;
- dealing with residents' complaints about other residents;
- maintaining good relations with brokers, community organizations, and local government;
- maintaining good relations with managers of neighboring apartments to share information on bad residents and work together on security and other common problems; and
- developing budgets and operating plans.

Clearly, with all these responsibilities, finding good managers for a property is an essential task.

The Basics of Apartment Property Management

A stable occupancy rate with low turnover and high-quality residents who pay market-rate rents punctually is every property manager's goal. But even the best managers encounter problems. The following advice represents lessons learned by many developers over many years.

- If you make promises, deliver.
- Check the credit history of new residents through credit agencies and previous landlords.
- Collect the first month's rent plus a security deposit from new residents to guard against their leaving without giving notice.
- In a slow market, the trick is to hold on to your current residents. Make sure that your incentives to managers adequately reward lease renewals.
- For lease renewals, have your manager meet with the resident 45 days before the lease expires.
- Deal with problems quickly and efficiently. Problems that are not resolved only grow.
- Fewer callbacks by residents on maintenance and repairs mean lower turnover.
- Property management problems are usually about people, not property.
- When cash flow is low, try to minimize cutbacks on maintenance, repairs, and replacements. Cutbacks dispirit on-site staff and lead to a lower standard of maintenance.

Source: Adapted from Richard B. Peiser and Dean Schwanke, *Professional Real Estate Development: The ULI Guide to the Business* (Chicago: Dearborn Financial Publishing and ULI–the Urban Land Institute, 1992), p. 202.

■

The Management Structure

The nature of the relationship between the developer and the property manager depends, in large part, on the property's size, the extent of the developer's property portfolio, and the nature and structure of the business. The manager can be the developer, the developer's employee, a subsidiary or in-house department of the development/property company, or an individual or third party management company under contract. Most large apartment property companies, including REITs, manage their own properties through an in-house department or owned subsidiary company.

For most apartment projects, the decision whether or not to use an outside property manager is based on the developer's willingness to invest time in the project.[8] Properly addressing residents' needs and maintaining the property are extremely time-consuming. Most developers prefer to delegate these responsibilities to a qualified property manager.

Management, operations, and maintenance for individual properties are handled in a variety of ways: by the developer or property management firm's on-site employees, by the developer's central office or the property manager (employees who work on or in a number of properties), or by tradespeople and contractors hired as needed.

The larger the property and its operating budget, the more likely it can accommodate specialists such as equipment engineers, gardeners, painters, or guards on staff. Many developers consider 150 or 200 units the minimum number necessary to support a full-time maintenance staff consisting of property manager, assistant manager, maintenance worker, and porter.[9] Projects of 300 to 400 units offer opportunities for even more operating efficiencies. And the emergence of high-volume apartment owners and operators has opened up opportunities for significant networking and economies of scale for bulk purchases of supplies, staffing and training, marketing, and office functions.

Management of small properties is by necessity a more informal undertaking. For instance, Century West Development, an apartment developer in Santa Monica, California, employs a resident manager for an 18-unit building. This person receives a free apartment and around $25 per unit per month. Century West believes in looking for stability in a manager—someone who has lived in the area for several years, who is aggressive, friendly, and a good leasing or sales agent. Such mom-and-pop management arrangements may be less expensive in the short run than professional managers, but for investments of any size, they are inadequate in today's market.[10]

Developers with multiple properties in a single market can dispatch centralized maintenance and management staff (and equipment and supplies purchased in bulk) where needed to achieve efficient operations. For example, Drever Partners, Inc., of San Francisco owns and manages 52 multifamily properties in the Houston area. To operate this portfolio cost-efficiently, Drever formed a Houston-based asset and property management sub-

figure 9-1
Ten Largest Multifamily Property Managers, 2000

Company	Headquarters	Apartment Units Managed
1 Apartment Investment and Management Company	Denver, Colorado	362,468
2 Equity Residential Properties Trust	Chicago, Illinois	234,756
3 Lincoln Property Company—Residential	Dallas, Texas	100,946
4 Pinnacle Realty Management Company	Seattle, Washington	98,656
5 United Dominion Realty Trust, Inc.	Richmond, Virginia	81,180
6 Archstone Communities	Englewood, Colorado	67,208
7 Sentinel Real Estate Corporation	New York, New York	59,000
8 Camden Property Trust	Houston, Texas	56,060
9 Trammell Crow Residential	Atlanta, Georgia	48,799
10 ConAm Management Corporation	San Diego, California	45,250

Source: National Multi Housing Council Web site: http://www.nmhc.org/top50/default.html.

sidiary, Concierge Management, to handle all the properties. In mid-1995, Concierge was the second largest property management firm in the Houston metropolitan market.[11]

Alternatively, developers can hire experienced outside managers to operate their properties based on a mutually satisfactory management agreement. Many large development companies offer for-fee apartment management services. Other companies are exclusively property management companies.

What to Look for in a Property Manager
Professional property managers should be skilled at maintaining high occupancy rates and achieving low operating costs. In assembling a management team or selecting a third party manager, a developer should consider four factors:

- management philosophy;
- apartment management's knowledge, including familiarity with the market segment(s) targeted;
- knowledge of the local market; and
- compatibility of the management group's accounting and reporting procedures with the requirements of the owner/investors.

When a third party manager is used, terms of the management contract are also an important consideration.

Established apartment developers and owners are a good source of information about the strengths and weaknesses of property management firms. Various professional organizations certify the education, experience, and affiliation of individuals and firms in the property management field, including:

- Institute of Property Management, which gives certified property manager (CPM) designations to qualifying individuals and accredited management organization (AMO) designations to qualified firms;

- Building Owners and Managers Institute, which runs a study program for professional managers leading to a designation of real property administrator (RPA); and
- National Apartment Association, which offers courses leading to a designation as certified apartment manager (CAM).

Developers are advised to "look for someone who recognizes that property management is something that happens on site at the property, not in the district or corporate office. Select a management company by shopping its properties. What impression do on-site personnel give you? Get references from other developers. Does the company get reports out on time? Are the reports understandable and informative?"[12]

For on-site staff and the resident manager in particular, people skills are essential. A motivated staff is as important as the physical property in maintaining high occupancy and low turnover rates: "People who are willing to get away from their desks are the ones you want. The property manager's abilities to motivate, to market, and to keep in touch with residents and staff are more important than skill at paperwork."[13]

Management Philosophy. Different apartment properties (and different investment goals) call for different management styles. Developers should determine priorities for the property's operation. For example, will aggressive marketing or an above-normal level of service be more important? Will careful selection and discipline of residents or operations cost control be paramount? Developers should match their own management team's strengths or a third party's management philosophy to the goals for the property. Ask potential managers to describe the approach they would take in managing the specific property and how they would add value.

Know-How. Apartment management is a complex service business, and developers may not always appreciate the technical or interpersonal skills it entails. The competence and personalities of the people who main-

The Domaine in Legacy in Plano, Texas, provides a wide array of services for residents, including a breakfast bar and massage therapy.

tain the property and deal with the residents are at the heart of successful management. Experience should be a key criterion in assembling or contracting for a management team. The management team's members, especially its top executives and top on-site managers, should be thoroughly experienced in the apartment management business. Ideally, they will have worked with properties of similar size serving similar markets. In assessing a management company's competence and experience, the developer should look at:

• Other Properties under Management—How many apartment units does the company manage? What is the range of sizes and rents under management? Experience with the same type of apartment property is probably the most important factor to consider. Look for companies with a good reputation for managing similar properties in terms of size, design, and residents' characteristics. Interview residents and owners of a few properties. Does the management style at another property match the developer's management philosophy?

• Staffing and Employment Policies—Given the importance of relations with residents on the bottom line, the management company's employment policies as they emphasize and reward customer service should be an important criterion for selection. Does the company use its own employees for maintenance and repair work? Are employees compensated in any way for outstanding customer satisfaction? Do service personnel

wear uniforms? Examine the company's employee policies book. Examine its training manuals. Visit some properties and talk to some of the staff people behind the desk, on the grounds, and in the corridors. Does the property management team include people at management levels who can relate to Asian, Hispanic, and African-American markets and residents? A diverse staff with a sensitivity toward other ethnic and cultural groups can be helpful.

• On-site Maintenance—What procedures are in place to handle ongoing maintenance and repairs? How is maintenance scheduled and verified? Developers should ask to see schedules and maintenance checklists for operating properties.

• Inspections and Audits—Who inspects properties and operations, and how often? Are off-site property managers responsible for inspecting and auditing on-site operations? Inspection checklists and audit procedures should be examined for their thoroughness and workability. Developers should review an example of an audit. An audit should be performed at least twice a year, preferably quarterly. The auditor, who should appear unannounced, should review collection reports, rent rolls, and individual leases, and inspect vacant units to ensure that no "skimming" is occurring.[14]

• Service Requests, Complaints, and Feedback—How does the company receive and record requests for maintenance and repairs from residents? What are its policies for handling requests and complaints, espe-

Addison Circle has brought urban density—and a sense of community—to a classic edge city. Located in Addison, Texas, a northern suburb of Dallas, the 80-acre mixed-use project is the result of a public/private partnership between Post Properties, Inc., and the town of Addison. Designed by RTKL Associates of Dallas, Addison Circle will ultimately comprise some 3,000 dwelling units intermixed with neighborhood shops as well as up to 4 million square feet of office and commercial space. At about 55 dwelling units per acre, the mostly rental project is more than twice as dense as the typical North Dallas garden apartment project. Yet Addison Circle has a sense of place and community not often seen in new development.

Attention to streets and open space is one of the qualities that make Addison Circle so appealing. The circle itself is the symbolic center of the project. In addition to its symbolic role, the roundabout serves to calm traffic that flows along Quorum Drive, a major thoroughfare that cuts through the middle of the site. The roundabout did not come into being without controversy; a special consultant was required to convince skeptical officials to permit construction of what was to be the first public traffic circle in the area in more than 50 years. To further establish the circle as the focal point of the project and the larger community, a design competition was held to create a sculpture for the center of the circle.

Substantial investment is evident in the treatment of Addison Circle's residential streets and boulevards. Sidewalks and crosswalks in many cases are paved in brick, with large shade trees planted at 25-foot intervals to give the streetscape the instant appearance of maturity. Bike racks, benches, litter containers, and other street furniture invite residents to use the public spaces.

Both the architecture and site planning contribute to the urban texture of Addison Circle. The residential buildings are four stories high; in some cases, three residential levels are located above a ground-floor level of shops and small service businesses. The building designs are modern, but they are domesticated by balconies, bays, gables, and brick. Window elements are used to create architectural diversity, and several window types are employed, including large bay windows painted to contrast with the brickwork. Facades are further articulated with cast-stone sills and lintels, painted metal balconies, and awnings.

Reversing the typical suburban norm of deep building setbacks and narrow sidewalks, the residential building facades at Addison Circle are close to the street and sidewalk widths are generous. Sidewalks are 12 feet

Attention to streetscapes and open space makes Addison Circle an appealing pedestrian-oriented community.

wide, and buildings are set just six feet back from the sidewalk, allowing for a landscape buffer between the sidewalk and building. Most residential buildings are built around courtyards. The units are located on both sides of interior corridors, with major entries and windows looking out over the street as well as over the interior pool and courtyard areas. The full-block closure building prototype is used to avoid functionally ambiguous space: one is either in the public realm, surveyed by the many windows overlooking the street, or enclosed within the security of the building.

Parking is provided in above-grade structures located behind each residential block, allowing residences and shops to open directly onto the street. One parking space per bedroom is allotted, a ratio that amounts to approximately 1.3 spaces per dwelling unit.

To a large extent, the market for Addison Circle is renters by choice—a mix of young, childless professionals and empty nesters, largely double-income couples ranging in age from 30 to 55. For this market segment, quality of life is a key issue. Developers are finding that pools and health clubs are a starting point but that for many renters, the idea of living in a community—of having everything from a dry cleaners downstairs to a coffee bar to a secure and attractive place to stroll or sit—is an increasingly sought-after amenity.

Source: Adapted from Steven Fader, *Density by Design: New Directions in Residential Development,* 2nd ed. (Washington, D.C.: ULI–the Urban Land Institute, 1999).

A well-maintained property is one of the responsibilities of the management team.

© Bloodgood Sharp Buster/Jess Smith

cially acknowledgment and response time? Does the company actively seek to measure residents' satisfaction and determine unmet needs? Is surveying residents or formally requesting their input standard operating procedure? Look at survey questionnaires that may have been used.

Knowledge of the Local Market. Property managers need to be familiar with local markets to carry out mar-

Useful Reports from Management

- Traffic Reports (monthly)—How many people come through the door each month to inquire about renting? How many of them are qualified prospects (in terms of income and lifestyle)? How many qualified prospects become residents? Answers to these questions can help owners determine the effectiveness of advertising dollars spent.
- Rent Rolls (monthly or quarterly)—Which apartments are rented? What are the demographics of the renters? When do current leases expire? Answers to these questions can help owners track occupancy, spot potential future problems with occupancy, and target marketing.
- Vacancies (monthly or quarterly)—Which units are vacant? How long have they been vacant? This report should include units that do not generate income.
- Income and Expenses (monthly)—This report should show gross potential income, actual income, nonrent income, and line-by-line expenses.

keting and leasing functions and to monitor rents to stay competitive. Local knowledge is also important to contract out maintenance and repair work, buy materials and supplies advantageously, work with utilities, deal with local governments on a variety of issues from taxes to zoning to crime, and even, at times, work cooperatively with neighboring apartment owners and managers on common tasks and mutual concerns.

Regional or national developers with their own property management groups nonetheless tend to seek local partners for on-site property management and construction management. In a tight market where carpenters, plumbers, electricians, and gardeners are in great demand, these tradespeople are more likely to trust and remain loyal to managers with whom they have worked before. Managers with local experience and contacts have a head start in the competition to attract the best talent.

Some developers do not subscribe to this approach, believing it is not difficult to find good local people even if the lead construction managers and the lead property managers are from the company's home office so long as the local contractors and other consultants can be sold on the development company's creditworthiness.

Accounting and Reporting Procedures. Managing apartments involves many detail-oriented tasks, including tracking the large volume of money transactions. For certain investors, like public REITs, the particular content, form, and frequency of reports provided by management can be important. Managers should be selected who will be able to tailor reports to meet the needs of the developer, the owner, or the investor. The degree of attention to details shown by management prospects and their accounting and reporting procedures are important criteria for selecting managers. Developers should check a management company's procedures for:

- Rent Collection—Procedures for issuing notices, handling on-site rent payments, transmitting payments to banks, and accounting for rental (and other nonrental) income.

- Control of Disbursements—Purchase procedures and systems for writing checks and accounting for expenditures.
- Reports—Structure of the management company's regular reports on financial performance (income and expense statements, rents, leasing activity, vacancies, traffic reports) and how often and when such reports are submitted. The developer should be able to work with the management company to change reporting methods as needed to meet the owner's and investors' needs.

Operations and Maintenance

For many of the day-to-day details of operation, various professional property management associations, including the Institute for Real Estate Management (IREM) and the National Apartment Association, offer practical advice and standards, including sample documents, forms, and checklists. IREM, for example, urges that the management company maintain separate accounts for funds belonging to the property owner and funds belonging to the management company to protect the owner's funds and prevent any commingling of different accounts required to operate the property.[15]

Operating Budget

Because the property manager and the maintenance supervisor are responsible for making the budget work over the long haul, they should prepare the operating budget.

Income and Expense Statement. Analysis of an income and expense statement requires a point of reference, sometimes multiple points of reference. The budget is the best tool for this comparison, because it tells how the project is doing compared with how the developer expected it to perform. Results from prior years can also be instructive, because they supply information about the same project over time and whether operations have improved. Industry standards are probably the least informative point of reference, "because all projects and operations are different and the nuances of a particular project are not reflected in industry standards. In some cases, an owner or property manager may wish to make all three comparisons . . . to properly analyze a project."[16]

Fine-Tuning Rates. The pro forma is hardly the last word in determining rents. Maximizing rents and adjusting rents to remain competitive in a changing marketplace are central functions of ongoing property management. In most markets for well-positioned properties with flexible management, there is room to be creative in maximizing rental rates. Making sure that the management team includes the requisite marketing and leasing talent (and is given the requisite authority) to keep rents as

A project's design and features must be viewed in terms of how they will affect the bottom line.

high as they can be without generating vacancies can pay off in the long run.

The most common method of determining rents is based on a project's physical characteristics measured against the physical characteristics of competitive projects. Increasingly, residents search not simply for the lowest rent but for the best value—a highly subjective quality—for which they may be willing to pay higher rents. Thus, apartment owners, marketers, and managers should shift their attention to "enhancing income by designing an aggressive, value-driven [unit pricing] strategy capable of capturing every dollar" that projects with special qualities can command.[17] Some renters are willing to pay more for such attributes as construction quality, staff quality, building reputation, and security.

Market research initially determines what amenities and services renters will pay premiums for, and getting those premiums is often a matter of marketing. But managers are in the best position to identify qualities that promise rent premiums on an ongoing basis. One management group, for example, has discovered that it can obtain premiums in exchange for offering more flexible lease terms. Post Properties, in response to competition from the homebuying market, offers different durations of leases, ranging from very short terms to two years. Renters pay for this flexibility with premiums that may range from $20 to $200. Post has seen no detrimental effects on turnover from these innovations.[18]

In some situations, owners may be forced by loan requirements or other investors to charge too much rent. To keep apartments leased, it may be necessary to offer extras that make the effective rent more competitive. A number of ways are available to lower effective rents without reducing face rents:

• Reduce the deposit required;
• Offer accruing deposits whereby residents make little or no initial deposit and earn deposit credits at the

At Jefferson Estates in Richardson, Texas, top-notch recreational amenities appeal to those who rent by choice.

Post Properties is known for its apartment communities' manicured landscaped areas.

rate of $20 to $30 a month, which they receive at the end of six months or so;

- Provide cable TV or other services that normally carry a monthly charge free of charge;
- Install additional appliances, such as microwave ovens, ceiling fans, and washer/dryers (which represent a permanent capital improvement to the unit);
- Offer privileges at health or other clubs in the community.[19]

Controlling Operating Expenses. Buying in bulk potentially can reduce costs for all aspects of apartment development, including operations. Large operations responsible for multiple properties in particular can lower costs this way. For instance, submetering utilities by units or buying electricity and gas in bulk and reselling them to residents saves on operating costs and can lower costs for residents.

Staffing and Employment Practices

Property management is one of the fastest-growing specializations in the real estate profession, "emerging as a managerial science. Today, property managers must have at their fingertips the knowledge, communication skills and technical expertise needed to be dynamic decision makers. They also must be versatile because they may be called on to act as market analysts, advertising executives, salespeople, accountants, diplomats or even maintenance engineers. Interpersonal skills are needed to deal effectively with owners, prospects, tenants, employees, outside contractors and others in the real estate business."[20]

In this emerging era, recruiting, training, and compensating staff are important considerations for property management companies or developers with property management departments. In a service industry, the most effective employees have a service mentality. Many managers emphasize this mentality as well as professional skills in hiring staff and seek to reinforce it with training and compensation.

Some experts advise that smaller developers should look for managers who have been trained by major property companies, companies that might give the best training but not necessarily the best commissions. Visit companies' properties, evaluate their leasing and management programs, and hire their people. It is possible to attract experienced managers by offering them more control and responsibility and the ability to make decisions quickly, with no layers of bureaucracy to navigate.[21] On the other side, Howard Ruby, chair of R&B Realty Group, admits that many R&B employees have taken jobs elsewhere in the industry, where, they have found, having gone through "R&B University" has been an asset.[22]

One criterion for hiring individuals in Post Properties's management division is good service skills or potentially good service skills (with training). New employees—from groundskeepers to property managers to company executives—meet with members of the top management group, who seek to impress upon them the fact that service is one of their most important duties. Every employee goes through an annual reorientation in resident service.

Psychological testing can help identify people with a knack for pleasing customers. R&B Realty has started working with testing companies to develop personality tests, based on its own best and worst employees in terms of customer service. The tests will be used to determine whether prospective employees have the kinds of qualities needed for customer service representatives. R&B Realty tends to recruit people from hotels, another industry with a strong customer service orientation.

Training is another key element in providing excellent service. R&B Realty offers a number of standard workshops for staff, including an entry-level course called "Focus on the Customer." All new hires are required to attend the course, which includes a one-day workshop on communications skills and a week-long series of half-day workshops that have been developed through feedback from regional managers. Subjects offered at the half-day workshops include writing customer service follow-up letters, basics for dealing with non-English-speaking persons, and sensitive issues. The company's marketing department also publishes a monthly newsletter for employees, *At Your Service,* giving tips on customer satisfaction and service.

Beyond hiring and training, a third component of effective customer service is feedback and reward. Leading apartment management companies tend to stress the bottom-up "culture of service" in their organizations, based on closely monitoring residents' satisfaction and compensation schemes that reward employees for keeping residents satisfied.

The key is to have on site the highest-quality people possible. AvalonBay values long tenure in its on-site employees, the people closest to the customers, and encourages it by giving good employees subjective as well as objective reinforcement (compensation). The company makes a point of celebrating management's successes.

Toscana, AvalonBay's property in Sunnyvale, California, carries out a contemporary Mediterranean design theme that suits the climate and terrain.

© Mert Carpenter

© Mert Carpenter

Summit Properties allows new residents to move out within 30 days if not satisfied. Residents also have 90 days to relocate to any other Summit community without penalties.

It also works on convincing employees that being in the apartment business is meaningful: "We're not selling hams. We're not selling cars. We're providing homes for people, and we have a real chance to make a difference in people's lives."[23]

Owners need to communicate regularly with their managers and staff to help them understand the owners' goals and objectives and to learn and understand managers' and staffs' concerns. This advice may be especially pertinent when the owner puts the property up for sale. On-site staff "should be informed about the developer's goals and given some financial incentive to motivate them to help put the apartment in the best possible condition, physically and financially, for sale."[24] According to experienced developers, however, residents should not be informed of a pending sale but informed immediately, by letter, of a completed sale. For most other events in the common life of an apartment community, open reporting is the best policy.

Resident Relations

Most managers view the exchange of information as a key factor in residents' satisfaction and, consequently, low turnover rates. Information needs to flow both ways—from management to residents about problems, policies, changes, services, and events, and from residents to management about likes and dislikes.

Keeping Residents Informed. Both the content of information communicated to residents and the means of communication are important. Managers should make sure they inform residents, preferably in writing, about:

- rules and regulations;
- the details, including the timing, of any planned maintenance or construction that may disrupt their normal activities;
- incidents of crime and any security problems;
- new services and changes in existing services;
- upcoming public events in the apartment community.

R&B Realty property managers use a standard letter to report to residents when specific crimes occur on the premises and to urge residents to take an active role in their own security. The following letter was delivered to residents of Oakwood Mid-Wilshire Apartments.

Dear Resident,

While enjoying the conveniences that are provided by living in a major metropolitan area, we must realize that crime in our society is real and plagues cities large and small across the nation. This letter is to advise you that the management office has received information that there has been a robbery within the Oakwood Mid-Wilshire Apartments on [date] at approximately 9:00 p.m.

Three suspects approached the victim while he was in the building #1 upper parking lot and demanded money. The victim was not injured even though a weapon was seen. The suspects fled on foot in an unknown direction. No additional information was given. If you require greater details, please contact the Rampart division of the Los Angeles Police Department.

The owners and management respect your right to know about this incident and bring the matter to your attention so that you can use caution to protect yourself against similar crimes.

Please take an active role in your own security. Even the most secure buildings cannot provide 100% protection. Make sure you contact the Los Angeles Police Department at [phone number] or call "911" should an emergency situation occur. You should always call the local authorities first as this will facilitate the quickest response to all emergencies, and greatly reduce any unnecessary problems. While our security officers are here to observe and report, neither they nor we can guarantee your personal safety or the security of your personal property.

Should you have any questions, please don't hesitate to contact me at [office phone number].

Sincerely,

Property Manager
Oakwood Mid-Wilshire

Another standard letter R&B property managers send when break-ins occur contains the following suggestions: "Please take the time to remember to secure all doors and windows when leaving your apartment, and use your deadbolt lock. We also recommend that you purchase renter's insurance to cover the personal possessions kept inside your apartment. The insurance is relatively inexpensive, and it covers losses due to fire, theft, and other perils, should they occur. Contact your local insurance agent for details on renter's insurance. For some general security tips please refer to the flyer contained in your move-in package. Should you have any questions, please do not hesitate to contact the manager's office."

Source: R&B Realty

Managers can provide an additional service to residents by providing information to live by—community events, nearby resources, available public transportation, and nearby stores, service establishments, and restaurants.

The methods of providing general information to residents range from the simple to the technologically complex, with an accordingly wide range of costs:

- bulletin boards and tables with brochures in the management office and other common areas;
- move-in packages that include, for example, the apartment community's rules and regulations and local public transportation route maps;
- letters, flyers, and other printed materials distributed door to door;
- phone calls and voice mail;
- computer networks and Web sites;
- dedicated cable channels;
- a community newspaper;
- concierge service;
- meetings and resident committees.

Taking the time to put together an attractive move-in package with information for new residents generally pays off in residents' satisfaction and their understanding of their responsibilities as renters. Special attention should be paid to effective communication of the community's rules and regulations. They should be clearly written and illustrated in a nonthreatening manner and include practical information about personal and government services, shopping, churches and other institutions, and transportation services in the neighborhood. Such a package can get the resident-landlord relationship off to a good start.

When well conceived and appealingly written and formatted, management-issued community newspapers or newsletters (or now intranets) can be an important component of resident relations. Indeed, such materials can

Besides being a recreational amenity, the swimming pool is usually a major design focal point for the development.

help market the community to prospective renters. "The trick is to resist the temptation of letting [the newsletter] read as if it were titled *The Landlord Speaks.* . . . If you violate this principle, you may very well prompt a resident group to . . . produce a newsletter for airing their grievances."[25]

New technologies provide new tools for property managers to successfully manage their communities and communicate with their residents. A number of firms, such as Windsor, Connecticut–based SS&C Technologies and Timberline Software Corporation in Beaverton, Oregon, provide integrated computer-based software systems addressing all property management functions. Similarly, firms like ClearWorks in Houston and Real Page in Carrollton, Texas, provide bundled voice, video, and data services to community residents, including Web-based services such as community intranets. These intranets allow residents to contact managers about service or other concerns as well as to see community notices,

maintenance schedules, and announcements from the management office.

Learning about Residents' Concerns. For its Oakwood Apartments, R&B Realty provides suggestion forms on postage-paid self-mailers addressed to the divisional vice president. The firm calls this communications device "home office hotline." The home office responds to comments and suggestions received via the hotline within one week of receipt.

Some managers have developed procedures for measuring residents' satisfaction to give them a better idea of what they are doing well and where improvements are possible, as well as to provide a basis for incentives for employees.

Post Properties polls every resident annually, asking questions about the attitudes, responsiveness, and skills of the office, maintenance, and landscaping staffs, and about residents' peace of mind. The result is a single objective measure of effective service that is used as a

The business center at AMLI's property in St. Charles, Illinois, provides residents with the tools they need for working at home.

benchmark tied to incentives throughout the organization. Post sets goals for itself and then ties incentives to meeting those goals.

At Oakwood Apartments, about 1,700 residents are surveyed once per quarter by phone (by an outside market research company); properties are ranked by performance based on the results. Feedback from the survey is circulated among the staff to point out where improvements are needed.

Resident Services. "While community amenities are important, they will move to second place behind services as the lifestyle market [people who can afford to buy but who chose to rent] develops."[26] Better services are in demand across the market spectrum. Older age cohorts bear particular watching, as the propensity to rent among older households is growing and they tend to be more demanding.

Exact returns from a bundle of services are hard to measure, says AvalonBay's Robert Slater, who believes strongly that providing extraordinary resident services adds value, which shows up in rent increases and high renewal rates. AvalonBay asks its on-site employees to deliver services "so outstanding that people will tell other people about us." No reasonable request is refused. A resident who tells someone else "They did this for me!" is, the company believes, more effective than any advertising it could concoct.[27]

Discovering what services will produce the biggest bang for the buck is often a simple matter of asking the residents. Post's Jeffrey Harris offers advice rooted in experience: "In terms of services offered, we've made the biggest mistakes when we tried to guess what the residents would want. Services that we've offered based on residents' input—from survey questionnaires or from informal polling around the pool—have been much more successful. We've also been more successful when we've shortened the list of potential services and focused on fewer items but done them well."[28]

The possible range of services management might consider is quite large, so costs and benefits must be considered very carefully in putting together a package of services. Will adding a particular service really help lease or re-lease apartments? More and more, the potential of various services to produce income is an important consideration. The property manager must make an informed business decision when adding services and conveniences, ensuring that they will yield a reasonable return on the investment of time and money. Depending on the market and the competitive environment, an apartment community may have to offer some services—convenience shopping, transportation, daycare, doormen, business services—as a matter of course to attract or retain residents. Certain niche markets, such as affordable housing or seniors' housing, can be extraordinarily service-intensive businesses, with the former often requiring extensive counseling services and the later often involving health care services.

Although "service" is a management philosophy that many experts think is crucial to the bottom line of apartment communities, the particular content of the service package can vary widely from one property to another. Innovation and experimentation are widespread. At the same time, many large-scale operators with multiple properties seek to standardize amenities and services to establish a brand identity for their apartment communities. Industry leaders have experimented with several services in recent years:

- Convenience Stores—Although in general retail operations are feasible only in large or mixed-use complexes, some properties include convenience stores in buildings with as few as 400 to 500 units.
- Visitor Units—Making apartments available for residents' relatives or friends for short stays is a popular option, especially in Florida communities.
- Home Services—Cleaning units, doing residents' laundry, walking/feeding pets, running errands.
- Community Gardens—Allowing residents to work three- by four-foot garden plots is a good use of space that would otherwise be dead, and it provides much enjoyment for those who tend them.
- Debit Cards—Residents pay for laundry services with magnetic swipe cards. New residents are given a starter card containing $1.00 to $3.00, which can be recharged at machines in the laundry rooms. Machines to read prepaid or billed plastic cards cost about $350 and are usually maintained and tabulated by the laundry vendor. The use of such cards can be fairly easily ex-

tended to other facilities and services, such as parking, purchases from vending machines or on-site stores, or equipment rentals.

Responsiveness. The number one rule of resident services is quick response to complaints. Most good managers recommend a policy of making repairs and handling other complaints within 24 hours. Some management companies guarantee a fast response time, promising to respond to requests for repairs within 24 hours, although actually fixing the problem may take longer.

At AvalonBay, maintenance employees are compensated to make good on these guarantees. They receive bonuses for turning around service requests within 24 hours, as well as a bonus that comes out of net operating income, which would diminish if the company had to pay a lot of money on the guarantees. Because of these incentives, at least 95 percent of service requests are handled within 24 hours.

Business and Media Centers. The spread of home-based work and telecommuting has created a market in many residential locations for business services. An increasing number of companies provide business centers, and the response has been favorable. They are usually very popular and relatively inexpensive to provide. Not only do they serve home businesses, but they also have become popular as an after-school center in properties with children. Most properties built in the last several years have such a center. A typical business center at Post Properties's com-

munities is about 180 square feet, with a conference table and some built-in spaces for fax machines, conference calling, and two or three loaded PCs; residents can access it 24 hours a day with magnetic swipe cards. The hardware and equipment cost less than $10,000. A side benefit is less traffic in the property's leasing and business office.

At some developments, business centers operate under a franchise arrangement with an operator who leases the space and offers computers and secretarial services. Typically, business centers include computers, fax machines, printers, and conference facilities. Media centers offer facilities for viewing movies and sporting events and for giving business presentations.

Wired. A number of forces make wiring a hot topic in multifamily housing. Communications technology is making rapid advances. Miles of fiber-optic cable are being installed every week in the United States. Households of all kinds, but perhaps most tellingly young households (aged 25 to 40) and old households (over 60) are increasingly seeking access to interactive entertainment and education resources and services. With the growth in telecommuting and home-based businesses, many households put a premium on sophisticated at-home communications capacity. Last but not least, far-reaching changes in telecommunications policy and deregulation have brought many new players into the telecommunications arena and have led to the creation of multiservice, multi-regional providers—many of which specialize in the multifamily industry.

Video screening rooms are an increasingly popular amenity. AMLI's St. Charles has comfortable sofas for viewing in a relaxed atmosphere.

Bundled communications—that is, integrated voice, video, and data services—using high-tech cabling is the current must-have for apartments. The signs that management put up a few years ago announcing that apartments had cable connections are now announcing that they accommodate high-speed and high-volume multifunctional communications applications—phone, TV, computer networks.

Many of the providers of bundled communications offer custom telephone, television, and computing services with one-stop shopping. Residents benefit from not having to deal directly with phone or cable companies, a long menu of options from which they can choose customized services, and instant hookups with no three-day waits. Owners and developers derive some additional income from such services. The infrastructure provided can be easily upgraded to handle new information services and entertainment options as they become available, including fiber optics. Some features of wired apartments include:

- Entertainment TV centers with vast programming options and interactive capabilities for home shopping, banking, and the like.
- Multimedia home office systems incorporating voice and videoconferencing capabilities, access to the Internet, and integrated messaging (voice, fax, and E-mail).
- Remote cameras for security or monitoring children.
- Programmable energy systems, security, and appliance management.

Such features are today's luxuries but will be tomorrow's standard in mid-level and even less costly properties that wish to remain competitive.

Smart features can come with smart price tags. Although the demand for communications technology is increasing at a pace owners and managers can no longer ignore, the hardware and software that drive interactive, on-demand services and improved operating efficiencies are now affordable for many apartment properties.[29]

Concierges and Cruise Directors. Full-fledged concierge services are becoming common in luxury apartment communities. The more an apartment community's concierge can do for busy households, the more competitive the community will be. At the Colony at Fashion Island in Newport Beach, California, a full-time concierge arranges theater tickets, restaurant reservations, travel assistance, and valet, maid, and handyman services.

For affluent households, one of the main advantages of renting is that it gives them more time away from yardwork and home maintenance chores for whatever they prefer doing, and because time is becoming an increasingly scarce commodity, the more time a high-end community saves, the more likely it appeals to its market. Expanded phone services providing two-digit dialing to selected vendors—restaurants, hair salons, video stores, and so forth—constitute a kind of electronic concierge

(and some extra income through fees vendors pay to be included in the menu).

Services as Income Generators. Earning a little more of the resident's dollar from sources other than rent is often a key reason for adding services. One goal is to be creative in coming up with "other income," that is, income that is not counted as ordinary rental income.

Apartment rents can be structured to include the costs of delivering services, or services can be viewed as add-on charges. Add-on charges appear to be used increasingly for even standard services, and the multifamily housing industry appears to be doing what the auto industry did a while back. That is, operators are going from a fixed price that includes everything to a system of à la carte services, even such fundamental services as trash collection and utilities.

Increasingly, monthly fees are charged for trash pickup, which can quickly add up to a sizable sum for the property owner. Many optional, nonstandard services—maid service, dry cleaning pickup and delivery, cable TV, on-site storage space—can generate income on the "other income" line of the property's financial statement. Frequently, such services are provided by third parties, who pay a fee or percentage to the apartment community's management for access, space, referrals, and other considerations. Alternatively, management companies can develop specialized service businesses such as linens, furnishings, cleaning, wiring, and apartment management itself for their own projects and for other properties (under third party contracts) whose owners prefer to concentrate on other aspects of their business.

Some apartments charge an extra fee for the right to use various amenities. For example, AvalonBay charges a one-time fee for the use of on-site amenities. The "amenities rent," which is not charged on renewals, is a big source of "other income" for the company. Many owners also charge a monthly fee for the privilege of having a pet, and most pet owners are glad to pay it.

Basic utility services—electricity, gas, and water/sewer—can be included in rents, allocated on a per-unit basis, or separately metered. Separate meters were rare until soaring utility bills in the 1970s virtually mandated them. The added front-end cost of separate meters can usually be recouped fairly quickly, especially if residents are billed directly by the utility company or the metering service. Renters tend to prefer having separate HVAC controls, and having separate meters is an advantage if the project is converted to condominiums. It is a safe bet that in most situations utility rates will rise faster than apartment rents, making direct unit-based utility charges a better alternative than including utilities in the basic rent.

Metering water and sewer use is something all property managers should take a hard look at. The meters themselves and reading the meters are provided by a company that provides utility metering services. Meters are currently read magnetically by wands; soon, they will be read over phone lines. The meter service collects from the residents each month for water use and remits the money to the owner/manager, who pays the utility.

Imagine an apartment community where someone comes to pick up your dry cleaning once a week, where you can order food and drinks while sitting by the pool, and where the concierge can arrange tickets to the great new show that just opened downtown. In more and more apartment communities across the country, such a scenario is becoming a reality. Apartment owners have long known that they could make extra income by providing amenities like laundry facilities or vending machines. By providing a broader selection of goods and services that residents want, however, owners and managers of apartment communities are realizing that they are in a great position to provide outstanding service to their residents while making additional profits at the same time.

Allen Cymrot, former chair of the National Multi Housing Council, points out that a typical renter spends about $15,000 a year on services like dry cleaning, child care, travel, and health clubs. Apartment owners should therefore ask themselves how they can make life easier for their residents by bringing those services to them at home. Developer Matt Perrin of Mark-Taylor Residential did just that at one of his firm's apartment communities in Scottsdale, Arizona. The poolside food and beverage service and concierge have been big hits with residents. "We wanted to bring in something that we knew our residents would enjoy but do something that we knew we could also make a little profit with as well," Perrin says.

Apartment owners and managers are positioned to offer this variety of goods and services to their residents. Unlike most business owners, apartment owners know a lot about their residents from their lease and credit applications, including their incomes, and they also have exceptionally good access to the residents themselves through newsletters, bulletin boards, and other forms of communication. By using this information and access, apartment owners can ensure the amenities provided are the right ones and that they are successful.

To identify the services to provide, it is essential to know who the residents are, what kinds of goods and services they really want, and how much they are will-ing to pay for them. It is also essential to understand the costs of providing a given good or service and to determine whether or not it makes sense to provide that good or service in the apartment community. If it does make sense to proceed, providing these types of amenities can greatly enhance residents' satisfaction—as well as the community's bottom line.

Adapted from Lila Baltman, "Ancillary Income Streams," *Units,* November/December 1998, pp. 30–34.

■

The service receives its payment from a monthly fee charged to the building owner or in some cases billed to the resident. Similar arrangements are also possible without the installation of metering devices by using billing systems that allocate costs of services to units. Often referred to as "RUBS" or ratio utility billing systems, they are very effective in unbundling water, sewerage, and trash removal charges, especially in older buildings. In setting up proprietary delivery services or metering systems for utilities, the building owner should carefully consider whether it wants to step into the shoes of the utility company for billing; in most cases, leaving the responsibility for billing to the outside service is the better choice. The strategy for and actual switching of utility billing to residents is an important management process. In most cases, all units can be changed over within 18 months.

Communications services can also be an important revenue generator for apartment owners. Private phone and cable systems are generally installed and operated by the vendor, with the building owner sharing in the profits based on percentage of income, rate of service penetration, or some other formula.

Rental rates reflect property taxes, which typically are the biggest expense for apartments. Some apartment owners suggest that property taxes be included in monthly rent bills or even that residents write a separate check each month for their share of the tax to sensitize them to the tax burden and perhaps impel them to bring some political pressure on local governments to control the escalation of taxes for multifamily properties.

Security. Security is a key issue in the multifamily housing industry today. In the United States, apartment properties are the most sued business, after hotels. Verdicts in Texas, for example, are staggering—often in the millions of dollars—as companies are found guilty of gross negligence (not mere negligence) and punitive damages are awarded. For apartment managers, gearing up for improvements in security has two dimensions: physical measures and communication with residents.

Security is a primary concern in the design of most new projects, and the major apartment owners and managers are spending considerable amounts of money on retrofitting their buildings. Instead of focusing on management procedures—making sure master keys are accounted for, getting residents to sign security release forms, and making sure all outdoor and common area lights are working—they are shifting the emphasis to "hard assets"—devices and infrastructure that regulate access. Most crime involves crimes of opportunity—an unlocked sliding door or open window. Not allowing nonresidents easy access to an apartment property thus can reduce the incidence of crime.

But controlled access can be inconvenient. Delivery people and visitors get very upset when they cannot gain entry. Police and emergency personnel face delays.

Individual garages improve both security and convenience for residents.

Residents and prospects may consider chain link fencing unattractive (ornamental fencing and barbed wired in certain situations are alternatives). It is important to be honest with residents about these problems, explaining that the management's goal is to restrict the property's use to them and their guests. Increasing security with these hard assets is a competitive necessity in some markets; in some cases, such security measures have produced a clear, although hard to measure, rent premium.

Lighting is a key component of exterior security, and, like fencing, it can sometimes annoy residents. The lighting at some properties has been increased to such an extent that the grounds resemble a baseball stadium during a night game—making some residents unhappy and others very, very happy.

Security of individual units is a second major area of concern. Where crime is an issue—which is practically everywhere—units are being designed with or retrofitted with key-operated window locks, deadbolt locks on steel doors, Charlie bars for securing sliding glass doors (a major point of entry for burglars across the United States), and the like. Alarm systems are sometimes offered. In Post Properties's experience, only about 10 percent of the residents having in-unit alarm systems use them, while in R&B Realty properties, only 15 percent of residents sign up for available in-unit alarm systems. Systems that allow residents to see callers before letting them through entrances they control, remotely or directly, are becoming more in demand in higher-end, urban apartment communities.

Today's apartment managers are moving away from master key systems for providing access to units, because it is too easy for a master key to fall into the wrong hands. Now, magnetic bar code key systems use unmarked keys, require users to type in a personal code, and keep track of outstanding keys.

Communication with residents is the other side of the security coin. One of AvalonBay's big pushes in this area is informing residents that their own safety is their responsibility, not the landlord's. The company's "Resident Security Notice and Acknowledgment," which residents sign when they sign the lease, begins "The Management of this apartment community (including the Owner and Owner's authorized property manager) does not promise, warrant, or guarantee the safety or security of resident's personal property against the criminal actions of other residents or third parties. Each resident has the responsibility to protect himself or herself and to maintain appropriate insurance to protect his or her belongings." The signed document releases management from claims arising out of criminal actions by third parties and puts residents on notice that, no matter what they were told or understand otherwise, the owner/ manager does not guarantee their security. AvalonBay trains its leasing people to get this message across. To the prospect's question "Is this a safe place to live?" they have been trained to respond, "No, we cannot guarantee your safety."

In some regions, fencing and controlled entrance gates are common security measures.

Good lighting should provide security and enhance the property.

Camden Property Trust

No matter how well a property is protected, crimes against residents are bound to occur. Managing residents' concerns about crime and their reactions to threatening situations has become as important as the physical improvements that are installed to deter crime. Standard letters to report specific crimes can be used to inform residents about major incidents, such as an armed robbery. Managers may set up meetings between the police and residents to discuss crime prevention.

Future Trends

Lines of Responsibility

As noted, property management has become increasingly important in companies with large apartment portfolios. Many companies are now struggling over how to organize the functions of property management and asset management. Some companies have separate asset management groups; others assign re-

An urban mixed-use development, Tent City in Boston includes retail activities facing commercial streets while creating a protected residential environment within.

© Steve Rosenthal

sponsibilities for asset management to property management departments.

Some industry leaders believe the problem many companies are having stems from their tendency to consider asset managers as inspectors of property managers or as responsible for the performance of the property management team. But asset management has a strategic role that should not be conflated into property management. Asset managers predict changes in demographics and determine when to enter or exit a market, when to sell, when to refinance, and whether to undertake extensive capital improvements. These strategic decisions should not be left to property managers or property management departments.

Some companies are giving property managers many of the responsibilities their asset managers used to have to better use the talents of their asset managers. Part of the goal is to reduce the number of layers between the

CEO and the property. Today's property managers are generally better educated and much more capable of interacting with lenders than before, but the development partners still need to be involved in the project over the long term.

Other Sources of Income

The apartment industry's increased focus on property management and services (and the simultaneous pressure on rents caused by cyclical overbuilding) is likely to inspire owners to seek other sources of income from apartments. According to Howard Ruby, residents in a building might collectively have $5 million to $10 million in disposable income, but only $1 million of it pays the rent. There are other ways of making money out of the building. A much more expansive view of residential services—concierges, delivery of prepared food, rental cars, or a hundred other possibilities—is beginning to take hold. Owners will make money by providing such services directly or by sharing in the service providers' take—a fee for giving the provider access to residents. A much more conscious effort on the part of owners to extract more of the goods and services dollar from their residents, says Ruby, can enhance yields by as much as two to three points.

Owners making considerable income from "other sources" will then face another challenge: getting potential purchasers of the property to recognize other income in their price calculations.

Notes

1. Richard B. Peiser with Dean Schwanke, *Professional Real Estate Development: The ULI Guide to the Business* (Chicago: Dearborn Financial Publishing and ULI–the Urban Land Institute, 1992), p. 151.
2. Elliott A. Lewis, remarks at a ULI professional development seminar, "Developing Multifamily Housing," 1995.
3. Peiser and Schwanke, *Professional Real Estate Development*, p. 151.
4. "Cascade Court Apartments," ULI *Project Reference File*, Vol. 25, No. 18, October–December 1995.
5. Coates & Jarratt, Inc., *The Future of the Apartment Industry: A Report to the National Multi Housing Council and National Apartment Association* (Washington, D.C.: National Multi Housing Council, 1995).
6. Peiser and Schwanke, *Professional Real Estate Development*, p. 196.
7. Ibid., p. 206.
8. Ibid.
9. Ibid., p. 197.
10. Edward N. Kelley, *Practical Apartment Management*, 3rd ed. (Chicago: Institute of Real Estate Management, 1990), p. 26.
11. "Wimbledon Apartments," ULI *Project Reference File*, Vol. 25, No. 7, April–June 1995.
12. Peiser and Schwanke, *Professional Real Estate Development*, p. 201.
13. Ibid., p. 202.
14. Ibid., p. 201.
15. Ibid., p. 42.
16. Kevin P. MacLatchie, "Know the Numbers: Reviewing the Income Statement for Accuracy," *Journal of Property Management,* March/April 1995, p. 27.
17. Laurence C. Harmon and Kathleen M. McKenna-Harmon, "Shifting the Apartment Pricing Paradigm," *Journal of Property Management,* September/October 1995, p. 32.
18. Jeffrey A. Harris, remarks at a ULI professional development seminar, "Developing Multifamily Housing," 1995.
19. Peiser and Schwanke, *Professional Real Estate Development*, p. 196.
20. Floyd M. Baird, Marie S. Spodek, and Robert C. Kyle, *Property Management*, 6th ed. (Chicago: Dearborn Trade, 1999), p. 1.
21. Peiser and Schwanke, *Professional Real Estate Development*, p. 202.
22. Howard F. Ruby, remarks at a ULI professional development seminar, "Developing Multifamily Housing," 1995.
23. Robert H. Slater, remarks at a ULI professional development seminar, "Developing Multifamily Housing," 1995.
24. Peiser and Schwanke, *Professional Real Estate Development*, p. 202.
25. Kelley, *Practical Apartment Management*, p. 206.
26. Donald L. Williams and Sally M. Dwyer, "Market Intelligence: Long-Term Success in the Apartment Industry Requires a Fresh Approach to Discovering, Tracking and Communicating with the Customer," *Multi-Housing News,* April/May 1995, p. 34.
27. Robert H. Slater, remarks at a ULI professional development seminar, "Developing Multifamily Housing," 1995.
28. Jeffrey A. Harris, remarks at a ULI professional development seminar, "Developing Multifamily Housing," 1995.
29. Ronald Litke, "Smart Apartments," *Journal of Property Management,* March/April 1995, pp. 16–19.

10. Multifamily Niche Products

A number of specialty products in the multifamily development industry offer savvy developers the prospect of substantial returns on investment. As our population becomes more diverse and as more people choose to live in nontraditional households, demand increases for a greater variety of apartment products. Changes in lifestyle and demographics encourage the multifamily sector to take a closer look at niche markets.

What are some of these emerging niche products and markets? This chapter discusses student housing; military housing; executive rental services, corporate apartments, and extended-stay hotels; adaptive use and apartment conversions; rehabilitation and repositioning of apartment buildings; and housing for seniors. It explains some of the ins and outs of developing these niche multifamily housing products and identifies what makes each product type distinctive, the pros and cons of developing for these markets, and what it takes to be successful. For smart developers with the right product, these niche markets can be very profitable indeed.

The key to succeeding in niche markets is to be able to identify the market segments that are looking for an unconventional type of housing and to provide a product that meets their needs. Doing so has to involve good market research and both the willingness and expertise to design and operate a product with atypical designs and

Montgomery Place in Chicago is a rental residence for active seniors that offers full nursing care on two levels.

layouts, unusual locations, or specialized packages of services and amenities. Developers working in multifamily niche markets still have to have the fundamentals down, and they must develop special expertise in the niche segment to succeed.

Student Housing

According to the U.S. Census, nearly 2 million students lived in dormitories in 1990.[1] Studies by the National Center for Education Statistics (NCES) indicate that enrollments at institutions of higher education between 1986 and 1996 increased approximately 14 percent, from 12.5 million to 14.3 million.[2] Very little new student rental housing has been developed since the mid-1980s, however, and much existing student housing is deteriorating or no longer meets the needs of today's demanding students. College enrollments have been increasing in recent years, and as the baby boomers' children begin to enter college, the demand for student housing will continue to grow. Indeed, NCES forecast a 6 percent increase in enrollments among those under the age of 25 between 1996 and 2000. Schools are beginning to realize that providing modern, comfortable housing contributes greatly to recruiting and retaining students.[3] Developers have significant opportunities in this market niche if they can learn what it takes to build successful student housing.

Apart from the fact that more people will seek to occupy student housing in the future, students' needs and desires have changed. Existing student housing is no longer satisfactory for many young people. Some existing student housing is functionally obsolete, allows no privacy, and is not wired for recent technological advances. Students today want more security and privacy, they want access to a variety of services and amenities, and they want access to the latest communications and computer technologies. And they still want to have a social life. Living with other students, on or off campus, is an important part of the college experience for many students. Meeting these varied demands is what makes developing student housing a special challenge.

But despite these needs, many universities and colleges find it difficult to pay for new construction. More and more schools look to the private sector for some or all of their housing construction and operations.[4] Management of existing student housing by third parties is a growing trend, and joint ventures between a university and a private sector developer offer the opportunity to develop the right kind of product on campus. Many of the same considerations apply whether the housing is on campus or off.

Design of the units differentiates student housing from conventional multifamily development. Privacy ranks as one of the biggest concerns for students today, and most would rather not have to live in double- or triple-occupancy rooms. The old common bathroom has fallen out of favor

The Graduate Living Center at Georgia Tech in Atlanta provides housing for 347 residents in furnished four-bedroom units.

as well. Therefore, suites with single bedrooms grouped around a kitchen and living room have become popular, and some developers are finding four-bedroom, four-bath layouts successful. Students may not have lived away from home before, so providing furnished units greatly facilitates the move. Given that most students need and have computers today, all bedrooms should be wired to allow at least two phone lines to let residents have phones and high-speed Internet connections.

Good amenities in student housing meet residents' recreational, academic, and social needs. Clubhouses with amenities like exercise rooms and tennis courts and 24-hour work centers with copiers, faxes, and computers are in great demand.[5] Students (and their parents) are concerned about security, so developers should consider the need for gates, electronic access systems, and alarms, depending on local conditions.[6] Finally, in looking for a site for off-campus housing, developers should bear in mind that many students do not have cars, so good transit or bicycle access to campus and shopping facilities should be available.

Leasing can be one of the most troublesome aspects of student housing. The inherent seasonality of students' housing needs presents the biggest problem. Therefore, developers and property managers need to be tuned into the local university's academic calendar. Unlike conventional multifamily projects, almost all the units in a student housing project will turn over once per year, often at the same time. Therefore, it is absolutely essential to be ready to lease a new project when students arrive for the beginning of the academic year or be prepared to face a whole year of low occupancy.

Some firms have developed leasing strategies to deal with seasonality. For example, the Picerne Real Estate Group uses a five-tiered leasing system in which rents are highest for leases running from September to December, lowest for full-year leases beginning in July, and in between for other groups depending on the length of the lease and when it was signed. This system has helped

Industrial conversions have been phenomenally successful in many urban areas. In the Deep Ellum section of Dallas, Adam Hats Lofts was once a Ford Motor Company assembly plant, then a hat factory. Today, the four-story building houses 90 rental apartments.

the company to achieve high occupancy levels, even during the summer.[7] Another strategy appropriate for student housing is to lease by bedroom rather than by unit. JPI, an apartment development and management firm, says this system saves a lot of headaches for management and residents. If one tenant has problems paying the rent, that person's suitemates are not held liable. In any case, flexibility should be the key word in leasing student housing, as students often have special requirements, such as extending a lease for an extra semester, breaking a lease early for a new job, or subletting a unit (or a bedroom) for the summer.

Property management is an important factor in developing and operating a successful student housing project. Operating student housing is very different from managing a conventional multifamily property. The need is greater to provide support services for residents. Going away to school for the first time can be stressful in itself, and, coupled with the intense academic and social pressures of university life, supportive advice or counseling is often necessary. Sometimes doing so can be as simple as hiring an older student to serve as a resident assistant to deal with day-to-day problems or simply to talk with younger students. Management also needs to respond quickly to requests for maintenance, although reports of crazed students destroying the property are greatly exaggerated. In fact, companies working in this field report that damage to units is comparable with that found in conventional apartments.[8]

Marketing student housing presents another challenge, but companies working in this area find that they need to spend relatively little money marketing projects. Word-of-mouth advertising (whether positive or negative) is more important in this market.[9] Telling the university housing office about the project is an essential step in building this awareness. On the other hand, developers and managers will need to take market research seriously. Surveys and focus groups are necessary to determine what amenities and features are most in demand in a given market. Finally, developers and property managers need to remember that they are marketing the project not just to prospective residents but also to students' parents, particularly if a project is targeted at freshmen and sophomores. Parents' perception of the project's quality and safety will have a major bearing on successful lease-up.

Clearly, the student housing market has its limits. Research indicates much potential in this product niche, but it is essential to be aware of local market conditions. It can be very difficult, if not impossible, to build in volume in the student housing market. Therefore, it is important to look for efficiencies in design, layout, and materials to keep costs down. Student housing, as a niche market, is accepted more in the capital markets than it once was. But as more and more national developers and property managers begin to enter the market, it is becoming quite competitive. Still, for firms that can develop an attractive product at the right price with the right mix of amenities and with professional management and leasing, the student housing sector will continue to be lucrative.

Students are more demanding than ever. Student apartments at JPI's Jefferson Commons at Clemson University in South Carolina offer furnished two- or four-bedroom units with a wealth of amenities.

Military Housing

At first glance, military housing may not seem like an attractive market niche.[10] There has been much more news over the past decade about military base closings than about new development opportunities. Since the passage of the Defense Authorization Act (more commonly known as the military housing privatization initiative [MHPI]) in 1996, however, the openings in this

Jardin des Fonderies is the most extensive conversion of an industrial property into housing in Brussels, Belgium. The project aims to attract residents to a declining neighborhood.

market have grown tremendously. Studies by the military in the early 1990s indicate that dissatisfaction with military housing contributed to low morale and was one of the biggest barriers to retaining personnel. Most existing military housing was built during the 1950s and today is functionally obsolete and poorly maintained. Moreover, the overall demand for housing among members of the military services and their families is not being met, a situation compounded by the fact that off-base

The Privatization of Military Housing

The military services nominate sites with large housing deficits or sites where housing needs to be renovated. They visit and evaluate the sites with private sector finance experts, identify problems, determine which authorities will best address the problems and issues at the specific sites, hold industry forums to introduce the projects to the private sector, and draft and issue requests for proposals. Once the requests are issued, the military branch holds local preproposal conferences so officials can meet with developers and financiers who may have questions and want to learn more about the specifics of the process and project. DoD then reviews and evaluates the proposals and selects a contractor.

DoD notifies Congress of the proposed contract. After the contract is executed, the developer obtains final zoning, site plan approval, and financing. Construction should begin immediately after award. It should take approximately seven to nine months before the contract is awarded, and construction should take another 12 months. The total time required to develop housing is approximately 21 months from beginning to end, depending on the size of the project.

Source: DoD Web site: http://www.acq.osd.mil/iai/hrso/hrsohome.htm (November 1999). ∎

housing is often too expensive for personnel to afford on their incomes and housing allowances.

The scale of the problem is immense. The military currently owns approximately 300,000 units of family housing and 450,000 barracks both on and off bases. The Department of Defense (DoD) estimates that more than 60 percent of these units need to be renovated or replaced and that using traditional military approaches would take 30 to 40 years and $30 billion. The DoD hoped that the MHPI would allow it to use the knowledge and skills of the private sector to leverage public funds to fix its housing problems more cheaply and more quickly than it could have had it developed the housing itself.

Under the MHPI, the DoD has set out five major guidelines for the privatization of military housing:

1. To ensure proper housing for service members and their families;
2. To leverage public funds with private capital;
3. To involve local governments in the development process;
4. To integrate any new military housing projects with private sector housing with a comparable mix of home sizes; and
5. To keep any new projects within a reasonable commuting distance from bases.

The MHPI allows the services to employ loan and rental guarantees, conveyances or leases of property and facilities, differential lease payments, investments in limited partnerships or ownership of stocks and bonds, and direct loans to develop new housing or to renovate existing housing, which may be used individually or in combination.

A major problem with the implementation of the MHPI thus far has been that although the DoD sets the overall guidelines for privatization, it leaves the decision of what should be privatized and how to the individual services and base commanders.[11] Each service has its own process for soliciting bids, and each privatization requires its own solicitation. The cost of responding to requests for proposals has been very high in the past. For example, in one case each bidder for an Army privatization project had to spend $200,000 to $500,000 on its submission. Such high costs have clearly created a major barrier for developers, especially smaller, less experienced ones, and the services have revised guidelines somewhat by switching, for example, to a two-stage process for proposals.

The process has thus far favored large developers with strong track records and the ability to contribute millions of dollars in equity to projects. Most of the privatization projects so far have involved large projects with hundreds or thousands of housing units. Some future projects are expected to be smaller, however, and awarding smaller contracts exclusively for managing military housing has been discussed.

Aside from the complexities of privatization, a further challenge has been created by the military's high standards but relative lack of funds to pay for new housing. So far the military has demanded the construction of housing units with the features and amenities of market-rate housing, but service members receive housing allowances of only $300 to $500 per month for off-base housing. Clearly, developers working in this sector need to be able to keep project costs down while delivering an acceptable product. The military has used its considerable assets as a bargaining tool with developers. It is willing to rent, sell, or give away specific assets to developers as a way of closing the gap between construction costs and the somewhat limited revenue stream generated by residents of the new project.[12]

Despite the problems thus far, privatization has been somewhat successful. As of March 1999, six projects with more than 4,000 housing units were undergoing requests for proposals or were about to be awarded. At the time, solicitations for more than 21,000 units at seven other sites were to be issued, and feasibility studies were in process

at 26 sites. From the military's perspective, the program has succeeded in saving money. Because the program allows developers to build to local construction standards instead of more stringent military construction standards and because of the efficiencies the private sector can achieve in development, the DoD has estimated that it has already saved more than $1 billion.

The development firms involved, many of which have teamed up to make submissions for these contracts, have done very well for themselves. Their experience indicates that the right product can achieve very high occupancy levels and solid returns on investment. Moreover, if the program continues as expected, it offers the opportunity to build thousands of housing units all over the country. Unfortunately, some doubt lingers about the future of the program. The current legislation authorizing the program expires in 2001. At that point, Congress must decide to extend, make permanent, or terminate the legislation authorizing privatization. If it is continued, the program offers the potential for substantial profits for a winning development and management team.

Executive Rentals, Corporate Apartments, and Extended-Stay Hotels

The purpose of executive rental services is to match businesspeople who must travel on long assignments with corporate apartments in their destination cities. This niche product is seeing increasing competition from the extended-stay hotel sector, but it has grown tremendously in recent years. Because of the high returns these products can generate, a frenzy of construction and acquisition is occurring in the sector. Given its growth, this market segment is one that multifamily developers should watch.

Executive rental services typically target business travelers who must travel on extended assignments, often for several months at a time. Despite improved communications technology, the number of people traveling for

About 10 percent of the units at Columbus Shore in Irving, Texas, are leased as corporate apartments.

work-related reasons has surged. Consultants, training staff, auditors, construction crews, and even relocating executive staff are all candidates for corporate housing. These services are very popular with business travelers because they offer the prospect of a much more comfortable, convenient, and affordable stay than traditional hotels.

Executive rental services sometimes own, but more often sublease, corporate apartments of various sizes. Corporate apartments are somewhat like conventional apartments and are often located in otherwise conventional apartment buildings, but they are furnished and offer additional amenities. For example, many corporate apartments provide maid service (at a less than daily frequency) and assistance with grocery shopping, and the units are equipped with appliances, televisions and VCRs, and at least one phone line. Amenities vary widely depending on the type of complex where the unit is located. The goal is to make business travelers feel at home, pro-

With more than 330 properties, Residence Inn is one of the largest extended-stay hotel chains.

vide them with a more convenient and productive place to live and work, and do so for less money than a hotel room would cost for the same amount of time. A single weekly or monthly payment is required for corporate housing units, which usually includes all utilities, local phone service, and maid service. Executive rental services are in the business of third-party property management rather than the direct provision of lodging.

A closely related but distinct product is the extended-stay hotel. Like corporate apartment providers, firms in the extended-stay hotel sector target long-term business travelers. They also aim to offer more home-like environments at a lower cost than traditional hotels. But extended-stay hotels and corporate apartments differ in important ways. First, extended-stay hotel rooms are not fully equipped apartments. They typically lack a fully equipped kitchen, which corporate apartments do have, and the required minimum stay is much shorter. Further, extended-stay hotels tend to offer more amenities on site than corporate apartments, although amenities do not match those of hotels. Moreover, the extended-stay sector includes different price and quality categories, and amenities and services vary widely. Extended-stay hotels differ from all-suite hotels, which much more closely approximate traditional hotels.

The corporate housing and the extended-stay sectors have become more and more intertwined in recent years, and the lines between the two are becoming more and more blurred. ExecuStay, a corporate housing provider with more than 6,000 units in 44 states, is owned by Marriott. The company is unusual in the corporate housing sector in that it allows customers to participate in Marriott's frequent traveler reward system and offers a central reservation system for all its properties. Marriott also owns two extended-stay hotel chains: Residence Inn and Towne-Place Suites. An outgrowth of the increased overlap of these two sectors is that more and more hotel companies are partnering with multifamily developers to build new extended-stay properties.

The market for these types of products has grown tremendously in recent years. Extended-stay hotels lead the hospitality industry substantially in both occupancy and profitability. Residence Inn, the extended-stay market leader pioneered by Marriott in the mid-1970s, posted an 81.3 percent average occupancy rate in 1999 in its more than 330 locations, despite adding 41 hotels totaling 5,000 rooms to its system during that year. Rates for Residence Inn average $90 to $120 per night, but profit margins have remained well above 40 percent.

As for corporate apartments, the market leader is Oakwood Corporate Housing. It has 20,000 apartment units under management worldwide and annual revenues of more than $500 million. Marriott's ExecuStay is also a strong presence in the corporate housing sector. ExecuStay owns no real estate but instead works through leases set up with conventional apartment owners and managers. ExecuStay has also been expanding its offerings at a tremendous rate, for example by acquiring the corporate housing division of JPI.

ExecuStay

Some corporate housing providers, like ExecuStay, provide housing through long-term lease agreements with existing apartment communities. Such providers typically select communities that offer a good range of amenities.

Mergers and acquisitions have played a major role in this sector. For instance, Globe Corporate Stay International acquired 14 competitors between June 1996 and March 1999. Marriott has been growing in similar fashion, while Oakwood continues to acquire smaller firms, as it did with Great West Corporate Housing in August 1999. Apart from a desire to improve profitability and market share, one of the main factors driving this consolidation is the strategic benefit of having a national presence. While some firms in the business remain decidedly local, great benefits accrue to those with a national presence. Large size means the possibility of increased brand recognition and loyalty while offering corporate customers the convenience of arranging all their accommodations with one firm. This strategy is now being carried to its logical conclusion as more and more firms in the sector are expanding into international markets.

Property Management for Business Residents and Long-Term Residents

- Business residents expect more technological amenities such as fax machines and Internet access. Residents of corporate apartments need housekeeping service.
- Generally speaking, business residents make one payment per month, which includes utilities, phone service, and other services like cable TV and voice mail.
- Corporate apartments are furnished.
- If demand is sufficient, corporate apartments can generate greater cash flow than unfurnished rental apartments.
- Given the extra costs for items such as furniture and appliances, it is more expensive to carry corporate apartments if vacancies go up.
- More services are provided for corporate apartments than for standard rental apartments. It is a challenge to successfully meet the needs of both types of residents.
- The presence of corporate residents may upset long-term noncorporate residents.
- Different operating systems are necessary for corporate apartments, especially to keep track of services and billing.
- Startup marketing is much more important for corporate apartments, because they are much less visible than long-term apartments and because a business, not the renter, is the client.
- Wear and tear on corporate apartments may be less than in conventional apartments, particularly if corporate apartments are left vacant for extended periods.

Note: *Business residents* refers to the residents of corporate apartments, while *long-term residents* refers to the residents of conventional noncorporate apartments. Business residents can reside in corporate apartments for extended periods of time.

Source: Douglas R. Woodworth and David Flando, "To Incorporate Corporate Apartments into Your Property," *Real Estate Today,* November/December 1995, pp. 50–54.

Originally built in 1903, the Wilson Building in downtown Dallas was considered the premier commercial building west of the Mississippi. Post Properties has converted the structure into luxury loft apartments and corporate apartments.

World Wide Holdings Corp.

71 Broadway in lower Manhattan was an office tower until it was converted to 237 luxury apartments in 1997.

The design and location of extended-stay hotels and to some extent corporate apartments require special considerations.[13] First, given their business orientation and the fact that these properties do not rely on walk-in customers, locations need not be highly visible; they are often located near suburban office parks or other employment centers. Some companies, however, particularly in the corporate housing sector, focus their efforts on high-profile, downtown locations in major cities. Two of the most critical issues in designing a project are to keep the number of staff down and to avoid "amenity creep" (the process of adding more amenities, such as restaurants or conference rooms, that add greatly to the project's cost but that do not matter to customers). Low cost is one of the main reasons extended-stay hotels and corporate housing have become so popular, and preserving that level of value is very important. The impact is abundantly clear when one considers that the development cost of an extended-stay hotel can be as little as $30,000 per room, compared with more than $300,000 per room for a high-end full-service hotel.[14]

The considerations in the feature box on the previous page apply less to corporate apartments, because they are conventional multifamily products that contain units rented on a temporary basis to business travelers. In terms of management, it is a good idea for corporate apartment units in a multifamily project to blend in seamlessly with conventional apartment units. While some hotels are now being developed to include corporate housing units, the possibility also exists that conventional apartments could be converted to corporate housing to improve a multifamily project's occupancy rate and cash flow. Given past market conditions, conversion may well be a good idea, but apartment owners and managers considering this route should make sure that they are aware of the differences between managing a building for long-term residents and managing a building for business travelers.

Debate rages about the future prospects for executive rental services and extended-stay hotels. The crux of the debate centers on how deep the market for this product really is. Some argue that the trends that spurred the sector's growth in the last several years will continue and that a large demand for extended-stay housing units is not currently being met. Therefore, the argument goes, demand should remain strong in the future because of the value these products offer to businesses. Others have noted, however, that business travel usually falls significantly during an economic downturn.

The consensus seems to rest at the optimistic end of the spectrum, given that the sector has continued to perform very well despite the extremely rapid construction of units in recent years. Corporate housing units and extended-stay hotels can be a very attractive niche because construction is similar to conventional multifamily developments and returns can be significantly higher. Nevertheless, developers, owners, and managers of multifamily products should look carefully before they leap into this sector. To be successful, they need to have a solid understanding of who the target market is, and they need to understand the subtle characteristics that define the different product segments in this niche.

Adaptive Use/Apartment Conversions

All around the country, developers are discovering that a tremendous supply of vacant or underused buildings is ideally suited to being converted into apartments. These buildings could be older, Class B and C office buildings in downtown locations, former industrial buildings and warehouses, or even institutional buildings such as schools and churches. Provided that local market conditions are right, more and more cities are breathing life back into their downtowns by encouraging the conversion of these aging buildings into apartments. Of the conversion projects that have taken place across the country, many have been for condominiums, particularly in the loft segment, but given the apparent trend toward downtown living today, developers who choose the right project in the right location can succeed with rental apartment conversions as well.

Changing market conditions encourage such projects. In the late 1980s and early 1990s, for example, this country saw an overbuilding of office space, a weakening economy, and a soft real estate market that allowed tenants to upgrade from Class B to Class A offices for comparable prices. According to estimates by the Society of Industrial and Office Realtors and Landauer Real Estate Counselors, 35.6 percent (1.1 billion square feet) of Class B office space in 1994 was vacant in the United States. While these numbers improved along with the rest of the economy in the second half of the 1990s, other factors contributed to increased office vacancies in older buildings: increasing standards for communications technologies, changing building codes and safety requirements, and changing needs for office space and floor plans. The need for the adaptive use of these structures was clear.

City governments have been eager to encourage this redevelopment, and many have since put in place policies to encourage the conversion of old offices and other buildings to residential uses. In New York City, Toronto, Philadelphia, and London, the process has been quite successful. In New York, the Lower Manhattan Economic Revitalization Plan created a variety of tax and energy cost abatements to facilitate conversions, and with the high demand for residential space in that city, the program has been a notable success.[15] Cities have also helped by removing some of the regulatory barriers to conversions, such as relaxing stringent building codes in recognition of the fact that renovations have inherent limitations that new construction does not. New Jersey, for instance, has seen a jump in the conversion of historic structures since it updated its building codes to facilitate conversions. Nonprofit organizations increasingly serve as intermediaries in the development process. Moreover, in converting a historic building to rental apartments, developers can use federal historic preservation tax credits

A public/private partnership converted the historic Hotel Hamilton in Laredo, Texas, to affordable housing for seniors. The original architectural detailing has been preserved.

to cover 20 percent of the project cost with a dollar for dollar tax deduction, or they can sell them to investors in exchange for equity.

A developer should look for a number of features in planning the conversion of an office building to multifamily use, several of which can benefit tenants.[16] For example, office buildings often offer higher ceilings and larger floor plans than typical multifamily developments. Similarly, office buildings can offer unbeat-

The days of friendly attendants and personal service may seem like a distant memory in today's hectic world, but an adaptive use project called Firestone Upper West Side in Fort Worth, Texas, has restored the charm and attention to detail that made those days seem so great. The new garden apartments were designed to complement the focal point of the project, the 13,000-square-foot Firestone Station building.

Built in 1929, the two-story building originally was an automotive service center. In 1999, it was redeveloped as a leasing office, business center, clubroom, and fitness center for the apartment development. The service bays were converted into a half-court basketball court and the upstairs storage area into a cardiovascular fitness center. The revitalization of the existing building involved rebuilding the structure and matching new and existing terra-cotta tiles.

The newly constructed portion of the project, an 11-building complex of 350 residential units, incorporates downtown Fort Worth's existing street pattern. The project offers all the amenities that today's residents expect, including high-speed Internet access, oversized patios and balconies, solariums, an indoor basketball court, and a clubroom with a billiards table and shuffleboard court, among others.

The major goal of the project was to preserve an old idea while adding the modern touches that discriminating residents demand. Firestone is designed to appeal to the urban professional who appreciates both modern amenities and the preservation of a historically significant structure.

■

Firestone Upper West Side includes 350 rental units in newly constructed buildings.

A 1929 service station now houses a leasing office and community amenities.

able locations. Developers should look for floorplates that are not too large and buildings that offer many windows for apartment units. Finding L- or U-shaped buildings can help tremendously in this regard. Features like multistory lobbies, interesting brickwork, and original moldings can help add to the project's attractiveness. Such features are often impossible to duplicate in new buildings and can have great marketing appeal. Converting a property can also allow the developer to get a product to market in significantly less time. Although conversions can offer significantly lower development costs than new construction, developers should be careful because conversion costs, particularly for historic structures, may end up being greater than for new construction.

But higher than expected conversion costs are only one of many obstacles that may arise.[17] Perhaps the biggest obstacle is that once construction begins, it may become apparent that more work needs to be done on the building than originally was thought necessary. For instance, plumbing, flooring, and walls of an older building may all need to be replaced because of unforeseen damage or an otherwise hazardous condition such as asbestos. These contingencies need to be thoroughly investigated early in the development process, and they need to be included in the budget. Development costs can also be increased by having to comply with strict regulations and high labor costs. Moreover, residential buildings require very different plumbing and vertical circulation systems from offices and warehouses, and the developer may have to make major structural changes to mitigate the problems.

Notwithstanding the efforts some cities have made to facilitate apartment conversions, major regulatory barriers can still prevent or delay the project's getting off the ground. Zoning for the property plays a significant role, and the developer may have to pursue changes to the property's zoning to go ahead with the project. A designated historic building may limit the extent to which the developer can change the building to enhance its marketability. As with any kind of project, the developer should thoroughly investigate market demand for the product, something that is often more difficult for rehabilitation projects because of a lack of comparable properties and limited data to estimate demand.

Marketing apartment conversion projects can be tricky. Depending on local conditions, consumers may be averse to living in a downtown area that has traditionally lacked housing. Indeed, the area may lack a number of amenities and services that make for a viable residential neighborhood, such as grocery stores, recreational facilities, or schools. The target market for this type of housing generally consists of either empty nesters or young adults who want to be close to work, so the marketing plan should target the appropriate demographic groups. The marketing plan will have to attract attention to the project and will have to convince people that there is no need to fear living downtown. The project may thus require additional security features such as gates, a doorman, or an electronic access system. If a project includes attractive features such as on-site retail shops, marketing plans should emphasize them.

While lenders are beginning to accept apartment conversions, many still hesitate to back a project with a lot of question marks. Although they might use public funds like historic preservation or low-income housing tax credits, developers must still demonstrate the project's viability to lenders.[18] Lenders will want to know in detail about the ways the project's risks have been addressed, what the exit strategy is, and whether demand exists for the project. In a given market, the project might not be able to achieve the rents required to make the numbers work, which has contributed to several apartment conversion projects' ultimately being sold for condominiums.

Many questions remain about the depth of the market for downtown housing, but current demographic and lifestyle trends suggest that the recent surge of interest in such projects will continue to grow. Conversion projects offer an outstanding opportunity to bring attractive and distinctive apartment buildings to market. Developers with the patience and skills to undertake these conversions will find that they can not only become financially successful by doing so but also contribute to the increased vitality and livability of our cities.

Rehabilitation and Repositioning

The rehabilitation of older apartment units is a major trend in the multifamily industry that often gets lost in all the discussion about new construction.

> Between the luxury and the subsidized segments of the apartment industry is the dominant, if underpublicized, middle market. In addition to ongoing new construction, in years to come the middle market should see huge outlays to renovate existing apartment communities. Nearly half of all multifamily rental housing in the United States is at least 25 years old, and [in 1997] owners of multifamily rental housing spent $8 billion on physical improvements to those properties. It seems certain that owners who are repositioning older apartment communities will continue to invest billions of dollars annually on property improvements.[19]

The market for rehabilitated apartments derives from the fact that consumers' preferences have changed and that people do not want to live in outdated, inconvenient, worn-out apartment units. The possibilities for undertaking rehab and repositioning are virtually unlimited. Tastes change, and rehab can be as simple as redecorating units and upgrading fixtures. For example, tastes in colors, appliances, and floor coverings have changed, and lighter colors and nature-inspired materials are more in vogue. People care more about their bathrooms and kitchens than previously. Rehabilitation could involve refurbishing or replacing kitchen cabinets and countertops. A small investment in adding to or improving fixtures and appliances can pay big dividends.[20] At the other

Rehabilitating and repositioning older developments is an important part of the business. Shown is Cedar Ridge in Daly City, California, before (left) and after renovation.

end of the spectrum, a rehab could be very extensive, involving the removal of walls to change an apartment's layout, the wholesale replacement of roofs, windows, and plumbing, the removal of hazardous materials such as asbestos and lead paint, and the virtual reconstruction of the building. Clearly, where a given project sits on this spectrum depends on what the building's initial condition was and what the ultimate target for the repositioned product will be.

Rehabilitating and repositioning a building have a number of advantages over new construction.[21] For instance, rehabs may offer outstanding locations unavailable on vacant sites. Rehab offers the possibility of avoiding NIMBYists' opposition, because the use already exists and the rehab may even make the project a better neighbor than before. Indeed, governments may be eager to assist in a rehab project by providing tax abatements, grants, tax credits, or zoning changes. As is the case with

At first glance, it would be hard to think of much to do with a hotel built in 1911 that had been vacant since 1975 and had fallen into such disrepair that rain was coming through the roof and moss was growing on the walls. For Chattanooga Neighborhood Enterprise (CNE), however, a nonprofit developer of affordable housing, this old hotel presented an opportunity.

The Grand Hotel once served travelers that came and went by train to Chattanooga. The decline in train travel spelled the end for the hotel, however, and the surrounding neighborhood of industrial and commercial uses similarly declined. CNE wanted to preserve this landmark building and provide much needed affordable housing. After purchasing the structure for $200,000 in 1995, CNE used low-income housing tax credits and historic preservation tax credits to cover 63 percent of the total development cost. Since opening, the project has been running at full occupancy and has a growing waiting list.

The Apartments at the Grand features 36 one-bedroom units. The project also provides approximately 4,500 square feet of ground-floor retail space, including a traditional, and very popular, English tearoom. The lobby of the building features decorative tile flooring salvaged from the original building. Moreover, despite being an affordable housing development, the apartments themselves were built to a high standard, with solid oak kitchen and bath cabinets and ceramic tile in the bathrooms.

The development has played an important role in the city's redevelopment plans for the Southside area. The adaptive use of the Grand Hotel has stimulated interest in similar projects in the downtown area, including loft developments and the conversion of an old Army store into restaurant and office space. The Apartments at the Grand demonstrates the potential for adaptive use projects to revitalize declining urban areas and preserve a city's architectural legacy.

The Apartments at the Grand in Chattanooga, Tennessee, feature 36 one-bedroom units of affordable housing. The street level includes a popular English tearoom.

office-to-apartment conversions, developers may be able to exploit distinctive architectural features and amenities to increase the property's value. And there is no mystery about what the neighborhood and its amenities and services will be like because they are already there. It is known what the schools and parks will be like, and the advantages of the site's accessibility are clear.

But many of these factors can work in reverse. There may be good reasons why a building lies vacant and de-

teriorated. The neighborhood may be in decline, a process that one apartment rehab project may be powerless to turn around. Adequate amenities and services may not be available in the neighborhood, and the neighborhood's reputation may keep prospective tenants away no matter how attractive the completed property is. Particularly for much older buildings, significant costs can be imposed by having to comply with current building codes and requirements for accessibility. The complexities of rehabilitating a property merit serious consideration, but meeting the challenge can be very rewarding.

To successfully rehabilitate a property, the key is to expect the unexpected. As with conversions from one use to another, rehab projects often bring surprises, and developers need to be prepared for them by doing surveys and inspections to understand exactly what they are getting into. In planning a rehab project, the first requirement is to figure out just how much rehabilitation is necessary. The developer must maximize the asset's value but should not overimprove it. Characteristics inherent in the property, such as its location, may inhibit its ability to compete with new Class A units, for example. In that case, it may make sense to keep the upgrade more basic. On the other hand, it does not make sense to do a superficial rehab if doing so means the developer has to do more substantial rehabilitation five years down the road.

Rehab involves many of the same details as new construction, plus a few more. Developers must reconceptualize a project to give it a new look. Some other questions need to be addressed: What amenities will be provided? How will the repositioning be achieved through the marketing campaign? Does the building comply with current codes and standards? Rehab can offer substantial savings over new construction. For example, when Metric Property Management took over Skyline Heights, an aging apartment property in Daly City, California, it found that even a major upgrade would cost only $68,000 per unit, compared with a replacement cost of $95,700 per unit.[22] Construction phasing can be difficult in a rehab project, especially if the developer attempts to work around current tenants. The cash flow received by doing so may not make up for the additional costs imposed by having to work at a slower pace.

Ultimately, rehab has to make sense in just the same ways that a new development does. With proper planning and good execution, those undertaking rehab and repositioning stand to gain tremendously while providing the market with up-to-date, livable, attractive housing units.

Most developers hope to achieve a big bang for the buck by adding amenities that add considerable value to the project. Whether it means replacing some appliances or gutting and redoing the building, the prospect of higher rents and retention rates can be very tempting.

Housing for Seniors

The multifamily market niche that has gotten the most press coverage in recent years has surely been the seniors' housing market.[23] As the population ages and as more developers begin to recognize the housing needs of seniors, the seniors' housing market will continue to grow for some time. The seniors' housing market is really a set of distinct submarkets.

Figure 10-1 shows the projected size of the seniors' housing market. It is immediately apparent that the senior population will grow in both absolute and relative terms until well into this century. It is also worth noting that seniors in different age and lifestyle categories require different types of housing.

Five distinct types of housing fall under the term *seniors' housing*. Generally speaking, seniors' housing refers to housing that is restricted to those aged 55 and older; the different types of housing are distinguished by the increasing levels of service and care provided to the residents.

- Active adult houses or apartments are targeted to people 55 years and older, and may formally prohibit rentals to younger people. The communities offer residents complete independence, and few, if any, services are aimed specifically to residents' age or health. Homes may include such universal design features as grab bars and doorways that allow wheelchair access. These communities often have a recreational focus, such as golf, and services are typically offered on a pay-per-use basis. Active adult commu-

figure 10-1
Projected Growth of the Population 65 and Older, 2000 to 2050

Year	65 to 74		75 to 79		80 to 84		85 and Older	
	Number (000)	Percent of Total Population	Number (000)	Percent of Total Population	Number (000)	Percent of Total Population	Number (000)	Percent of Total Population
2000	18,136	6.6	7,415	2.7	4,900	1.8	4,259	1.6
2010	21,057	7.1	7,124	2.4	5,557	1.9	5,671	1.9
2020	31,385	9.7	9,435	2.9	5,940	1.8	6,460	2.0
2030	37,407	10.8	13,962	4.0	9,555	2.8	8,455	2.4
2040	33,013	8.9	16,004	4.3	12,664	3.4	13,552	3.7
2050	34,731	8.8	13,927	3.5	11,977	3.0	18,223	4.6

Source: U.S. Census Bureau, *Population Projections of the United States by Age, Sex, Race, and Hispanic Origin: 1995 to 2050,* Current Population Reports, Series P-25, No. 1130 (Washington, D.C.: U.S. Government Printing Office, 1996).

In Parkville, Maryland, Oak Crest Village provides a mix of independent-living, assisted-living, and skilled-nursing units for middle-income seniors.

nities tend to attract seniors at the younger end of the spectrum. Very little special regulation applies to this category; the size of projects varies widely, from 20 to more than 1,000 units.

- Congregate-care or independent-living housing is targeted to residents in their late 70s and older. In addition to housing, such projects usually provide limited additional amenities such as transportation, assistance with or provision of meals, and assistance with household tasks. Units are normally rented on a monthly basis, with additional fees for specific services used. These types of development are not heavily regulated. The average size of a project is 70 to 250 units.

- Assisted-living housing is directed at the more frail elderly and is often mixed with congregate-care housing. Assisted-living projects offer higher levels of service, such as daily assistance with personal and household tasks. Typical residents are older than 80 years and are usually women. Some recent projects focus on

the needs of residents with Alzheimer's disease or other forms of dementia. Residents are usually provided with three meals daily. Skilled-nursing facilities may be available in limited cases. These types of projects are subject to increasing licensing and regulation and may also be eligible for financial assistance from government sources. Average projects range from 50 to 75 units.

- Nursing homes offer a distinctly different environment from the projects in the previous categories, because they provide full-time nursing care for residents, many of whom have serious medical problems. Nursing homes are subject to the heaviest regulation. They have increased dramatically in number, partly because of a trend toward shorter hospital stays. Nursing homes that provide skilled nursing care should be thought of as more like a medical or institutional facility; they are mentioned here only to provide readers with a complete picture of the range of housing avail-

figure 10-2
HUD/FHA Programs for Seniors' Housing

Section Number	Program Name	Program Features	Comments
Section 8	Housing Assistance Payments	Assists low- and very-low-income households in meeting their housing costs. The subsidy equals the difference between 30 percent of the household's income and the fair market rent.	Many of the variety of programs under Section 8 have been changed or eliminated since the establishment of the Section 8 programs.
Section 202	Supportive Housing for the Elderly	Provides capital advances and rent subsidies for the construction and rehabilitation of supportive housing for very-low-income seniors.	Capital advances do not have to be repaid if project serves very-low-income elderly persons for 40 years. Rental assistance covers the difference between HUD-approved cost per unit and tenant's rent.
Section 213	Mortgage Insurance for Cooperative Units	Insures mortgages for the construction or rehabilitation of cooperative housing projects.	Cooperatives may use Section 221(d)(3) insurance instead of Section 213.
Section 221(d)(3)	Mortgage Insurance for Rental Housing	Insures mortgages for the construction or rehabilitation of rental and cooperative housing.	This section is used by nonprofit and cooperative sponsors. Sponsors receive an insured mortgage on the full amount of the estimated replacement cost of the project.
Section 221(d)(4)	Mortgage Insurance for Rental Housing	Insures mortgages for the construction or rehabilitation of rental and cooperative housing.	This section is used by for-profit sponsors. Sponsors can receive a mortgage for a maximum of 90 percent of the estimated replacement cost of the project.
Section 223(f)	Mortgage Insurance for Purchase or Refinancing of Existing Multifamily Housing Projects	Insures mortgage loans for purchase or refinancing of rental housing, including nursing homes and assisted-living facilities.	This section may not be used for substantial rehabilitation. Usually these projects cannot otherwise be refinanced without causing an excessive rent burden on existing residents.
Section 231	Rental Housing for the Elderly	Insures mortgage loans for construction or rehabilitation of rental housing for the elderly.	This section insures private lenders. In recent years, many more projects use Section 221(d)(3) and 221(d)(4).
Section 232	Mortgage Insurance for Nursing Homes and Assisted-Living Facilities	Insures mortgage loans for the construction or rehabilitation of nursing homes, assisted-living facilities, intermediate-care facilities, and board-and-care homes.	For new construction and substantial rehab, the insurance covers 90 percent of the value of the improvements and equipment, 95 percent for nonprofit borrowers.
Section 236	Interest Reduction Payments		This program is inactive.
Section 241(a)	Supplemental Loans for Multifamily Projects	Insures loans to finance repairs, additions, and improvements to multifamily rental housing and health care facilities.	This program applies to projects that already carry HUD-insured or HUD-held mortgages.
	Congregate Housing Services Program	Grant funds to provide meals and other supportive services for frail elderly residents in federally assisted housing.	This program is project-based rather than tenant-based.
	Multifamily Housing Service Coordinators	Provides three different types of assistance to support the provision of supportive services to elderly and disabled persons living in federally assisted multifamily housing.	This program intends to extend the amount of time where the elderly and the disabled may live independently.

Source: Department of Housing and Urban Development Web site: http://www.hud.gov/senior.html.

able for seniors. Skilled-nursing facilities may be combined with other types of seniors' housing.

- Continuing-care retirement communities (CCRCs) also occupy a special category of seniors' housing. They typically offer two or more of the housing types listed above in the same project. The guiding concept behind CCRCs is that they attempt to provide a variety of housing units and services to meet residents' changing needs and preferences over time so that residents are not forced to relocate as they age. These projects average more than 200 units and can be found in a wide variety of configurations and densities, depending on the project's location. They offer amenities comparable to other kinds of housing along with services and features designed to facilitate "aging in place." In CCRCs, residents pay an entrance fee and monthly service charges, or they rent units on a monthly basis.[24]

Seniors' housing is often subsidized. The subsidies can apply to the development of the project, or the funds may assist in operation of the facility. Figure 10-2 explains some of the HUD/FHA programs that subsidize housing for the elderly.

Much of the seniors' housing constructed in recent years has fallen into the assisted-living category. While a need clearly exists for this type of housing, some indications are that too much building is occurring in this market segment and not enough in the others. For example, according to the American Seniors Housing

With the character of a single-family neighborhood, J.E. Wall Victoria Manor in Riverside, California, includes 112 rental apartments in a fourplex configuration. The project is designated for low-income seniors.

Association, 44 percent of all new units under construction at the end of the first quarter of 1999 were free-standing assisted-living communities, 24 percent were combined assisted-living and skilled-nursing projects, 11 percent were congregate-care and assisted-living communities, and 20 percent combined congregate-care housing with independent-living units. A recent survey by the National Investment Conference on Senior Living reports, however, that the potential market for active adult

Harmony Creek is a development of seniors' apartments in Orange, California.

Newbury Court in Concord, Massachusetts, is a congregate-care facility with 75 apartments.

units stands at 35 to 50 percent of the overall seniors market, although not all of these units would be multi-family units.[25] Therefore, developers will have to carefully consider what type of seniors' housing is in demand in their local market.

The key to developing successful housing projects for seniors is to understand the different needs of different groups of residents and to provide not only a quality housing product but also levels of service and amenities appropriate to the age and condition of the residents. No matter what the age of the residents, a good mix of services and amenities is the hallmark of a successful seniors' housing product. In the past, many seniors' housing developments were modeled after hospitals, and the stigma of seniors' housing as cold and institutional persists. Surveys overwhelmingly show that most seniors would rather continue living in the homes where they currently live instead of moving to a new community. Therefore, it is essential to make senior communities

attractive and inviting places that people would actually prefer over their current homes.

Providing opportunities for recreation and social interaction is very important, no matter what the age of the residents. For younger seniors, it may mean organizing golf or tennis tournaments. For older seniors, it may mean organizing games or classes on how to use the Internet. This kind of "soft programming" has become a very important amenity in seniors' housing. Moreover, the amenities offered in a senior community need not be on site. More and more projects offer transportation to nearby shopping centers, medical facilities, places of worship, and educational institutions. Having a solid network of referrals in the community can be a big help in this area. As in any development, good market research and an understanding of the preferences and values of the targeted residents will help to identify what services matter most. And having well-trained and experienced staff to work with residents is essential.

Several considerations are important in the location and design of seniors' housing projects. Because many seniors are no longer able to drive, it is important to consider the project's location with respect to community facilities like shopping centers and to ensure that transit is accessible. Seniors are particularly vulnerable to crime, and the project's design and location should take this factor into account. Many seniors want to be close to their families and friends, so the project's location should consider where prospective residents will be moving from. The design of the project and the interior spaces should accommodate the changing abilities of people as they age. An extensive literature is available on architecture and design for seniors and those with mental and physical disabilities, but attention to safety and spatial orientation are typically paramount.

Marketing a new seniors' housing project must focus on who the target market is and what kind of lifestyle they aspire to.[26] Particularly for younger seniors, images of people leading healthy, active, fulfilling lives will be much more appealing than the stereotypical picture of an old couple sitting on the porch in their cardigans. Even if the project is an assisted-living project with extensive medical and other care facilities, it is still important to point out the factors that make the project an attractive and enjoyable place to live. Firms such as Leisure Care, which is a market leader in assisted-living housing, have succeeded in part because they focus on "relationship marketing," not just selling a real estate product. Another innovative aspect of Leisure Care's business plan is to reach out beyond residents to people who may become residents some day by offering services—access to its travel network and wellness center, for example—to the community at large.

With each passing year, seniors' housing is becoming increasingly accepted by lenders, and there are even fears that financing has become so easy that more marginal projects are being built.[27] Institutional investors are increasingly interested in housing for seniors, and experts forecast that investment will increase in a greater variety of seniors' housing products. In addition to conventional financing, affordable housing tax credits often provide a major source of financing for seniors' housing. Depending on the levels of care provided at a facility, funds may be available from government programs like Medicaid to help cover the costs of operation. Property managers must be sure, however, to get good advice from a consultant well versed in the medical aspect of property management. Lease-up of seniors' housing projects is typically slower than for conventional apartments, often because seniors take a longer time to decide whether they want to move and will visit the site many times. Further, turnover is higher because residents die or move to facilities that provide higher levels of care as their needs change.

Notwithstanding the overbuilding of some types of senior housing in some markets, the overall market for seniors' housing today is very strong, and demand is set to grow as baby boomers age. This niche market even stands to lose its status as a niche. A recent survey by the National Association of Home Builders found that more than half its multifamily builders planned to build some kind of seniors' housing in the next few years. Working in this market niche requires substantial skills and expertise, but for those firms that are able to climb the learning curve, prospects are for increasing returns.

Notes

1. U.S. Census Bureau, Database C90–Summary Tape File 3–C1 (Washington, D.C.: U.S. Dept. of Commerce, 1990).

2. National Center for Education Statistics, *Digest of Education Statistics, 1998* (Washington, D.C.: NCES, 1998).

3. John Browne, director, Residence Development, University of Toronto, personal communication, November 1, 1999.

4. Dorothy Lindstrom, "Nontraditional Housing Opens Doors for Goldstein, Truitt, Jones," *Multi-Housing News,* September 1998, pp. 42–46.

5. Miriam Lupkin, "Creating Profits by Going Back to School," *Multifamily Executive,* February 1999, pp. 46–51.

6. Julian E. Barnes, "Luxury 101," *New York Times Magazine,* September 5, 1999, p. 32.

7. Steve Bergsman, "Avoiding Animal House," *Journal of Property Management,* March/April 1999, pp. 24–28.

8. Ibid.

9. Ibid.

10. This section relies heavily on information from the Department of Defense. The Competitive Sourcing and Privatization Office (formerly known as the Housing Revitalization Support Office) oversees the military housing privatization initiative. Reports, congressional testimony, and other information about the initiative can be found on the department's Web site (http://www.acq.osd.mil/iai/hrso/).

11. For a discussion of some of the obstacles facing the privatization program, see Ellen Romano, "Uncle Sam Wants You to Manage His Housing," *Journal of Property Management,* March/April 1999, pp. 30–35.

12. See Gregory G. Gotthardt, "Privatizing Military Housing," *Urban Land,* July 1999, pp. 18–21, for more information.

13. Bradley C. Grogan, "Extended-Stay Hotels," *Urban Land,* May 1997, pp. 43–45+.

14. *Building Design & Construction,* August 1998, p. 20.

15. For more information about New York's program, see Francis Greenburger, "Office Conversions Drive Downtown Revitalization," *Multifamily Trends,* Spring 1999, pp. 20–24.

16. Jane Adler, "Boardrooms to Bedrooms," *Journal of Property Management,* September/October 1997, pp. 20–24.

17. Kenneth H. Lurz, "City Spaces: Avoiding Loft Conversion Pitfalls," *Multifamily Executive,* April 1999, pp. 64–66.

18. For more information on the Secretary of the Interior's guidelines for historic preservation, rehabilitation, and restoration, see the department's Web site: http://www2.cr.nps.gov/tps/tax/rehab-standards.htm.

19. Jack Goodman, vice president of research and chief economist, National Multi Housing Council, cited in "The Multifamily Outlook," *Urban Land,* November 1998, p. 92.

20. Amy L. Spencer, "Enhancing the Pivotal Spaces," *Multi-Housing News,* March/April 1998, pp. 74–76.

21. Ted Trivers, "Apartment Rehabilitation," *Multifamily Trends,* Fall 1999, p. 44.

22. Jeffery J. Morris, "Filling the Middle Market," *Journal of Property Management,* May/June 1998, pp. 30–32.

23. This section draws extensively from Paul A. Gordon, *Seniors' Housing and Care Facilities: Development, Business, and Operations* (Washington, D.C.: ULI–the Urban Land Institute, 1998).

24. Douglas R. Porter et al., *Housing for Seniors: Developing Successful Projects* (Washington, D.C.: ULI–the Urban Land Institute, 1995); and Bonnie Solomon et al., "Retirement Communities: Designing for the Aging Rental Market," presentation at the 1998 Multi Housing World Info Expo, April 17, 1998.

25. Jerry L. Doctrow, "Where Is the Demand?" *Multi-Housing News,* January/February 1998, pp. 38–40.

26. Laura Otto, "Old? No Way!" *Journal of Property Management,* May/June 1999, pp. 66–69.

27. Brad Berton, "Seniors Housing Finance: Historical or Hysterical?" *Multi-Housing News,* May/June 1998, pp. 66–68.

11. Case Studies

Urban Projects, New Construction

Avalon Cove/The Tower at Avalon Cove
An upscale mid-rise project in Jersey City, New Jersey, that provides an urban lifestyle and riverfront views.

Church Street Housing
A publicly funded urban infill project in Brisbane, Australia, for singles and couples.

Gramercy on Garfield/Greenwich on the Park
Mid-rise, public/private infill development in Cincinnati, Ohio, part of a long-range plan to bring housing to downtown. The projects include moderate-income and market-rate housing.

The Mercado Apartments
Affordable rental housing in San Diego, California, developed by a local nonprofit organization with architecture reflecting the community's Hispanic heritage.

Pearl Court Apartments
Affordable housing on a brownfield in downtown Portland, Oregon. Today the surrounding neighborhood supports a wide variety of residential and commercial development.

Urban Projects, Renovation

The Cotton Mill
The historic preservation and rehabilitation in New Orleans, Louisiana, of what was once the largest cotton mill in the South. The project brings 287 residential units to the city's warehouse district.

Denver Dry Goods Building
A historic department store in downtown Denver, Colorado, rehabilitated to create a mixed-use development that includes retail, office, and rental and for-sale residential uses.

The Exchange
Adaptive use of a historic high-rise office building in New York City's financial district. The project was one of the first to use the city's tax abatement program to encourage revitalization of lower Manhattan.

Suburban Projects, New Construction

The Colony at Fashion Island
A high-end, mid-rise rental community in Newport Beach, California, in the master-planned community of Irvine. The project emphasizes luxury and service.

Franciscan Village
Continuing-care retirement community in Lemont, Illinois, developed and managed by the Franciscan Sisters of Chicago for middle-income seniors. A full continuum of housing and care options enables seniors to remain independent for as long as possible.

McNeil House
A community in Austin, Texas, with a homespun design melded with state-of-the-art amenities to create comfortable homes for young high-tech workers and entrepreneurs.

Peakview Apartments
A mixed-income development in Lafayette, Colorado, in a high-cost suburban community near Boulder. The project emphasizes high-quality design and uses "green" building methods and products.

Phillips Place
A pedestrian-oriented retail center in Charlotte, North Carolina, with residences above stores. This mixed-use development brings urban forms and lifestyles into the suburbs. More traditional garden apartments complete the mix.

UCLA University Village
A development of 912 apartments in Los Angeles, California, for married graduate students and their families. The complex provides a quiet, affordable refuge in a densely populated urban neighborhood.

Suburban Project, Renovation

Wimbledon Apartments
The renovation and repositioning of an underperforming 161-unit complex in Spring, Texas. An investment of $25,000 per unit covered the purchase and transformation of the development into a Class A property.

Avalon Cove/The Tower at Avalon Cove

Jersey City, New Jersey

Avalon Cove is a 504-unit mid-rise apartment community developed on one of the last significant parcels of land on the Jersey City waterfront. The project, consisting of two U-shaped buildings oriented toward both the waterfront and the community, offers spectacular views of lower Manhattan and features one- to four-bedroom units. Standing in contrast to the existing high-rise residences on the waterfront, Avalon Cove creates variation and offers a more human scale while preserving views of the waterfront from nearby buildings. Developed and managed by Avalon Properties (now AvalonBay), Avalon Cove targets the high end of the housing market with an abundance of amenities and an emphasis on high-quality service to residents. A second phase of the project with 269 luxury units, the Tower at Avalon Cove, was recently added to the development.

Completed in 1997, Avalon Cove is an upscale apartment community that offers one-, two-, three-, and four-bedroom units. The Tower at Avalon Cove, its newly built neighbor, features 269 units in a 25-story building along with a detached four-level parking garage. The community is located in the heart of Jersey City's Hudson River waterfront district, which features a view of the Manhattan skyline. The developer, Avalon Properties, overcame environmental constraints and limited access to the surrounding neighborhood to construct the first new rental housing on the Jersey City waterfront in more than a decade.

Avalon Cove consists of two U-shaped buildings; each is five stories high, with the fifth floor "disguised" by a mansard roof. The apartments on the top level are two-story duplexes, and each unit type is available in four different floor plans. Surface-level parking is available to all residents, and some apartments have access to a surface-level garage. Recreational amenities include a swimming pool, an indoor half-court basketball court, a fitness center with two indoor racquetball courts, and two outdoor tennis courts. Avalon Cove also includes several special telecommunications features: the entire community is served by fiber-optic cable, and each apartment can accommodate six separate phone lines without additional wiring.

The Tower at Avalon Cove, the second phase of the project, was completed in 1999. It borders the Avalon Cove property to the northwest and extends east to the Hudson River. Like Avalon Cove, the units in the Tower at Avalon Cove feature excellent views of the river and the Manhattan skyline. Features and amenities include a 24-hour concierge in the lobby, an outdoor swimming pool, a fitness center, and a landscaped courtyard with barbecue area. Residents of the Tower at Avalon Cove may also use the community amenities available at Avalon Cove.

Avalon Cove was developed by Avalon Properties, a self-administered and self-managed equity REIT concentrating exclusively on acquisition, construction, development, and management of apartments in markets where barriers to entry are high. In 1998, Avalon Properties merged with Bay Apartment Communities to become AvalonBay, Inc. The Tower at Avalon Cove was developed during the merger.

The Site

The 11-acre site adjacent to the Hudson River was vacant when Avalon Properties purchased the property in the early 1990s. It was part of a larger parcel of land slated for an ambitious redevelopment plan in the early 1980s, when Jersey City received one of the largest urban development action grants awarded to any jurisdiction by the U.S. Department of Housing and Urban Development. Although no development had taken place on the site, Jersey City officials nevertheless recognized its importance because of its strategic waterfront location.

Despite its convenient location and views of the Manhattan skyline, the Jersey City waterfront had seen no new residential development from the time of the stock market crash in October 1987 until the completion of Avalon Cove in 1997. The property, formerly a railyard for Conrail, had been designated a brownfield site in the 1980s. Before Avalon Properties's acquisition of the site, the New Jersey Department of Environmental Protection determined that contamination levels were relatively modest and decided that development could proceed on the site with minor environmental mitigation, such as covering the site with a layer of clean soil and/or an impermeable surface like a parking lot or building. The agency's decision to limit liability if the proper measures were taken cleared the way for the site's development.

When Avalon Properties first purchased the site, it had no frontage road or any other access to the site from the surrounding neighborhood. Nevertheless, Avalon recognized the site's potential for development: the parcel was located just one-third mile from the Holland Tunnel and less than two blocks from a PATH train station, and it offered spectacular views of lower Manhattan. The rail station near the site is the only waterfront PATH station where passengers can connect to lower and midtown Manhattan without having to transfer. Transit times of

Avalon Cove, built on one of the few remaining parcels on Jersey City's shoreline, offers residents spectacular views of Manhattan, upscale services, and many amenities.

The buildings at Avalon Cove were arranged to form two private courtyards for recreational facilities. Both courtyards look out on the Hudson River.

six minutes to lower Manhattan and 12 minutes to midtown Manhattan convinced Avalon Properties that the site would be ideal for residential development.

Planning/Engineering/Architecture

The overall concept for the site was to build a residential community on a human scale. Because all the existing housing on the Jersey City waterfront consisted of high-rise apartments, Avalon Properties decided that building Avalon Cove as a mid-rise apartment community would help differentiate it from other projects in the area. Its less intimidating scale was seen as an attractive feature that would appeal to the targeted segment of the market, mostly high-income singles and married couples. The Tower at Avalon Cove used a very different development concept, but this 25-story building has been just as successful as Avalon Cove.

From inception, the development team wanted the project to be open to both the city and the waterfront. Achieving that effect was not easy, however; the Hudson River borders the site on the east, and street access to the site is on the west, directly opposite the waterfront. The streetscape on the west was designed to be pedestrian oriented and open to the city, with as much passive, open green space as possible.

Avalon Cove's architectural character is eclectic, with traditional elements such as corner pieces and quoins. The buildings were limited to five stories so that residents could comfortably walk down to the ground level if they chose not to use the elevator. The pitched roofs feature turned gables, and the exterior is made of multicolored brick and precast stone that soften the scale of the structures. The Tower at Avalon Cove is clad in limestone, granite, and two colors of brick. The design uses windows and bays extensively to soften the visual impact of the building and to provide it with more interesting facades.

The highly varied depth of the bedrock presented a significant engineering challenge. Both U-shaped buildings were placed on pilings that vary from six to 90 feet, becoming progressively deeper the closer they are to the river to anchor the buildings to the bedrock and ensure that they rest on a solid foundation.

Site Design

The development team at Avalon Properties produced a building layout and site design that relates well to the existing street grid in the adjoining parts of Jersey City. The site design also focused on taking advantage of the adjacent waterfront as much as possible. The riverfront portion of both Avalon Cove and the Tower at Avalon Cove is characterized by a waterfront walkway that includes benches, lighting, and bike racks; the walkway is part of an easement granted by the developer to the public, which is required by the state of New Jersey for all new waterfront development. This requirement, aimed at creating a publicly accessible, continuous waterfront promenade, coincided with the development team's desire to use the waterfront as much as possible in site planning.

The prohibitive expense was one factor in rejecting a structured parking garage as an option, but the desire to preserve as many views as possible of the river and the Manhattan skyline was equally important. In addition, the development team wanted to create an attractive streetscape along the city side of the site; putting a parking garage there would create a hard, uninviting edge between the community and the rest of the city. With the development of the Tower at Avalon Cove, however, AvalonBay decided to add a greatly needed four-story parking garage. Residents of both phases of the development share the 266 spaces in the garage, which was sited to preserve views of the water and the skyline.

The project's U-shaped configuration was chosen to increase the amount of building frontage that faces Manhattan, resulting in views of the river or the Manhattan skyline from 80 percent of the apartments. Similarly, the Tower at Avalon Cove was sited so as to maximize views from the apartments at the same time it minimizes the extent to which the building blocks existing views from the city. Using the waterfront as an amenity to attract residents was deemed important enough to create views of the river from as many vantage points as possible, including the main lobby of each building. By orienting the buildings as it did, Avalon Properties can achieve view premiums ranging from $100 to $800 per apartment per month. The interior courtyards feature gazebos, green space, tennis courts, a pool, a deck, and other amenities. At the Tower at Avalon Cove, each ground-floor unit features a private garden.

Public Approval
A myriad of agencies were part of the approval process, reflecting the complexity of developing real estate in a large urban area with many overlapping jurisdictions, each having its authority over land development projects. The process took 18 months from start to finish. The public agencies involved included the Jersey City Redevelopment Authority, the planning board of the city of Jersey City and Hudson County, the New Jersey Department of Environmental Protection (the waterfront division and the water resources division), and the city of Jersey City (for tax abatement).

Avalon Cove was built at a density 20 to 30 percent less than permitted by zoning for the site to construct a mid-rise apartment community on a human scale. City officials did not immediately support this approach, because they viewed the 11-acre parcel as one of the last significant tracts of undeveloped land along the waterfront and felt that to develop the property at the lower density would be to squander an opportunity to develop it to its greatest potential.

The development team at Avalon Properties was able to convince city officials to accept the lower density by pointing out that it made sense to have some variation along the waterfront. If the project had been constructed at the highest density permitted by the city, the result would have been a continuous wall of structures with

no relief. Moreover, a mid-rise apartment community would preserve many views from existing nearby buildings, whereas developing the site to its maximum density could have resulted in a blank wall that obstructed valuable views.

Marketing/Financing/Legal Arrangements
Because Avalon is a self-financed REIT, the project was financed internally. Moreover, no significant legal arrange-

The mid-rise height of Avalon Cove offers residents urban living on a relatively small site while preserving views of the waterfront for nearby buildings.

Elegant, sophisticated common areas appeal to urban renters.

ments or relationships were involved, as Avalon Properties developed and manages the property.

AvalonBay strives to provide service that exceeds customers' expectations. It offers dry cleaning service, pet walking when residents are traveling, and a guaranteed 24-hour maintenance program with the promise that if no repairs are made within 24 hours, no rent is charged until repairs are complete.

AvalonBay's two principal operating strategies are to increase operating cash flows and long-term value for stockholders. To achieve these objectives, management attempts to generate increased revenue at each apartment community it operates through high occupancies and value pricing. Further, new development projects that are in markets with high barriers to entry are ideal for making the goal of high occupancy a reality. The development of the Tower at Avalon Cove has allowed AvalonBay to diversify its holdings and better compete in the Jersey City market. The leasing offices of the two development phases have been combined to achieve operating efficiencies and economies of scale by streamlining operations and providing better service to the residents of the community.

Northern New Jersey was experiencing significant growth in new households at the time Avalon Properties purchased the Hudson River site; at the same time, no new residential properties had been built in Jersey City for several years. As a result, the rental vacancy rate was exceedingly low. In addition, the relocation of firms from Manhattan to northern New Jersey made the office market in the Jersey City area one of the most dynamic in the state. All these factors indicated that demand was sufficient for new rental housing in the market.

The residents at Avalon Cove come primarily from northern New Jersey (40 percent) and Manhattan (20 percent). The rents at Avalon Cove are two-thirds those of similar upscale properties at Battery Park City, just across the river in Manhattan. The fact that 50 percent of Avalon Cove residents work in Manhattan is testimony to how the community has been able to attract residents from Manhattan and those who work in the city. Residents are evenly split between couples and single people. Although rents compare favorably with those for Manhattan apartments, they are the highest in the Jersey City market. In fact, rental rates are more than $500 over initial pro forma projections.

Experience Gained

Despite the favorable vacancy rates and the growth in households that characterized this market, development of Avalon Cove was not without risks. It was a new market and a new product for Avalon Properties, whose specialty had been garden apartments. A change in product type demands different consultants, such as architects and engineers, who must have a different set of skills if the project is to be a success.

Mid-rise apartment communities beg for simplicity, including the design and management of the building. The more diverse the number of floor plans, the more

Avalon Cove offers one- and two-level units that include one to four bedrooms.

complex the construction and the more cumbersome the leasing process.

Experience demonstrated that a number of pre-school-aged children live at Avalon Cove. Therefore, a tot lot or a children's playroom would have added to the value of the amenity package.

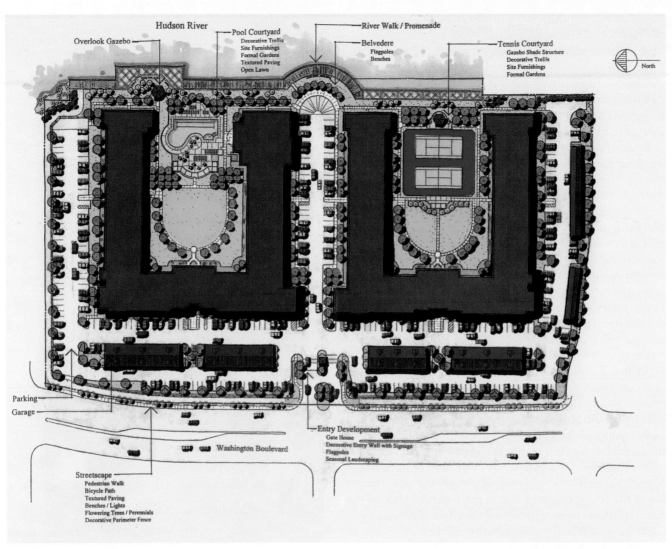

Site plan.

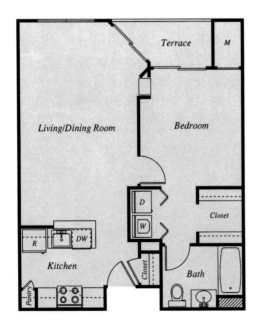

One-bedroom floor plan.

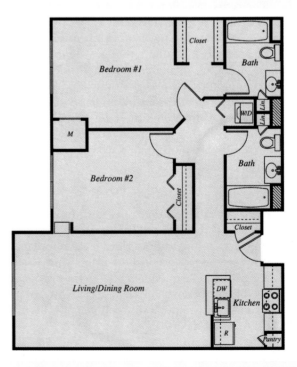

Two-bedroom floor plan.

Project Data: Avalon Cove/The Tower at Avalon Cove

Land Use and Building Information

Site Area	11.15 acres
Total Dwelling Units	504
Gross Density	50 units per acre

Land Use Plan

	Acres	Percent of Site
Buildings	5.15	46.2%
Roads/Paved Areas	1.50	13.4
Common Open Space	3.50	31.4
Other	1.00	9.0
Total	11.15	100.0%

Residential Unit Information

Phase I—Avalon Cove

Unit Type	Unit Size (Square Feet)	Number of Units	Rent Range
1-Bedroom	680–1,454	206	$1,607–3,025
2-Bedroom	1,106–1,719	222	$2,030–3,870
3-Bedroom	1,483–1,781	50	$3,334–3,353
4-Bedroom	1,853	26	$4,505–4,647

Phase II—The Tower at Avalon Cove

Unit Type	Unit Size (Square Feet)	Number of Units	Rent Range
1-Bedroom	600–724	167	$1,567–1,734
2-Bedroom	925–1,173	94	$2,054–3,170
3-Bedroom	1,456	24	$3,030–4,080

Development Cost Information (Phase I—Avalon Cove)

Site Costs

Site acquisition	$8,529,562
Site improvement	7,269,881
Total	$15,799,443

Construction Costs

General requirements	$9,878,897
Structures	49,532,608
Amenities[1]	991,597
Leasing office	424,564
Freestanding garages/carport	1,239,122
General contractor fees	323,749
General conditions	1,771,489
Rebates (city of Jersey City)	(261,888)
Total	$63,900,138

Soft Costs

Architecture/engineering	$1,123,469
Marketing and promotion	721,101
Legal and closing costs	516,100
Permits and fees	1,683,422
Financing fees	393,197
Construction interest	5,506,209
Office overhead	608,290
Total	$10,551,788

Total Development Cost	$90,251,369
Total Development Cost per Apartment	$179,070
Construction Cost per Square Foot	$158

Developer

Avalon Properties (now AvalonBay Communities, Inc.)
535 Fifth Avenue, 18th Floor
New York, New York 10017
212–370–9269

Architect

Minno & Wasko
80 Lambert Lane
Suite 105
Lambertville, New Jersey 08530
609–397–9009

Landscape Architects

Melillo & Bauer
300 Hawthorne Avenue
Point Pleasant Beach, New Jersey 08742
732–295–9630

Development Schedule

1991	Planning started
1992	Site purchased
12/1994	Construction started
Mid-1997	Project completed

Note

[1] Community center, swimming pool, tennis courts.

Church Street Housing
Brisbane, Queensland, Australia

Church Street Housing is a publicly funded, developed, and managed low-income housing project in an emerging suburban renewal area of Brisbane, Australia, called Fortitude Valley. The infill development is the result of the efforts of the Queensland Department of Housing, known at the time as the Queensland Department of Housing, Local Government, and Planning (DHLGP).

The 42 units are a mix of one- and two-bedroom apartments stacked in six adjacent buildings designed to look like separate developments. Buildings are walkups of three stories or three stories plus lofts. The project set the standard for high-quality design for public housing and was a vanguard project for urban renewal of the area.

Funded by the state within the context of a three-tier national government program, the project was intended to provide much needed low-income housing in the largely hitherto neglected inner suburbs of Brisbane and to act as a catalyst for the renewal of the immediate neighborhood. The 59,200-square-foot site was part of an underused grade-level parking lot in a commercial neighborhood on the edge of the historic Fortitude Valley Centre. The site is bounded on three sides by roads, two of which are heavily traveled and noisy. On the remaining side, the project faces a historic church located across a quieter urban street.

The housing department engaged three architectural firms to work together to create varied designs for different parts of the project to generate an appropriate urban scale and a noninstitutional look and feel. The housing department wanted the project to have the appearance of market-rate housing to increase its market flexibility and for reasons of social policy. The units are designated for adult singles and couples who pay up to 25 percent of their income as rent, as is the practice for housing provided by the state housing authority.

The Government's Role
Since the end of World War II, most nonprivate low-income rental housing in Australia has been provided by state public housing authorities, substantially funded by grants and long-term loans from the federal government. While such state-owned rental housing represents about 5 percent of total housing across Australia, the amount, type, quality, and management policies vary from state to state.

At the beginning of the 1990s in Queensland, only a small percentage of low-income housing was publicly owned. Most was low-density, single-family detached dwellings. The multifamily housing that had been developed was often in undesirable locations, clustered in large groups, and seen by the community as uniform, easily identifiable, and of poor quality.

In the early 1990s, a new government set about to radically revamp the housing agency and substantially increase the amount and improve the quality of new housing. By late 1992, the Queensland DHLGP, having begun to demonstrate its changed approach in a series of suburban and regional town projects, was in a position to propose a significant community plan. It suggested a development in the largely commercial and run-down suburb of Fortitude Valley. The project would be a state contribution to the federally created "Building Better Cities" program and would support Brisbane's proposed Inner North East Urban Renewal initiative. The housing department began the process of gathering support for the idea, especially among key players in city hall.

The Site
The site was part of an underused surface public parking lot, just over a mile from city hall in the central business district. The gently sloping area was used mainly by local workers for a park-and-ride lot and on weekends by patrons of a nearby public swimming pool complex.

The neighborhood was predominantly low-density commercial of mixed quality: car showrooms and lots, offices, warehouses, a police station, a church, a bus depot, a school, and so on. Virtually no residents lived within one-third mile.

On two sides were busy one-way urban streets. One was a main route out of the downtown, edged by some significant mature trees and four heritage-listed unattractive World War II bomb shelters. Across the quieter street that formed the third side, the site faced a historic church and associated buildings. On the fourth side were an old, deteriorating two-story duplex that was being used for marginal commercial activity and additional public parking. The land's ownership was a mix of state and city with tenures that bore no relation to likely development strategies.

Development Process
Officials decided to explore the project's potential, and work began on three interactive fronts: developing a potential housing brief, negotiating the amalgamation and acquisition of a site, and garnering support from relevant city, state, and federal agencies.

Major demographic changes in Queensland were pushing the DHLGP to realign its housing stock to accom-

A model of the project shows its urban context.

modate more one- and two-person households, such as empty nesters and the elderly. But Fortitude Valley (and especially this site) was too harsh a place in the early 1990s for the elderly or for small children. In time, this and other projects might help change those conditions. In the meantime, the project became focused toward young and middle-aged childless households, still a major component of demand for housing.

The city began to promote the potential of the immediate area to become a more mixed-use neighborhood, perhaps a strongly residential one. Officials spoke of re-routing traffic, making local environmental improvements, instituting transit to the site, and making available other nearby city-owned sites for housing. This public project, which did not need to depend on market acceptance as would a market-rate project, would be a catalyst for renewal, to be quickly followed by others. Perhaps as conditions improved, the Church Street units could be suitable for later use by the elderly or by single parents with older children.

Although there was almost no public housing in the area and no other sites available, the DHLGP saw the potential yield of 40-plus apartments on one site as too great a concentration of low-income housing. Under evolving policies in response to the regrettable practices of the 1970s and 1980s, two separate sites of 20 units would be better in terms of dispersing low-income residents throughout a community. But what if another nearby site for further public housing never transpired? John Byrne, proj-

ect director for the DHLGP, bargained for pursuing the 40-plus project but building possible exit strategies for part of it into the design.

Putting the site together was complicated. Although the city did not own the entire parking lot, it maintained control. How much of it was the city prepared to give up? Would it affect the imminent offering of management rights to the city-owned swimming pool? How committed was the state to the renewal idea, still in its infancy? The DHLGP was not the state agency in control. Would state treasury officials support the necessary land negotiations and under what terms? After considerable delays that took the project until late 1993, the parking lot site was made available at minimal cost to the housing department. The swimmers would have to park somewhere else.

Critical to gathering support, acquiring a site, and identifying possible stumbling blocks was the very early attempt to paint a picture of what the project might be like. The early words and sketchy diagrams (initially by Byrne and then in greater detail by consulting architect John Clarke) embodied a strong, high-quality urban design that related well to its surroundings. The project ultimately was built based on these original concepts.

The housing department began to explore the response to adjacent heritage structures, to generate the idea of adding a community park, and to form the basis for the radical split of design responsibilities—including the question of what to do with the old adjacent duplex that the DHLGP had now bought. Historic restoration was unlikely, but could it be renovated in a way that acknowledged its original residential character? Could a supportive community use be found to justify a restoration? A youth and drug program was suggested, but some felt it would jeopardize the housing project and the project's role as a catalyst for further redevelopment.

Approvals

As a state agency, the DHLGP did not require statutory approval from the city. Indeed, the city's approval of the project would have likely placed significant and lengthy obstacles in the way of a development of the kind envisioned if in the hands of a private developer. The housing department, however, had adopted the practice of seeking expressions of support from the city or town for its projects and needed the city of Brisbane to be on its side. Fortunately, the sophistication of relevant parts of its bureaucracy, the political philosophy of the incumbent administration, and its interest in pursuing urban renewal made it likely.

Apart from halving the parking lot, few critical issues arose from the essentially commercial neighborhood. The adjacent church community expressed its support for the project as well as for the emerging idea of a pocket park to be constructed by the project team and then managed by the city.

The principal sticking point came when municipal engineers wanted to apply suburban standards to the new rear alley proposed as part of the design. Their agreement was legally required to proceed with the subdivision process and essential for delivering municipal services. Precedents set elsewhere eventually prevailed, and the engineers agreed to more urban standards.

Financing

As early as the initial discussions regarding the project, the DHLGP had assumed that the funding would come from its annual construction budget. Along with several thousand other dwellings under development, it would create and manage this public housing as well. In the end, however, this project's costs became part of the Queensland government's contribution to the Australian government–sponsored "Building Better Cities" program, because it was located in the urban renewal project in Brisbane's Inner North East area, one of five identified program initiative sites in the state. The program required the cooperation of all three tiers of government, so more than the usual number of federal and city eyes focused on this public housing project.

Planning and Design

Architectural design began late in 1993. The project's broad form, content, and urban relationships had largely been defined by the department's urban housing brief and the subsequent studies. It was expected to include several components:

- a mix of one- and two-bedroom apartments;
- three-story walkups with no balcony access from the street (for privacy, security, and climatic reasons);
- strong recognition of the public streets and a "facing the street" approach where possible;
- recognition of the two noisy frontages in the internal design;
- as many ground-floor units as possible accessible by wheelchairs;
- significant private balcony space for all units for livability and crime prevention through environmental design (CPTED);
- retention of the significant trees on the noisy frontages;
- retention and creative use of the heritage structures;
- a new pocket park;
- minimal amounts of parking area;
- vehicle access from the less-used Church Street side only in the form of a new public alley to facilitate both the creation of separate lots with rear vehicular access for some buildings and refuse collection and

Balconies facing Church Street provide "eyes on the street."

tenants' access to a shared parking lot for other buildings.

Byrne also sought considerable variety of design for the complex to create an appropriate urban scale and to maintain the rhythm of the neighborhood; to provide legibility for tenants and their visitors through variety and human scale, and dignity through identification as more than an identical bit of a large institutional whole; and to make the development along Church Street seem like three separate buildings to facilitate later sale to investors, if so decided. Byrne therefore persuaded the DHLGP to commission three prominent design firms to work cooperatively. Each firm would work on two of the six buildings identified in the initial studies. The three groups, working within an agreed-upon framework of materials and with the help of a common landscape architect, further refined and enriched the design.

The result is 42 apartments: 17 one-bedroom units, 16 one-bedroom plus alcove units, and nine two-bedroom units. The project consists of six three-story (or three-story plus loft) buildings. Three buildings face Church Street with an array of private balconies and courtyards. Living spaces face the front, bedrooms the rear. Parking is protected by building overhangs and is accessed by the new Bonney Lane at the rear. Two buildings line the busy roads, presenting strong urban facades behind the dense trees but functionally turning their backs to the streets and facing inward onto the central courtyard. The living areas, bedrooms, and balconies or courtyards face northeast and southeast onto the central space; parking is accessed from Bonney Lane. The last building turns sideways to one of the busy roads, with its balconies and courtyards facing the new pocket park.

At the same time, the department was also exploring (with a different architect) the renovation of the duplex, and the city was developing designs and documentation for the pocket park with the help of community artists.

The three sets of drawings from the three architectural firms were combined into a single proposal. Construction began in July 1994, and the project was turned over to the city in August 1995.

Public Response

The deputy prime minister, the state minister, and the lord mayor jointly celebrated the project's completion on December 15, 1995. It subsequently won awards in Queensland from the Royal Australian Institute of Architects, the Royal Australian Planning Institute, and the Australian Institute of Landscape Architects. It has been well received by tenants and potential tenants, and the city uses it frequently as a reference point for urban design. Although some private citizens have criticized Church Street Housing as "too good," the state housing agency continues to seek to match or exceed its design standards in other works.

A simple renovation of the duplex was undertaken to accommodate the youth program. Taming the traffic and improving transit have not been instituted, and the

The project enhances its urban setting. Low walls and fencing offer privacy for the first-floor units without acting as a blank wall. Newly planted shade trees will eventually form a canopy of shade for pedestrians.

other potential sites for housing have been sold for other uses. The city's urban renewal program has been very successful in generating substantial private investment in housing in adjoining areas. Although other public housing has been built in those areas, gentrification has accelerated.

Experience Gained

The early conceptualization of the project proved critical for identifying issues and selling the vision to the key political players.

The basic strength of urban design, with its varying response to the different streets and its commitment to climatically livable and CPTED-oriented dwellings, has been essential to its success and in dealing with changing neighborhoods.

The use of three design firms on a relatively small project, working cooperatively and with an interventionist designer client, was controversial but delivered greater variety than using a single firm. Were this process to be repeated, the department would define some common approaches to details during the conceptual stage and use only one firm to document the whole project.

In the pursuit of variety, as perceived by citizens, the department believes that color is more important than form, although both are necessary. In the Church Street project, the use of a common palette of colors by the three firms proved counterproductive and tended to overly unify the different buildings.

A good project has significant power to influence responses on subsequent projects. Precedents or benchmarks are important for evolving practice.

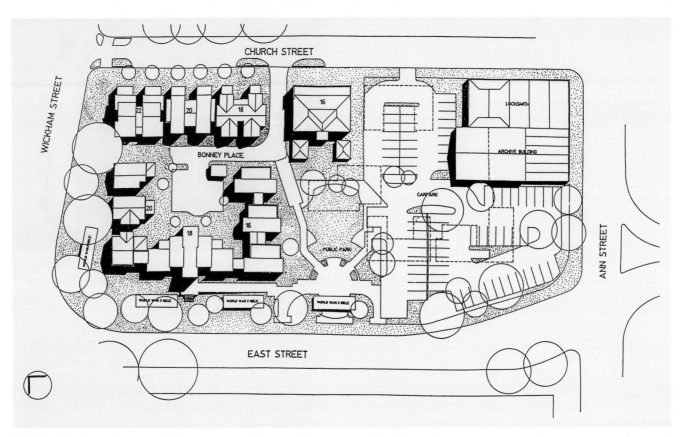

Site plan.

The slatted design of the balconies maintains privacy and shade and allows air circulation, important in the subtropical climate.

Varying the colors and articulating the buildings break up the horizontal forms.

Project Data: Church Street Housing

Land Use and Building Information

Site Area	1.36 acres
Total Dwelling Units	42
Gross Density	30 units per acre
Off-Street Parking	21 spaces

Land Use Plan

	Square Feet	Percent of Site
Buildings	13,240	22%
Private Ground-Level Courtyards	7,535	13
Parking/Paved Areas	11,302	19
Public Alley	3,550	6
Pocket Park and Landscaping	23,573	40
Total	59,200	100%

Residential Unit Information

Unit Type	Unit Size (Square Feet)	Number of Units
1-Bedroom	549–710	17
1-Bedroom plus Alcove	646–818	16
2-Bedroom	840–947	9

Development Cost Information[1]

Site Costs

Site acquisition	0
Site improvement	
Excavation/grading	$57,960
Sewer/water/drainage	67,200
Paving/curbs/landscaping/irrigation	207,200
Fees/general conditions	184,800
Total	$517,160

Construction Costs

Superstructure	$1,086,400
Electrical	157,920
Plumbing	184,800
Finishes	135,520
Total	$1,564,640

Soft Costs

	–

Total Development Cost $2,081,800

Developer/Owner

Queensland Department of Housing, Local Government, and Planning
111 George Street
Brisbane, Australia 4000
61–7–32278236

Architects

John Clarke
St. Lucia, Australia 4067
61–7–33716023

Michael Rayner
Brisbane, Australia 4000
61–7–32100844

Shane Thompson
Fortitude Valley, Australia 4006
61–7–38522525

Landscape Architect

Gamble McKinnon
South Brisbane, Australia 4101
61–7–38461103

Development Schedule

Late 1992	Planning started
11/1993	Site formally committed
Second half 1993	Design started
7/1994	Construction started
8/1995	Construction completed
8/1995	Rental started

Note
[1] U.S. dollars.

Gramercy on Garfield/Greenwich on the Park

Cincinnati, Ohio

Gramercy on Garfield and Greenwich on the Park are two mid-rise rental apartment buildings located in downtown Cincinnati. They are the first two phases of a six-phase master plan for housing in the neighborhood. Together, the buildings offer 212 housing units, parking garages, a fitness center, a rooftop pool, and on-site accessory retail space. Both projects were developed in partnership with the city of Cincinnati, and they represent the first successful downtown housing developments in a number of years. By replacing surface parking lots with attractive apartment buildings designed to complement the surrounding area, these projects have helped to fill a hole in the city's urban fabric.

The two phases feature two new moderate-income rental apartment buildings with parking and accessory retail space. The first phase of the project, the six-story Gramercy on Garfield, was completed in 1992 and features 148 residential units with 15,000 square feet of ground-floor retail space and a 429-stall parking garage. The garage has two floors above grade and two floors below, with the roof of the garage forming an outdoor courtyard for the building. The garage also provides structural support for the remainder of the building.

The second phase of the project, the four-story Greenwich on the Park completed in 1996, has 64 residential units and 43 garage parking spaces. The Greenwich also includes an 1,800-square-foot restaurant on the ground floor. Twenty percent of the units at the Greenwich (13 out of 64) are affordable to households earning 50 percent of the area median income.

The projects, the first housing built in the downtown area in more than ten years, are located on the northern edge of Cincinnati's central business district. The city, which granted the developer a ground lease for the project sites and contributed substantial amounts of funding, was critical to the project's feasibility. With a design that defines the street edge and complements the surrounding area, the Gramercy and the Greenwich have been very successful and have contributed to the ongoing revitalization of downtown Cincinnati.

Development Process and Planning

The Gramercy and the Greenwich have a prominent location framing the western end of Piatt Park. Created in 1817, Piatt Park is the oldest park in Cincinnati. The park currently rests, boulevard-like, in the middle of Garfield Place. The location of the residential develop-ments is notable, because they are at the northern edge of the central business district, where newer, high-density office buildings and retail stores make a transition to older, smaller buildings with a greater variety of uses.

The city of Cincinnati was very interested in seeing these sites developed for housing and had prepared a master plan for housing for the area. The city had acquired the project sites (as well as others in the area) over a number of years using a combination of negotiated purchases and eminent domain. The city initially wanted high-rise, luxury housing on the sites, but the market would not support such a use. Two different developers who had been chosen by the city to develop the sites ultimately chose not to proceed.

Eventually, the city changed its approach to the sites and, after a request for proposals, selected Towne Properties to begin developing them. Towne Properties, founded in 1961, has extensive experience developing residential and other properties throughout Ohio and Kentucky. Its owners believed that the sites should be developed with lower-density, mixed-income housing with accessory retail space. In fact, the two phases were built at a significantly lower density than the zoning for the sites permitted.

Financing

The two phases of the project were financed separately. Financing for the first phase, the Gramercy, consisted of a conventional loan from a local lender and a community development block grant from the city. The conventional loan was difficult to acquire because few other successful downtown housing developments were available for comparison for the feasibility analysis. What made the project work was Towne Properties's ability to get a 65-year ground lease from the city, which allowed it to avoid site acquisition costs. Instead of a fixed price for the land, the city receives a percentage of the project's yearly net cash flow. The city paid for the parking garage for this phase under a separate contract, for which Towne Properties was the subcontractor. The parking garage, which is operated by the city, is an amenity for the residents of the Gramercy, because parking in the garage is discounted for them. In contrast, the parking garage at the Greenwich is reserved exclusively for residents.

Financing for the Greenwich, the second phase of the project, was more complex. A ground lease from the city again helped to avoid the prohibitive cost of site acquisition. The city contributed CDBG funds, made a conven-

Gramercy on Garfield and Greenwich on the Park are two mid-rise buildings totaling 212 residential units, 17,000 square feet of retail space, and garage parking for 472 vehicles.

Brick, stone, tiles, and other high-quality materials were used. Details such as the corner towers and bay windows recall the architecture of the older buildings in the neighborhood.

Replacing surface parking lots, the residential buildings fill a hole in the urban fabric. The project faces Piatt Park, the oldest park in Cincinnati.

tional loan, made a grant of funds to cover site preparation expenses, and issued more than $3 million in general obligation bonds, one of the first projects in Ohio to do so. Towne Properties also contributed its own equity to make the project work.

Under the terms of the development agreement for these sites, the city receives a percentage of the yearly net cash flow. Moreover, the city will also receive a percentage of the proceeds when or if the projects are sold or refinanced. In the case of the Gramercy, for example, the city would receive 25 percent of the profits from a sale. A stipulation of the bond issue for the Greenwich was that the project provide affordable housing units. Therefore, 20 percent of the units in the Greenwich are affordable to households earning 50 percent of the area median income. These units must remain affordable for the life of the bonds, that is, 20 years. Rents from the retail space in both the Gramercy and the Greenwich contribute to the project's cash flow.

Design and Construction

Both the Gramercy and the Greenwich were designed to respect the traditional character of the surrounding neighborhood. Both buildings use brick, stone, tiles, and other high-quality materials, and the facades recall those of the older structures in the area. The buildings also feature contemporary-style metal-clad towers that define the corners of the blocks. The scale and massing of the structures complement Piatt Park, providing an urban street edge to the blocks where they are located.

For Phase I, the developer expected that the target market for the units would be young, recently formed households or older, empty nest households looking for a smaller place to live. Therefore, studios and one-bedroom units were strongly emphasized (129 units out of 148). What the developer discovered, however, was great interest in two-bedroom units, a demand that the Gramercy could not meet. At the Greenwich, therefore,

37 of 64 units were developed as two-bedroom units, which have been very well received by the market.

Units in the Gramercy are designed with a comfortable, contemporary feel. They are average in size for the market, and all units are equipped with kitchen appliances, walk-in closets, and eight-foot, four-inch ceilings. Many units have balconies, and all units have individual climate control. Building amenities include a fitness center, a club room, and a pleasantly landscaped outdoor courtyard and pool on the roof of the parking garage. In addition to the standard apartment units, two-story townhouse units with front stoops face Piatt Park. The Greenwich's amenities are similar to the Gramercy's, but the interior design alludes to the Arts and Crafts style with its careful use of wood and tile. The rear elevation of the building helps to form a mid-block mews with additional landscaping and traditional paving stones.

The commercial uses in the project—restaurants, dry cleaners, and a market—help to enliven the street level. The stores and services are oriented toward neighborhood convenience, and the target market includes the residents of the project and the surrounding neighborhood as well as the many people who work in nearby offices.

Marketing and Management

Towne Properties manages all the projects it develops. For both phases, lease-up of the buildings proceeded very rapidly (three months for Phase I and four months for Phase II). Both phases remain at 98 percent occupancy, and they are meeting pro forma expectations.

Conventional marketing tools, such as direct mail and open houses, were used to advertise the projects. Both phases also benefited greatly from receiving positive coverage in the local media. In addition, the Gramercy won an award for best new construction in the National Apartment Association's magazine *Units* in 1994. Among its efforts at tenant retention, Towne Properties conducts yearly surveys of residents and organizes occasional parties and other social events. Residents are also offered bonuses for referring new tenants.

Experience Gained

To be successful, a developer must be in touch with the demands of the market. In this case, the city held firmly to its idea of high-density luxury residential units, but the market did not support this model of development. The alternative model identified by Towne Properties proved to be very successful, however.

Developers must be willing to work with local governments when developing downtown housing, especially when acquiring the land would be prohibitively expensive without public support.

Developers must be flexible and willing to change the product over time, particularly for multiphase projects, to conform to changing market conditions and the needs of customers.

Neighborhood and convenience retail space is a very important component of successful downtown housing

A central courtyard with a swimming pool offers residents a quiet setting away from the activity of the street.

Many units feature balconies or bay windows.

projects. It enhances marketability of the units and can improve the project's cash flow.

When analyzing the feasibility of downtown housing projects, developers need to find truly comparable developments to consider. Previous downtown housing developments in Cincinnati were not comparable with the proposed project: they had failed, but not because of an inherent resistance to downtown living. Those earlier projects were the wrong type of product for the market.

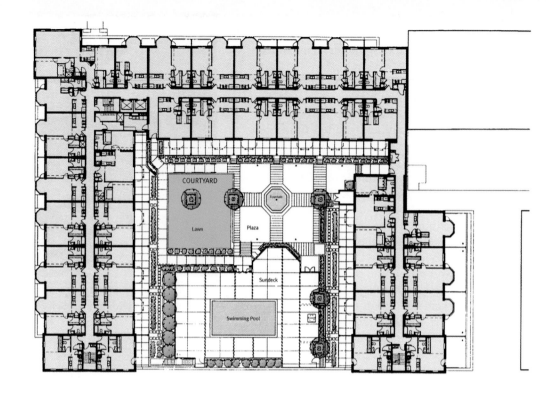

Third-floor plan.

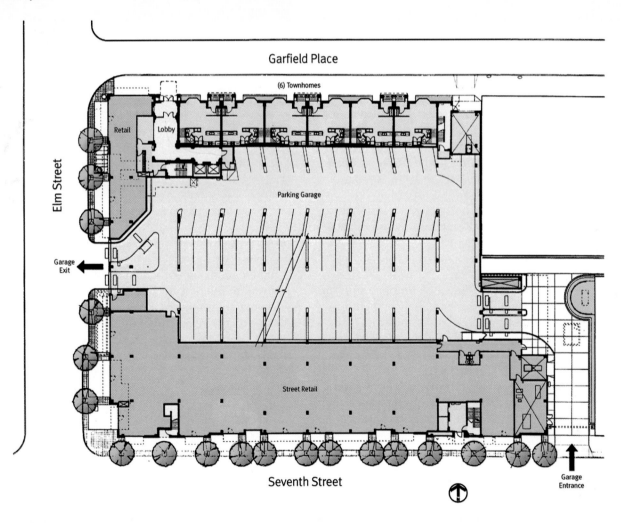

First-floor plan.

Project Data: Gramercy on Garfield/Greenwich on the Park

Land Use and Building Information

Phase I

Site Area	1.1 acres
Total Dwelling Units	148
Gross Density	135 units per acre
Parking Spaces	429 (public garage)

Phase II

Site Area	0.67 acre
Total Dwelling Units	64
Gross Density	100 units per acre
Parking Spaces	43

Residential Unit Information

Unit Type	Unit Size (Square Feet)	Number of Units	Rent Range
Phase I			
Studio	554	16	$450–485
Studio	592	18	$450–505
1-Bedroom	698–748	95	$560–825
2-Bedroom	1,167	8	$695–715
2-Bedroom	1,277–1,407	5	$750–795
2-Bedroom Townhouse	1,468	6	$895
Phase II			
Studio	550	19	$375–545
1-Bedroom	625	8	$625–695
2-Bedroom	1,044–1,204	37	$775–830

Development Cost Information

Phase I

Site Costs	
Site acquisition	$0[1]
Site improvement	0[2]
Construction Costs	$ 8,230,000
Soft Costs	$ 1,820,000
Total Development Cost	**$10,050,000**
Total Development Cost per Apartment	**$67,905**
Construction Cost per Square Foot	**$59**

Phase II

Site Costs	
Site acquisition	$0[1]
Site improvement	$65,000
Construction Costs	$5,927,000
Soft Costs	$832,000
Total Development Cost	**$6,824,000**
Total Development Cost per Apartment	**$106,625**
Construction Cost per Square Foot[3]	**$61**

Developer

Towne Properties
1055 St. Paul Place
Cincinnati, Ohio 45202
513–381–8696

Design Architects

Gruzen Samton
304 Park Avenue South
New York, New York 10010
212–477–0900

Executive Architects

PDT Architects
8044 Montgomery Road
Cincinnati, Ohio 45236
513–891–4605

Contractor

Turner Construction
250 West Court Street
Cincinnati, Ohio 45202
513–721–4224

Development Schedule

Phase I

1/1990	Planning started
5/1990	Site leased
6/1992	Construction started
10/1992	First occupancy
12/1992	Leasing completed

Phase II

9/1993	Planning started
10/1994	Site leased
12/1994	Construction started
2/1996	First occupancy
5/1996	Leasing completed

Notes

[1] Ground lease from city.

[2] Paid in construction of parking garage.

[3] Including one-level parking garage and 1,800 square feet of retail space.

The Mercado Apartments
San Diego, California

The Mercado Apartments, developed by a nonprofit multi-purpose social services agency, provide affordable rental housing for 144 families in a community just over a mile southeast of downtown San Diego. Comprising 26 two-story buildings on 4.4 acres, the apartments' architectural design reflects the community's Hispanic heritage. Located one block from Chicano Park to the east and four blocks from San Diego Bay to the west, the Mercado Apartments provide a nucleus for the Barrio Logan community by creating a positive link to the overhead Coronado Bay Bridge, which divided and blighted this once vibrant community. Creative and complex financing, including tax credit equity, was critical to the project's development.

Site History

From the end of World War II until the early 1960s, Logan Heights, just southeast of downtown San Diego, was a vibrant community. The area was home to many Latinos who themselves or whose parents had immigrated from Mexico; indeed, it is the historical core of the Latino population in San Diego. Disinvestment began in the late 1950s with the planned construction of I-5 and the San Diego–Coronado Bay Bridge. The freeway and bridge bisected the Logan Heights community, which steadily deteriorated, resulting in a depleted housing stock and absentee ownership. The small portion of the community —no more than three miles by six blocks—between the freeway and port area was dubbed Barrio Logan, to give the area an identity distinct from that of the larger Logan Heights area, from which it had been cut off. Indeed, the population of approximately 5,000 in Barrio Logan represents only a small share of the roughly 30,000 people living in the entire Logan Heights area.

In 1970, the city of San Diego agreed to allow the state to put in a highway patrol facility on the site just beneath the Coronado Bay Bridge, reneging on a promise to the residents of Barrio Logan to build a park there. Community activists banded together to show their solidarity and have the park reinstated. Elderly residents and children stood in front of the bulldozers, and eventually the city and the state gave back the site on which Chicano Park, with its world-famous murals, now stands.

Despite the residents' steadfast commitment, the decline continued, the result of inconsistent zoning, political apathy, and years without monitoring of environmental regulations. In 1977, a city-sponsored study of the area presented a revitalization plan for the Barrio Logan area; however, it was not until 1990 that the plan actually began to be implemented. The San Diego Redevelopment Agency created the Barrio Logan Redevelopment District, allowing the use of tax increment financing. Because Barrio Logan is a designated redevelopment area, the city now can reinvest all the increase in property tax revenues resulting from the redevelopment back into the community. The city also was able to obtain federal grants for needed street improvements and grants and loans to acquire property for redevelopment. This renewed commitment by the city was the catalyst needed to begin realizing the community's vision for the future.

Initial community studies conducted by the architect for the Mercado revealed a distinctive neighborhood. Despite years of neglect and industrial rezoning, the people and their homes had survived. The community is pedestrian oriented and well served by buses and a light-rail system. Small storefronts dot the neighborhood along with churches, schools, social service facilities, and one bank, all within walking distance. To the immediate west of the Mercado, sandwiched between the Mercado and the bay, are businesses; to the east and south are located primarily residences. To the immediate north of the Mercado Apartments, separated only by the overhead Coronado Bridge, is the seven-acre site for a retail center that also will be developed by the Metropolitan Area Advisory Committee (MAAC) Project.

Development Strategy

MAAC Project, the developer of the Mercado Apartments, is a nonprofit multipurpose social services agency that has been serving the San Diego metropolitan area for more than 34 years. Unlike many community development corporations, MAAC Project is a large and stable organization with a staff of 250 employees and an annual budget of more than $11 million. Before 1990, MAAC Project had no experience in housing development; it had been advised by many intermediaries to start small, with a maximum of 15 to 20 units of housing. But Richard Juarez, director for community development at MAAC Project, had never forgotten a quote by planner Daniel Burnham (1846–1912): "Make no little plans; they have no magic to stir men's blood." The developer's goal then was to build a project of sufficient size to have a substantial impact on the community. The ancillary revitalization efforts in progress in the entire Barrio Logan area are testimony that the 144 affordable rental homes of the Mercado Apartments, nearly ten times the recommended number, did indeed have a substantial impact.

The Mercado Apartments provide affordable rental housing for 144 families in the Barrio Logan neighborhood of San Diego.

The apartments provide a positive transition to the overhead Coronado Bay Bridge, which once divided and blighted the community.

Juarez, who was once director of planning for the Model Cities Program for the San Diego area, has a strong planning background. But he had no hands-on experience in residential development, so an experienced residential development firm, Odmark and Thelan, was brought into the project at its inception as a development consultant.

The developer knew the importance of neighborhood support for the project. Accordingly, neighborhood participants were included in the process from the beginning. During the design phase, the development team met with local business associations, social groups, and community planning committees to identify neighborhood goals, needs, and aspirations for future growth. It became apparent during this phase that residents felt that the earlier loss of housing had robbed the community of its vitality and identity. It was not enough simply to replace the housing; the Mercado had to be "more than housing."

Project Design

The most successful affordable housing projects respond to the needs of the neighborhood, needs that cannot be fully met without neighborhood input into a project's design. In the case of the Mercado Apartments, the architect worked closely with residents and community groups to develop a design that respected and promoted their lifestyle, their traditional housing types, and their objectives for the community plan. Community members suggested that the design for the Mercado Apartments re-

flect the neighborhood's Hispanic heritage, and it does, drawing inspiration from Mexican urban townhouses and courtyard bungalows of the early 1930s and 1940s. Extensive use of flat roofs with varied parapet lines and shallow barrel-tile accents recalls a familiar architectural style. Private interior courtyards promote pedestrian circulation with direct access to all apartments. Each courtyard provides an outdoor space for gathering, visiting, and other passive activities.

Architects of the Mercado Apartments avoided suburban housing models and opted to orient the homes toward the street to address community groups' first concern—safety. Although prospective tenants in the community wanted protection from crime and vandalism, they explicitly stated that they did not want walls to cut them off from the community. The solution was to join buildings by gates with limited access; thus, residential units that face the street (some front the courtyards) take ownership of the streets with generous porches, front doors, and second-floor balconies.

Parking is divided into two smaller areas and located toward the interior of the development. The landscaping uses a combination of drought-tolerant plants and low-maintenance ground cover to maximize aesthetic appeal while minimizing maintenance cost. Each courtyard is beautifully interspersed with shade trees and a generous array of tropical plants and flowers. The various paths and walkways encourage human interaction by inviting neighbors to stop and chat. The interplay between living space and landscape creates a feeling of home that goes beyond the boundaries of each family's living area and its courtyard balcony, stretching down the courtyard to the neighbor's living space and balcony. The sidewalks were designed to keep most of the pedestrian traffic away from the open courtyards, and the courtyards were designed to naturally impede high traffic flow. The project complements the existing street grid, while the on-site parking areas are internalized to minimize their impact on pedestrian circulation. The architecture and landscaping combine to complement and enhance the entire community.

Tenants were instrumental in the design of individual units. Making concessions is critical to trying to create a comfortable living environment while keeping the unit cost at a level that will not jeopardize the project's feasibility. For example, prospective residents traded off dishwashers for additional storage space. Mealtime is often the only time that family members have to catch up with each other, and it was little wonder that many prospective residents concentrated on amenities that related to this activity. Tenants preferred gas stoves to electric, because it is difficult to heat tortillas on electric burners. A pass-through between the kitchen and the dining area was important so that the cook and the guests could continue to talk to each other.

Construction and Engineering

Innovative construction methods and service programs make the Mercado Apartments a prime example of how

The project comprises 26 two-story buildings architecturally styled to reflect the community's heritage.

community revitalization can be economically viable. In addition to addressing important social issues, the project needed to respond to a limited construction budget. Extra effort was put into trimming costs, undertaking extensive value engineering, and holding construction change orders to a minimum. Minimizing costs is of paramount importance in developing affordable rental housing when subsidized financing and tax credits are involved. Because the rent the landlord can charge is restricted by law, high development costs cannot be passed on to tenants.

Simplified architectural elements and building infrastructure kept costs to $75 per square foot. Only readily available, low-cost materials, such as aluminum windows, stucco, and flat roofs with tile accents, were used. The architect and his consultants placed bathroom plumbing in common walls and minimized mechanical ductwork to control costs. The final cost of slightly more than $86,000 per unit made the Mercado Apartments one of the most affordably built residential developments in San Diego. The per-unit cost was the lowest for tax credit projects in the entire state of California, with the exception of one project in the Fresno area whose land and labor costs were lower.

In addition to construction costs, some of the greatest costs involved infrastructure. More than one-fifth of the costs for sitework involved relocating electric transmission lines that extended across the property from San Diego Gas and Electric's generating plant, just two blocks away. MAAC Project, with some help from the city, also had to pay a substantial amount for the replacement of a sewer line to be extended to the project.

Development Process and Financing
The approval process went smoothly, reflecting the city's commitment to revitalizing the area. At 32.7 units per acre, the planned development was well below the maximum permitted density of 52 units per acre. Required parking ratios were reduced because the project is lo-

cated near a transit node, and the public approval process was accelerated because the project is in the Barrio Logan redevelopment area. A city staff person walked the project through the entire approval process so that it did not get lost among all the pending applications.

Real estate projects were experiencing a credit crunch during the early 1990s, so securing financing for the project was a challenge. At a time when projects involving minimal risk were unable to secure financing, the chances of a residential development in an inner-city neighborhood in which no housing had been built in more than 30 years appeared slim, even to the most optimistic observer. The Local Initiatives Support Corporation (LISC), a national intermediary that provides financial and technical assistance to community organizations to revitalize underserved communities, provided predevelopment financing.

Both public and private sources were tapped to finance the development itself. San Diego's housing com-

Homes are oriented to provide eyes on the street with front doors, porches, and second-floor balconies facing the street.

Architecture draws from Mexican townhouses and courtyard bungalows of the 1930s and 1940s.

mission provided a significant first piece of financing with a $1.4 million plus loan from its housing trust fund. The commission also has a long-term silent second loan of $1.1 million. The Federal Home Loan Bank loaned $800,000, the largest loan from California's affordable housing program made to that point. Bank of America stepped up to the plate with a $3 million loan. The California Equity Fund (established by LISC) was instrumental in syndicating tax credits and raising nearly $5 million

Interior courtyards allow private space for children to play and for pedestrian circulation.

in equity from their sale. A utility deposit refund and a CTCAC (California Tax Credit Allocation Committee) refund provided another $125,000. A gap of just over $1 million remained, which the San Diego Redevelopment Agency closed—and the final piece of the puzzle was in place.

Marketing and Tenant Selection
One of the Mercado's larger objectives was to serve the immediate community. Thus, the homes were marketed in concentric circles around the Mercado, waiting for rentals to slow down in one circle before marketing to families in the next larger and farther removed circle. Marketing involved primarily flyers, word of mouth, and local newspapers. Unlike many market-rate residential projects, the Mercado did not have to do a lot of hard selling because of the large pent-up demand for decent, affordable housing. The target market for the apartments is the working poor. Because the Mercado is a tax credit property, the units are set aside for low-income families. Thus, households with incomes that exceed a certain percentage of the area median family income are ineligible to live there. (Eligibility is reexamined each year.) Those with no income or incomes that classify them as extremely poor would be hard pressed to afford the rents, however, which run up to $600 per month for a three-bedroom apartment.

Selecting tenants was an interactive process involving the prospective tenant, and representatives of MAAC, the management company, and community agencies. Prospective tenants were required to bring their entire family to a rather lengthy interview; because the Mercado was looking for residents who are committed to the success of the community, failure of any family member to show up disqualified the family. All Mercado tenants sign a binding agreement that all family members will remain drug and crime free. One striking measure of the success of the screening process is the lack of a single incident of graffiti or vandalism in five years of operation.

The Mercado was developed to be "more than housing." That phrase is stated on all material related to the Mercado Apartments, and for MAAC Project it is more than just another marketing ploy. Cuatro Properties, Inc., founded with the assistance of MAAC Project to operate and manage the Mercado Apartments, employs a full-time staff member supervised by both Cuatro and MAAC to act as tenant services coordinator. That person's duties include organizing activities for residents, from adult education classes to movies for children to trips to baseball games and the opera; assisting tenants with preparation of the agenda for the monthly tenant association meeting; running the Fifth Dimension program, which provides residents' children with help on their homework in a structured learning environment; and dealing with other tenant relations.

MAAC Project realized early that if it wanted to provide homes for the working poor, it had to focus on *working* so that residents would not fall from the ranks of the employed to welfare recipients. The downstairs of the 2,500-square-foot on-site office building therefore is devoted to an affordable child care and Head Start facility. Neighborhood children aged three to five are eligible to attend. Currently, more than 40 children are in the Head Start program. A tot lot and a recreation area provide space for play. Above the child care center are a community room with a kitchen for the monthly tenant association meetings and other activities, a computer resource center with Internet access where the Fifth Dimension homework program is held, a social services/employment services room, an office for the tenant services coordinator, and the management office. Besides providing 144 families with quality affordable housing and enrolling

more than 40 children in the Head Start program, the project has provided 48 children with home-based Head Start educational services, trained 51 individuals in entrepreneurship and counseled 200 in business startup and development, offered job training and development services for adults in the area, increased collaboration among service providers, increased resources, and reinvigorated the community's spirit.

Tenants are expected to participate actively in bettering their community and empowering themselves. They are expected to come to monthly tenant association meetings, where issues affecting them are discussed and plans for future activities are formalized. Their input is encouraged, and the meetings have become standing-room-only events.

Experience Gained

Tenant selection is critical to the success of an affordable housing project whose long-term objective is to further community revitalization. Tenants and their families must be carefully screened to ensure that they will be committed to their own empowerment and to the betterment of their community.

The tenant services coordinator has been critical in encouraging tenants' involvement. The coordinator binds tenants together in a cooperative effort to maintain the housing and promote social interaction and a feeling of pride and ownership in their community.

Multiple layers of financing are needed to make affordable rental housing feasible. Indeed, the best-laid financing plans often go awry when the economy is weak, but financing usually resumes for good projects when the economy turns around.

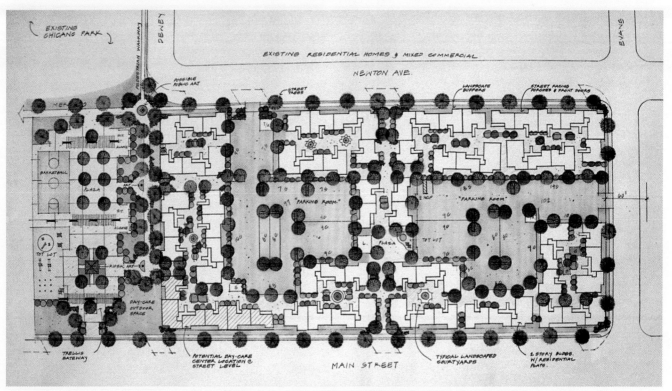

Site plan.

Project Data: The Mercado Apartments

Land Use and Building Information

Site Area	4.4 acres
Total Dwelling Units	144
Gross Density	32.7 units per acre
Off-Street Parking Spaces	212

Land Use Plan

	Square Feet	Percent of Site
Buildings	76,772	40.0%
Paved areas/common open space	114,892	60.0
Total	191,664	100.0%

Residential Unit Information

Unit Type	Unit Size (Square Feet)	Number of Units	Rent Range
1-Bedroom	650	18	$341–545
2-Bedroom	850	60	$360–635
3-Bedroom	1,050	66	$379–715

Development Cost Information

Site Costs

Site acquisition	$1,440,000

Hard Costs

Construction costs	$5,776,752
Site improvement costs	1,656,130
Off-site costs	213,413
Security service	85,060
Total	$7,731,355

Soft Costs

Interest during loan	$195,543
Insurance/bond costs during loan	17,849
Bank loan fee	47,600
Government fees	1,358,379
Appraisal/construction services	38,549
Title/recording/escrow fees	24,008
Design architect/engineering	484,560
Legal fees	59,671
Promotion/advertising	58,810
Other consultants	197,152
Other costs	767,293
Total	3,249,414

Total Development Cost	**$12,420,769[1]**
Total Development Cost per Apartment	**$86,255**

Financing

California Equity Fund	$4,937,022
City of San Diego Housing Commission Housing Trust Fund (first agency note)	1,425,000
City of San Diego Housing Commission Housing Trust Fund (second agency note)	1,094,656
Bank of America	3,000,000
Federal Home Loan Bank (affordable housing program)	800,000
Utility deposit refund	81,000
CTCAC refund	43,727
San Diego Redevelopment Agency (gap financing)	1,039,372
Total	$12,420,777

Budget (1998)

Income

Gross potential rent	$860,571
Daycare center income	28,092
Less: vacancy (7%)	(60,240)
Less: concessions	(1,200)
Less: lodging for manager	(15,312)
Other income	43,560
Total	$855,471

Expenses

Direct expenses

Advertising/promotion	$2,400
Credit checks	500
Elevator maintenance/supplies	1,176
Equipment rental	14,400
Exterminating	1,320
Facilities services	13,824
Fire protection services	924
General repairs	10,400
Insurance (liability/fire)	16,570
Landscape maintenance	20,400
Maintenance supplies	14,400
Make-ready expenses	6,600
Management fee	48,000
Other expenses	1,200
Resident relations expense	10,000
Security services expense	28,800
Tenant activities	6,880
Trash removal	10,500
Utilities	102,600
Total	$310,894

Notes

[1] All amounts less than $1.00 were excluded; original costs totaled $12,420,777.

[2] Used to pay deferred developer fees.

General/administrative expenses	
Accounting	$13,000
Administration	6,600
Bank charges	180
Legal fees	1,200
License fees	500
Office supplies/expense	2,400
Postage/Federal Express	600
Payroll	137,651
Total	$162,131

Debt service	
Note payable to Bank of America	$19,800
Interest	296,400
Total	$316,200

Other expenses	
Operating reserves	$24,357
Replacement reserves	16,239
Partnership management fee	10,000
Total	$50,596

Total Expenses	**$839,821**

Net Income	**$15,650[2]**

Developer

Metropolitan Area Advisory Committee Project
22 West 35th Street
Suite 100
National City, California 91950
619–426–3595

Architect

Rodriguez-Simon Design
2359 Fourth Avenue
Suite 200
San Diego, California 92101
619–544–8951

Other Team Members

Wakeland Housing and Development Corporation
225 Broadway
Suite 1700
San Diego, California 92101
619–235–2296

Catellus Residential Development
1262 Kettner Boulevard
San Diego, California 92101
619–231–3602

Development Schedule

12/1992	Site purchased
1990	Planning started
1/1993	Construction started
6/1994	Rental started
8/1994	Project completed

Pearl Court Apartments

Portland, Oregon

Pearl Court Apartments, completed in September 1997, is a full-block development at the edge of Portland, Oregon's, emerging River District, a new neighborhood between downtown Portland and the Willamette River. The building's 199 apartments are rented at rates that residents earning 40 to 60 percent of the area median income can afford. The building features a library, a formal two-level lobby with a fireplace, numerous lounges and outdoor decks, and a large bicycle room. The apartments enclose a landscaped courtyard.

Pearl Court was the first affordable housing project —and only the fifth project overall—to be developed in Portland's emerging River District, an area of approximately 70 acres bordered by downtown Portland on the south and by the Willamette River on the east. Most of the area is vacant land that once was used as a railyard.

Unlike many affordable housing developments, Pearl Court was begun by a private developer. The 199-unit apartment building, developed by Prendergast & Associates for the Housing Authority of Portland, offers studio and one- and two-bedroom apartments. The building's exceptional design sets the standard for future affordable housing developments in the neighborhood and proves that high-quality affordable housing can be developed without large public subsidies.

Despite the complexity of the undertaking, which involved cleanup of a brownfield, intricate financing, and myriad public/private partnerships, Pearl Court was put on a fast-track development and construction schedule. Although many tax credit projects entail two to three years of planning before construction starts, the developer closed on the financing one year after planning began and completed construction less than a year after that. From the start, the architect, developer, and contractor worked together, helping the project stay on schedule and on budget.

Site History

The city of Portland had been studying the area's potential for redevelopment since the early 1980s and acquired about 30 acres on its fringe—including the passenger train station—in the late 1980s. Planning began in earnest in 1990 when a local developer, Pat Prendergast, purchased 40 acres from Burlington Northern Railroad. A committee of civic leaders, property owners, citizen activists, and city officials convened in 1991 to develop a vision for the district. Whereas earlier plans treated the area as an extension of downtown, the committee recommended building a new medium-density residential neighborhood as part of Portland's strategy to contain urban sprawl and use existing infrastructure more effectively.

In 1995, Portland's city council adopted an ambitious plan for the River District, calling for the creation of 5,000 or more housing units to accommodate residents of all incomes in a pedestrian- and transit-oriented neighborhood connected to downtown and the river and served by a mix of retail uses, new parks, and a new streetcar line.

Development and Construction

Built at a density of more than 211 units per acre, Pearl Court exceeds the density of any project built in the area to date as well as that of most projects in Portland. It thus furthers one of the main goals of the city's River District plan: to stem sprawling development in the metropolitan area and capture growth within the central city by locating housing close to employment, retail outlets, and services. In addition, the site's proximity to downtown, the transit mall (which provides free bus service in the central city area), the light-rail line, and a planned streetcar line allowed the developer to build at a very low parking ratio of only 18 spaces for 199 apartments.

Prendergast & Associates already had built market-rate condominiums and townhouses on four sites in the area. The Pearl Court site—next to a viaduct ramp and the city's main post office parking lot—made it more suitable for rental apartments than for-sale housing. Moreover, the developer viewed Pearl Court as an opportunity to realize one of the central goals of the River District plan —to create a mixed-income neighborhood.

Unlike many affordable housing developments, Pearl Court Apartments was developed by a private company rather than a nonprofit or a public agency. Prendergast knew that the Housing Authority of Portland (HAP) wanted to ensure a permanent supply of affordable housing in the River District, so he offered to sell HAP the Pearl Court parcel and to develop it.

HAP made an attractive partner because of its ability to issue low-cost tax-exempt bonds and because it would be a responsible long-term owner. The developer in turn brought the land, development expertise, and working capital to the project. Prendergast established a limited partnership with HAP as the general partner. The developer sold the tax credits to Fannie Mae, making it the sole limited partner of Pearl Court Limited Partnership. Prendergast & Associates assumed full development responsibilities, and HAP assumed responsibility for management after completion.

The first affordable housing development in Portland's emerging River District, Pearl Court offers housing to residents earning 40 to 60 percent of the area median income.

Pearl Court received the first permit issued in the city for a five-story, wood-frame building and was the first project approved under the newly adopted River District design guidelines. The project also obtained approval for an experimental stormwater system. In addition, it went through a lengthy process to vacate streets and reattach a triangular piece of land that had been dedicated to the city years earlier.

The River District plan called for densities of 80 to 120 units per acre, far greater than in any other Portland neighborhood. Pearl Court Apartments was built at 211 units per acre, with an exceptionally low parking ratio of 1:11. The developer started with a ratio of 1:6, but when it decided to increase the number of units from 170 to 199, it found there was no room for additional parking to serve the extra 18 units and decided to offer them as low-income rentals without parking. One of the keys to developing affordable housing at greater densities is to limit the amount of space devoted to parking.

Pearl Court was part of a large brownfield site; its soil was contaminated by railroad operations and its groundwater by an old manufactured gas plant nearby. Burlington Northern Railroad had been working with the Oregon Department of Environmental Quality (DEQ) on a risk and feasibility assessment of the entire 40-acre railyard area. As part of assembling the site for Pearl Court, the developer asked Burlington Northern and DEQ to accelerate the assessment and remediation of the one-acre parcel. Although both parties were concerned about setting a precedent, they agreed to the cleanup program.

Burlington Northern quickly cleaned up the soil, and DEQ agreed to issue a prospective purchaser agreement to remove any liability to HAP, the partnership, lenders, or investors for any existing conditions. It was the first time a prospective purchaser agreement was used in conjunction with a project involving a Section 42 low-income housing tax credit. It also was the first time DEQ had

The building's height was modulated to suggest a more residential scale. The roof was carved out at the four outside corners and was stepped up above the east and west entries to give the appearance of a fifth floor.

used a prospective purchaser agreement for a residential project.

The developers were committed to making Pearl Court as environmentally sustainable as the budget permitted. They worked with the local utility company, Enron Portland General Electric, which provided an environmental consultant and a comprehensive set of guidelines for constructing an "Earth smart" building that recommended recycling construction site materials, using nontoxic (or low-toxic) paint and other materials, installing a continuous ventilation system, using recycled-content materials, providing for tenants' recycling by having a large recycling room on each floor, and installing an innovative stormwater system that discharges part of the roof runoff back into the ground rather than into the public storm sewer system.

Planning and Design
As the first example of new, affordable housing in a mostly upper-end neighborhood, Pearl Court would set the standard for future affordable and mixed-income developments in the River District. The developer therefore wanted to build a beautiful building and thought it especially important to use a higher level of design, finishes, and architectural details than usually is associated with tax credit projects.

A major challenge was to design a building that was open to the street and contributed to an active streetlife while providing residents in the still-emerging neighborhood with a sense of safety and security. The solution was to build a full-block building around a private interior courtyard that would offer residents a welcome haven from the bustling neighborhood that will soon surround them. Three formal entrances are located at street level, allowing pedestrians to see through the building into the landscaped courtyard. Common decks, built on the upper floors above each of the three entries and above the parking entry, provide further animation for the area adjoining the street.

Another challenge was to fit the apartment building into an area surrounded by massive warehouses and still express its residential character. The developer chose an industrial red brick veneer with alternating panels of synthetic stucco for the building exterior, which blends well with the neighborhood. The stucco panels that project beyond the brick line like bay windows and the black wrought-iron window boxes with terra-cotta planters underscore the building's residential nature.

Building height also was modulated to suggest a more residential scale. The roof was carved out at the four outside corners and was stepped up above the east and west entries to give the appearance of a fifth floor. Besides emphasizing the entries, the additional space contains the elevator shafts and rooftop stairs.

One goal was to create a hierarchy that would differentiate the four sides. To that end, a straight horizontal line was maintained at the roof on the south side, where residents enter the parking garage, to identify it as the back of the building. A partial fifth story of living area was added on the north side, where the elevator tower gives the appearance of a sixth story. This additional massing is in scale with the wider and deeper horizontal articulation of the building and marks the north side unmistakably as the formal entrance to the building. The fifth story was built under the first permit issued in the city for a five-story, wood frame building. The process was simplified because the fifth floor includes only 3,000 square feet. To avoid the cost of an additional elevator stop and stair tower, the five apartments in this section were made into two-story units.

Because the building occupies a full block, the developer wanted to avoid the appearance of a massive, solid box and to create a pedestrian-scale environment. In downtown office buildings, such environments can easily be accomplished by providing retail space on the first level. Developers in the residential River District, however, needed to find ways to do so with apartments on the ground floor and without sacrificing the privacy of the tenants. The design solutions used in this case to break up the building's mass included recessed corners and large, raised planting areas that break down the apparent length of the building. The building also was stepped back in increments at each of the three entries, where raised planters, small benches, and large projecting canopies were added to create visual interest at the ground level.

The first floor was raised three feet above the sidewalk so that window sills were six feet above grade. While doing so solved the issue of privacy, it created a blank wall that did not improve the quality of the pedestrian environment. To add variety to the facade, an 18-inch-wide landscaped strip was planted on the sidewalk, and a rowlock course of brick and a raised panel scoring pattern were added in the concrete base. Wrought-iron window boxes also enliven the streetscape.

Three separate entries open into the interior public spaces and encourage circulation in the courtyard.

The entries connect directly—both physically and visually—to the courtyard, thus encouraging tenants to cut across the courtyard to get their mail or go to the laundry room. The mailroom and laundry room face the courtyard.

Pearl Court features higher-quality indoor and outdoor common area amenities than are generally associated with tax credit projects. Instead of building one large community room, as frequently is done in low-income rental projects, the developer, believing that such a large space would tend to discourage socializing, opted instead to create a series of smaller, intimate gathering spaces throughout the building. The main public area is the light-filled, two-story lobby that overlooks the private courtyard. Winter-weary residents can sit awhile and warm themselves in front of a crackling fire in the fireplace. The space—decorated in rich, warm colors with large, comfortable chairs, wood furniture, and plenty of lighting—is a favorite place for residents to read their

An interior courtyard offers residents a secure outdoor environment in the still-emerging neighborhood.

morning newspapers or open their mail. An open stairway leads to a balcony framed by a wood railing that overlooks the lobby and provides access to a deck above the courtyard. A smaller sitting area that opens to the side of the main entry is a good spot to wait for visitors and eventually will be a popular place for watching pedestrian activity on the street in front of the building.

Another popular gathering place is the library off the main lobby, which features the same style of decor as the lobby. Residents have donated books and established their own lending library.

The laundry room has a connecting lounge area with a large picture window that looks out on the interior courtyard. Residents also have use of five separate lounges on the upper floors and 14 covered outdoor decks that provide views of the Willamette River, downtown Portland, and the West Hills neighborhood.

The courtyard was designed as a series of smaller, intimate outdoor rooms with an abundance of seating and attractive places for residents to mingle and converse. Seating areas are sprinkled throughout the courtyard to take advantage of both sunny spots and shaded areas. A fence and pergola that eventually will be covered with vines were added to screen the courtyard from the parking garage behind. The parking garage was built slightly below street level so that cars entering the garage are not visible to someone standing in the courtyard, which is located at the first-floor level.

Rather than providing only one handicapped-accessible entry, as required by law, the building is fully accessible on all four sides. After the first level was raised three feet, too little space was available on the east and west sides for ramps, so double-sided elevators were installed. Wheelchair-bound residents can enter through the east and west doors and ride the elevators up three feet to the elevator stop on the first floor. Pearl Court has ten fully accessible units, but a number of other units also are rented by tenants in wheelchairs because they find the entire building so accessible.

Pearl Court has access to a broad range of public and private transit services within a five-block area, including local and long-distance buses, light-rail trains, and a soon-to-be-completed streetcar line. A main goal of the River District plan is to locate housing close to employment, retail outlets, services, and entertainment as a way of encouraging walking, biking, and use of public transit. The plan designates NW Kearney Street, which runs on the north side of Pearl Court, as a main pedestrian thoroughfare. NW Ninth Avenue, which runs on the east side of Pearl Court, will be a primary north/south bicycle route, connecting the River District to downtown. NW Tenth Avenue will be the route for the new streetcar line, which will connect the neighborhood to Portland State University on the south edge of downtown and to major employment centers to the west.

Pearl Court features a bicycle room with 72 locking bicycle racks that each can hold two bicycles. River District residents will walk, bicycle, or use transit for an estimated 50 percent of their daily trips outside the district.

Marketing and Management

The Housing Authority of Portland contracted out marketing, sales, and management services to Seattle-based Pinnacle Realty, a large residential real estate management firm. The primary marketing tools were newspaper ads, banners on the building, and advertising in local rental apartment magazines. Because of the high quality of the development, Pinnacle took a much more market-driven approach than is usual for tax credit projects. The key to the strategy was not to treat Pearl Court as low-income housing; instead, the company marketed Pearl Court as if it were one of the most expensive buildings in town. Leasing agents wore business suits, and Pinnacle hired temporaries to answer the telephones and added extra leasing staff rather than turn people away.

Eighteen units were reserved for households earning up to 40 percent of the area median income, 91 units for households earning up to 50 percent of the area median income, and 90 units for households with incomes up to 60 percent of the area median income. HAP is committed to keeping the housing affordable for at least 60 years. In contrast, the vast majority of new development in the River District so far has been decidedly upper end. For example, a project completed at the same time and located one block west of Pearl Court features luxury townhouses priced around $400,000. Units now being completed in that project are selling for around $700,000.

Pearl Court leased up at a rate of 50 units per month, an impressive feat given that HAP changed management companies mid-stream and brought on Pinnacle just six weeks before the building opened. Although there was little time for preleasing and lease-up took place during the Thanksgiving and Christmas holidays, the building was fully leased and occupied four months after opening.

The site had a number of significant drawbacks that easily could have discouraged potential residents. Although located within blocks of the Pearl District—a rapidly gentrifying area of art galleries, trendy restaurants, and loft housing—the site was both visually and physically separated from the neighborhood by an on-ramp to a viaduct system. (The ramp was removed in 1999 and the city street system extended.) The site also was bordered by a vacant lot, an empty warehouse, and a truck parking lot for the main post office.

Renters, however, recognized the long-term opportunities. Drawn by the high-quality design, affordable rents, and close-in location, they were willing to look beyond

some short-term unattractive conditions to secure an apartment. Since Pearl Court opened, a park has been created immediately to the west of Pearl Court, the empty warehouse nearby is being restored, and a new grocery store has been built just northwest of the project.

Financing

The capital structure of tax-exempt bonds, low-income housing tax credits, a Portland Development Commission (PDC) loan, and a bridge loan for the tax credit equity created a complex and time-consuming financing process. The first step was for HAP to obtain an allocation of tax-exempt bonding authority from the state's private activity bond committee.

In December 1995, HAP applied unsuccessfully for an allocation from the state's unused carryover that was reallocated at the end of the calendar year. These allocations could be used anytime in the following three-year period. Competition was fierce, and Pearl Court had started much later than other projects on the list.

Bonding authority issued in regular cycles had to be used within 75 days or be returned. (It was possible to obtain an extension, but doing so could hurt future applications.) Because the project was not slated to start construction until September, HAP would not apply again until late spring, also pushing back the commitment of the 4 percent tax credits because they cannot be allocated by the state's housing finance agency until a project has received an allocation for the bonds.

Unit interior.

Raised planters, small benches, and large projecting marquees add visual interest and create a more pedestrian scale at the street edge.

The timing meant that the developer had to proceed almost to the start of construction without any major financing. Fortunately, the bond and tax credit allocations were received on schedule, and with these two pieces in hand, the developer could begin negotiating the sale of LIHTCs in earnest. The terms of the sale included deferring the investors' pay-in of equity for three years, allowing them to pay a much higher price for the tax credits while maintaining the same yield. To ensure enough capital during construction, the developer needed to obtain bridge financing to substitute for the equity.

This complex financing structure and careful budgeting helped to reduce the amount of subsidy required from the city.

Experience Gained

As the first affordable housing development in the emerging River District area, Pearl Court set the standard for future affordable development in the neighborhood and demonstrated that low-income housing can be attractive and blend well with adjacent high-end development.

Pearl Court demonstrates that the cost of including numerous environmentally sustainable and energy-conserving features need not be prohibitive and that those features are just as appropriate for affordable housing as for market-rate development. In fact, energy savings are especially important to a low-income population. The developer followed the "Earth smart" standards of the local utility company, employing features to lower

heating and lighting expenses for residents. The utility company ran several public service announcements highlighting the development's environmental features, which contributed to the project's quick lease-up.

In hindsight, the developer says he would have started earlier and allotted more time for incorporating the environmental features. Although most of the participating entities—contractor, architect, landscape architect, HAP, and interior designer—supported the basic concept of building an environmentally responsive project, their tendency was to rely on the standard specifications they were accustomed to because they involved less effort, risk, and expense. As a result, the developer spent more time than he anticipated researching the various environmentally sustainable materials and construction technologies, rather than relying on others to come up with the information.

In a development located in an emerging neighborhood, such as Pearl Court, it is important to take a long-term perspective. Otherwise, it is easy to be discouraged by temporary conditions (the viaduct ramp and adjacent parking lots, for example) and build a lower-quality development. The lesson is to focus on a good product and to build it rather than become distracted by existing conditions that are likely to improve in the future.

The developers started with a higher parking ratio. But when they looked at increasing the density from 170 to 199 units, they found that there was no room for additional parking to serve the extra 18 units and decided instead to build them as low-income rentals without parking. Thus, one of the keys to developing affordable housing at greater densities is to limit the amount of space devoted to parking.

Pearl Court demonstrates that low-income housing can be well designed with attractive, high-quality amenities at relatively low cost without large subsidies. Whereas most Portland tax credit projects require loans from the city's urban renewal agency of $20,000 or more per unit, Pearl Court borrowed only $7,000 per unit. Using a similar financing strategy, the city potentially could increase the amount of low-income housing it produces. Moreover, the financing was structured so that the housing authority will receive substantial cash flows from the development, which it will use to replace expiring federal subsidies on other projects serving even lower-income tenants.

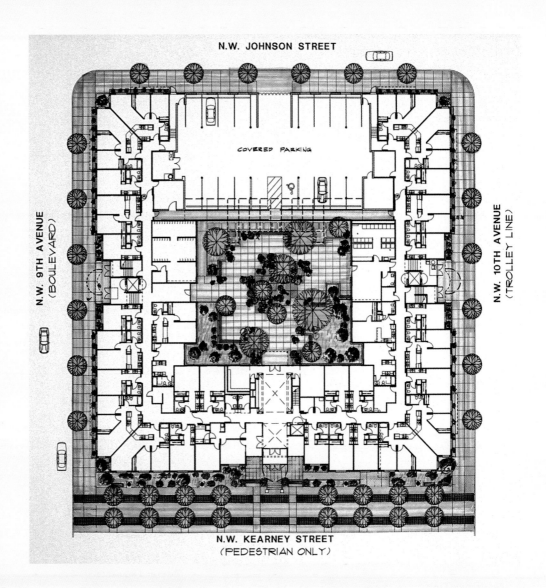

N.W. JOHNSON STREET

N.W. 9TH AVENUE
(BOULEVARD)

COVERED PARKING

N.W. 10TH AVENUE
(TROLLEY LINE)

N.W. KEARNEY STREET
(PEDESTRIAN ONLY)

Project Data: Pearl Court Apartments

Land Use and Building Information

Site Area	0.94 acre
Total Dwelling Units	199
Gross Density	211 units per acre
Off-Street Parking Spaces	18

Land Use Plan

	Acres	Percent of Site
Buildings	.72	76.6%
Roads/Paved Areas	.02	2.1
Common Open Space	.20	21.3
Total	.94	100.0%

Residential Unit Information

Unit Type	Unit Size (Square Feet)	Number of Units	Rent Range
Studio	312–422	112	$331–504
1-Bedroom/1-Bath	543–821	59	$495–539
2-Bedroom/1-Bath	695–1,148	28	$595–643

Development Cost Information

Site Costs

Site acquisition	$750,000

Site Improvements

Excavation/grading	259,698
Sewer/water/drainage	85,019
Paving/curbs/sidewalks	145,205
Landscaping/irrigation	61,500
Fees/general conditions	59,299
Total	$610,721

Construction Costs

Superstructure	$3,353,454
HVAC	186,276
Electrical	963,512
Plumbing/sprinklers	806,929
Finishes	1,604,588
Graphics/specialties	86,103
Fees/general conditions	751,499
Other	241,683
Total	$7,994,044

Soft Costs

Architecture/engineering	$300,850
Project management	272,095
Marketing	112,019
Legal/accounting	80,162
Taxes/insurance	34,952
Title fees	16,141
Construction interest and fees	517,091
Debt service/operating reserves	724,383
Other	801,550
Total	$2,859,243

Total Development Cost	**$12,214,008**
Total Development Cost per Apartment	**$61,377**
Construction Cost per Square Foot	**$61.65**

Annual Operating Budget (2000)

Revenue

Rent income	$1,080,156
Vacancy	(43,206)
Other revenue	101,018
Total	$1,137,968

Expenses

Administrative	$135,821
Payroll	216,746
Utilities	73,667
Turnover	16,619
Maintenance	35,145
Taxes and insurance	31,048
Total	$509,046

Net Operating Income	**$628,922**
Principal and Interest	524,389
Capital Expenditures	14,041
Net Cash Flow	**$90,492**

Financing

Source	Construction Financing	Permanent Financing
Tax-Exempt Bonds Issued by HAP	$7,137,222	$7,137,222
Portland Development Commission	1,417,497	1,417,497
PDC Bridge Loan	600,000	
Bank of America Bridge Loan	3,009,489	
LIHTC Equity (Fannie Mae)	10,000	3,619,489
Utility Rebate (Portland General Electric)	39,800	39,800
Total	$12,214,008	$12,214,008

Developer

Prendergast & Associates, Inc.
1930 NW Irving Street
Portland, Oregon 97209
503–223–6605

Architect

William Wilson Architects
133 SW Second Avenue
Suite 200
Portland, Oregon 97204
503–223–6693

Development Schedule

1990	Site purchased
10/1995	Planning started
10/1996	Construction started
8/1997	Rental started
9/1997	Construction completed
1/1998	Project 100 percent occupied

The Cotton Mill

New Orleans, Louisiana

The Cotton Mill is the rehabilitation and conversion of a historic former mill into 287 apartment and condominium units. The mill includes six large three- and four-story structures that ring an entire city block, creating a 25,000-square-foot courtyard in the project's interior. Special care was taken to maintain the historical and industrial feel of the property, both for aesthetic reasons and to secure historic preservation tax credits. The original wood floor was restored, and units feature exposed brick interior walls and timbers. The project's massive five- by 12-foot double-hung cypress windows were stripped and repaired. The developer also sponsored an initiative to salvage objects from the mill to create on-site sculptures.

In 1882, Ambrose A. Maginnis and Sons began construction of a large textile manufacturing plant in the warehouse district of New Orleans. Before construction of the mill, the site had been occupied by a series of plantations dating back to 1765. By 1884, the mill was fully established, and it remained the largest cotton mill in the South until it ceased operations in 1944. When the HRI Group purchased the property in 1996, the mill was vacant except for one small textile manufacturing tenant.

Since then, the Cotton Mill has been rehabilitated and converted into 269 rental apartments and 18 condominium units (the latter constructed on the roof of the existing structure). The massive renovation project was the largest of its kind in New Orleans's warehouse district and one of the largest in the country. Its presence has injected a welcome dose of vitality into the emerging warehouse/arts district adjacent to downtown New Orleans.

Development and Design

The 323,000-square-foot Cotton Mill is actually a composite of six three- and four-story structures that ring the block, enclosing a one-half-acre courtyard. The buildings were constructed in the traditional manner, with load-bearing brick exterior walls and interior columns and beams of heavy timber. Huge five-foot-wide by 12-foot-high double-hung cypress windows punctuate the facade at regular intervals.

In addition to the primary mill structures, the complex included several smaller structures abutting the main buildings, primarily within the courtyard. A few of these structures, including a transformer vault and an overhead bridge, were removed to open up the interior and increase the natural light in the courtyard. The selective demolition provided space for a swimming pool, a per-

gola constructed of salvaged metal gratings, and a raised concrete "stage" area that sits on the foundation of the removed transformer vault. Within the 25,000-square-foot open space, several smaller, more intimate courtyards and spaces have been created by retaining some of the original brick walls.

Although some peripheral structures were removed, several others that contribute to the mill's historic identity were preserved. The largest of them, the mill's water tower, was stripped of its lead-based paint and emblazoned with the Cotton Mill name. It is visible for miles around. In addition to its marketing value, the water tower serves as a telecommunications station and is leased to a local cellular service. The mill's bell tower and a 120-foot cylindrical brick boiler stack were also retained.

Taking its preservation philosophy a step further, the HRI Group also sponsored an archeological survey of the site and funded an initiative to search for salvageable items and turn them into art. Local artist Paul Fowler took remnants of the mill's infrastructure—old boiler pipes, flues, and the like—and turned them into sculpture for the site.

Renovation of the Cotton Mill included cleaning and repairing the mill's extensive brickwork, which was pressure washed both inside and outside. A water containment system was used on the interior to avoid damaging the wood floors. Much of the brickwork had 100-year-old paint on the interior side, some of which was failing; much of it was lead-based and had to be treated as a hazardous material. The pressure wash was designed to remove only the unsound paint; well-adhered paint was left in place as a reminder of the mill's industrial past. In accordance with HUD requirements, however, all lead-based-paint surfaces were repainted up to a height of 48 inches from the floor with a special lead-encapsulating paint. The result, as HRI intended, is that the gritty history of the Cotton Mill remains intact, a feature that seems to appeal to the young, urban crowd that has leased the Cotton Mill apartments.

To comply with National Park Service standards for historic preservation, the 1,200-plus cypress windows were refurbished and reused. The monumental windows were removed from their frames and shipped out of state to strip the paint using chemicals. A workshop with nine workstations was established on site to repair and reinstall the windows as they returned from being stripped. On most windows, the upper sash was fixed in place and sealed to conserve energy—and to minimize tenants' utility bills—while the lower sash was made operable. The

Once the largest cotton mill in the South, the original 1882 structure was rehabilitated to house 269 rental apartments and 18 condominium units.

As much of the original structure as possible was retained. Cypress-frame windows were removed, refurbished, and reinstalled. Where possible, wood strip flooring was reused.

stripped windows were left unpainted on the interior side to reveal the natural beauty of the wood.

In most cases, the wood flooring of the mill was refurbished. After the existing interiors were gutted, the acres of remaining wood flooring were sanded and coated with polyurethane for protection. In areas where the wood flooring could not be saved, the floors were filled in with plywood panels or fitted with color-stained concrete slabs. Although the plywood was intended as a subflooring for carpet, it was later decided to coat the plywood with a clear finish and use it as a finished floor in keeping with the industrial ambience of the Cotton Mill.

The rooftop condominiums created extra challenges. Although the buildings' original structure permitted construction on the roof without upgrading the foundations, it did require localized reinforcement of columns and beams as well as construction of additional support beams. The bigger issue, though, was how to integrate the new construction with the old without destroying the historic

design and how to screen the required air-conditioning units that were to be mounted on the roof.

These issues were more than aesthetic questions. Approval of the project's historic tax credits—the financial linchpin of the project—was contingent on approval by the state historic preservation office and the National Park Service. Months of design studies and sight-line studies—even a full-size mock-up on the roof—were required to come to agreement on the massing of the rooftop construction. A related issue was the materials to be used for the facades of the condominium units. The Park Service would not allow brick because it would imitate the historic original, and stucco was judged too expensive and hard to maintain. Aluminum panels were the final choice. The solution for the air-conditioning units was to set the units in a specially built trough within the condominium roofline, separated from the condominiums by several inches of sound-deadening concrete.

Renovation and buildout of the Cotton Mill apartments were accomplished in phases because of the project's size. Initially, two phases were planned, corresponding to the building's major fire wall demarcations. Construction was staged "like a GM production line," notes Gary Meadows, president of HCI Construction & Design (HRI's in-house construction and design division), "with crews of each trade cycling through the buildings." Eventually, based on the evident market demand for the apartments, the project was divided into three phases so that portions of the building could be occupied sooner than originally planned. The first tenants moved in 12 months after construction began. Construction was completed, except for some of the rooftop condominium work, in 18 months.

Because each of the six buildings had its own floor-plate configuration, more than 30 different unit plans were required. Most of the apartments have luxurious 12-foot ceilings, and some top-floor units have partial 20-foot ceilings. To further accentuate the historic character of the Cotton Mill, the mill's heavy timber structural columns were exposed in the apartments and hallways rather than buried in drywall partitions. Similarly, the timber beams and metal tie rods were left exposed, for both economy and visual interest.

To maintain an open feeling, some interior partitions were built only eight feet high. Most kitchens are open to the adjacent space, and all units have side-by-side or stacked washer/dryer units. Each dwelling unit also has two telephone lines, with high-speed Internet access and standard cable television. Project amenities include the pool, courtyard, game room, and a 1,500-square-foot fitness center. A full-time concierge is stationed in the main lobby.

One corner of the ground floor is occupied by Spice, Inc., a gourmet food and takeout shop owned and operated by Susan Spicer, one of New Orleans's premier chefs. Spice, Inc., which also offers on-site cooking lessons, is "an amenity for the tenants," notes Tom Crumley, vice president and project manager for HRI, "as valuable to the marketing and livability of the project as the swimming pool and fitness center."

The interior courtyard was rehabilitated to become a series of landscaped areas and now includes a pool.

Original brickwork and timber beams give a gritty industrial character to the project that is enhanced by elements like concrete flooring, steel staircases, and new exposed ductwork.

The rooftop condominium units, which average about 1,600 square feet, have panoramic views in two directions. The units are reached from a mezzanine, newly constructed by HRI within the existing 20-foot-high top floor. The units have hardwood floors and granite countertops, features that originally were offered as upgrades but that were requested so often that the developer has retrofitted all the units to this standard.

Financing

The Cotton Mill was developed through a partnership, with HRI as the general partner and AmerUs Mutual Life Insurance Company as the limited, tax-credit partner. AmerUs provided $6.5 million in equity through the purchase of the project's historic tax credits as well as the purchase of tax credits generated from the donation of a preservation easement for the Cotton Mill's facade. HRI provided an additional $3 million in equity financing. The remainder of the project's $32.2 million cost was financed through a first mortgage insured through HUD's 221(d)4 loan program and sold to a pension fund as Ginnie Mae securities.

Market Acceptance

Restoration of the Cotton Mill clearly struck a chord in New Orleans. The progress of the restoration, the archaeological dig, and the art initiative were widely reported in the local press, and the project was featured on the cover of *New Orleans* magazine. In response, leasing of the Cotton Mill apartments proceeded at twice the expected rate; the units were 95 percent occupied in 12 months, a rate of more than 20 units per month. In addition to the rapid absorption rate, rents exceeded the project's pro forma by more than 7 percent. Condominium sales proceeded less rapidly but generally met pro forma expectations, selling at base prices ranging from $235,000 to $384,000 and averaging sales of two units per month. Base sale prices exceeded the originally budgeted prices by approximately 10 percent.

Experience Gained

The Cotton Mill has taken a building of little economic use—whose deterioration could be expected to contribute to the disintegration of its inner-city neighborhood—and used it as a vehicle to regenerate the neighborhood. Not only has a chapter of New Orleans history been preserved, but a neighborhood has also been strengthened in the process.

The industrial character of the Cotton Mill has been particularly appealing to young New Orleans residents, and the developer has made a conscious effort to retain this aesthetic aspect in the renovation. Turning salvaged objects into art reinforced that effort while serving as a bridge to the New Orleans arts community, which has pioneered the revitalization of the warehouse district.

The retail component of the Cotton Mill, although limited, is a highly visible aspect of the project and a valued amenity for tenants.

© 1998 Ron Calamia

The developer salvaged objects from the mill to create on-site sculptures, helping to link the project to its historic past.

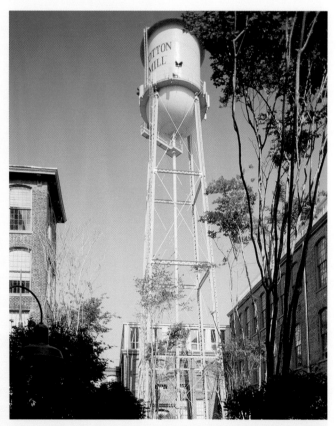

The water tower is a recognizable landmark that identifies the Cotton Mill and also brings additional revenue. It has been leased to a cellular telephone service for use as a communications tower.

More than 30 different floor plans make up the unit mix at the Cotton Mill. Most of the units feature 12-foot-high ceilings and kitchens open to the adjacent space.

Building section.

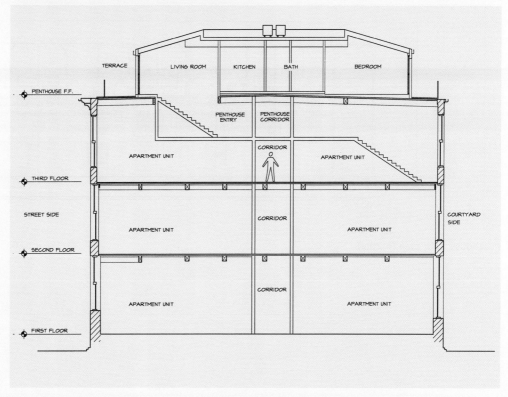

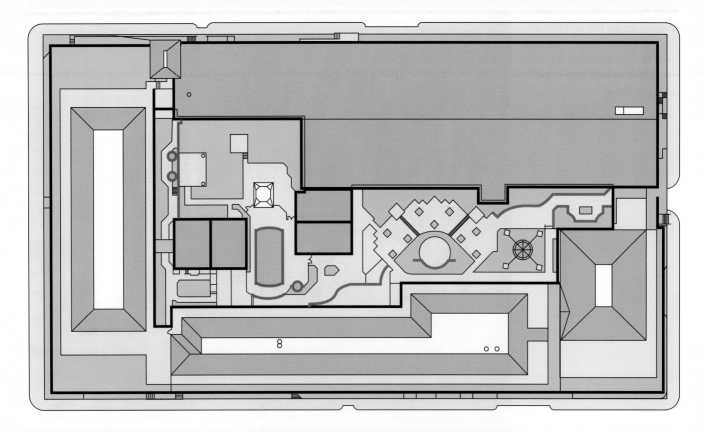

Site plan.

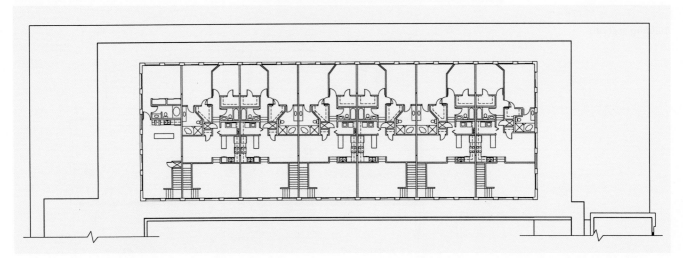

Penthouse floor plan (partial).

Project Data: The Cotton Mill

Land Use and Building Information

Site Area	2.836 acres
Total Dwelling Units	287
Gross Building Area	323,333 square feet
Gross Leasable Area	253,408 square feet
Gross Density	101 units per acre
Parking	190 off-site spaces
Parking Ratio	0.66 space per unit

Land Use Plan

	Acres	Percent of Site
Residential	1.92	68%
Recreation/Amenities	0.69	24[1]
Open Space	0.23	8[2]
Total	2.84	100%

Residential Unit Information

Unit Type	Unit Size (Square Feet)	Number of Units	Rent or Price Range
Efficiency	639	27	$722
1-Bedroom	580–1,515	162	$655–1,712
2-Bedroom	984	66	$1,112
3-Bedroom	1,551	14	$1,753
Rooftop Condominium	1,545	18	$235,000–$384,250

Development Cost Information

Site Costs

Site acquisition	$3,513,000
Site improvement	500,000

Construction Costs	20,358,000
Soft Costs	7,839,000
Total Development Cost	$32,210,000
Total Development Cost per Apartment	$112,230
Construction Cost per Square Foot	$100

Developer

Historic Restoration, Inc.
210 Baronne Street
Suite 1717
New Orleans, Louisiana 70112
504–566–0204

Architect

HRI Group
210 Baronne Street
Suite 210
New Orleans, Louisiana 70112
504–679–5040

Contractor

HCI Construction & Design
210 Baronne Street
Suite 210
New Orleans, Louisiana 70112
504–679–5040

Development Schedule

10/1996	Site purchased
10/1996	Construction started
6/1997	Leasing and sales started
2/1998	First closing
7/1999	Leasing and sales completed

Notes

[1] Interior courtyard.

[2] Exterior green space.

Denver Dry Goods Building

Denver, Colorado

The historic six-story Denver Dry Goods Building, built in 1888 in downtown Denver, has been renovated for affordable and market-rate housing, retail, and office uses. The building's 350,000 square feet of space was subdivided and repackaged using 23 different financing sources.

For nearly 100 years, the Denver Dry Goods department store served as the retail heart of downtown Denver. Built in 1888 and enlarged three times over the years, the 350,000-square-foot Denver Dry was the city's premier department store for generations of Denver residents. But fortunes changed, and in 1987 the building was sold and the store closed.

With the beloved Denver Dry facing reincarnation as a parking lot, the Denver Urban Renewal Authority (DURA) stepped in and purchased the building in 1988. After several false starts, DURA selected the Affordable Housing Development Corporation (AHDC) as project developer, and together DURA and AHDC have managed to resurrect the Denver Dry, fashioning it into a vibrant mixed-use project of affordable and market-rate housing, retail stores, and office space. The key to the Denver Dry's resurrection was an echo of its past: just as the building was built in increments, so its reconstruction and reuse were accomplished piece by piece. The mammoth structure was broken down, figuratively and legally, into smaller condominium units to provide for more manageable and "financeable" packages for development. The smaller, separate housing, retail, and office units could be planned and then variously repackaged for financing and construction.

The Site and Building

The Denver Dry Goods Building occupies the entire frontage of California Street from 15th Street to 16th Street. Strategically located where the 16th Street Pedestrian/Transitway Mall joins the light-rail system, which began operations in fall 1994, the Denver Dry also links the convention center, retail business district, and downtown hotels.

The Denver Dry Goods Building was erected as a three-story structure occupying half of the California Street frontage closest to 16th Street. The red brick, sandstone, and limestone structure was designed by Frank D. Edbrooks, architect of several notable Denver buildings, including the historic Brown Palace Hotel. In 1898, a fourth story was added to the original structure, and in 1906, a six-story addition was constructed on the 15th Street side of the original building. During the last ex-

pansion in 1924, an additional two stories were constructed on top of the original building, which became the location of the Denver Tearoom.

Development Process

The city of Denver regarded the preservation of the Denver Dry Goods Building as critical to the health of downtown. The department store had closed, and the vacated building was becoming an eyesore and was threatened with demolition. In the depressed real estate market of the late 1980s, no private buyer emerged to save the Denver Dry. As a last resort, the city of Denver and DURA stepped in and purchased the building for $6.9 million. The city financed approximately half the purchase price, with the remainder financed by a consortium of local banks and union pension funds.

Over the next two years, several developers responded to DURA's requests for proposals, offering a variety of adaptive use schemes, including a retail mall, a hotel, an aquarium, movie theaters, and upscale housing, but none were able to obtain leasing or financing commitments.

Out of these failed attempts, however, a new concept emerged: breaking the building down into smaller pieces. Based on this concept, DURA sold two floors of the building to the Robert Waxman Camera Company, a strong local retailer that had operated in the downtown market for 30 years.

The plan that ultimately took shape provided for three development phases. Phase I consisted of 51 units of affordable and market-rate housing, 73,370 square feet of retail space, and 28,780 square feet of office space. Phase II consisted of an additional 42,000 square feet of retail space. Phase III provided 77,000 square feet of residential loft space.

Planning, Design, and Construction

The first phase of development, completed in October 1993, concentrated on the 15th Street building and one floor of the 16th Street building. Waxman's Camera and Video took over the first floor and basement of the 15th Street building. National retailer TJ Maxx committed to taking most of the second floor of the 15th Street and 16th Street buildings with the proviso that an escalator be installed to provide direct access from the street to the second floor. The remainder of the second and third floors of the 15th Street building was improved for office use, and the top three floors of the building were renovated for housing. The housing takes advantage of its high elevation and the building's large windows to afford spec-

The Denver Dry Goods Building is a landmark department store structure in the heart of downtown Denver that has been reborn as a mixed-use development including both affordable and market-rate housing.

tacular views of Denver and the Rocky Mountains beyond. Construction of this phase lasted ten months.

During Phase II, the first floor and basement of the 16th Street building were converted to retail space and leased by Media Play. Phase II took seven months to complete. The remaining portions of the 16th Street building, floors three through six, have been redeveloped into 66 for-sale residential lofts.

Renovation of the building's exterior included the removal of more than 30 layers of white lead-based paint, exposing the original orange-red brick, sandstone, and limestone surface of the building. This process took eight months to complete at a cost of $800,000. The original wood-framed windows were renovated and retrofitted with double-pane glass. In addition, new canopies and signage were installed.

The interior of the Denver Dry Goods Building was gutted (except for certain historic elements) to allow building in phases. Architectural plans for the reconfiguration of the approximately 50,000-square-foot floorplates provided for separate, dedicated elevators for the housing and office uses, reusing the existing department store elevator banks. New, direct access was provided to the second-floor retail space.

Significant fire and life safety improvements were made for the entire building during the initial phase. In addition, new HVAC and electrical systems and tenant finishes were installed for Phases I and II. Evapo-

The original four-story building, circa 1910.

rative coolers were installed in lieu of central air conditioning in the apartments, and city steam was used for heating.

For the housing component, the challenges for designers were to use the deep bays of the existing space and to bring light to the deep interiors. They solved the problems by building wide hallways with adjacent leasable storage units and providing clerestory windows to light interior bedrooms.

For the office space, the greatest challenge was to provide space for new HVAC systems while respecting the high window openings of the historic structure. Designers decided to construct dropped soffits in part of the space while maintaining the original 18-foot-high ceilings along window walls and other significant areas.

Financing

Twenty-three separate sources of funding were pieced together to finance the multiple uses and phases of the project. Financing sources included pension funds, state bond issues, tax increment bonds, HUD urban development action grants, the sale of low-income housing and historic tax credits, and loans and equity investments from public agencies and private nonprofits, private bank loans, and the developer's equity.

The development of Phase I was split between two limited partnerships: Denver Dry Retail L.P. and Denver Building Housing Ltd. The latter was responsible for the development of the 51 units of rental apartments and office space for the Denver Metro Convention and Visitors Bureau. This partnership was made up of two entities, the Federal National Mortgage Association, which purchased the tax credits that provided the equity for the deal, and the Denver Dry Development Corporation, a nonprofit 501(c)(3) corporation formed by DURA. The partnership selected AHDC and its president, Jonathan F.P. Rose, as the fee developer for these portions of the project.

The second partnership for Phase I, Denver Dry Retail L.P., was responsible for development of the entire second floor of the building, where the TJ Maxx store and office space for DURA were to be located. The Denver Dry Retail Corporation, an affiliate of AHDC, is the general partner of Denver Dry Retail L.P.

The development team for Phase II of the redevelopment consists of a single limited partnership, Denver Dry Retail II, L.P., also an affiliate of AHDC. This partner-

The first floor of the building was renovated for commercial use during the first phase of development. Clockwise from above left, the first floor before, during, and after renovation.

Renovation of the exterior of the building included the removal of more than 30 layers of white lead-based paint to expose the original orange-red brick, sandstone, and limestone facade.

ship was responsible for the development of the Media Play store in the basement and first floor of the 16th Street building.

The adaptive use of the Denver Dry Goods Building has been successful for the developers and for the city of Denver. The two national retailers that have leased space in the project are the first national large-space retailers to locate in downtown Denver in ten years. The housing component, which was fully leased in just two months, now has a 200-name waiting list and has become a catalyst for six other residential projects in downtown Denver. More generally, the renovation of the Denver Dry has acted as a catalyst for eight other historic renovation projects in downtown Denver.

Experience Gained

Although large, unconventional adaptive use projects such as the Denver Dry Goods Building may not be feasible when viewed in their entirety, redefining the project into smaller components and packages may allow for a variety of development and financing options.

Housing can be a valuable partner in a commercial project by providing a 24-hour presence and stimulating an active retail environment.

A public/private partnership, such as that between DURA and AHDC, can be most successful when the approach is open on both sides and the parties work by consensus.

A typical residential unit.

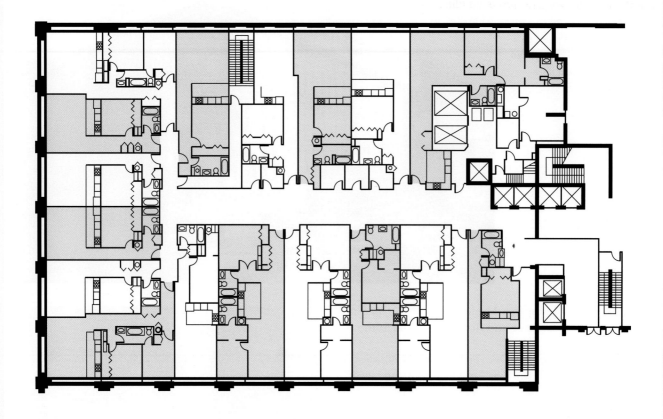

Floor plan.

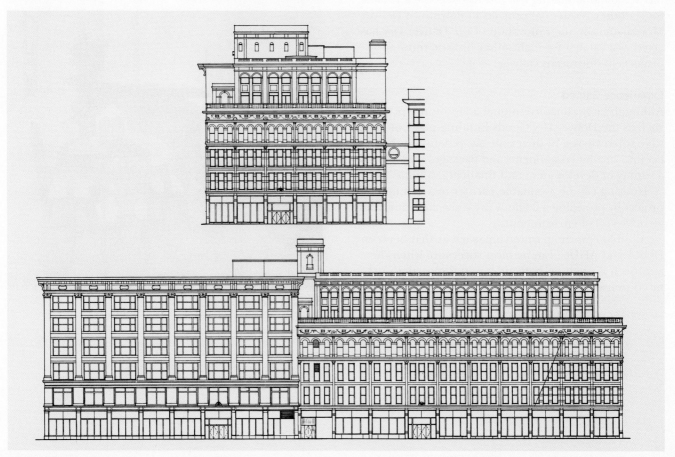

Building elevation.

Project Data: Denver Dry Goods Building

Land Use and Building Information

Site Area — 1.15 acres

Gross Building Area — 350,000 square feet

Building Plan	Square Feet
Office	28,780
Retail	115,370
Residential	124,235
Circulation and common areas	81,615
Total	350,000

Residential Unit Information

Unit Type	Unit Size (Square Feet)	Number of Units	Rent Range
Affordable			
1-Bedroom	590–950	31	$615–659
2-Bedroom	1,100–1,400	9	$775–790
Market Rate			
1-Bedroom	890–950	2	$950
2-Bedroom	1,100–1,265	9	$1,195–1,325
Total		51	

Commercial Tenant Information

Average Annual Rents

Office	$13 per square foot
Retail	$10 per square foot

Average Annual Retail Sales — $250–650 per square foot

Length and Type of Leases

Office	10–15 years full service
Retail	15–20 years triple net

Major Financing Sources

Affordable Housing Development Corporation
Bank One
City of Denver Housing Trust Council
Colorado Historical Society
Colorado Housing and Finance Authority/Bank One
Denver Dry Retail II, L.P.
Denver Urban Renewal Authority
Dominion Bank
Federal National Mortgage Association
First Bank of Republic Plaza
First Interstate Bank of Denver (Norwest)
Rocky Mountain Investors
Tax credits
United Bank of Denver
U.S. Department of Housing and Urban Development
Women's Bank

Development Cost Information

Site Costs

Site acquisition	$6,900,000[1]

Construction Costs

Superstructure	$ 8,443,000
HVAC	2,800,000
Electrical	2,120,000
Plumbing/sprinklers	1,961,600
Fees/general conditions	1,801,000
Graphics/specialties	100,000
Tenant improvements	11,367,034
Total	$28,592,634

Soft Costs

Architecture/engineering	$1,202,530
Leasing/marketing	760,769
Legal/accounting	743,356
Taxes/insurance	201,773
Construction interest and fees	1,589,719
Other	3,071,010[2]
Total	$7,569,157

Total Development Cost — $43,061,791

Sponsor

Denver Urban Renewal Authority
1555 California Street
Suite 200
Denver, Colorado 80202
303–534–3872

Developer

Affordable Housing Development Corporation
33 Katonah Avenue
Katonah, New York 10536
914–232–1396

Architect

Urban Design Group
1621 18th Street
Suite 200
Denver, Colorado 80202
303–292–3388

Development Schedule

7/1988	Site purchased
7/1988	Planning started
1/1993	Construction started
7/1993	Sales/leasing started
10/1993	Phase I completed
5/1994	Phase II completed
8/1999	Phase III completed

Notes

[1] Includes $900,000 for asbestos removal.

[2] The lofts' share of the parking garage was $1,455,000.

The Exchange
New York, New York

The Exchange, located at 25 Broad Street directly across from the New York Stock Exchange in lower Manhattan's financial district, is a pioneering residential conversion project that led the way for development of a more vibrant downtown district. Before its conversion to apartments, the vintage 1899 office building was Paine Webber's corporate headquarters.

History of the Neighborhood

With an estimated 400,000 employees, the Wall Street district is the third largest commercial district in the United States. In the early 1990s, the national economy was in the midst of a slump and Wall Street was experiencing a major decline. By 1994, office buildings in the financial district had vacancy rates as high as 30 percent, accounting for an estimated 25 million square feet of space. Much of the space had become obsolete for office use and would need major renovations to be attractive to new users, even if demand were to improve. At the same time, residential vacancies throughout the city remained low and rents stayed high, averaging about $2.50 per square foot per month.

In 1996, the city formulated the Lower Manhattan Revitalization Plan, which included a tax incentive package to encourage residential conversions in the financial district. It was a rare case in which the city government, preservationists, and developers all shared common goals: in addition to stemming serious decline of the district, they sought to create a mixed-use, 24-hour community in lower Manhattan by encouraging residential development.

The tax incentive plan specifically targets residential conversions of nonresidential buildings in lower Manhattan for an exemption and abatement from property taxes. For a landmark building like 25 Broad Street, the plan exempts the assessed value of the conversion from property taxes for 13 years at 100 percent for the first nine years and allows declining abatements for the next four. In addition, the existing assessed base is exempt from taxes for ten years, with declining exemptions for the next four years.

Because of the city's and developers' common goals, the city was extremely helpful in facilitating conversions. In addition to creating the tax incentives, the city formed the Alliance for Downtown New York, a partnership between business and government that administers the downtown business improvement district. The city eliminated obsolete zoning that would have prohibited residential conversions and assisted with day-to-day operations, such as street cleaning and trash removal.

Development Concept

Crescent Heights is a national firm that specializes in high-rise multifamily properties, particularly high-end conversions and rehabilitations. The partnership has completed several landmark residential rehabilitations in southern California and south Florida. The Exchange is the firm's only project in New York.

Partners of Crescent Heights purchased 25 Broad in October 1994, before the tax incentives came into effect. They believed that the property was so undervalued at that time that even storage space would be an economically viable use for the property. Once the tax program came about, it was the major factor that determined the new use for the property. It should become residential and, more specifically, rental residential property, so that the tax credits would remain with the owner/developer.

It took owners of the Exchange 18 months to secure financing. Finally, after the city's tax credit plan was in place, CS First Boston agreed to finance the project, granting the first large-scale construction loan in lower Manhattan in many years.

Turning the financial district into a residential neighborhood posed a number of challenges. It lacked the retail and other services found in other residential neighborhoods in Manhattan. Many people found it aesthetically unattractive as well, lacking the desirable views and streetscapes found in other neighborhoods.

To compensate for these disadvantages, Crescent Heights's strategy was to offer a product that would be both better and cheaper than the competition. The goal was to create a residential product that offered more spacious units and was aesthetically superior and more affordable than high-quality apartments in the more established neighborhoods of Manhattan. Crescent Heights's managers realized that this newly developing neighborhood would draw residents only if they found the project superior in every way to those in established neighborhoods. Further, if the project did succeed, it would spur other nearby conversion projects and would then compete with others right in the neighborhood. Therefore, it was crucial that the project remain very competitive for the long term.

Design and Renovation

The Exchange is a 21-story, 376,000-square-foot building originally constructed as an office building between 1897 and 1899. It was one of the first skyscrapers ever constructed, with a modern elevator system and steel frame supporting non-load-bearing masonry walls. At the time,

This historic 1899 office building located in Manhattan's financial district was converted to residential units in the mid-1990s using a city tax credit plan to encourage such conversions.

it was the most valuable building in New York. Originally designed by the architectural firm of Clinton & Russell, the building is Italianate style with intricate limestone garlands and other carvings adorning its stately facade. Hand-carved fluted columns flank the grand Broad Street entrance.

The original lobby has been restored. Granite floors and marble walls with pilasters topped with gilded Corinthian capitals create an opulent setting. Coffered ceilings are outlined with carved friezes. Twin marble staircases at one end of the lobby take visitors to the second floor leasing office. Of the original elevators, 12 were removed to create additional floor space. Five remaining elevators were refurbished with mahogany paneling. An oval concierge desk in the lobby's center houses security cameras and staff. During most of the day, one doorman attends the entrances; two are stationed there at rush hours. Amenities include a video rental room, a valet, a concierge, a well-equipped gym, two executive-quality conference rooms, and a rooftop sundeck.

Upper floors have been carved into 345 units ranging from studio to three-bedroom apartments. Units range from 735 to 2,931 square feet. All new electrical, plumbing, and HVAC systems were installed throughout the building. The new state-of-the art telecommunications system includes high-speed Internet access for every apartment and a building-wide intranet system.

Each floor has a laundry room, although three-bedroom units have their own laundry rooms. Each floor contains approximately 16 units. One of the building's major drawbacks was the lack of desirable views. Many of the apartments face only narrow, canyon-like spaces at the center of the building or between adjacent buildings. The developer compensated for unattractive views by making the units themselves as appealing as possible. Units are large by urban standards, with ceilings as high as 16 feet, and contain quality architectural detailing such as deep baseboard moldings and raised-panel doors. All units feature parquet wood flooring in living areas and ceramic flooring in kitchens and bathrooms. Typical one-bedroom units are 800 square feet, compared with the more typical 650 square feet in most New York apartments. Bathrooms are unusually large and include two sinks. Pocket doors close off the bath area from what can serve as a powder room for guests. Most units have walk-in closets.

The building's retail space is leased to Vine Restaurant, Market, and Catering. The establishment includes a 55-seat restaurant and gourmet market on the street level and a 7,000-square-foot catering space in the original bank vaults in the lower level of the building, all of which are attractive amenities for the building's residents as well as the surrounding neighborhood.

Landmark Status

The building was placed on the National Register of Historic Places in April 1998 and has been designated by the New York City Landmarks Preservation Commission as a historic property. Placement on the National Register makes the building eligible for certain tax credits as well as ensures that the historic structure will be preserved.

Upper-floor windows were replaced with more energy-efficient units of the same style. Carved limestone garlands grace the refurbished windows of the lower floors.

The richly detailed granite and marble lobby was restored to its original opulence.

Marketing and Management

The Exchange's major initial market attractions were its large units, high quality, and relative affordability. Occupancy has remained near 100 percent since initial lease-up. No advertising has been necessary. The Exchange is one of the few rental apartment buildings in Manhattan that is 100 percent market rate and not subject to rent control.

The philosophy of management for the Exchange is to provide the level of service and amenities of a quality hotel along with top-notch surroundings. The developer initially believed the building, as the pioneering project in the neighborhood, had to be outstanding to attract residents to a newly developing neighborhood. Once the neighborhood became more established, it remained important for the building to be outstanding to remain competitive with new entries to the market. The Exchange continues to strive to remain the most exclusive building in the Wall Street neighborhood, while maintaining the value of its units.

Experience Gained

One of the major factors of success is to be first in and first out. By being the pioneer developer in a neighborhood, a purchaser can take advantage of deflated property values. Although the risks are greater, so is the potential for profitability. Crescent Heights paid about $10 per square foot for the building. Developers who came later to the Wall Street area paid $30 or more per square foot, greatly reducing the potential for profit. Construction costs for historic rehabilitation projects are difficult to gauge beforehand, because it is impossible to determine many of the structural factors until work begins. Construction costs for the Exchange ended up over budget; the developer would thus recommend negotiating a construction contract for a guaranteed maximum cost.

The owners expected to draw singles or couples who worked in the financial district, but this sector has made up only about half the residents. Management also reports a surprising number of families are drawn to the

Twin marble staircases lead to the second-floor leasing office.

building because of the large units and relative affordability compared with similar quality units in uptown neighborhoods. The building has also drawn reverse commuters who prefer city life even though they may not work in the neighborhood.

At this point, the neighborhood is still in transition. The financial district suffers from massive buildings on long blocks, which are not conducive to the small first-level retail spaces necessary for pedestrian activity. The kinds of urban amenities that draw residents to more settled neighborhoods are still lacking. But the situation is improving. Some restaurants, retailers, and services have moved into the neighborhood, and the city, working with the Alliance for Downtown, continues its efforts to transform downtown into a 24-hour neighborhood.

A rooftop sundeck with a view of Manhattan is one of the Exchange's amenities.

Corridors are spacious and elegantly appointed.

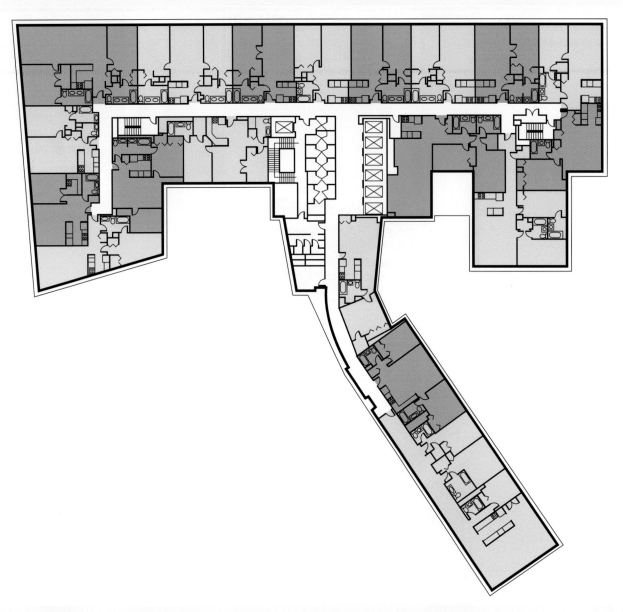

Building floor plan.

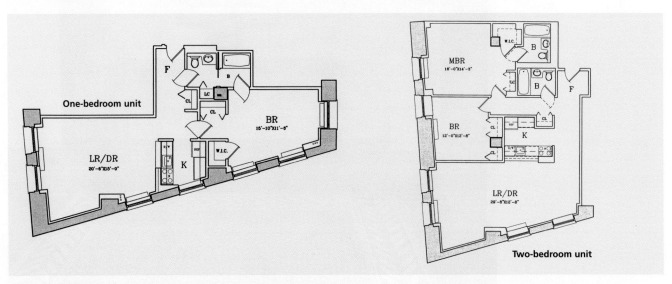

One-bedroom unit

LR/DR
20'-6"X15'-0"

K

BR
15'-10"X11'-8"

F

B

CL

LC

CL

W.I.C.

REF

MBR
16'-0"X14'-3"

W.I.C.

B

B

LC

F

BR
12'-0"X12'-8"

CL

REF

K

CL

LR/DR
29'-8"X12'-8"

Two-bedroom unit

Typical unit floor plans.

Project Data: The Exchange

Land Use and Building Information

Site Area	25,000 square feet
Building Gross Square Feet	525,000
Rentable Square Feet	376,092
Total Dwelling Units	345

Residential Unit Information

Unit Type	Unit Size (Square Feet)	Number of Units	Rent Range
Studio	735–922	2	$2,000–3,100
1-Bedroom	683–1,042	177	$2,000–4,200
2-Bedroom	927–1,533	145	$2,500–4,500
3-Bedroom	2,554–2,931	21	$4,800–10,000

Developer/Owner

Crescent Heights
555 NE 15th Street
Miami, Florida 33132
305–374–5700

Architect

Costas Kondylis & Associates
3 West 18th Street
New York, New York 10011
212–727–8688

Development Schedule

10/1994	Property purchased
8/1996	Construction started
4/1997	Rental started
1/1998	Project completed

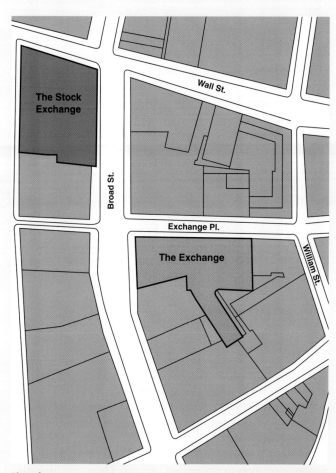

Site plan.

The Colony at Fashion Island

Newport Beach, California

The Colony at Fashion Island sits in the heart of Newport Center in Newport Beach, Orange County, California, toward the southern end of the greater Los Angeles metropolitan area. Newport Center is a mixed-use development that is part of the Irvine Ranch, one of the nation's largest master-planned communities, a 90-square-mile development that includes the cities of Irvine, Newport Beach, and Tustin Ranch. Irvine Ranch was developed and is owned by the Irvine Company. The mixed-use Newport Center includes offices, hotels, restaurants, and a premier retail center, Fashion Island, a mall with 200 stores, 40 restaurants, and two multiplex theaters. Irvine Apartment Communities (IAC), an affiliate of the Irvine Company, developed and built the Colony.

The Colony represents the first high-density luxury apartment complex developed by IAC. The company wanted to capitalize on the exclusivity of the Fashion Island address and thus included "Fashion Island" in the property's name. The property is also the first residential development built in recent years in the Newport Center complex. The Colony at Fashion Island fills a need for housing in this area of high-tech industry and commercial development.

Site and Development Process

The property was the only parcel zoned for residential development in Newport Center. The approval process was fairly routine, and the site required no unusual infrastructure or grading. With height restricted to 100 feet, it would have been permissible to construct a ten-story building, but IAC believed that low rises would appeal best to residents of a rental property. Moreover, designers decided a low profile would enhance the natural landscape. To minimize the visual impact of the parking, they designed a partially underground garage.

IAC understood that the concept and marketing strategy for the Colony would have to be different. The units would have to be considerably larger than the company's standard apartment units. The Colony's floor plans average 200 square feet larger than IAC's typical apartment units, ranging from 1,008 square feet for the smallest one-bedroom unit to 1,546 square feet for a two-bedroom unit with den. IAC also understood that the project would require top-notch amenities in luxury surroundings.

Project Design and Architecture

The Colony is a 245-unit low-rise, infill apartment complex consisting of four elevator buildings, each four stories tall.

The contemporary stucco apartment buildings surround a large clubhouse with a generous pool and spa; a separate health club is also among the amenities. The complex features a mix of six floor plans, including one-bedroom, one-bedroom-plus-den, two-bedroom, and two-bedroom-plus-den units. All 612 assigned parking spaces are in a two-level parking structure located partially below grade, a new concept for IAC. Thus, no surface parking lots mar the site plan.

The project features four different themed courtyards, each accessed by a two-story archway. The courtyards provide a neighborhood identity for each building in the complex, creating the feel of small communities. Each theme is carried out in fountains, artwork, and pavement materials.

- The pavement in Beach Court is reminiscent of ocean waves, with alternating paving materials in a wave pattern. A fountain features bronze dolphins.
- The nature-inspired theme of San Joaquin Hills Court emulates the surrounding coastal hillsides. Artwork depicts scenes of the hills from the 1930s. The grand fountain features native plants and rock gardens.
- The casual, rustic atmosphere of Back Bay Courtyard is inspired by the nearby marshlands. The court includes bronze sculpture and other art depicting local plant and animal life.
- Fashion Island Courtyard reflects the plazas and paseos found at the adjacent Fashion Island retail mall that the project was named for. In contrast to the others, this court is urban in feel, with paving and landscaping organized in a grid and the lighting and fountain more contemporary in design.

Amenities and Services

A wealth of amenities and services make up the luxury lifestyle package at the Colony. A full-time concierge is on staff to arrange everything from valet service, restaurant reservations, and theater tickets to catering and travel assistance. Daily or weekly maid service and handyman services are available. When residents travel, they can rely on the on-site staff to walk their dogs and pick up mail and newspapers.

Security is enhanced by a staffed entry gate with a monitoring system for guests' access. The units also include alarm systems. Other amenities include a resort-style clubhouse with catering kitchen, 24-hour fitness center with personal trainer and fitness classes, an outdoor junior Olympic pool, and a Jacuzzi with hotel-like

The Colony at Fashion Island is a luxury apartment building in the mixed-use development of Newport Center, part of the 90-square-mile Irvine Ranch master-planned community.

services, including pool towels and beverages. Unlike most low-rise projects, the Colony has elevators.

Each unit is assigned two reserved garage parking spaces. All apartment units have windows on at least two sides, and the largest floor plan has windows on all four sides, offering attractive views in all directions. Units include alarm systems, six telephone lines, and high-speed Internet access. Gourmet kitchens feature gas cooktops and microwaves. No refrigerator is pro-

vided because residents generally prefer to purchase their own.

Units have generous walk-in closets, a separate laundry area with a full-sized washer and dryer, gas fireplaces, and nine-foot ceilings. A program initiated at the Colony allows residents to customize their units. At an on-site home decorating center, residents may select custom options, including upgrades for flooring, window treatments, custom closet fittings, and moldings.

Four different themed courtyards help provide a neighborhood identity for each building and create the feeling of small communities.

The developer opted for a low-rise, four-story design to enhance the surrounding landscape and appeal to high-end renters.

Courtesy of Irvine Apartment Communities

The Colony's apartment units feature large windows affording plenty of natural light and attractive views.

Courtesy of Irvine Apartment Communities

Marketing and Management

IAC is among the largest owners and operators of multi-family properties in Orange County. The company began developing apartment communities in 1969. After three decades of developing projects exclusively at Irvine Ranch, the firm has now expanded into other regions of the state, including Silicon Valley, San Diego County, and West Los Angeles. The company now owns and manages 71 rental apartment communities totaling 24,000 units.

IAC is currently a wholly owned subsidiary of the Irvine Company. In 1996 and 1997, when IAC was developing the Colony, the firm was a publicly held REIT, but in 1998, the Irvine Company bought back the stock it did not own. IAC is headquartered in Newport Beach, California.

Marketing the Colony began in July 1997, about six months before the anticipated opening of the project. IAC operated an apartment-locating center, where housing specialists could refer prospective renters to the prop-

erty. An on-site leasing trailer attracted more attention. Flags, signage, and landscaping were used to capture the attention of drive-by traffic, resulting in about 50 to 60 prospects per week.

The property also was advertised in newspapers and local magazines and promoted through press releases. *The Orange County Register* published a feature article on the project in the Sunday real estate section. Advertising and other materials created the local buzz that the Colony would be the first luxury apartment property built in the area since the early 1990s. IAC held a VIP event for community leaders, including the mayor, city council, and owners of local businesses, and an open house for realtors and brokers. IAC offers a broker referral service to local agents, with a 3 percent commission to brokers who bring in a lease. All these efforts paid off, resulting in a waiting list of 1,800 prospective residents.

The waiting list was whittled down to about 800 serious prospects. Information on the project, including floor

The contemporary stucco buildings surround a large clubhouse with a generous pool and spa.

The clubhouse provides comfortable space for socializing.

plans, was sent to those prospects soon after rents were established. IAC had to further pare down the waiting list and sent letters asking for a deposit of $1,000. The $1,000 deposit was a departure from IAC's usual policy, which was to collect a deposit of $100. Prospects were given a deadline to make the deposit after seeing models and choosing the floor plan they wanted, and then were given three days to change their minds. Those who returned a deposit were considered priority candidates for the units of their choice. The strategy worked well. Those who sent in $1,000 were strongly interested in renting a unit, and no significant cancellations were reported.

Lease-up averaged 20 units per month, with regular rent increases along the way. Because interest in the project was so overwhelming, IAC was able to pare down the advertising budget, even pulling scheduled ads from local news media.

The primary target market was empty nesters, with professional singles and couples viewed as a secondary market. At lease-up, about 60 percent of the residents were over the age of 45, and 32 percent were between 26 and 45. About 45 percent were single-person households, and 31 percent were married couples. The remainder were unmarried couples or roommates. Nearly 70 percent had incomes over $100,000, with the average household income $195,000. Today, there has been very little turnover. The average income of renters is $210,000.

Management Philosophy

IAC is dedicated to quality in design and construction. Because the firm retains ownership of all the projects it develops, it has a vested interest in their long-term profitability. At the Colony, service became a crucial element

Formal public areas are enhanced by inlaid marble flooring, brass railings, and elegant furnishings.

Courtesy of Irvine Apartment Communities

of concern as well. IAC decided to provide hotel-level customer service in an environment of luxury. A wide range of services provides the Colony's residents with everything they need and want.

Experience Gained

IAC's policies and procedures had to be reexamined for the Colony because of the anticipated upscale clientele. Enhanced customer service was necessary to fulfill residents' high expectations. IAC found the experience gained at the Colony, in what was a new type of market for the firm, useful in developing and leasing other high-end properties.

In retrospect, IAC believes that demand existed for larger, more expensive units and that it undersold the project, not capturing the high-end market to the fullest extent possible. Officials think that including a more up-

scale penthouse-type unit would have helped to capture an even higher-end market niche.

The custom decorating program turned out to be an extremely popular way for renters to personalize and upgrade their units. About 30 percent of tenants have had custom features added to their units, ranging from window treatments to laminate flooring.

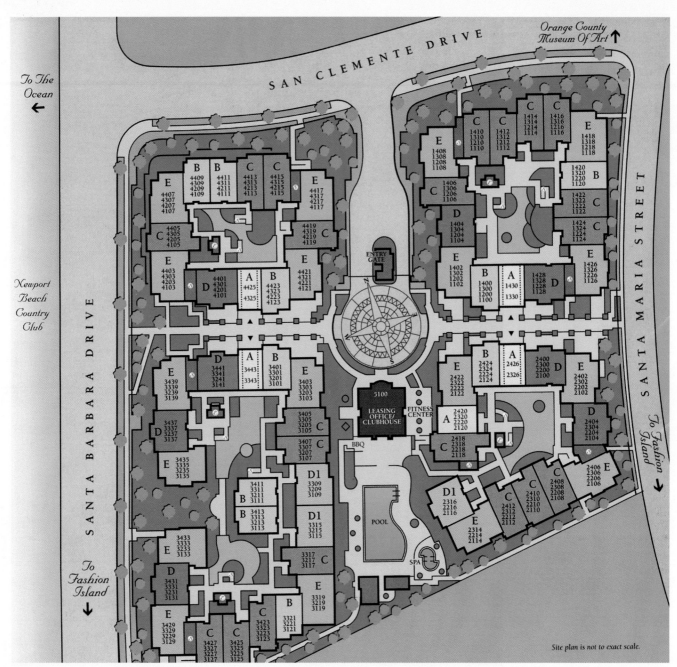

Site plan.

Project Data: The Colony at Fashion Island

Land Use and Building Information

Site Area	6.4 acres
Total Dwelling Units	245
Gross Density	40 units per acre
Off-Street Parking Spaces	612[1]

Residential Unit Information

Unit Type	Unit Size (Square Feet)	Number of Units	Rent Range at Lease-Up
1-Bedroom/1-Bath	1,008	12	$1,600–1,675
1-Bedroom/1-Bath + Den	1,087	39	$1,725–2,125
2-Bedroom/2-Bath	1,273–1,414	124	$1,885–3,445
2-Bedroom/2-Bath + Den	1,546	70	$2,635–4,760

Development Cost Information

Construction Cost	$25,000,000
Construction Cost per Square Foot	$75.77
Construction Cost per Unit	$102,040

Owner/Developer

Irvine Apartment Communities
550 Newport Center Drive
Suite 300
Newport Beach, California 92660
949–720–5500

Architect

McLarand, Vasquez & Partners
695 Town Center Drive
Suite 300
Costa Mesa, California 92626
949–809–3300

Property Manager

Irvine Apartment Management Company
8 Executive Circle
Irvine, California 92614
949–862–6400

Builder

Regis Contractors
2111 Palomar Airport Road
Carlsbad, California 92009
760–918–0400

Development Schedule

1/1995	Planning started
8/1996	Site purchased
8/1996	Construction started
7/1997	Rental started
5/1998	Project completed

Note
[1]Subterranean carport.

Franciscan Village

Lemont, Illinois

A 33-acre continuing-care retirement community (CCRC) developed and managed by the Franciscan Sisters of Chicago, Franciscan Village is targeted for middle-income seniors. The project provides a continuum of housing options, ranging from cottages for independent living to acute-care nursing facilities, allowing residents to continue living at Franciscan Village as they age and their needs change. The project was carefully designed to afford residents a seamless transition from independent living to more comprehensive care. The development fulfills the Franciscan Sisters' traditional mission of serving the aged while filling an underserved market niche of middle-income retirees. The campus-like setting provides a range of personal services, including convenience shopping, a library, a bank, exercise facilities, and restaurant-style dining facilities.

Located in Lemont, Illinois, a small town about 30 miles outside Chicago, Franciscan Village is sponsored and managed by the Franciscan Sisters of Chicago. The project includes 50 single-story cottages known as coach homes, 150 independent-living apartments, and 30 assisted-living apartments known as the Village Inn. It also includes the Mother Theresa Home, a 150-bed skilled-nursing facility. The Village Inn, the independent-living apartments, and Mother Theresa Home are connected by a mall that provides direct access to the common areas of the campus. The mall features a convenience shop, restaurant-style dining facilities, deli, library, bank, beauty/barber shop, activity rooms, exercise facilities, and the heart of the Franciscan Village campus, the St. Francis of Assisi Chapel.

Franciscan Village and the Mother Theresa Home thrive in part because of the Franciscan Sisters' commitment to serving the senior community beyond simply providing long-term care. Through management and operations, the sisters also promote the concept of a "community of companionship and caring" to alleviate the trauma seniors often feel when they are uprooted from their homes of many years and go through various phases of their mature life. The sisters played a pivotal role in the development of Franciscan Village, ensuring that their philosophy and vision were implemented in every aspect of the project.

Site and History

The history of Franciscan Village begins with the Mother Theresa Home, which before 1964 existed as a convent for the Franciscan Sisters of Chicago. In 1963, in keeping with the sisters' mission of serving the elderly, the convent was converted into a nursing home for 57 residents; it served as the local intermediate-care facility for some 25 years. The new construction project included the building of a new Mother Theresa Home and increasing the number of nursing beds to 150. Upon evaluating the site and infrastructure, the sisters determined it would be more feasible to build a new assisted-living facility than to renovate the existing structure. It also would allow for more efficient operations and use of space than the original building.

After studying three different sites, the sisters determined that the Lemont site was most suitable. At the time, the site was located just outside Lemont in unincorporated rural Cook County, occupying five acres surrounded by undeveloped green fields. The rural location would provide a country-like environment, although redevelopment would require additional land as well as a new drainage and water retention system. The existing building was left vacant with the intention of converting it into an assisted-living unit. Development of the retirement facility balanced environmental and economic concerns.

The sisters asked O'Donnell Wicklund Pigozzi and Peterson Architects, Inc. (OWP&P), to prepare several possible concepts for the site. They decided to develop a facility for moderate-income seniors that would serve not only the sick elderly but also healthy seniors, and from that decision came the idea of building an entire campus to house seniors throughout their mature lives. The result is now a 33-acre CCRC graced with mature trees that has a small-town feel and European ambience. The park-like setting features landscaped areas throughout, flowering gardens, and a gazebo.

Planning and Development

Development of Franciscan Village began in 1987, at a time when the idea of a CCRC was relatively new to the area. Being unfamiliar with the idea, the townspeople initially resisted development; they were concerned about the project's density, public safety, use of community resources, and parking. Planning therefore entailed a great deal of community outreach and education.

The sisters shared their vision and goals for the CCRC at a public meeting that was followed by a series of informational and educational sessions with the village planning board, architects, and county administrators. The sessions occurred regularly until construction began, by which time community residents and officials were quite supportive of the concept and the plans for the CCRC.

Unlike many CCRC developments, the nursing facility at Franciscan Village was the first phase of the project to be completed.

The local community's acceptance led to approval of the project by Cook County, which at that time had jurisdiction over unincorporated Lemont Township.

The Franciscan Sisters resolved to complete the Mother Theresa Home first because the need for a skilled-nursing facility was most acute. In this respect, the development of Franciscan Village was unusual. Typically, housing is completed first, with the promise of a nursing facility to follow, which often never does. Also significant was the phasing of the development, which allowed the sisters and the development team to accommodate and adjust to new legislation and regulations that came into effect during construction. Phasing also allowed for continual redesign to accommodate growth and change.

Although development was carried out in four individual phases, the overall process was continuous. Phase I included development of the Mother Theresa Home and the construction of some of the coach homes, which were

Franciscan Village features a range of life-care housing options. Independent-living cottages to skilled-nursing facilities allow residents to age in place. The design of Franciscan Village strives to provide a seamless transition for its residents as they move to different levels of care.

built in clusters. Phase II saw completion of the mall, 78 apartments, and the remainder of the coach homes. The assisted-living units and the administrative offices for the Village Inn were completed during Phase III. The final phase included the completion of 72 additional independent-living apartments.

Design

The Franciscan Sisters selected OWP&P to design the project because of the firm's experience in designing housing for aging populations. The sisters knew exactly what they wanted, and the architects helped them realize their vision. It was thus a partnership in which the sisters were involved in every step of the design, and their hands-on approach greatly influenced the look and feel of the village.

The design was driven by program and service requirements, the need for efficient operations, and aesthetics. Specifically, facilities on campus were designed to look and feel like home, regardless of residents' functional capacity. In this respect, a seamless design was an important feature of the village in both exteriors and interiors. The sisters wanted to ensure that no disruption or trauma would be associated with residents' moving to a different type of dwelling.

Continuity and consistency are evident in the color scheme and materials used in the village. The facade of the mall, the Village Inn, the apartment units, and the Mother Theresa Home are built of red brick, colored concrete, and cream and yellow stucco, while the coach homes are covered in cream-colored vinyl siding. Most interiors feature similar colors, design, and lighting throughout, using neutral finishes. The common areas, such as the library and dining halls, use light tones for surface treatments as well as rich solid and patterned accents. The corridors in the residential units have individual color schemes so that they can be easily distinguished from the common areas. Brighter, more intense colors are used in the acute-care areas, creating contrast

for the benefit of residents who may have diminished visual acuity. In addition to visual continuity, physical continuity is created by connecting all residences to the mall and chapel.

Still, the various facilities are distinct and independent, and each has its own points of entry and control. The coach homes and apartments surround the mall in clusters, promoting residents' privacy while making them feel part of the community.

The design of the village took into consideration the importance of natural light and neutral colors, privacy, and common spaces. Because most residents would spend a significant amount of time in their units, it was decided to provide more private than common space. The mall features a three-story octagonal atrium finished with beige walls and white mill work that provides access to all common areas; the main dining hall, which seats 80, features large windows and French doors to provide plenty of natural light. The library, adjacent to the atrium, is distinguished by upholstered seating, a marble fireplace, and boldly patterned wallpaper.

Marketing

The Franciscan Sisters, who had no experience in marketing, relied on their reputation and experience and on the community's trust to market Franciscan Village. Although the sisters initially hired a marketing consultant, they subsequently assumed the task themselves, taking their cues from potential residents and demographic trends as they continuously implemented the most appropriate responses to issues and changes affecting seniors.

The sisters have created a market niche for the village by offering a variety of levels of care in rental units to middle-income seniors, most of whom cannot afford the life-care housing contracts often associated with CCRCs and assisted-living facilities. The sisters developed one of the first CCRCs in Illinois to provide rental housing to seniors at various levels of dependence in a campus setting at an affordable price.

The most successful marketing, according to the sisters, was through word of mouth. As a result of the monthly information and education sessions held throughout the planning and development process, the community gained a great deal of understanding of and trust in the sisters' mission. Many of the attendees were children of seniors for whom the campus was being planned. Following the meetings, potential residents and their family members exchanged information about Franciscan Village, which also was available through print media.

The sisters' greatest marketing asset is their outstanding reputation; they are well known throughout Chicago and the surrounding area for their knowledge, dedication, and provision of quality care to seniors. Reflecting that reputation, occupancy reached 96 percent within 13 months and typically lingers at around 98 percent. In addition, the Mother Theresa Home was awarded the Illinois Governor's Award for Excellence in social programming in 1991 and the Theresa Dudzik Service Award in 1993 for its outstanding interdisciplinary team approach to the overall health and well-being of residents.

Operations and Management

Franciscan Village is composed of two separate corporations. The Mother Theresa Home, Inc., is a skilled-nursing facility regulated and licensed by the state of Illinois, while Franciscan Village operates as an independent housing corporation. Though legally separate, they share services and facilities. The Village Mall is known as the campus "bridge," bringing management facilities and services together in one central location. All residents share the common areas throughout the mall, including the deli, dining halls, chapel, barber/beauty shop, and kitchen, and the human resources department, finance department, and administrative and residential offices located on the first level of the Village Inn serve the entire campus.

Sharing services and facilities has been economically feasible in most respects. The sisters consider the campus as a whole when planning and operating the facilities,

while providing individual attention and care to the various segments of the resident population. Despite the dual management structure, all residents are admitted to either the village or the Mother Theresa Home. Applicants are screened for suitability for and compatibility with the facility and with respect to established health and financial parameters. They undergo a personal interview, which includes questions about their desire to live in the village. A fee is required to secure a unit or dwelling on campus. Internal and external waiting lists are maintained for admittance to Franciscan Village and the Mother Theresa Home, but priority is given to current residents who wish to move to another level of care. If no units are available, potential residents are referred to another facility for seniors in the area for temporary placement. Village staff contact potential residents on the waiting list monthly.

Regardless of dwelling type, financial dealings are with Franciscan Village only; no outside sources or agencies fund the operation. The coach homes require a monthly service fee of $911 and a 90 percent refundable entrance fee of $79,000. This entrance fee, required only for the coach homes, is among the lowest in the area. The 960-square-foot homes are single level, with two bedrooms and two bathrooms, eat-in kitchens, attached patios, laundries, and garages. The monthly service fee ensures that residents receive security services, home and lawn maintenance, transportation, an emergency response system, planned social events and activities, semiannual cleaning, and all utilities except telephone and cable television.

The apartments include efficiencies and one- and two-bedroom units ranging from 468 to 950 square feet. The 150 units offer individual entrances, lounge areas, on-site laundry facilities, and patios or porches on each floor. In addition, residents have direct access to the mall, the Village Inn, and the Mother Theresa Home. Monthly service fees range from $1,193 for the smallest efficiency to $2,183 for the largest two-bedroom apartments. This fee includes the main meal each day in the dining rooms,

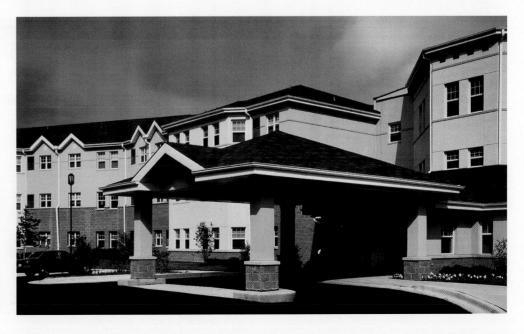

The exteriors of the mall, Village Inn, apartment units, and nursing facility are clad in red brick and cream and yellow stucco.

security services, transportation, biweekly housekeeping, social events and activities, an emergency response system, maintenance, and all utilities except cable television and telephone. A second occupant pays an additional monthly fee of $350. Patios and storage facilities are an additional $15 each per month.

Offering 30 private efficiencies ranging from 323 to 438 square feet, the Village Inn assisted-living apartments carry a monthly service fee of $2,048 to $2,213, depending on the size of the unit. The fee includes all the services offered to those in the apartments plus three meals daily and a 24-hour snack service, reminders to take medication, access to assistance if necessary 24 hours a day, seven days a week, and weekly housekeeping services. A $550 monthly fee is assessed for a second occupant in the unit.

The Mother Theresa Home provides comprehensive, licensed care to 150 residents, who are charged a daily rate that is assessed monthly. Accommodations include a private or semiprivate furnished room, and residents receive assistance with bathing, dressing, laundry, housekeeping, and medications as well as constant evaluation and monitoring. Three levels of care are offered. The first level, known as sheltered care, is for seniors who need personal care and assistance in meeting their daily needs. The second level is intermediate care, which can be broken down further to three sublevels of care: light intermediate care for those who need daily monitoring, some nursing services, and minimal assistance with dressing, bathing, and diet; general intermediate care for those who need assistance with several daily activities and moderate supervision; and heavy intermediate care for seniors who depend on staff for the majority of their daily needs and who require rehabilitative services and a great deal of intervention and redirection. The third level of care provided is skilled care. At this level, seniors who require a licensed nurse or personnel to tend to their daily needs are offered a semiprivate or private room. This service is typically for seniors who are in a postacute phase of

an illness or are experiencing recurrence of a chronic illness.

The ultimate goal of the staff at the Mother Theresa Home is to focus on the individual's capabilities rather than disabilities, and the staff provides programs for residents and their families to promote their overall wellness. The administration is dedicated to providing restorative care, activities, pastoral care, and social services while accommodating residents' dietary, nursing, and psychosocial needs. Staff do not focus on recreation but on "re-creation," encouraging independence and social interaction.

The staff constantly evaluates residents in the village as they age. The resident services director evaluates residents to make sure they are placed in appropriate housing and receive the correct level of care. Every level of care includes internal assessments, adequate staff and nursing, available professional experts, and close working relationships with residents' families.

Franciscan Village also has a close working relationship with the surrounding community. The sisters provide educational outreach and seminars to the local community on aging and related issues, and local college interns and nursing students gain practical experience in caring for seniors at Franciscan Village, particularly the Village Inn and Mother Theresa Home. Other programs include an intergenerational volunteer program through which seniors, children, young adults, and adolescents are bought together for social interaction and programmed activities. Franciscan Village also operates a successful job training program in which Lemont High School students are trained to work in various capacities at the village.

Impact and Impressions

Franciscan Village has had a tremendous impact on the surrounding community and the development of CCRCs in general. With more than 400 residents, the town of Lemont views the village as important to its overall growth

Common areas such as the main dining hall feature pastel colors accented with rich solids and patterns. Such a palette improves livability for those with deteriorating eyesight.

Floor plan.

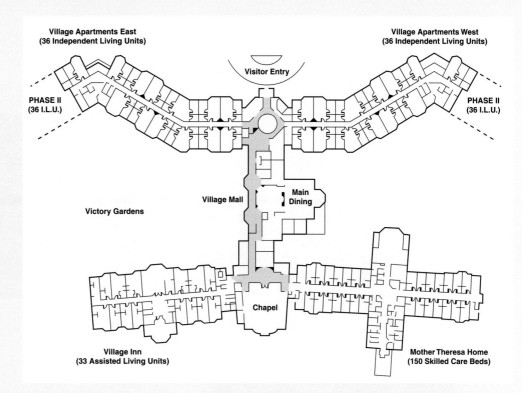

Village Apartments East
(36 Independent Living Units)

Village Apartments West
(36 Independent Living Units)

Visitor Entry

PHASE II
(36 I.L.U.)

PHASE II
(36 I.L.U.)

Main
Dining

Village Mall

Victory Gardens

Chapel

Village Inn
(33 Assisted Living Units)

Mother Theresa Home
(150 Skilled Care Beds)

and requested the village to be annexed to the town in 1994. The village provides nearly 300 local jobs; it is committed to using local vendors and services whenever possible. Its community outreach program helps educate the public on issues related to aging and serves as a training site for health care professionals and local high school students. Franciscan Village residents go into Lemont for shopping, services, and various activities, enhancing the town's economic base.

Franciscan Village has been recognized in Illinois as a model for CCRCs; other senior service providers frequently contact village staff for insight and advice. Recognized by the Retirement Research Foundation as "exemplary" in the provision of services to seniors, it also provides a social model for assisted living that allows residents to remain as independent as possible for as long as possible. The sisters maintain an open-door policy for other developers and architects interested in pursuing this model of seniors' housing development.

The Franciscan Sisters believe that having a mission and being willing to take risks are vital to the development of CCRCs and that those traits explain their success in developing Franciscan Village. The sisters chose OWP&P as the architects for Franciscan Village because of the firm's knowledge of and commitment to the seniors market. They were essential to the success of the project and to fostering the intimate involvement of all team members in all its aspects. Also critical to success was all members' flexibility throughout the development process.

Plans for future development based on current needs and Illinois demographics include the potential for additional coach homes and the expansion of health care services to serve the village and the local community through the provision of a wellness center for seniors.

In addition, a greater number of residents are being admitted with some form of dementia; the sisters therefore are looking at developing specialized units within the Mother Theresa Home to serve residents with dementia, including Alzheimer's disease. Finally, the village is exploring the possibility of offering rehabilitative and subacute-level services. The Franciscan Sisters' long-term expectations for Franciscan Village include simply serving the community and accommodating legislative and demographic changes as well as residents' needs, always remembering that the village is the place residents call home.

Experience Gained

Issues surrounding zoning and community support of the project were most problematic. The sisters engaged in a significant community outreach and education effort to gain local support.

Besides antidevelopment sentiments, several regulatory obstacles had to be overcome. When planning first began, retirement housing was considered simply another multiunit housing project. During construction, the Americans with Disabilities Act and other regulations governing assisted living became effective and had to be complied with.

Flexibility is essential in designing and developing new product types. The sisters' vision allowed for innovative design and programming to resolve issues as they arose and to plan for future regulatory constraints.

Site plan.

Project Data: Franciscan Village

Land Use and Building Information

Site Area	33 acres
Total Dwelling Units	380
Gross Density	11.5 units per acre
Off-Street Parking Spaces	270

Land Use Plan

	Acres	Percent of Site
Buildings	4.4	13.3%
Roads/Paved Areas	4.0	12.1
Common Open Space	13.6	41.2
Other	11.0	33.3
Total	33.0	100.0%

Residential Unit Information

Unit Type	Unit Size (Square Feet)	Number of Units (Planned/ Built)	Entrance Fee	Monthly Rent
Coach Homes[1]	960	62/50	$79,000	$911
Apartments[1]	468–950	200/150	0	$1,193– 2,183
Apartments[2]	323–438	45/30	0	$2,048– 2,213
Skilled-Nursing Units	–	150/150	0	Variable

Development Cost Information

Site Improvement	$2,158,000
Construction	30,036,000
Soft Costs	1,806,000
Total	$34,000,000

Annual Operating Expenses

Franciscan Village	$5,000,000
Mother Theresa Home, Inc.	$6,000,000

Financing

Tax-Exempt Bond	$24,125,000
Franciscan Sisters of Chicago Equity Contribution	$10,000,000

Developer/Manager

Franciscan Sisters of Chicago
14700 Main Street
Lemont, Illinois 60439
630–257–3994

Architect and Interior Design

O'Donnell Wicklund Pigozzi and Peterson Architects, Inc.
111 W. Washington Street
Suite 1200
Chicago, Illinois 60602
312–332–9600

Contractor

Pepper Construction Company
643 North Orleans
Chicago, Illinois 60610
312–266–4700

Other Team Members

Dickerson Engineering—electrical engineering
Brian Berg Associates—mechanical engineering
Branecki Virgilio & Associates—civil engineering
David McCullum & Associates—landscaping

Development Schedule

1987	Planning started
1989	Construction started
1989	Sales/leasing started

Notes

[1] Independent-living units.

[2] Assisted-living units.

McNeil House
Austin, Texas

Apartment developers are facing demands from residents clamoring for more technology-friendly housing. Today's two-income households typically have some form of home office and require many more data ports and the necessary wiring to accommodate high-speed Internet access and other computer-related needs. "Technology architect" has become a new specialty to meet these high standards, particularly in high-tech areas such as Silicon Valley and Austin, Texas. Nestled in the heart of Austin's high-tech area, McNeil House strikes a balance between housing the latest high-tech gadgetry and creating a cozy, home-like atmosphere. Developer Tami Siewruk took homespun images of an old farmstead and blended both high- and low-tech dimensions into a comfortable environment. Facing a tight budget, Siewruk had to make tough decisions about design and amenities. The constraints led her to find creative solutions using the highest-grade finishes, and providing amenities and the technology package desirable for residents' lifestyles.

The Site and Development Process
Austin was chosen for McNeil House because of the city's continued growth as a high-tech center and its status as one of the best places to live and work in the United States. The semirural feel of the site appeals to the market niche the developer was trying to attract; more-over, it is located near several major advanced technology employers, such as Dell Computers and Cisco Systems. Much of the area, including the site of McNeil House, was already zoned for multifamily development, and it is surrounded by numerous other multifamily properties and single-family homes.

An unusually large number of old-growth trees on the site were retained to the extent possible. The soil went down to a depth of only two to six feet; below that level was solid rock. When excavating, builders found an underground cave that had to be filled. The retention area built in the cave was designed to look like a dam. It is now planted with wildflowers, and vines have been introduced to cover the massive structure so that it appears as a natural part of the landscape.

The project's exterior amenities include a newly planted peach and pear orchard, herb and wildflower gardens, a potting shed, and a pleasure garden. The pleasure garden includes a horseshoe pit, reading grottoes, a bocce ball court, a putting green, and a rose garden. Other recreational amenities include a full-scale fitness center with personal trainer, a sports pool, and a pool pavilion with an outdoor billiard table. A business center

and an executive conference room complete the amenity package.

Design and Architecture
The leasing center is designed to look like an old-fashioned farmhouse, creating the image of a longstanding community that might have been erected on the site. The architectural concept creates a distinctly quaint, small-town feel. Marketing materials tell the story of a fictitious family that settled at the site during the Texas land rush of the late 1880s. The 16 residential buildings are meant to mimic a small Texas town, with mature shade trees and broad avenues contributing to the ambience. The community's architectural design offers the look and feel of a traditional single-family development, with steeply pitched rooflines, numerous gables, and chimneys. Each unit has a private front-porch entry and its own driveway leading to a direct-access garage. Grass is planted in strips down the middle of the driveway and around the garage areas to break up the look of a sea of concrete. All one- and two-bedroom units have a one-car garage, and all three-bedroom units have a two-car garage.

Interior spaces were designed to be open and admit as much natural light as possible. Of the 11 floor plans offered, four are three-story townhouse units and the remaining one- and two-bedroom plans are stacked flats. Storage space is generous, with storage areas built into any area of the apartment that would typically have hollow wall space, such as under staircases. Built-in shelving, alcoves, and "net nooks" (computer areas) offer utility and character. Most units include fireplaces, and some have vaulted ceilings.

Upscale fixtures, crown moldings, raised-panel doors, antique-style brass hardware, Berber carpeting, and custom upgrade options lend an air of luxury, fine craftsmanship, and individualization. Kitchens include pantries, furniture-quality cabinetry, double sinks, undercounter lighting, and upgraded appliances, including refrigerators with ice makers. Master suites are oversized, and baths are intended to feel like relaxing retreats, with oval Roman tubs and built-in vanities with cultured marble countertops.

High-Tech Amenities
The many technological extras include state-of-the-art enhanced Category 5 wiring for Internet access. Wiring has the capacity for surround-sound home theater, the capability for whole-house music distribution, built-in surge suppression throughout the unit, and an energy management system. Units are furnished with a software

Located in the high-tech business area of Austin, Texas, McNeil House features high-tech amenities in a cozy home-like atmosphere.

package that allows residents to turn lights on or off and to control the energy management system with a key fob remote control or to activate the system with a keypad. An indicator light on the keypad informs residents when the mail has arrived. Project amenities include a cyber-café where residents can socialize and have a snack while using the Internet.

Energy management systems in each unit include advanced thermostats that allow temperatures to be set for both occupied and unoccupied times using digital read-out wall controls. The system is programmed along with the security system, so that when the security system is disarmed, the temperature automatically returns to the "occupied" thermostat setting. Further, the system includes an option for setting the water heater in an economy mode when the unit is unoccupied.

Ownership and Financing

Developer Tami Siewruk formed the Siewruk Development Company in 1997 and operates with a general development partner, Kent Conine of Conine Residential Group. McNeil House is the premier project for the Siewruk Development Company, which still retains ownership of the community.

Siewruk is chief executive officer and president of both Siewruk Development Corporation and Sales & Marketing Magic Companies, the latter based in Tampa, Florida. She is one of only a handful of female multifamily developers. The companies specialize in provid-

ing the most effective leasing, marketing, management, and training information and seminars available for the multifamily housing industry.

Siewruk acquired the site for McNeil House for $1.26 million in August 1996. Birmingham, Alabama–based SouthTrust Bank provided a construction loan and permanent financing of approximately $13.5 million. Siewruk Development put up all the equity, $1,533,833.

Leasing and Management

ZOM Residential was the original leasing and management company. The marketing program focused on the community's advanced technology and the project's traditional single-family look and feel. Marketing materials were designed for simple, single-color printing on unbleached recycled paper. Brochures provided thorough information, including all floor plans, detailed descriptions of each unit type, and an extensive introduction to the amenities, high-tech features, and options. Full-color advertising was placed regularly in the area's major apartment publications and on billboards; radio advertising also was used. Rather than investing in expensive brochures, Siewruk developed a multimedia videotape because she thought it would be difficult to fully capture the technological features in printed material. Leasing agents played the tape in the model to demonstrate all the electronic and environmental control features, thus allowing prospective residents to experience the units' high-tech capacity for themselves.

The leasing office is designed to look like an old-fashioned farmhouse.

Pitched rooflines, chimneys, driveways with direct-access garages, and private entrances help give the units the look and feel of single-family housing.

The project includes a range of one-, two-, and three-bedroom units, all with private garages and porches.

Leasing began in December 1997. Applicants with solid credit histories who met the community's minimum annual household income of $38,000 were offered leases. The community attracted mostly single men and women in their early 30s who worked in nearby high-tech companies. More than 80 percent of the residents are employed; the remainder are homemakers, students, children, or retirees. Nearly one of every three residents came from out of state. Slightly more than one in ten residents previously had owned their own home.

Initial marketing tried to capture the "renter-by-choice" niche. With its extra features, amenities, and high-quality design, McNeil House appealed strongly to discretionary renters. The community rented quickly and lease-up was completed by August 1998, two months after construction of the final units was complete.

Today, the occupancy rate remains stable at about 93 percent. The three-bedroom units are the most popular and easiest to rent, but the one- and two-bedroom units are also relatively easy to keep occupied. ZOM is no longer the on-site management company, having been replaced by Bridge Property Management. Currently, the tenant mix is fairly diverse. About half the units are occupied by singles, with the larger units generally housing couples and families. Because of the project's location across the street from an excellent elementary school, it draws quite a few families with young children. More than half of the resident households have incomes higher than $60,000. About one-third have relocated from outside the area.

The community gives residents the tools they need to live and work conveniently, and offers services and amenities that provide a carefree lifestyle so important to this market. For instance, the community intranet offers residents a way to send requests for maintenance via E-mail, and they can pay rent on line. The community offers many luxury conveniences, such as a pool concierge who lends radios, earphones, magazines, and floats to residents using the swimming pool. Executive services, such as valet dry cleaning, catering, car care, and pet sitting are also available. Seminars are hosted on tax and estate planning, investments, health and wellness, and professional development.

Experience Gained

The amount of thought given to developing McNeil House resulted in an excellent product that appeals to the upscale market. With a wide variety of floor plans, it is easy for leasing agents to find one that suits most prospective tenants.

The nostalgic design and small-town feel of the project are probably the major reasons that renters choose McNeil House over the many other rental developments in the area. Residents like the variety of floor plans, the styling, and the quality of the product. The only element that has not worked well is the Berber carpeting, which is difficult to clean and maintain.

The high-tech amenities are popular, and they are one of the major marketing tools that draw residents. The management believes that the added costs were well worth it.

The interior of the leasing office exudes old-fashioned warmth.

Squire Haskins Photography, Inc.

Squire Haskins Photography, Inc.

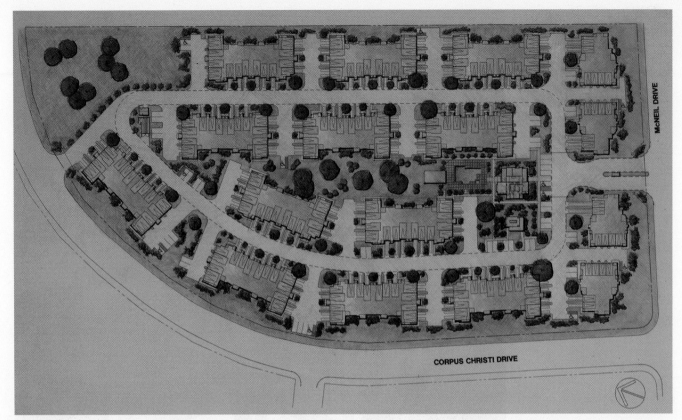

Site plan.

Outdoor amenities at McNeil House include a fitness center and pool, a bocce ball court, and numerous reading grottoes.

Project Data: McNeil House

Land Use and Building Information

Site Area	10.9 acres
Total Dwelling Units	192
Gross Density	17.65 units per acre
Off-Street Parking Spaces	468

Land Use Plan

	Acres	Percent of Site
Buildings	3.05	28%
Parking/Roads/Sidewalks	3.49	32
Landscaped and Common Open Space	3.49	32
Other	0.87	8
Total	10.90	100%

Residential Unit Information

Unit Type	Unit Size (Square Feet)	Number of Units	Initial Rent Range
1-Bedroom/1-Bath	677–859	60	$695–895
1-Bedroom/1.5-Bath	1,116	24	$825
2-Bedroom/2-Bath	1,012–1,267	24	$1,025–1,240
2-Bedroom/2.5-Bath	1,154–1,271	48	$1,165–1,265
3-Bedroom/2-Bath	1,936	36	$1,485
Total		192	

Development Cost Information

Site Acquisition Costs	$1,479,900
Construction Costs	11,097,200
Soft Costs	2,356,700
Total	$14,933,800

Annual Operating Expenses

	Annual Cost	Cost per Unit
Taxes	$6,000	$31.25
Insurance	27,828	144.94
Maintenance	27,775	144.66
Janitorial	3,500	18.23
Utilities	44,950	234.11
Management	103,137	537.17
Administrative, legal	41,081	213.96
Advertising	89,104	464.08
Grounds	47,336	246.54
Payroll	201,630	1,050.16
Total	$592,341	$3,085.10

Developers

Siewruk Development Corporation
58 Bahama Circle
Tampa, Florida 33606
813–254–9258

Conine Residential Group
12770 Coit Road
Suite 924
Dallas, Texas 75251
972–789–1999

Architect

Womack + Hampton
3000 McKinney Avenue
Dallas, Texas 75204
214–252–9000

Interior Designer

D.V. Preiser Designs, Inc.
4807-A Bayshore Boulevard
Tampa, Florida 33611
813–831–7099

Civil Engineer

Gray, Jansing & Associates
8217 Shoal Creek Boulevard
Austin, Texas 78757
512–452–0371

Technology Architect

RRH Associates
5 Cross Creek
Suite 100
Ormond Beach, Florida 32174
904–676–2725

General Contractor

C.F. Jordan Construction
13154 Coit Road
Suite 101
Dallas, Texas 75240
972–234–4400

Development Schedule

7/1996	Planning started
8/1996	Site purchased
2/1997	Construction started
11/1997	Leasing started
6/1998	Project completed
8/1998	Leasing completed

Peakview Apartments

Lafayette, Colorado

A 160-unit, mixed-income apartment complex comprising one-, two-, and three-bedroom units, Peakview Apartments was designed as moderately priced rental housing for a mix of families and adult households. Tax-exempt bonds and low-income housing tax credits were used to finance the project. The general partner incorporated the tax credits into a limited partnership offering instead of using a third-party syndicator to raise equity.

Peakview Apartments offers income-restricted and market-rate rental units. Forty percent of the complex's 160 units are required to serve households with incomes at or below 60 percent of the area median income. Potential tenants must show that they have been at their present job at least six months and that they have verifiable income and a satisfactory credit history. The existing tenant roster has a well-rounded mix of two-person working households, seniors, and families.

The property is located in Lafayette, Colorado, a city of approximately 19,000 people that was originally a Boulder bedroom community. With Boulder's approaching buildout, people have migrated into surrounding communities such as Lafayette. Over the past decade, employment has become more decentralized, and housing costs have escalated in Lafayette and other Boulder County communities.

Peakview's developer, Peak Properties and Development Corporation, is a small, closely held corporation formed in 1988 that has developed and managed seven projects in Colorado. The company prefers to develop 80- to 200-unit entry-level, multifamily projects for sale and for rent. The team at Peak Properties structured public/ private partnerships to enhance financial viability and help meet a community's need for affordable housing.

The Site

Peakview's 11.55-acre site is an optimal location with no physical impediments to development. An elementary school is located adjacent to the site on its northern edge, and a park and public swimming pool are located directly across a road to the south. To the west, a vacant parcel separates the site from Lafayette City Hall; plans for this parcel call for construction of a mixed-use office, retail, park, and residential development. Mobile homes lie to the east of the property. A variety of retail stores are nearby, and Lafayette's downtown area is about one-half mile away. The site, only 20 minutes from nearby Boulder, Longmont, and metropolitan Denver, is convenient for commuters. It offers views of the mountains to the west.

Planning, Design, and Construction

The development of Peakview took almost three years from project design to completion of construction. The city of Lafayette was a significant partner in planning decisions and zoned the parcel for multifamily development with a maximum density of 14 units per acre. A two-acre open space/park area containing roughly 1.5 miles of trails and walkways was created in the project's interior by positioning the buildings around the access road that forms the perimeter of the site. The seven two- and three-story buildings in the rectangular complex are oriented diagonally toward South Boulder Road.

Special design features include hip roofs, oversized windows, French doors, balconies or patios for each unit, a choice of four floor plans, 12-foot ceilings in some units, washer/dryer hookups in the three-bedroom units, private exterior entrances, and carports. The appealing exterior of the buildings avoids the institutional appearance often associated with large low-income apartment complexes.

The city police department became involved, as it does routinely, in helping to plan the project to mitigate crime through site design. Police advisers addressed lighting, the size of rocks used in landscaping, design of the carports, peepholes, and type of locks installed.

Five public hearings were held during the one-year city review period. Some neighbors opposed the specific project, but most citizens opposed growth in general. They were sensitive to the amount of growth in the area that resulted from rapid population increases over the previous five years. During winter 1995, a citizens' initiative was adopted by referendum that limited the number of building permits that could be issued each year. The developer was uncertain whether the apartment complex, representing 13 percent of total growth permitted over the next six years, could be built, even though approvals for the complex already had been granted. A moratorium had recently passed, but because of the project's high quality and the developer's commitment to "green" development and to providing much needed affordable housing, opposition was overcome.

More than 200 prairie dogs had to be relocated from the site to undeveloped open areas. And the commitment for HUD mortgage insurance was about to expire when all federal offices were closed in November 1995 as the result of a federal budget stalemate, delaying the project for more than two months.

The developer's sensitivity to environmental concerns resulted in the use of available "green" alternatives during the project's construction. Peak Properties initially

Peakview Apartments is a mixed-income apartment complex in Lafayette, Colorado, on the outskirts of Boulder.

used recycled paint on both the interior and exterior of several buildings, but the paint's unsatisfactory consistency prevented its use for the balance of the project. Stain-resistant carpet made from recycled plastic soft drink bottles was installed in all units.

Marketing and Management
During the public approval process, the complex became known as an "affordable" property, leading to some negative perceptions about potential problems with low-income residents. Greater market exposure throughout the region, however, made this apprehension short-lived. Because of Boulder County's relatively high median income ($58,300 in 1996), incomes for those qualifying for market-rate units were similar to those qualifying for tax-credit-restricted units.

Strong relations with the Lafayette chamber of commerce and area real estate agents aided in promotion of the apartments. No other apartment complexes were located in Lafayette, so Peakview's management established a referral network with property managers in nearby towns. Advertisements were placed in Boulder-area publications and Denver apartment rental guides.

Absorption of units was slower than anticipated primarily because of the time of year the units reached the market. The federal government's closure delayed completion until September, a historically poor time for leasing in Boulder County. Thus, the developer needed

larger reserves for the lease-up period. Delays in finishing the units also deterred leasing. Nevertheless, Peakview reached full occupancy four months after construction was completed.

Financing
The project was funded primarily through low-income housing tax credits and tax-exempt bonds. Peak Properties applied for a noncompetitive 4 percent tax credit program from Colorado's allocation. Sixty-four units (40 percent) are set aside to serve persons whose incomes are 60 percent of the area median. The remaining 96 units are market rate.

Peak Properties established a limited partnership and issued its own offering to qualified investors in Boulder County. Handling the offering in-house saved a significant amount of money because no commissions or mark-ups were involved. Fifty partnership interests sold in four months at a price of $45,000 per unit, raising slightly more than $2.2 million in equity. Each unit is expected to generate an annual tax credit of $3,500 for ten years.

Participants were enthusiastic about the investment because of the returns and the opportunity to participate in a local affordable housing project. Investment returns come from three sources: tax credits (8 percent), anticipated cash flow from the market-rate units (4 percent), and appreciation from the sale of the property once the tax credit period expires.

Peakview's location, adjacent to an elementary school, makes it a desirable residence for households with young children. A park and public swimming pool are also attractive amenities for families.

Each of the 160 units has its own balcony or patio and optional carports.

The other primary source of funding was a $10.96 million tax-exempt private activity bond issued by Boulder County at 6.4 percent interest for 40 years based on the anticipated revenue stream from the project. HUD's 221(d)4 program provided mortgage insurance, creating a AAA rating for the bonds. In addition, the Colorado State Division of Housing provided a $325,000 contingency loan at 6 percent for 40 years to assist with operating expenditures.

Experience Gained

The developer proved that attractive affordable rental units can be constructed in a high-cost community despite financial impediments and local opposition. The town's zoning requirements limited density, so the developer had to invest additional funds in landscaping and open space. City fees totaled more than $1.4 million ($9,000 per unit). Low-income housing tax credits and

tax-exempt bonds offered by the state were essential in countering the financial difficulties.

A high-quality product can sustain itself if it has an optimal location and is properly sized to maximize benefits resulting from economies of scale.

If unscheduled delays occur, it is financially more prudent to postpone construction until the project can be completed when leasing in the area typically is at its peak. The cost of holding undeveloped land is significantly less than the cost associated with a slow lease-up period.

Community support was important to Peakview's success. Developers should beware of the stigma associated with "affordable" projects and use models, renderings, and other physical representations to focus on design rather than occupants.

Developers should pursue environmentally friendly alternatives in construction. "Green" products may be similar in price to traditional materials. Some will work

Private open space was created by arranging the buildings around the perimeter of the property.

The clubhouse (left) features a view of the Rocky Mountains to the west.

better than others, but experimenting with them could provide a cost-effective solution.

Potential residents' preferences for amenities should be considered along with the cost of those amenities. For instance, washer/dryer hookups were available for only three-bedroom units, yet residents in the smaller market-rate units also would have paid for them.

Site plan.

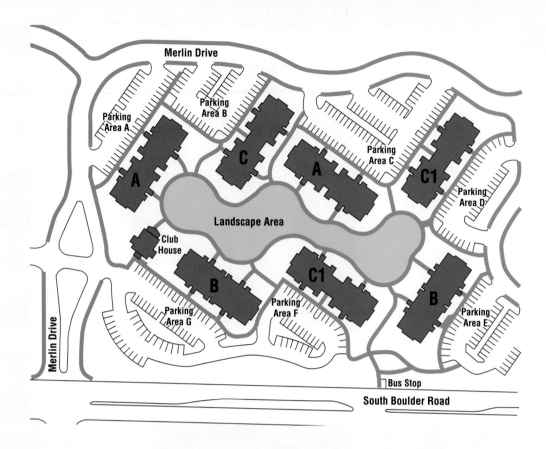

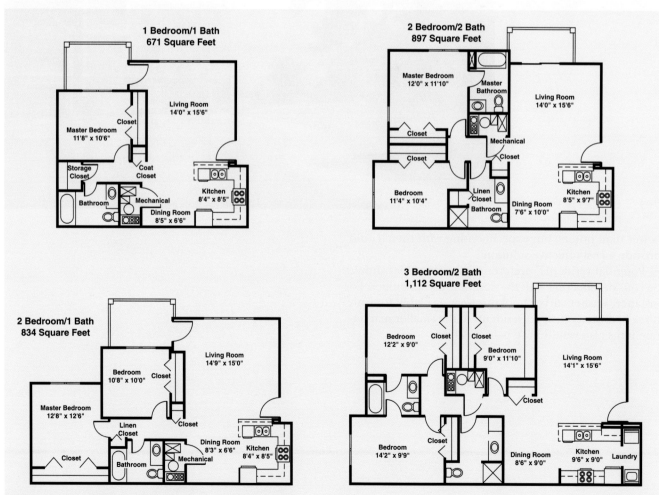

Typical floor plans for one-, two-, and three-bedroom units.

Project Data: Peakview Apartments

Land Use and Building Information

Site Area	11.55 acres
Total Dwelling Units	160
Gross Density	13.86 units per acre
Gross Square Feet	168,193

Residential Unit Information

Unit Type	Average Unit Size (Square Feet)	Number of Units	Market Rent	Income-Restricted Rent
1-Bedroom/1-Bath	671	42	$640–650	$575
2-Bedroom/1-Bath	834	42	$765–775	$685
2-Bedroom/2-Bath	897	32	$815–840	–
3-Bedroom/2-Bath	1,112	44	$975–1,000	$830

Sources and Uses of Public Funding

Source	Amount	Use
Private activity bond, Boulder County and Colorado	$10,500,000	Construction/mortgage
Federal Low-Income Housing Tax Credits	2,250,000	Equity/construction
Deferred fees on $1 million, City of Lafayette	50,000	Interest/operating costs
Total for Construction	$12,800,000	
Colorado Division of Housing Loan	325,000	Operating costs
Private activity bond, Boulder County and Colorado	460,000	Operating reserve
Total	$13,585,000	

Development Cost Information

Site Costs

Site acquisition	$574,827
Site improvement	1,010,354
Total	$1,585,181

Construction Costs

Construction Costs	$7,829,328

Soft Costs

Architecture/engineering	$367,205
Marketing	40,000
Legal/accounting	32,703
Taxes/insurance	39,086
City fees	1,466,792
Syndication	72,586
Loan fees/interest	771,312
Developer fee	650,000
Miscellaneous	5,207
Total	$3,444,891

Total Development Cost	$12,859,400
Average Construction Cost per Unit	$48,933
Average Construction Cost per Gross Square Foot	$47
Average Development Cost per Unit	$80,371
Average Development Cost per Gross Square Foot	$76

Developer

Peak Properties and Development Corporation
1877 Broadway
Suite 701
Boulder, Colorado 80302
303–444–3020

Architect

Lantz Boggio Architects
5650 DTC Parkway
Suite 200
Englewood, Colorado 80111
303–773–0436

Site Planner/Engineer

Downing Thorpe James Architects
1881 Ninth Street
Suite 103
Boulder, Colorado 80302
303–443–7533

Development Schedule

3/1994	Planning started
3/1995	City approvals obtained
12/1995	Site acquisition
12/1995	Construction started
7/1996	Marketing started
9/1996	Leasing started
12/1996	Construction completed

Phillips Place

Charlotte, North Carolina

A suburban mixed-use development on 35 acres in the SouthPark area near Charlotte, North Carolina, Phillips Place features 130,000 square feet of retail space, 402 residential units, 124 hotel rooms, and a multiplex cinema organized around a main street. The project includes a pedestrian-scale main street within a traditional low-density suburban area. The three-story buildings on the main street feature retail uses on the ground level and apartments on the second and third floors. The classically influenced architecture and the significant emphasis on high-quality streetscape design and lighting combine to create a pleasant and safe pedestrian experience.

The challenge was to develop a thriving, mixed-use town center for a traditional low-density suburban business district and residential neighborhood. The developer sought to achieve this goal by creating a main street with a hotel anchoring one end and a multiplex cinema anchoring the other, apartments built over retail stores on one side of the street, and several separate apartment buildings located behind the main street.

The Site

The site is located 15 to 20 minutes from downtown Charlotte, the airport, and I-485, Charlotte's major outer loop. SouthPark, known for its high-quality office and retail development, well-established neighborhoods, and strong demographics, includes the Carolinas' second largest business district and also has a residential base with one of the highest income levels in the Southeast. Half the residents of SouthPark have annual household incomes of more than $50,000, and nearly 25 percent are 25 to 35 years of age, ideal demographics for upscale apartments.

The site includes substantial frontage on Fairview Road, southeast Charlotte's major east/west thoroughfare, but it is not served by any other adjacent streets. Thus, all access to the project, including three separate entrances, is provided by Fairview Road, a constraint that limited the ability of developers and designers to connect the project to its surroundings. Residents to the south, however, did not want any significant connection, especially additional traffic flowing through their neighborhood on the way to and from Phillips Place. Commercial properties lie to the north and west, residential properties to the south and east.

Other features and constraints that affected the development and its design include high-tension power lines located at the front of the property along the arterial frontage, an electrical substation adjacent to the property to the east, and a terrain that slopes from north to south.

Development Process

From the outset, the developers pursued the idea of a mixed-use town center for the property. This concept was desirable and highly marketable for SouthPark and for the specific site, which is in a prime location and sufficiently large for the concept to work.

The site originally was owned by a family trust, the D.L. Phillips Trust, and some of the family members live adjacent to the property to the south. Thus, they not only had a strong economic interest in developing the land but also were interested in a development that did not detract from the surrounding residential areas. As a result, they exercised considerable influence on the nature of the project and its impact on their neighborhood.

To develop a mixed-use project on the property required rezoning. In the South District Plan, the site was recommended for multifamily housing at a density of 22 units per acre. This zoning would potentially have allowed 800 units, which would have generated significant traffic during peak hours. The developers sought to amend the plan to incorporate nonresidential uses, which they successfully argued would reduce peak traffic, avoid placement of housing adjacent to high-tension power lines, and provide retail stores not presently in the Charlotte market and public spaces that would be an amenity for the surrounding area, while still providing the multifamily housing originally targeted by the plan.

To complicate the rezoning approval process, the county had no zoning classification for mixed uses. Thus, the developer had to apply for an amendment to the GC–General Commercial zoning category to allow residential above retail uses, lengthening the approval process, even though city staff and elected officials supported the project. The conditional rezoning plan required sensitivity to the surrounding land uses and residents, as it involved achieving residential densities higher than those previously approved for the area.

The master developer, the Harris Group, sought several partners to make the complicated concept work. Although the company had extensive experience in retail and hotel development, it had not pursued a substantial residential project, nor was it a hotel operator. It therefore sought a partner to develop the apartments, finally settling on Post Properties, a major real estate investment trust that develops, owns, and operates apartments. It also sought a hotel partner and operator, settling on the Panos Hotel Group, a hotel operator. The group chose TBA2, a local firm with which it had worked extensively, as architect.

The entrance to Phillips Place identifies the project and sets the tone with the same architectural style and quality as the buildings.

The developers used essentially one contractor to handle the retail, hotel, and cinema development, eliminating numerous issues of coordination that could have arisen if more than one contractor built the project. The general contractor's attention to detail and to coordination of the utilities that service the project—and the contractor's insistence on staying a phase ahead on site work—allowed the project to be delivered on time. Construction began in November 1995, the first phase was completed in June 1997, and the entire project was completed in March 1998.

The retail and entertainment component, which includes 130,000 square feet of space configured as an open-air retail village along a main street, targets specialty retailers and upscale restaurants; the program currently includes 28 tenants, including four restaurants, six clothing stores, six gift/specialty stores, four home furnishings stores, and a ten-theater cinema that incorporates stadium seating and an attractive marquee visible from most points along the main street.

The residential portion of the project is made up of several components, all developed and owned by Post Properties. It includes 32 apartments/townhouses that face the main street over the retail uses in three-story buildings, and 68 units that surround a garden area in three-story buildings just off the main street. The residential component also includes 302 apartments in 12 separate garden apartment buildings with attached and detached garages. Apartment residents have access to a

clubhouse, a residential business center, a fitness center, a swimming pool, and two tennis courts. The apartments facing the courtyard near the main street are designed to include urban-style lofts with 14-foot ceilings and two-story townhouse apartments.

Planning and Design

The developers and designers were challenged to create a pedestrian-scale town center along a heavily traveled six-lane arterial. The solution involved internalizing the main street, which provided a slower, more controlled environment than the rapidly moving, auto-oriented environment on surrounding thoroughfares. Contrary to standard suburban retail design, the storefronts along this internal street are not visible from the adjacent thoroughfare, although some of the larger stores have signage that is visible and some also have back entrances that face the thoroughfare. The development team considered the layout essential to the success of the pedestrian environment they sought.

One of the premises on which the project is built is that the spaces between the buildings are just as important as the buildings themselves. Two landscaped courts terminate the east/west axis of the main street and showcase the two anchors, the hotel and the cinema. These two buildings establish the visual endpoints of the main street, and they serve as primary destinations and activity generators, enhancing pedestrian movement along the street. Several octagonal pavilions help to shape the courts

Broad, well-landscaped sidewalks create a pleasant pedestrian-oriented environment for residents and shoppers.

at both ends of the street, which include traffic circles surrounding water fountains that feature four heraldic-style standing lion sculptures holding the fountain bowl. Angled parking with landscaped dividers also is provided along the street.

The streetscape and lighting were emphasized to ensure that the pedestrian experience, during the day and in the evening, would be pleasant and safe. Brick sidewalks and outdoor seating encourage people to relax and enjoy themselves. Decorative street signs can be found in all areas of the project. The general lighting level is less intense than that typically found in shopping centers, but it gives pedestrians a sense of safety and invites strolling. The glow of the subdued lighting also enhances the romantic nighttime mood of Phillips Place. Special attention was given to the lighting of the fountains, the theater marquee, and the hotel porte cochere to give them the necessary presence along the main street.

The project's architectural influences range from the commercial streetscapes of Charleston and Savannah to the public gardens and residential townhouses of Bath, England. Colorful awnings over streetside windows accent the beige, taupe, and peach exterior walls inspired by historic Charleston's Rainbow Row. Building surfaces are made of synthetic stucco using an exterior insulation and finish system. Variegated Mexican sandstone forms the exterior building bases, and classical columns are abundant. Gabled and mansard roofs are accented with twin domes at the center, further enhancing the European ambience.

All the stores front the main street, and they have numerous large windows. The retail buildings on the north side of the main street are two stories high to balance the three-story buildings to the south; however, zoning for the property does not allow the second level to be developed as retail space. As a result, with 24- to 26-foot ceiling heights, retailers on this side of the street have opportunities to use the space creatively—as storage or as attractive high ceilings, for example—depending on their needs. Retail buildings on the south side of the street have more conventional ceiling heights, as these spaces include second- and third-level residential apartments, some of which have balconies. The mixed-use buildings use post-tension concrete slabs on the roof of the retail stores and wood-frame construction for the residential units above.

The developers emphasized the continuity of design along the main street. All of the buildings and facades along the street—including the retail and residential spaces, hotel, and cinema—were designed by TBA2 Architects, and they draw from a coordinated palette of colors and architectural themes.

The project includes three two-level parking structures, two of which are divided between retail and residential uses, with the retail component using the upper level and the apartments using the lower; there is no shared parking on the property. The sloping site benefited the design for the parking structures. Because of the slope, the top retail parking level is at grade with the main street and

Traditional architectural details help to create a town-like atmosphere.

Fountains are the focal points of each end of the main street, and extensive lighting at night encourages evening strolls.

Most parking is located in structures at the rear of the buildings so that it does not intrude on pedestrian spaces.

is not an obtrusive visual element when viewed from the main street. The lower residential parking level can be accessed at grade from the south, but only by residents or guests, who must pass through the security gate to get to the lower-level parking entrance.

The apartment community on the southern half of the site is gated. The architecture of these units is more conventional for suburban development than that used in the commercial portion of the project. Access to the apartments is through two separate road entrances. All units are in walk-up buildings, and many include balconies; some of the floor plans include direct access to garages.

Land available to meet stormwater retention requirements for the site was limited, so vaults were constructed under tennis courts and a large stormwater management pond was created as an amenity along the southern border of the property for the residential area.

The large residential lots to the south, including the residences of the landowners, required considerable buffering and careful attention to preserving trees and landscaping along the southern property line.

Marketing/Management/Finance
Construction of the project was phased, starting with the 302 garden apartments, the cinema, and 20,000 square feet of retail space adjacent to the cinema. The second phase included the remainder of the retail space, 100 additional residential units, and the hotel. Parking was a

challenge when the cinema first opened, as not enough spaces were available. The problem was remedied upon completion of the second phase, which created more parking behind the cinema but also required an amendment to the administrative site plan.

Each major component of the project is separately owned and managed: the Harris Group owns and manages the retail properties, Post Properties owns and manages the apartments, and a partnership of the Harris Group and the Panos Hotel Group owns the hotel, with Panos managing the property. Ownership of the residential and retail portions of the buildings that include residential over retail space is divided between the residential and retail owners/developers.

Post Properties, the Harris Group, and the hotel partnership share responsibility for maintenance of the landscaping along the entrances. The hotel pays a set monthly fee for its share of landscaping and lighting. Retail tenants pay for their share of common area maintenance costs based on the size of their space. Most of the retail tenants finished their own space with a tenant allowance.

The concept of a town center with specialty retail and entertainment attractions helped draw desirable nationally known retailers to the project. National tenants not previously in the Charlotte area were attracted to the project; most of them have only one store in the market to provide Phillips Place with a special collection of tenants. The project was marketed to retailers as a regional destination.

Behind the main street development are more standard suburban-style garden apartment buildings.

© Steve Hinds Photography

© Steve Hinds Photography

An executive for one of the signature retailers in the
project—Restoration Hardware—notes: "As a retailer,
we love the outdoor plaza environment. Our customers
love going back to 'Main Street,' where there is an outside presence and a meandering atmosphere. We wanted
a place where there are a host of interesting tenants so
our customers could walk from shop to shop and sample
the fare. We like the fact that Phillips Place has hints of
a historic nature."

Apartment rents range from $720 per month for 650
square feet to $2,920 per month for 2,200 square feet—
generally about $1.10 to $1.30 per square foot per month.
Rents are highest in the areas nearest the retail stores,
especially those directly over retail stores. The residential portions achieved 98 percent occupancy shortly
after opening, and they are now 100 percent leased.

Southtrust Bank provided construction financing
for the retail portion of the project, while Compass provided construction financing for the hotel. First Union
later provided two separate permanent loans for those
elements. A ten-year, nonrecourse permanent loan for
$25.3 million at 6.79 percent interest for the retail por-
tion was closed on March 12, 1998. The developers
found that the retail portion of the project required
substantially more equity than a typical retail development, but financing sources nonetheless received the
project well.

Experience Gained

Phillips Place is a prime example of how a mixed-use
town center can be successfully developed in a rapidly
growing suburban business district. The project provides
an important urban gathering place for the surrounding
low-density suburban community and illustrates how the
relatively dense mix of a variety of uses can create synergy
and a whole that is greater than the sum of its parts. Leasing the retail spaces and apartments was quick, and those
portions easily achieved pro forma rents. The hotel occupancy rate is higher than the average for the area, and

sales per square foot are above average for a retail center of this type.

Although Phillips Place is pedestrian oriented, it remains very much a suburban development that is reached
primarily by car. The apartment residents and hotel guests
can and do walk throughout the center, but few of those
living or working in the surrounding community are likely
to come to the project on foot, as no attractive pedestrian pathways are available that serve the project. The
project could not be integrated with an existing street
system—it is served by only one roadway—and it is separated from adjacent residential neighborhoods by fences.
Moreover, few major generators of pedestrian traffic
are within easy walking distance, even if suitable pathways existed.

Phillips Place brings to the Charlotte suburbs a new
urban element, giving its residents the opportunity to
walk to many conveniences and providing visitors and
nearby residents and workers with a combination of dining, shopping, and entertainment in one location. It is a
major step in the right direction for suburban place making and pedestrian-oriented mixed-use development.

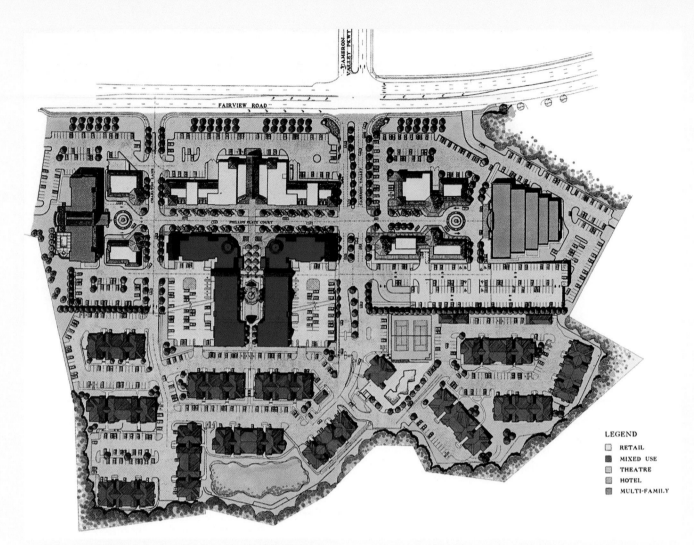

Site plan.

LEGEND
☐ RETAIL
■ MIXED USE
☐ THEATRE
☐ HOTEL
▨ MULTI-FAMILY

Project Data: Phillips Place

Land Use and Building Information

Site Area	35 acres
Retail Spaces	129,394 square feet
Total Dwelling Units	402
Hotel	124 rooms (80,000 square feet)
Parking	790 spaces (200,000 square feet)

Residential Unit Information

Unit Type	Unit Size (Square Feet)	Rent Range
1-Bedroom/1-Bath	650–1,050	$720–1,260
2-Bedroom/2-Bath	965–1,335	$1,170–1,680
3-Bedroom/3.5-Bath	1,980	$2,470
3-Bedroom/3.5-Bath	2,200	$2,920

Development Cost Information

Site Costs

Site acquisition	$11,950,000
Site improvement	3,907,842
Total	$15,857,842

Construction Costs

Parking deck	$1,700,000
Retail	14,254,000
Residential	38,000,000
Hotel	8,000,000
Total	$61,954,000

Soft Costs

Leasing	$1,600,000
Construction interest/fees	786,825
Startup costs	167,000
Legal and accounting costs	45,000
Total	$2,598,825

Total Development Cost | $80,410,667

Master Developer/Retail Developer

The Harris Group
Rotunda Suite 175
4201 Congress Street
Charlotte, North Carolina 28209
704–556–1717

Apartment Developer

Post Properties
3350 Cumberland Circle
Suite 2200
Atlanta, Georgia 30339
404–846–5076

Architect

TBA2 Architects (now called LS3P Associates Limited)
112 South Tryon Street
Suite 200
Charlotte, North Carolina 28284
704–333–6686

Site Planner

LandDesign
P.O. Box 11938
Charlotte, North Carolina 28220
704–333–0325

Development Schedule

11/1995	Site purchased
11/1995	Construction started
6/1997	Phase I completed
3/1998	Project completed

UCLA University Village

Los Angeles, California

University Village is a 912-unit graduate-student housing development five miles south of the University of California at Los Angeles (UCLA). University Village replaced a deteriorated 507-unit student housing community that the university had acquired in 1964. To meet a substantial need for student housing, the university decided to demolish the old apartments and construct a new development. Rents for apartments at University Village are below market. The development includes facilities for both students and their families, such as a computer lab and a child care center.

The apartments are clustered around open courtyards that foster a sense of community. Located in a densely populated western Los Angeles neighborhood packed with residential and commercial development, one of California's largest apartment projects built since 1994 offers graduate students and their families a quiet, affordable refuge in primarily residential pockets tucked on either side of a major freeway.

One-, two-, and three-bedroom units rent for as much as $200 less per month than market-price rentals in the area. Children can play on the half-court basketball court or the playground and in the pool at the new multipurpose community center. University students can use the free computer lab for class projects. Parents can head for the university after dropping off their children at the new 14,000-square-foot child care center.

Site Description

In 1964, UCLA Housing, a self-supporting division of the public university, purchased yellow stucco apartment buildings originally constructed in 1948 and 1958 on Sawtelle and Sepulveda boulevards to house graduate students and their families. At the time, UCLA Housing paid $7.6 million for 647 units on a flat, 30-acre site bisected by the San Diego Freeway (I-405). Over time, as other off-campus housing was located nearby, the Sawtelle/Sepulveda apartments became the oldest properties in UCLA's off-campus housing inventory.

The framed stucco, three-story cement-slab apartment buildings were stacked with four units on each floor. Parking was available in separate garages. The units lacked most amenities, including air conditioning. By the late 1980s, the aging apartment buildings were deteriorating and their maintenance costs soaring. The units required new plumbing and electrical systems, expensive repairs to tackle asbestos and dry rot, and replacement cabinetry, heaters, window hardware, and shower pans. A sound buffer was necessary to reduce the noise and visual impacts of the adjacent freeway. In addition to other identified needs, an existing child care center and a maintenance building had seismic deficiencies.

Planning and Design

By 1989, UCLA faced a housing crunch. More off-campus units for graduate students with families were desperately needed. Total UCLA enrollment exceeded 35,000, including more than 10,000 graduate students. Lengthy waiting lists existed for all graduate student housing, including the old Sawtelle/Sepulveda units.

UCLA Housing conducted detailed studies to compare the cost of refurbishing the apartment units with building new ones. University officials concluded that demolishing the 507 old units on the 25-acre site and building 912 new units in their place made financial sense. The cost of new construction was only $21 million more than a complete refurbishment of the old buildings and would slash the high maintenance budget required to keep the aging units habitable.

New construction also would boost UCLA's off-campus housing inventory to 2,011 units. At the same time, UCLA could increase the availability of child care, add a community center, and address its needs for administrative and maintenance space. A 14,265-square-foot child care center for 171 children, a 4,614-square-foot community center/administrative office building, and a 5,000-square-foot maintenance shop were included in the construction plans.

Working with UCLA staff, architects Johannes Van Tilburg and Partners set out to design long-lasting, low-maintenance apartments addressing the needs of graduate students and their families while matching their expectations for low rents. The result was attractive, three-story apartment buildings clustered around courtyards. The courtyards provide public space for neighbors to visit, children to play, and greenery. Each apartment is equipped with a dining and study nook, air conditioning, modern appliances, and a private garage. Units near the freeway are fitted with double-pane windows to muffle noise. About 45 ground-floor units are accessible to persons with disabilities.

The new buildings include 80 one-bedroom/one-bath units of about 585 square feet; 307 two-bedroom/one-bath units and 474 two-bedroom/two-bath units ranging from 800 to 910 square feet; and 51 three-bedroom/two-bath units of 1,035 square feet.

The apartments were designed to last 50 to 60 years, incorporating elements that save money over the long run.

UCLA University Village is a housing complex for graduate students located five miles from the university in a densely developed western Los Angeles neighborhood.

UCLA Housing is charged with providing affordable student housing on a break-even budget. The project was privately financed by selling University of California bonds; below-market rents generate enough income to repay the bonds.

University Village is designed to meet the needs of modern-day graduate students. Amenities like a computer lab, basketball court, child care center, and playground help today's older graduate students manage family and school.

Old student housing was demolished for the construction of University Village. University officials concluded that demolishing the 507 old units on the 25-acre site and building 912 new units made financial sense.

For example, bay windows instead of high-maintenance balconies, stucco hallways that do not require paint, and heavy-duty hardware and carpets are part of the design. Water heaters accessible by roof make them easy to maintain or replace. Trash compactors lower the cost of transporting and disposing of garbage. Garage buildings constructed up against the freeway double as sound walls.

Financing

UCLA Housing is charged with providing affordable student housing on a break-even budget unsubsidized by public funds. Future rents must pay all construction, operation, and debt-financing costs for new projects. To evaluate the University Village project, university officials calculated future rental income, subtracted operating expenses and debt service costs, and arrived at a construction debt they could finance. The project was privately financed by selling University of California bonds worth $63.5 million at an interest rate of 6.41 percent. No state funds were used.

Once the financing was established, UCLA Housing had to build the project as designed and stay within the tight budget. Bid as a fixed-price design/build project to ensure that the builder would stick to the $65 million construction budget, the contract was awarded to Keller Construction. The company's bid fit the cost range targeted by university officials. Construction manager Stegeman and Kastner, Inc., came on board to monitor construction and spending.

Building only 1.25 parking spaces per unit helped University Village retain enough green space to give children a place to play and foster a sense of community among residents.

As planned, rental income repays the bonds that financed the project. Monthly rents range from $715 for a one-bedroom/one-bath unit to $1,000 for a three-bedroom unit. Those rents—about 20 percent below market rates—are a bargain in urban Los Angeles.

New apartments began opening for occupancy in late 1995, with additional buildings becoming available in 1996. By fall 1997, the final University Village units opened, snapped up by eager graduate students despite a higher rent than the older units. A waiting list is maintained for prospective tenants.

Experience Gained

Private sector solutions can help satisfy a public university's demand for housing. Using a design/build contract and hiring a professional construction manager helped keep construction costs down for University Village, making it possible for UCLA Housing to meet a tight budget driven by future rental income.

Below-market rental rates were possible because UCLA Housing did not have to purchase land for this project. Using acreage purchased long ago and owned free and clear before construction began made the entire project cost-effective.

Because the University of California Board of Regents is not subject to local ordinances, UCLA Housing saved millions of dollars by building only 1.25 parking spaces per unit and avoiding expensive below-grade parking and the elevators that would have been required to reach it.

This low parking ratio would not have been possible for a private developer subject to city planning requirements. University Village retained the same parking ratio as the old buildings, which left space for the attractive courtyards and extensive green spaces. It also allowed the apartment buildings to be constructed slab-on-grade, not typical in an urban area. Although some residents complain about not having reserved parking for two vehicles per household, the area is well served by public transit.

Building the project in three phases reduced the impact on the neighborhood and minimized disruptions to student tenants. The project broke ground in 1994 but proceeded section by section. Buildings were vacated while tenants were assisted with replacement housing and paid $400 in relocation funds. Old buildings were demolished one at a time before construction on new buildings began.

The innovative blueprint that produced University Village's unqualified success will be employed again at UCLA. A fourth phase of University Village—180 additional two- and three-bedroom units replacing 140 old units—already is planned. Demolition and construction are targeted for 2001, with new units becoming available for rental in fall 2002.

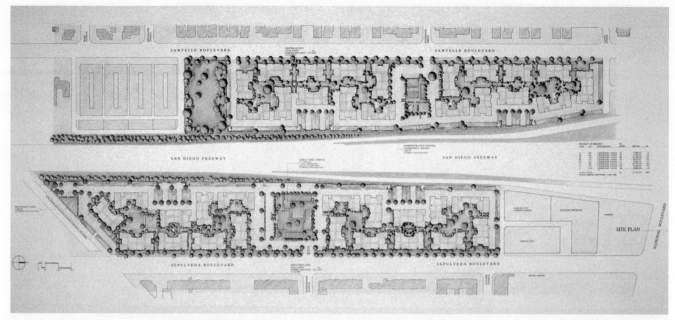

Site plan.

Project Data: UCLA University Village

Land Use and Building Information

Site Area	25 acres
Total Dwelling Units	912
Gross Density	36.5 units per acre
Off-Street Parking Spaces	1,148[1]

Residential Unit Information

Unit Type	Unit Size (Square Feet)	Number of Units	Rent Range
1-Bedroom	585–589	80	$715–770
2-Bedroom	797–912	781	$835–885
3-Bedroom	1,035	51	$1,000

Development Cost Information

Site Costs

Site acquisition	$7,613,000
Site improvement	$3,583,100
Total	$11,196,100

Construction Costs	$51,389,080
Soft Costs	$6,487,910
Total Development Cost	$69,073,090
Total Development Cost per Unit	$75,738
Construction Cost per Square Foot	$49.25

Developer

UCLA Housing
270 De Neve Drive
Los Angeles, California 90095
310–794–2653

Architect

Johannes Van Tilburg and Partners
225 Arizona Avenue
Santa Monica, California 90401
310–394–0273

Builder

Keller Construction
P.O. Box 4070
El Monte, California 91734
626–443–6633

Construction Manager

Stegeman and Kastner, Inc.
2601 Ocean Park Boulevard
Suite 300
Santa Monica, California 90405
310–450–9010

Development Schedule

1964	Site purchased
1989	Planning started
7/1994	Construction started
12/1995	Rental started

Note

[1] Includes 539 in detached garages, 373 in tuck-under garages, and 236 surface spaces.

Wimbledon Apartments

Spring, Texas

The renovation and repositioning of this underperforming and deteriorating 161-unit apartment complex with a 30 percent occupancy rate involved completely renovating the interiors of the 13-building complex and redesigning exteriors to look like townhouses. A new leasing and management office was part of the project. As a result of the renovation, monthly rental receipts increased more than 400 percent in just over three years.

The renovation of Wimbledon Apartments, originally built in 1977, illustrates the successful rehabilitation and enhancement of a distressed and underperforming multifamily real estate asset. Located in a suburb northwest of Houston, the complex includes 161 garden-style apartment units. Drever Partners, Inc., purchased Wimbledon Apartments for $1.8 million in February 1992. Before its acquisition and renovation, the complex had been poorly managed and was in dire need of repairs. Drever, an experienced player in Houston's multifamily housing market, successfully acquired and rehabilitated the apartment complex for just over $26 per square foot. The renovation transformed Wimbledon Apartments into a Class A property, making the asset an outstanding candidate for future resale, particularly to an institutional investor.

Before its redevelopment, the distressed property suffered from a 30 percent occupancy rate and had become a community eyesore. Drever's experience in rehabilitation of multifamily properties in the local market allowed the firm to successfully reposition the property to capture market demand cost-effectively, dramatically enhancing the complex's functionality, marketability, profitability, and aesthetic appeal.

Site and Development Process

Situated on 6.3 acres, Wimbledon Apartments occupies a highly visible location approximately ten miles from George Bush Intercontinental Airport and 25 miles northwest of Houston's central business district. The property is near many of Houston's major employers, including Compaq Computer and the many businesses around the airport. Located three blocks north of a major thoroughfare, Wimbledon offers its residents easy access to office centers, shopping malls, and entertainment resources. The complex acts as the gateway to Wimbledon Estates—a prestigious planned residential community. A swimming pool, a deck, and a picnic area are Wimbledon Apartments's primary amenities.

Before acquisition, the property was subjected to an extensive due diligence analysis. Because of the complex's physical deterioration, each apartment, whether occupied

or vacant, was examined individually. (Investors often conduct less extensive tests on a sample of units.) Due diligence "walk sheets," providing detailed inspection guidelines, were completed for all 161 units. Information gathered from the walk sheets was used throughout redevelopment, allowing accurate and detailed construction cost projections. Extensive interviews also were conducted with the maintenance staff, manager, and residents to gain information about the property's condition. The due diligence analysis showed that 103 of the 161 units were uninhabitable. These extensive investigations allowed Drever to carry a modest rehabilitation contingency of approximately $25,000.

Renovation and Construction

Immediately after acquisition, Drever began the renovation of Wimbledon, which took approximately eight months. Initially, rehabilitation focused on mitigating water damage and structural problems, and on preventing further damage. Roof repairs and enhancements continued throughout the project; two buildings received entirely new roofs. The complex's grading and water drainage system were improved in an effort to mitigate water damage, which was occurring on sidewalks, stair landings, and in underground storm sewers.

Together with the architectural firm Scruggs & Hammond and design consultant Jim Bartish, Drever had rehabilitated numerous multifamily properties throughout the Houston metropolitan area, gaining a tremendous amount of experience to use in determining the magnitude of renovations, specifications, level of amenities, and design parameters needed to reposition Wimbledon. The renovation's design focused on emulating the classic proportions of individual townhouses in a Federal style, successfully transforming the monotonous tone set by the complex's long brick buildings. To achieve the desired effect, architectural features such as false fire walls and chimney housings, well-placed shutters, moldings, brass hardware, kick plates, coach lamps, cast aluminum unit number plates, and nine-pane replacement windows were installed throughout the property. High-visibility areas received more attention and detail than those that were less visible; for example, unappealing building features such as roof dormers were removed in high-visibility areas but left in others.

Individual apartments, which range from 613 to 1,402 square feet, were renovated to some extent. All existing carpeting, wallpaper, linoleum flooring, light fixtures, and appliances were upgraded. In each living and dining

The repositioning of Wimbledon Apartments included constructing an attractive new clubhouse/rental information center that enhances the property.

area, new miniblinds, chair rails, and mirrored walls were installed. In the kitchens, cabinetry was salvaged wherever possible, and usable cabinetry from apartments throughout the complex was frequently mixed and matched to save costs. Each kitchen's plumbing was retrofitted for the installation of ice makers at a cost of approximately $50 per unit. Washers and dryers were attached to preexisting utility hookups, and new sinks were installed as well. Kitchen countertops were resurfaced in most cases and replaced in others. The bathrooms received new toilets and basins while retaining their original bathtubs. Vinyl flooring was laid in each bathroom. Inferior aluminum wiring throughout the complex was brought up to current code, adding significantly to the project's hard costs.

The renovation also included improvements to amenities and substantial landscaping. The pool area was greatly enhanced by the addition of a landscaped wooden deck and a spa. Decorative wrought iron fencing was also installed around the pool area. Given the growing demand for increased security, a limited-access gate and a perimeter fencing system were built to surround the property in an aesthetically appealing fashion. New signage was also added.

The Wimbledon redevelopment also included the construction of a $78,000 highly visible, architecturally attractive, 1,010-square-foot leasing and management office referred to as "the Clubhouse." The new office is located directly adjacent to the pool and one of the two entrance areas. The previous leasing office was converted into a 525-square-foot bachelor's apartment, enhancing the project's traditional design and adding rentable square footage to the property.

Financing and Management

Drever Partners, Inc., a San Francisco–based real estate development and investment firm, acquired Wimbledon in an all-cash deal for $11,250 per unit in February 1992. Drever projected a cost of $2,245,325 for the renovation's capital improvement budget and $2,281,083 for the final cost. The firm secured $2.5 million of nonrecourse mortgage financing through the Prudential Insurance Company at an interest rate of 6.99 percent. Annual debt service for the property is approximately $215,000, providing a 14 percent cash-on-cash return and a 2.0 debt coverage ratio.

Walden Residential Properties, one of the nation's largest multifamily REITs, purchased Drever Partners in 1997. In turn, Olympus Real Estate Corporation purchased Walden Residential in February 2000, resulting in one of the most significant public-to-private real estate transactions in history. Walden continues to operate under its own name; it maintains a headquarters office in Addison, Texas, and controls 157 properties with nearly 44,000 apartment units. Walden operates throughout Texas, Florida, Arizona, Oklahoma, and Tennessee.

The classic proportions and detailing of Federal-style townhouses improve the look of the project, which was originally constructed in 1977.

Dynamic marketing proved to be invaluable in the successful repositioning of Wimbledon Apartments. Concierge Management, the original management firm for the property, initially underestimated the amount of public relations and marketing work needed to counter the property's inferior reputation and tenant profile, resulting in a lease-up period that exceeded original projections. Concierge eventually overcame these obstacles through a strong public relations program that sought to educate the local community about the project. Marketing professionals actively solicited corporate human resource departments throughout the target market to get their message across.

Renovation and marketing of Wimbledon Apartments were successful. Monthly rental collections for Wimbledon Apartments rose from $15,810 when the property was acquired to $82,887 in April 1995, a 424 percent increase in slightly more than three years.

Experience Gained

Considerable experience is needed to successfully and cost-efficiently rehabilitate and reposition a multifamily asset. Understanding the local market is essential in determining the amplitude of renovation, level of improvements to amenities, and general design parameters for redevelopment. Successful rehabilitation can dramatically enhance an asset's functionality, marketability, profitability, and aesthetic appeal, but keeping the improvements and costs in line with market realities and targets is imperative.

The effort needed to surmount a distressed property's existing negative reputation should not be underestimated. Innovative and aggressive marketing must be initiated early in the development process. Projections for lease-up should accurately reflect these challenges.

Broad lawns replaced a parking lot in front of the renovated complex.

The swimming pool has a new deck, spa, Colonial-style wrought iron fencing, and improved landscaping.

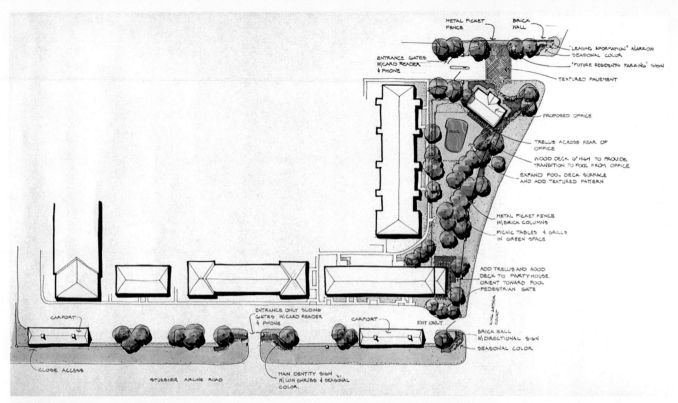

Site plan.

Project Data: Wimbledon Apartments

Land Use and Building Information

Site Area	6.3 acres
Total Dwelling Units	161
Gross Density	25.5 units per acre
Off-Street Parking Spaces	247

Land Use Plan

	Acres	Percent of Site
Buildings	1.9	30.1%
Roads/Paved Areas	1.7	27.0
Common Open Space	2.7	42.9
Total	6.3	100.0%

Residential Unit Information

Unit Type	Unit Size (Square Feet)	Number of Units	Initial Rents
1-Bedroom/1-Bath	613–847	49	$415–485
2-Bedroom/1-Bath	862	14	$545
2-Bedroom/2-Bath	978–1,061	84	$575–625
2-Bedroom/2.5-Bath	1,227	8	$700
3-Bedroom/2-Bath	1,402	6	$750

Development Cost Information

Site Costs

Site acquisition	$1,800,000
Site improvement	257,900
Total	$2,057,900

Construction Costs

Superstructure	$1,418,868
HVAC	78,253
Electrical	54,595
Plumbing/sprinklers	36,707
Finishes	85,622
Graphics/specialties	42,276
Total	$1,716,321

Soft Costs

Architecture/engineering	$69,285
Project management	122,611
Marketing	33,226
Legal/accounting	61,305
Taxes/insurance	20,435
Total	$306,862

Total Development Cost	$4,081,083
Total Development Cost per Unit	$25,348
Total Development Cost per Square Foot	$26.40

Developer

Drever Partners, Inc. (purchased by Walden Residential Properties)
5080 Spectrum Drive
Suite 1000 East
Addison, Texas 75001
972–788–0510

Management

Walden Residential Properties
5080 Spectrum Drive
Suite 1000 East
Addison, Texas 75001
972–788–0510

Architect

Scruggs & Hammond
1103 Schrock Road
Suite 301
Columbus, Ohio 43229
614–436–2622

Design Consultant

Jim Bartish & Associates
4869 Rudgate Boulevard
Toledo, Ohio 43623
419–841–1010

Development Schedule

1/1992	Planning started
2/1992	Site purchased
2/1992	Construction started
3/1992	Leasing started
10/1992	Project completed

12. Development Trends

Demographics

The U.S. apartment development industry spent the 1990s serving primarily new demand from baby boomers in their 30s and 40s, frequently singles or childless couples who opted to rent because the lifestyle suited them rather than because their finances were limited. These renters-by-choice did not expect to be lifelong renters. At that stage of life, however, they were drawn to new upscale apartments by the flexibility and the lack of maintenance that renting offered and by housing with numerous amenities they typically could not have afforded to buy at the same location. These time-constrained professionals also valued highly the extensive services offered by on-site management.

The housing needs of young adults and other households who find themselves priced out of the homeownership market are met primarily by rental apartments. This demand for more moderately priced apartments is fulfilled largely by the existing apartment stock rather than by new development, as the costs of building affordable units cannot be supported by market rental rates without some form of subsidy. The most common subsidy for affordable housing is low-income housing tax credits, which have produced 50,000 to 70,000 new units annually over the past decade.

Clubhouse at the Ranch at Ridgeview in Plano, Texas.

Two age groups will emerge to drive demand for rental apartments as the new century begins. First, baby boomers will move into their 50s and, as this generation did in the 1990s, will create demand for additional apartment development tailored to their lifestyles. While demand will span a wide spectrum of income levels, the building of more upscale new apartments that began in the 1990s will continue into the early years of the 21st century. Second, the children of the baby boomers—the baby boomlet—will begin to enter the workforce and thus the housing market in meaningful numbers from 2006 to 2010. This new crop of first-time renters will harken back to the 1960s and early 1970s, when their parents' generation came of age, and will produce the first net increase in the nation's under-25 renter market since the 1970s.

As these young adults begin to enter the housing market, U.S. household growth should accelerate from 2000 to 2010. In fact, those years will return the nation to its highest level of household formation since the 1930s. This upturn will reverse three decades of slowing growth, when gains slowed from an average of 1.6 million new households formed annually in the 1970s to 1.3 million in the 1980s to 1.1 million in the 1990s. This acceleration of household formation means rising demand for housing in general and, because of the return of an expanding young adult populace, will produce even faster increases in demand for rental housing early in the 21st century.

In the last three decades of the 20th century, social and economic trends reshaped how Americans chose

Evergreen Hills Apartments in Macedon, New York, successfully combined public and private financing sources, including low-income housing tax credits.

their housing. Key social changes impacted the housing markets in that era: a skyrocketing divorce rate, and a delay in the age of marriage and of childbearing. Economic changes, including the taming of domestic inflation and the rise of global competition, put pressure on U.S. companies. Absent inflation, homeownership did not provide the outstanding investment return of the 1970s and early 1980s. Global competition prompted wide-ranging layoffs in major companies across the United States and effectively ended the sense of career-long job security for many Americans. A more fluid employment market requires greater mobility. Thus, the ease of movement that rental housing offers appeals to a greater portion of workers.

These social and economic shifts have had major lifestyle implications for millions of Americans. In the 1990s, the primary growth segments in American society were single or divorced adults living alone and single-parent families—both groups more likely to rent than own, on average. These shifts in lifestyle pushed the propensity to rent higher across age groups through most of the 1990s, despite single-digit mortgage rates.

The impact of these social, economic, and lifestyle trends is evident in viewing the homeownership rates of the U.S. population. The propensity to rent remains highest among young adults and declines sharply by middle age. But boomers have been more apt to rent throughout their adult lifetime than the preceding generation. As a result, households across all cohorts under age 55 have shown a rising propensity to rent since the mid-1970s.[1]

These shifts in lifestyle show no signs of abating in the early 2000s and should translate into a more renter-oriented generation of 40- to 60-year-olds than seen previously in the United States. In addition, the limited earning power of young adults should continue the popularity of renting among those under 25. The renewed growth of this cohort of young adults will eventually exceed the lifestyle-driven demand produced by the older, more affluent boomers.

Another new trend that will somewhat reshape U.S. demography in the early years of the 21st century is the diversity of growth rates among various racial groups. From 2000 to 2005, 40 percent of the nation's population growth will occur among Hispanics, whose numbers will expand by almost 5 million in this period. Anglo and African-American segments will produce roughly equivalent volumes of growth (near 2.5 million persons), with another 2 million new Asian citizens in this five-year time frame. These trends are expected to hold in the subsequent ten years, as Hispanic Americans represent 45 percent of total growth expected (Figure 12-1).

Combining these various demographic trends into a forecast of renter households suggests that the early 2000s should be a golden era for the rental housing industry. In the 1990s, low mortgage rates and, more important, population growth dominated by ownership-prone 30- to 45-year-olds produced minimal growth of 130,000 rental households per year on average. Even against this slow-growth backdrop, the nation's apartment development industry prospered. Yet the period from 2000 to 2010 should produce an average of 250,000 to 300,000 new renter households annually and provide support for the most active period of demand-driven new apartment

figure 12-1
Population Growth by Race, 2000 and 2015

	2000		2015	
	Population (Millions)	Percentage of Total	Population (Millions)	Percentage of Total
Total Population	275.3	100.0	312.3	100.0
White, Non-Hispanic	196.7	71.4	204.6	65.5
African-American	35.3	12.8	42.4	13.6
Hispanic	32.5	11.8	49.3	15.8
Asian	11.3	4.1	17.4	5.6

Source: U.S. Census Bureau, National Population Projections Summary Files: Total Population by Race, Hispanic Origin, and Nativity, 1999–2100: www.census.gov/population/www/projections/natsum-T5.html.

construction the United States has experienced since the late 1970s.

Product Types

The 1990s began a new era of apartment products, with somewhat larger units and, more important, residences with so many amenities that the list of features rivaled those offered by many single-family custom homes. Historically, the newest apartments have always catered to the more affluent growth segments of the renter market, simply because these residents could afford to pay the rents needed to economically justify new construction. Why did the 1990s follow this trend yet leap several generations ahead in luxury features? Never in U.S. history had this many early-middle-aged singles and childless couples (30+ years of age) been in the market for rental

Post Shores in Irving, Texas, draws its success from rapid employment growth. Texas ranks among the top states for new apartment development.

Apartments increasingly resemble luxury single-family homes. A two-bedroom unit at Island Place Apartments in Tampa, Florida, features a spacious multilevel floor plan.

housing. Well-educated and ascending their earning curves, baby boomers were ready to enjoy a more luxurious form of housing, and many who found themselves single or without children living at home opted for dramatically upgraded new apartment communities.

Among the most notable features introduced in 1990s apartments (which could not be added to existing properties through rehabilitation) were nine-foot ceilings (often accented by heavy crown molding), direct-entry garages, oversized oval bathtubs, separate shower stalls, and kitchens with islands.

As a result of this new renter audience; unit square footage expanded to accommodate the material possessions accumulated by these 30- to 40-something adults. A larger share of the new units built incorporated multiple bedrooms and multiple bathrooms (Figures 12-2 and 12-3). For many, the additional bedroom served at least some of the time as a home office as working at home full time or part time grew in importance. Reflecting the need for electronic connectivity, the late 1990s saw new apartments designed with built-in computer desks, and high-speed Internet access grew from a curiosity in the middle 1990s to a common feature by 2000—and to an absolute necessity in markets with high concentrations of technology workers such as Silicon Valley, Boston, Austin, and Raleigh/Durham.

Even workers outside the technology field have seen the advantage of connectivity, as features like E-mail and the Internet proved huge time savers in a society where time arguably had become the scarcest resource. As a re-

sult, developers of new apartments have the opportunity to build in a technology infrastructure that differentiates their community from properties even a few years old. In the last decade, new apartments could thus enhance the quality of life of residents, addressing not only the housing tastes of affluent baby boomers but also their needs for saving time and convenience. Nearing middle age and growing more affluent, upper-end apartment renters also grew more concerned about crime. Video-monitored access gates allow residents to screen their visitors, perimeter fences encircle the property, and alarms are built into upscale units to provide a peace-of-mind package that these residents value highly.

The advancing age and affluence of boomers also brought a new awareness of the benefits of health and fitness. Once, a single-station Universal weight machine placed in a closet met the market's expectations for a fitness center. Today, developers recognize that new construction can gain a competitive advantage by incorporating the latest in fitness training. In some cases, this advantage comes from aerobics or other exercise classes in custom-designed rooms in a clubhouse; in others, the new community offers the latest in entertainment exercise equipment with a selection of audio and video channels to enjoy during the workout.

Now that the development industry has sharply honed these upscale amenity packages to meet the wishes of discretionary, early-middle-aged renters, the new century has brought two new growing groups of renters. All the nation's net new demand for rental apartments during

figure 12-2

Average Size of New Multifamily Units Started, 1985 to 1999

Year	Square Feet
1985	922
1986	911
1987	980
1988	990
1989	1,000
1990	1,005
1991	1,020
1992	1,040
1993	1,065
1994	1,035
1995	1,080
1996	1,070
1997	1,095
1998	1,065
1999	1,105

Source: U.S. Census Bureau, Selected Characteristics of Housing Units in New Privately Owned Buildings Completed with Two Units or More, Table 8: www.census.gov/const/C22/c22_char.txt.

figure 12-3

Percentage of New Multifamily Units with Multiple Bedrooms or Multiple Baths, 1985 to 1999

	2+ Baths	3+ Bedrooms
1985	37	7
1986	36	7
1987	39	7
1988	41	8
1989	41	10
1990	44	11
1991	43	12
1992	42	13
1993	45	17
1994	44	15
1995	49	16
1996	51	17
1997	49	16
1998	49	17
1999	54	19

Source: U.S. Census Bureau, Selected Characteristics of Housing Units in New Privately Owned Buildings Completed with Two Units or More, Table 8: www.census.gov/const/C22/c22_char.txt.

Apartment communities will need to keep up with the most desired amenities.

the decade from 2000 to 2010 will be produced by first-time renters in their early 20s and late-middle-aged renters in their 50s. For the first time in postwar history, the development industry has the opportunity to respond to two rather than just one major renter segments.

What features will these two disparate customer groups demand? New apartment communities of 2005 may hark back to the 1970s, with larger clubhouses as gathering places for socially active early 20s residents. Similarly, young renters are most likely to be on the early climb of their earning curve, so affordability will be a key factor, meaning more efficiency or studio units, more junior one-bedroom units, and more roommate floor plans with equal master suites. Along with these stereotypical images of the early 20s apartment renter, though, will come a new phenomenon—the most technologically astute generation in our history. E-mail, instant messaging, chat rooms, and surfing the Web will be as ingrained in their daily lives as television and stereos were in their parents'. As a result, tomorrow's young renters will seek even better technology infrastructure than the upscale communities built in the late 1990s. In 2005, a visitor to a new young adult–oriented apartment community will see a group of residents enjoying Web-connected home theater rooms equipped with very large wall-mounted, flat screens. One group may enjoy a live concert while another group works on a team presentation with colleagues in another city. While the capabilities of future technology are certainly unpredictable, the apartment developer of 2005 could be motivated to offer the latest and best hardware and software, amortized across the hundreds of apartments in the community. Because of the large concentration of consumers found in an apartment community, the multifamily industry will be a test site for E-commerce ideas.

As focused on affordability and technology as most young adult renters will be in the next decade, upper-income middle-aged singles or couples will seek quality housing with security and convenience. For those who can afford them, even larger and more lavishly appointed units will be in demand. Many services, almost to the level of personal assistant, will be provided to these professionals and empty nesters whose lifestyles and interests include extensive travel, volunteer work, new educational challenges, personal financial planning, and portfolio/investment management. Online connectivity will play a vital role in delivering these conveniences.

Demographics have determined that apartment development in the early 21st century will continue to reinvent product design, resident services, and locations. In a more automated society, the locations of work may become more flexible. To attract the key employees needed in a competitive labor market, quality of life and housing near work centers will be critical. Historical character may become increasingly valued in housing and neighborhoods. As the 20th century closed, most major cities had begun a renaissance of upscale housing in or near downtown, often reclaiming abandoned neighborhoods. More momentum may be added by young adults of 2000 to 2005, who have grown up watching popular television shows set in urban apartment buildings.

Regional Forecasts

Beneath these national trends, varying—in some cases, shockingly different—trends are emerging across regions of the country. The single force that most differentiates one region from another is the composition and motivation of *newcomers* to the region's cities. International immigration has reshaped portions of the West Coast, the Northeast, and south Florida. In most cases, these new residents seek personal freedom first and upward financial mobility second. For the growth markets of the South and Southwest, migration has been largely domestic rather than international, with newcomers seeking greater career opportunities and earning power.

Extending these patterns over time produces a stark contrast in future demographic patterns in America's

Bridgecourt Apartments was developed by the Catellus Residential Group in Emeryville, California, a small city between Oakland and Berkeley in the San Francisco Bay Area. The 220-unit mixed-income project was completed in June 1998. Bridgecourt won a Best in American Living award in 1999, and it has proven financially successful as well.

Catellus worked closely with the city of Emeryville, the city of Oakland, and neighborhood groups to create this community on a formerly industrial site. Ninety-one of the 220 units (41 percent) are affordable to households with 56 percent of the area median income. Moreover, renters can purchase their units after 15 years.

Three sources of funding were used for the project: tax-exempt multifamily revenue bonds issued by the city of Emeryville, a grant from Emeryville's affordable housing setaside fund to improve affordability for residents, and the sale of federal low-income housing tax credits to bring additional equity into the project. Creative use of these different financing techniques ensured that Bridgecourt provided highly affordable housing in an area that desperately needs it.

Bridgecourt has also been noted for its bold architecture. The site includes four buildings with three levels of apartments over one floor of at-grade parking. The design recalls the industrial heritage of the area through its massing and scale; it also employs strong colors and interesting window treatments and other accents to distinguish itself and to tie the project in with a neighboring retail development, also by Catellus.

New developments like Bridgecourt Apartments have led the way in the transformation of Emeryville from a city of heavy industry to one of highly accessible retail and residential uses.

Bold colors and design distinguish the award-winning Bridgecourt Apartments in Emeryville, California. The mixed-income housing project is built on a brownfield site.

figure 12-4
Regional Population Growth by Race, 2000 to 2005
Thousands

	White, Non-Hispanic	African-American	Hispanic	Asian	Other
Northeast	–544	351	631	394	12
Midwest	427	327	359	217	35
South	2,072	1,412	1,443	340	41
West	785	210	2,266	1,016	72
U.S. Total	2,740	2,300	4,699	1,967	160

Source: U.S. Census Bureau, National Population Projections Summary Files: Total Population by Race, Hispanic Origin, and Nativity: www.census.gov/population/www/projections/natsum-T5.html.

regions. The Northeast is forecast to experience a net outflow of Caucasians to other states in the country, while Hispanic, Asian, and African-American population expands to fill the void and push population to new record highs. In the West, more than one-half of the population increase will be Hispanic. Non-Hispanic whites will lead population growth only in the South, although African-American and Asian populations will also increase sharply. The Midwest is anticipated to show a relatively balanced mix in population gains (Figure 12-4).

Influences underlying these distinctive patterns of migration are the cost of living, the cost of doing business, and receptivity to growth in one region compared with another. In part because of their openness to growth, for example, the markets of the South and the Southwest will continue to be at greater risk of overbuilding than their counterparts. Being receptive to growth, however, may also translate into an ability to grow out of oversupplied markets more readily than the more growth-constrained markets of the West, Midwest, and Northeast.

As of year-end 1999, the highest vacancy levels were found in the South, where new apartment development activity has been strong since 1994. Although many markets have sustained a healthy balance between supply and demand, selected markets have clearly begun to suffer from excess supply, driving up the region's overall vacancy rate. Most markets that appear to be oversupplied began to see a slowdown in multifamily starts in 1999. For example, multifamily building permits fell by 47 percent in 1999 in Houston, 17 percent in Dallas, 64 percent in Fort Worth, and 42 percent in Las Vegas.

At the other extreme, the Northeast and parts of the West (specifically California) began to see meaningful amounts of new building only in the late 1990s. As a result, vacancy rates in those areas are well below the national average. New development began this cycle in the Midwest during 1994, but because of stiffer barriers to entry (in the upper Midwest in particular), overbuilding has been very limited in this region and vacancy rates generally remain quite healthy. With very strong occupancy rates, construction in markets where

barriers to entry are higher was up in 1999, and metropolitan areas like Chicago, Minneapolis, and Los Angeles approved 15 to 30 percent more new multifamily units than in 1998.

Patterns of Development

The unending outward march of new housing development continues in U.S. metropolitan areas, reinforced by the leapfrogging of affordably priced new housing to areas farther away from the core, the pursuit of newer

In New York's Chinatown, a nonprofit development corporation built Chung Pak/Everlasting Pines, a mixed-use project with 88 subsidized seniors' housing units, a health clinic, daycare center, and street-level retail stores.

Will You Marry Me? M&A in the Apartment World

Mergers and acquisitions (M&A) were a big story in the multifamily business in the 1990s. Some of the biggest players in the industry, such as Apartment Investment and Management Company (AIMCO) and Equity Residential Properties Trust, grew in part because of their M&A. In 1998, for example, AIMCO added almost 140,000 apartment units to its portfolio through two acquisitions alone. A number of forces have contributed to consolidation, and a few years ago many analysts were forecasting the emergence of a few dominant firms in the multifamily sector. M&A activity has slowed dramatically since 1998, however, as the market paused to take stock. Compared with other major industries in the United States, there remains a low degree of concentration in the multifamily business.

Some of the commonly identified factors encouraging consolidation in the real estate business include decreased capital costs, savings in operating costs, diversification by geographic region or asset class, and improved management for larger firms. Larger firms should be able to access capital markets more easily and on better terms compared with their smaller competitors. Larger firms can also spread their fixed costs more widely, and they should be able to achieve economies of scale in terms of purchasing, labor costs, and management compared with their smaller competitors. Merging with or acquiring firms operating in other regions or markets can allow a firm to grow more efficiently than if it had tried to build that expertise internally. This diversification can also serve as a hedge against local market fluctuations and can help to ensure stable revenue streams. A more substantial presence in many markets can also help a company to develop a widely recognized brand for its products.

On the other side of the coin, a number of factors limit consolidation in the multifamily sector. One commonly mentioned factor is the reluctance of many real estate executives to sell their companies. Another is the fact that the localized nature of the real estate business promotes the existence of smaller firms, expert in local markets, that resist acquisition by large national firms. Indeed, Jack Goodman of the National Multi Housing Council points out that REITs prefer to acquire large apartment communities but that only 25 percent of multifamily rental units are in communities with more than 200 units.

REITs have been responsible in large part for the consolidation witnessed in the multifamily sector in recent years. Some analysts, such as Anthony Downs of the Brookings Institution, however, believe that a number of conditions specific to the financial market in the 1990s and to REITs in general will discourage the massive consolidations expected by many other industry analysts. These conditions include the nature of the real estate cycle, current capital costs, and tax and other laws that determine how REITs behave as corporations. As for the other factors driving M&A, debate continues about their true importance. A recent paper published by the NMHC and *National Real Estate Investor* cites empirical studies that found that there were, in fact, some economies of scale and other benefits for large multifamily REITs, although in some cases these savings were smaller than expected or the effects of a firm's increased size were unclear.

AvalonBay Communities is a firm that knows the trials and tribulations of mergers very well. The company was formed in 1998 following the merger of Avalon Properties, Inc., and Bay Apartment Communities. Headquartered in Alexandria, Virginia, the company focuses on high barrier–to–entry markets on the East and West coasts. According to the NMHC, in 1999 AvalonBay was the 17th largest apartment owner in the country, and tenth largest in terms of management, with an ownership interest in more than 40,000 apartments. Richard Michaux, CEO and president of AvalonBay, points out that the merger of Avalon and Bay made a lot of strategic sense, although it turned out to be more difficult than initially thought. Avalon and Bay had similar strategies and similar histories, and the fact that each firm focused on one coast was complementary. Merging was seen as a way to improve financial flexibility, achieve economies of scale, and create added value for both shareholders and residents. Since the merger, the new firm has been quite successful, but there were some bumps on the road along the way.

Chief among the challenges that had to be overcome was the need to create a common corporate culture and a strategic vision that everyone could support. Despite the

retail services, traffic congesting underdeveloped roadways, employers moving farther from the core to be closer to their workers and future labor supply, and affordably priced new housing moving farther out still. And so the outward growth continues.

In many cities, however, new apartment developments following this progressive spiral outward have seen high turnover as residents move out to buy affordable homes nearby. As a result, the investment viability of new apartment developments in these fringe suburbs has come under question.

In somewhat more mature (and more expensively priced) suburbs, NIMBYists often nix new apartment zoning cases. Thus, at no time in the past 50 years has the development environment—for apartments specifically—differed so greatly between central cities and suburban communities. In the 1960s and 1970s, suburban jurisdictions hungry for a tax base opened fact that hundreds of employees were surveyed about their attitudes and ideas and despite the extensive use of consultants expert in mergers, Michaux says that many in the new firm were surprised at the extent to which the policies, practices, and norms in the two companies differed and had to be reconciled. There were strains at the executive level as well. Not everyone bought into the new corporate vision, and some important people left the firm. Eventually, the new AvalonBay was able to overcome these differences, but as Michaux says, "It took longer than we would have liked to get everyone on the same page."

The consensus apparently emerging in the multifamily sector is that consolidation in the industry will continue, albeit not at the breakneck pace seen a few years ago. Many of the factors driving consolidation continue to be present, and they will encourage further mergers and acquisitions. Given the lack of concentration in the multi-family industry, room is certainly available for more mergers. Some analysts point out, however, that new public offerings and spin-offs will also result in the cre-ation of new firms. Overall, these market dynamics will take longer to play out than previously thought.

For those contemplating a merger or acquisition, a num-ber of issues need to be considered. First, the firms involved need to have the underlying strengths to sug-gest that they will continue to be able to add value and grow over time. Similarly, the firms should have a com-plementary set of operational strategies and property portfolios. Making sure that corporate cultures and atti-tudes match is essential, as the absence of such an agree-ment has sunk many a merger deal. And senior managers need to be very realistic about the reasons a merger might be desirable and what the firm stands to gain and to lose, particularly given today's market conditions.

■

Many apartment dwellers seek an urban lifestyle. At Pentagon Row in Arlington, Virginia, a town center is being developed with residences on upper floors.

their arms to apartment developers, whose properties would provide relatively affordable housing and simulta-neously boost the tax base for the locality and school districts dramatically. Today, though, residents of these same suburbs attempt to raise the drawbridge in their communities, vociferously opposing new housing that is not on a par with (and preferably higher priced than) their respective residences. Apartments are often seen as the source of many of society's evils, notably over-crowded schools, crime, and congested traffic to name a few.

New housing development in central cities, on the other hand, had lost its vitality to less expensive land in the suburbs, to often superior suburban school systems, to new shopping centers, and to growing suburban employ-ment centers. Simultaneously, central cities felt an eco-nomic squeeze in multiple areas: 1) weakened central business district office markets that no longer supported the taxable value on which the city may have counted previously, 2) increasing traffic congestion as a result of the continued flow of commuters to central city jobs from suburban residential areas, and 3) potential penal-ties to economic development arising from the Clean Air Act. Many forward-looking cities have responded to these risks with mass transit plans that can once again make downtown the center of a hub-and-spoke system.

Fortunately for the development community, this newly found fervor for urban apartments is matched with a

willingness on the part of local governments to not only allow higher-density residential development but also offer economic incentives to facilitate such development. Depending on the city and the nature of the development, these incentives can include a streamlined entitlement or even rezoning process, property tax abatements, creation of tax increment financing districts to improve infrastructure necessary for the project's viability, and the waiver of local sales taxes on the materials used in the development.

Given the degree of traffic congestion affecting most major U.S. cities, mass transit became a well-accepted, even popular, mode of transportation beyond the el in Chicago and the subways of New York. MARTA in Atlanta, DART in Dallas, the Trolley in San Diego, and MAX in Portland provided popular alternatives. In turn, the success of mass transit in these cities now coming of age has also created opportunities for multifamily development around transit stations, an opportunity long understood by developers in the Northeast and Midwest but only recently recognized in the newer cities of the South and West.

Many large cities also have reinvented downtown entertainment districts, making central business districts regional draws and leveraging their highly accessible location as the hub of the region. In turn, these restaurant, nightlife, and sports venues make downtowns a more attractive place to live.

As baby boomers age, the demand for high-quality rental units in convenient infill locations is likely to accelerate. For many boomers seeking new experiences, suburban living falls under "been there, done that." Given the size of the upper-income segment of this generation and the scarcity of land in desirable intown locations, more high-rise residential construction is expected. Even in cities previously characterized by lower-density neighborhoods, new construction is moving toward greater heights and higher densities (Figures 12-5, 12-6, and 12-7).

figure 12-5

Multifamily Completions in Mid- and High-Rise Buildings, 1992 to 1999

4+ Stories

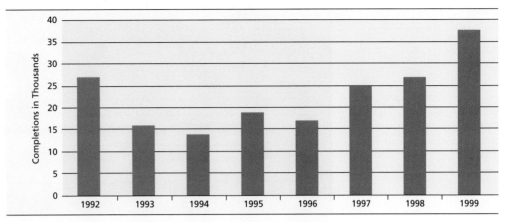

Source: U.S. Census Bureau, Construction Reports, Series 22, Housing Completions.

figure 12-6

Multifamily Completions in High-Density Buildings, 1992 to 1999

50+ Units per Building

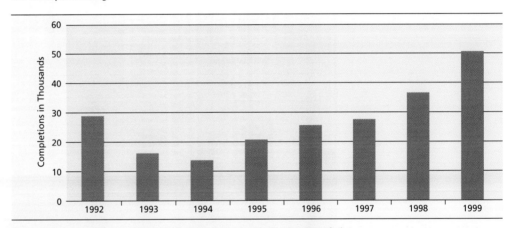

Source: U.S. Census Bureau, Construction Reports, Series 22, Housing Completions.

figure 12-7

Percentage of All Multifamily Starts in Higher-Density Buildings, 1992 to 1999

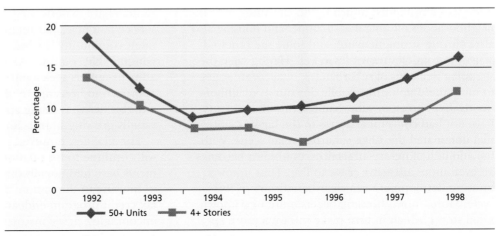

Source: U.S. Census Bureau, Construction Reports, Series 22, Housing Completions.

Ma On Shan residential complex in Sha-tin, Hong Kong, includes 725 units in six towers with harbor and mountain views.

Callison Architecture, Inc.

The resurgence of intown living has not escaped the notice of major retailers. While the more visible new multifamily communities offer the most obvious evidence of residents' return to the city, most close-in neighborhoods offering mid- to upper-end housing also are enjoying strong demand, and some see renewed activity in condominium sales as well. Having sated the shopping demands of suburbanites, retailers are eager to mine these upwardly mobile downtown neighborhoods. In contrast to suburbanites, intown residents have not had convenient access to the big-box stores that dominated the 1990s suburban retail scene. With the addition of new retail services, downtown becomes an even more attractive place to live. Thus, intown housing development is a clear beneficiary of this cycle. More intown housing begets more new intown retail stores, which in turn make intown a more appealing place to live and draw more residents to urban neighborhoods.

Magnifying this return to the city is the maturing of the baby boom generation and a parallel pursuit for new housing experiences. Many upscale 30- and 40-something renters have experienced every luxurious amenity and service in a new apartment development the development community has been able to invent, even with its considerable creativity. As a result, a growing number of affluent renters seek a different lifestyle as well as a fresh approach to housing. In almost every major American city, this desire is filling apartments in an active and rapidly growing intown housing market.

For all cities, however, providing affordable housing will continue to be a daunting challenge. Clearly, apartments have traditionally offered the most affordable form of housing in the nation, and the low-income housing tax credit program endeavors to continue that role by encouraging new construction. Many housing agencies are encouraging Congress to expand this popular program by increasing allocations to the states. Other pro-

figure 12-8
Construction Lending for New Multifamily Properties, 1981 to 1997
Billions of Dollars

	Banks	Thrifts	Credit	Other
1981	5.675	2.029	1.607	1.130
1982	5.969	3.113	2.015	0.971
1983	7.747	8.081	2.759	0.759
1984	11.835	8.046	2.402	0.562
1985	15.386	9.550	4.046	0.823
1986	20.735	8.761	7.218	0.797
1987	22.884	8.469	3.454	0.697
1988	23.184	8.247	1.370	1.004
1989	29.327	5.278	1.717	0.514
1990	20.317	2.921	1.613	0.392
1991	20.064	1.475	3.122	0.404
1992	14.107	0.696	1.390	0.173
1993	16.326	1.195	0.723	0.261
1994	12.254	1.378	0.763	0.120
1995	15.406	1.240	0.847	0.212
1996	18.066	1.341	0.681	0.309
1997	17.368	1.347	0.585	1.511

Source: U.S. Department of Housing and Urban Development, Survey of Mortgage Lending Activity, 1997.

grams at the local, state, and national levels will be necessary to fill the housing needs that are not met by LIHTCs, especially for very-low-income households.

Financing

In the aftermath of the overlending and overbuilding in almost all local markets in the 1980s, banking reform sharply reined in construction lending, beginning in the late 1980s. Simultaneously, risk-based capital requirements for insurance companies curtailed their appetite for direct real estate investment. The result was the real estate credit crunch of 1990 and 1991. The evaporation of capital for construction lending was evident by 1990 (Figure 12-8), as was the curtailment of longer-term mortgage lending for apartments.

In this capital-constrained environment, the federal low-income housing tax credit program drew new interest from traditional developers. The long-term residual value of a tax credit property offered limited economic incentive (because of the long period of enrollment in the program required to receive a tax credit allocation). Nonetheless, these developments did offer lucrative fees and an opportunity to continue to build new apartments. As a result, the tax credit program gained visibility in the early to mid-1990s; it has provided 50,000 to 70,000 units of new construction annually to serve middle-income renters who were not

figure 12-9
Multifamily Mortgage Borrowing
Billions of Dollars, Net

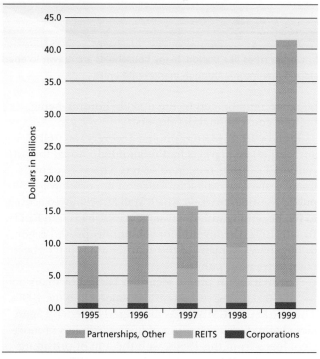

Source: Federal Reserve Board, Flow of Funds Accounts of the United States, Release Z-l, Data Series F219, June 9, 2000.

In vibrant cities like Boston, many households are drawn to apartment living. Langham Court includes a mix of apartments, from subsidized low-income through market-rate units.

being accommodated by the upscale housing being built by conventional developers.

Even by 1992, when economic recovery was well along and real estate markets had rebounded, capital for conventional projects remained scarce. This void of traditional real estate capital provided an opportunity for the public securities markets, which Wall Street moved actively to fill, beginning with the resurgence of interest in REITs. By late 1992, the investment community proved eager to buy shares as many of the apartment industry's best companies went public.

The market for public securities backed by loans on income-producing real estate also emerged in the 1990s. The market for CMBSs was pioneered by federal agencies charged with disposing of huge portfolios of mortgage loans from the 1980s, with the aim of providing liquidity for holders of commercial mortgages just as the public market had succeeded in providing liquidity to originators of home mortgage loans years earlier. This

effort proved very successful, and by the late 1990s, many traditional lenders had created "conduit" programs to originate apartment mortgage loans that would be packaged and sold in securities offerings. Figure 12-9 shows the volume of borrowing by corporations, partnerships, and REITs in recent years.

By 1995, banks again began to fund apartment construction and mortgages. By the end of the decade, traditional capital sources were active again in providing financing for apartments. In addition, the public markets for real estate debt (CMBSs) and equity (REITs) had also become quite efficient in providing capital to the apartment industry. This growing capability to place debt led to intensified competition and in turn to less strenuous underwriting standards.

Awash in capital made available at less and less stringent underwriting standards, the U.S. real estate market of early 1998 appeared out of balance and perhaps headed for another painful correction. Loans originated to be packaged for the public CMBS market had reached 90+ percent loan-to-value ratios, at very low interest rates (particularly low compared with the risk associated with first-loss positions). In early fall 1998, a global flight to quality swept capital away from the high-risk portions of securitized debt, touching off a repricing of real estate capital, both debt and equity. The second great real estate credit crunch of the 1990s thus bridled the overoptimism that had emerged in early 1998 and likely extended the record 1990s real estate expansion cycle.

This repricing in 1998 resulted in increased equity required for construction loans, higher equity returns demanded by equity investors, and permanent loans priced not only at a given spread above U.S. Treasuries but also with a floor rate attached. In this more stringent financing environment, fewer new developments proved financially feasible, and new construction slowed in 1999.

With the discipline shown by this first test of the public real estate capital markets, future real estate cycles should be smaller in amplitude than the severe swings evident earlier. Better market awareness coupled with a strong focus on short-term yields (as opposed to tax shelters or large residual value on sale) should mean more frequent adjustments in new construction starts and lessened volatility in supply and demand and thus property cash flows. Further, the volatility of earlier periods was tempered by the 1989 passage of the Financial Institutions Reform, Recovery, and Enforcement Act (FIRREA), which imposed a number of requirements on banks, including maintenance of a higher percentage of their capital base against real estate loans. The result was to make them more conservative lenders than in the past.

Nonetheless, the real estate markets will remain subject to notable imbalances in supply and demand, albeit likely less extreme than in the catastrophic 1980s. Because of the construction time required for significant real estate developments, developers' decisions depend on a view of the future, which will periodically prove wrong and result in too much new construction in a given market at a given time. This time-to-market lag is precisely what warrants the higher return expected on new development compared with alternative investments.

Note

1. U.S. Census Bureau, *Housing Vacancy Survey*, Table 7, Homeownership Rates by Age of Household, 2000.

401 East Ontario in Chicago is a 51-story tower with 394 units. Amenities include an indoor pool and a health club.

Bibliography
and Index

Bibliography

Books

Altshuler, Alan A., and José A. Gómez-Ibáñez. *Regulation for Revenue: The Political Economy of Land Use Exactions.* Washington, D.C., & Cambridge, Massachusetts: Brookings Institution & Lincoln Institute of Land Policy, 1993.

Barrett, G. Vincent, and John P. Blair. *How to Conduct and Analyze Real Estate Market and Feasibility Studies.* Second Edition. New York: Van Nostrand Reinhold, 1988.

Blakely, Edward J., and Mary Gail Snyder. *Fortress America: Gated Communities in the United States.* Washington, D.C.: ULI–the Urban Land Institute, 1999.

Bookout, Lloyd W., Jr., et al. *Residential Development Handbook.* Second Edition. Washington, D.C.: ULI–the Urban Land Institute, 1990.

Burchell, Robert W., David Listokin, et al. *Development Impact Assessment Handbook.* Washington, D.C.: ULI–the Urban Land Institute, 1994.

Condit, Carl W. *Chicago 1910–1929: Building Planning and Urban Technology.* Chicago: University of Chicago Press, 1973.

Dewberry & Davis. *Land Development Handbook: Planning, Engineering, and Surveying.* New York: McGraw-Hill, 1996.

Downs, Anthony. *A Reevaluation of Residential Rent Controls.* Washington, D.C.: ULI–the Urban Land Institute, 1996.

Fader, Steven. *Density by Design: New Directions in Residential Development.* Washington, D.C.: ULI–the Urban Land Institute, 1999.

Fisher, Robert Moore. *Twenty Years of Public Housing: Economic Aspects of the Federal Program.* New York: Harper & Brothers, 1959.

Mason, Joseph B. *History of Housing in the U.S., 1930–1980.* Houston: Gulf Publishing Co., 1982.

Miles, Mike E., Gayle Berens, and Marc A. Weiss. *Real Estate Development: Principles and Process.* Third Edition. Washington, D.C.: ULI–the Urban Land Institute, 2000.

Miles, Mike E., Richard L. Haney, Jr., and Gayle Berens. *Real Estate Development: Principles and Process.* Second Edition. Washington, D.C.: ULI–the Urban Land Institute, 1996.

National Association of Home Builders. *Impact Fee Handbook.* Washington, D.C.: Home Builder Press, 1997.

Nicholas, James C., et al. *A Practitioner's Guide to Development Impact Fees.* Chicago: Planners Press, 1991.

Parks, David C. *Environmental Management for Real Estate Professionals.* Chicago: National Association of Realtors®, Institute of Real Estate Management, 1992.

Peiser, Richard B., and Dean Schwanke. *Professional Real Estate Development: The ULI Guide to the Business.* Chicago & Washington, D.C.: Dearborn Financial Publishing & ULI–the Urban Land Institute, 1992.

Porter, Douglas R., Susan B. Brecht, Lee E. Cory, Randy A. Faigin, Mel Gamzon, and Stephen L. Taber. *Housing for Seniors: Developing Successful Projects.* Washington, D.C.: ULI–the Urban Land Institute, 1995.

Salvesen, David. *Wetlands: Mitigating and Regulating Development Impacts.* Second Edition. Washington, D.C.: ULI–the Urban Land Institute, 1994.

Simons, Robert A. *Turning Brownfields into Greenbacks: Developing and Financing Environmentally Contaminated Urban Real Estate.* Washington, D.C.: ULI–the Urban Land Institute, 1997.

Suchman, Diane R. *Developing Infill Housing in Inner-City Neighborhoods: Opportunities and Strategies.* Washington, D.C.: ULI–the Urban Land Institute, 1997.

ULI–the Urban Land Institute. *Dollars and Center of Multifamily Housing: 1999.* Washington, D.C.: ULI–the Urban Land Institute, 1999.

———. *Managing Environmental Mandates for Multifamily Housing: 1997. A Compendium of Federal Laws and Regulations.* Washington, D.C.: ULI–the Urban Land Institute, 1996.

———. *New Uses for Obsolete Buildings.* Washington, D.C.: ULI–the Urban Land Institute, 1996.

Warner, Sam Bass, Jr. *The Urban Wilderness: A History of the American City.* New York: Harper & Row, 1972.

Wentling, James W., and Lloyd W. Bookout, Jr. *Density by Design.* Washington, D.C.: ULI–the Urban Land Institute, 1988.

Wright, Gwendolyn. *Building the Dream: A Social History of Housing in America.* New York: Pantheon Books, 1981.

Journal Articles

Baar, Kenneth. "The National Movement to Halt the Spread of Multifamily Housing, 1890–1926." *Journal of the American Planning Association,* Winter 1992 (vol. 58, no. 1): 39–48.

Bartsch, Charles, and Edith Pepper. "Brownfields and Housing." *Land Development,* Winter 1997 (vol. 9, no. 3): 19–22.

Belsky, Eric S. "Housing and Commuting Behavior." *Housing Economics,* September 1994: 9–12.

Brown, Jim, and Kim Storey. "Rainwater in the Urban Landscape." *Places,* Summer 1996 (vol. 10, no. 3): 16–25.

"Coming: Housing That Looks like America." *Architectural Record,* January 1995 (vol. 183, no. 1): 84–93.

Fernandez, Kim. "Higher and Higher." *Units,* May 1997 (vol. 21, no. 4): 32–34.

Foong, L. Keat. "Just Like a Big House." *Multi-Housing News,* January/February 1997 (vol. 32, no. 1): 46–48.

"The Garden Spot." *Multi-Housing News,* June/July 1996 (vol. 31, no. 4): 34–35.

Goode, Ann Eberhart. "Promise and Problems in Brownfields Redevelopment." *Environmental Planning Quarterly,* Spring 1996 (vol. 13, no. 2): 3–7.

"Happy Medium." *Multi-Housing News,* April/May 1996 (vol. 31, no. 3): 36–39.

Leslie-Bole, Benjamin, and Mark E. Ransom. "Finding Green in Those Brownfields." *Journal of Property Management,* March/April 1997 (vol. 62, no. 2): 18–23.

Malizia, Emil, Richard Norton, and Craig Richardson. "Reading, Writing, and Impact Fees." *Planning,* September 1997 (vol. 63, no. 9): 17–19.

"Much Ado about Brownfields." *The Law and the Land,* Summer 1996 (vol. 10, no. 1): 1.

Ring, Gustave. "Modern Trends in Garden Apartments." *Urban Land,* May 1948 (vol. 7, no 5).

Rowley, Laura. "Local Custom." *Multi-Housing News,* November/December 1994 (vol. 29, no. 6): 43–45.

Strange, Gary L. "Infrastructure as Landscape." *Places,* Summer 1996: 8–15.

Welsh, Douglas, Bruce Adams, Michael O'Brien, and George Richard. "Dry Idea." *Planning,* September 1993: 12–17.

Zimet, Michelle J. "Mind Your Ps and Qs." *Planning,* September 1997 (vol. 63, no. 9): 19.

Journals

Apartment Finance Today. Alexander & Edwards Publishing, Inc., 220 Sansome Street, 11th Floor, San Francisco, CA 94104; Phone: (415) 546-7255; Fax: (415) 249-1595. http://www.housing-finance.com.

Architectural Record. American Institute of Architects, Two Penn Plaza, New York, NY 10121-2298; Phone: (800) 525-5003; Fax: (609) 426-7087. http://www.archrecord.com.

Architecture. BPI Communications, 1515 Broadway, New York, NY 10036; Phone: (800) 382-3322. http://www.architecturemag.com.

Environmental Planning Quarterly. Center for Urban Policy and the Environment. 342 North Senate Avenue, Indianapolis, IN 46204-1744; Phone: (317) 261-3000; Fax: (317) 261-3050. http://www.spea.iupui.edu/cupe/.

Housing Economics. National Association of Home Builders, 1201 Fifteenth Street, N.W. Washington, DC 20005-2800; Phone: (202) 822-0434. http://www.nahb.com.

Housing Market Statistics. National Association of Home Builders, 1201 Fifteenth Street, N.W. Washington, DC 20005-2800; Phone: (202) 822-0434. http://www.nahb.com.

Housing Policy Debate. Fannie Mae Foundation, 400 Wisconsin Avenue, N.W., North Tower, Suite One, Washington, DC 20016-2804; Phone: (202) 274-8000; Fax: (202) 274-8100. http://www.fannie-maefoundation.org.

Journal of the American Planning Association. American Planning Association, 122 South Michigan Avenue, Suite 1600, Chicago, IL 60603; Phone: (312) 431-9100; Fax: (312) 431-9985. www.planning.org.

Journal of Property Management. Institute of Real Estate Management. 430 North Michigan Avenue, Chicago, IL 60611; Phone: (312) 661-0004. http://www.irem.org.

Land Development. National Association of Home Builders, 1201 Fifteenth Street, N.W. Washington, DC 20005-2800; Phone: (202) 822-0434. http://www.nahb.com.

Managing Housing Letter. CD Publications, 8204 Fenton Street, Silver Spring, MD 20910; Phone: (800) 666-6380; Fax: (301) 588-6385. http://www.cdpublications.com.

Midwest Real Estate News. Intertec Publishing Corporation, 6151 Powers Ferry Road, N.W., Atlanta, GA 30339-2941; Phone: (770) 955-2500. http://www.mwrenonline.com.

Multifamily Executive. MGI Publications, Inc., 301 Oxford Valley Road, Suite 804, Yardley, PA 19067; Phone: (215) 321-5112.

Multi-Housing News. Miller Freeman, Inc., 600 Harrison Street, San Francisco, CA 94107; Phone: (415) 905-2200. http://www.multi-housingnews.com.

National Real Estate Investor. Intertec Publishing Corporation, 6151 Powers Ferry Road, N.W., Atlanta, GA 30339-2941; Phone: (770) 955-2500. http://www.internetreveiw.com.

Places: A Forum of Environmental Design. University of California at Berkeley, 390 Wurster Hall, Berkeley, CA 94720; Phone: (510) 642-1495; Fax: (510) 643-5571. http://www.places-journal.org.

Planning. American Planning Association, 122 South Michigan Avenue, Suite 1600, Chicago, IL 60603; Phone: (312) 431-9100; Fax: (312) 431-9985. http://www.planning.org.

Southeast Real Estate News. Communication Channels, Inc., 6151 Powers Ferry Road, N.W., Atlanta, GA 30339-2941; Phone: (404) 955-2500.

Units. National Apartment Association. 201 North Union Street, Suite 200, Alexandria, VA 22314; Phone: (703) 518-6141. http://www.naahg.org.

Urban Land. ULI–the Urban Land Institute, 1025 Thomas Jefferson Street, N.W., Suite 500 West, Washington, DC 20007-2501; Phone: (202) 624-7000; Fax: (202) 624-7140. http://www.uli.org.

Organizations

American Institute of Architects
1735 New York Avenue, N.W.
Washington, DC 20006
Phone: (202) 626-7300
http://www.aiaonline.org

American Planning Association
122 South Michigan Avenue, Suite 1600
Chicago, IL 60603
Phone: (312) 431-9100
Fax: (312) 431-9985
www.planning.org

Fannie Mae Foundation
400 Wisconsin Avenue, N.W.
North Tower, Suite One
Washington, DC 20016-2804
Phone: (202) 274-8000
Fax: (202) 274-8100
http://www.fanniemaefoundation.org

National Apartment Association
201 North Union Street, Suite 200
Alexandria, VA 22314
Phone: (703) 518-6141
http://www.naahg.org

National Association of Home Builders
1201 Fifteenth Street, N.W.
Washington, DC 20005-2800
Phone: (202) 822-0434
http://www.nahb.com

National Association of Real Estate Investment Trusts
1875 I Street, N.W.
Washington, DC 20006
Phone: (202) 739-9400
Fax: (202) 739-9401
http://www.nareit.com

National Association of Realtors®
700 Eleventh Street, N.W.
Washington, DC 20001
Phone: (202) 383-1014
Fax: (202) 383-7563
http://www.nar.realtor.com

National Multi Housing Council
1850 M Street, N.W., Suite 540
Washington, DC 20036-5803
Phone: (202) 974-2300
Fax: (202) 775-0112
http://www.nmhc.org

Property Management Association
7900 Wisconsin Avenue, Suite 204
Bethesda, MD 20814
Phone: (301) 657-9200
http://www.pma-dc.org

ULI–the Urban Land Institute
1025 Thomas Jefferson Street, N.W., Suite 500 West
Washington, DC 20007-2501
Phone: (202) 624-7000
Fax: (202) 624-7140
http://www.uli.org.

Index

National Association of Home Builders, 58, 227
National Building Code, 72
National Conference on Housing, 8
National Emission Standards for Hazardous Air Pollutants, 66
National Environmental Policy Act (NEPA) (1969), 62, 63
National Flood Insurance Act (1968), 62, 65–66
National Historic Preservation Act (1960), *62,* 63
National Housing Act (1949, 1968), 4, 13
National Investment Conference on Senior Living, 225
National Multi Housing Council (NMHC), 3, 203, 346
National Park Service, 160, 268, 270
National Priorities List, 63
National Real Estate Investor, 346
National Register of Historic Places, 63, 284
Natomas, California, *26, 28, 29*
Natural features, and site planning, *104, 105, 110*
Net operating income (NOI): and financial analysis, 143, 145–46; and financial feasibility analysis, 83, 84, 85, 86, 88, 89, 101; and management and operations, 184, 185, 187
Net present value (NPV), 89
New Jersey, 73, 79, 217
New Jersey Department of Environmental Protection, 229, 230, 233
New Orleans, Louisiana. *See* The Cotton Mill
New York City: adaptive use in, 217; cooperatives in, 4; and development trends, 15, 348; and history of multifamily housing, 6, 8, *8,* 12; mid-rise and high-rise buildings in, 6; mixed-use projects in, *107, 148, 345;* niche markets in, *216;* rents in, 78; and site planning, *107;* tax abatement programs in, 229; unit mix in, 112; zoning in, 68. *See also* The Exchange
New York City Landmarks Preservation Commission, 284
New York Stock Exchange, 282
Newbury Court (Concord, Massachusetts), *226*
Newport Beach, California, 202. *See also* The Colony at Fashion Island
Newport Center (Newport Beach, California), 290, *291*
Niche markets, 4, 16, 31, 103, 112, 168, 200. *See also specific market*
NIMBY (not in my backyard), 69–70, *70,* 220, 346
NOI. *See* Net operating income
Northlake Farms (Gurnee, Illinois), **177–79**
Northside Tenants Reorganization (Pittsburgh, Pennsylvania), 63

NPV. *See* Net present value
Nuisance lawsuits, 67
Nursing homes, 223, 224, 225

■

Oak Crest Village (Parkville, Maryland), *223*
Oak Park, Illinois, *131*
Oakland, California, *60*
Oakwood Apartments, 198, 199, 200
Oakwood Corporate Housing, 214, 215
Occupational Safety and Health Administration, 66
Odmark and Thelan, 252
O'Donnell Wicklund Pigozzi and Peterson Architects, Inc. (OWP&P), 298, 300, 304, 305
Olympus Real Estate Corporation, 333
Open space, 50, 66, 71, 110, 116, 121
Operating period, 83, *84,* 89, 93, *98–99*
Operations. *See* Management and operations
Options, on land, 149–50
Orange, California, *225*
Oregon Department of Environmental Quality (DEQ), 259–60
Orlando, Florida, *32*
Overbuilding, 4, 32, 207, 351
Ownership, of multifamily projects, 4–5, 136, 138–42, *138–39,* 153

■

Paine Webber, 282
Palladium Group, *150*
Panos Hotel Group, 318, 322
Park at Greenway (Houston, Texas), *97*
Parking, 6, 105, 106–8, **108,** 121, 166, 169, 184. *See also* Garages
Parks and recreation: and exactions and impact fees, 76; indoor, 109; and management and operations, 187; and marketing, 166, 167, 169; and senior housing, 226; and sites, 39, 44, 55, 108, 109, 110. *See also specific case study*
Parkville, Maryland, *223*
Partnerships, 138–39, *138,* 141, 142, 149, 153, 154, 352
Pasadena, California, *126, 161*
Paseo Colorado (Pasadena, California), *126, 161*
Patterns of development, 22, 345–51
PDT Architects, 249
Peak Properties and Development Corporation, 312, 313, 317
Peakview Apartments (Lafayette, Colorado), **229, 312–17,** *313, 314, 315, 316*
Pearl Court Apartments (Portland, Oregon), **229, 258–67,** *259, 260, 261, 262, 263, 265*
Pearl Court Limited Partnership, 258
Pecerne Real Estate Group, 210
Pedestrians, 41, *41,* 108, 119, 121. *See also* Phillips Place

Pension funds, 130, 148, 151, 153, 154, 155, 156
Pentagon Row (Arlington, Virginia), *347*
Pepper Construction Company, 305
Performance bonds, 76
Performance zones, 70
Permanent financing, 89, 93, **132,** 147–53, *148, 149,* **154–55,** 156–57, 161, *161,* 353
Perrin, Matt, 203
Pesticides, 66
Phillips Place (Charlotte, North Carolina), *45,* **229, 318–25,** *319, 320, 321, 322, 323, 324*
Phoenix, Arizona, 15, *117*
Phoenix Urban Housing (Phoenix, Arizona), *117*
Piatt Park (Cincinnati, Ohio), 244, 246, *246,* 247
Piggyback townhouses, 106
Pinnacle Realty Management Company, *189,* 262, 263
Pipeline, development, 28, *29*
Pittsburgh, Pennsylvania, *63,* **63**
Planned Unit Developments (PUDs), 70
Planners, 20, 54, 68, 103. *See also* Land planners
Planning commissions, 125
Planning/predevelopment: and alternatives, 116, 121, 122, 123; and amendments to plans, 126; and approvals, 116, 125, 126; and concept planning, 116, 118–19, 121–22, 123; and final plans/construction drawings, 123, 125–26; and financing, 147, 148, *148,* 156, 157, 161; and formal applications, 123; and management and operations, 184; and marketing, 163, 164–70; and meetings with government officials, 125; preliminary, 121–23, 125; and regulation, 116, 118, 119, 121; and review of plans, 125–26; strategic, 163, 164–70. *See also* Site planning; *specific case study*
Plano, Texas, *190, 339*
Plantation, Florida, *75*
Plater-Zyberk, Elizabeth, 71
Play areas, 108–9
"Plex" developments, and site planning, 106
Poco Way Renaissance (San Jose, California), *10, 105*
Point of depletion, **174–75**
Points, 151
Police, 76, 204
Polychlorinated biphenyls (PCBs), 66
Pools, 13, 108, 199, 205, *247, 335, 353*
Portland Development Commission (PDC), 263
Portland, Oregon, *62,* 348. *See also* Pearl Court Apartments
Portland State University, 262
Post Properties, Inc., *158,* 191, 194, 195–96, *195,* 199–200, 201, 204, *216,* 318, 319, 322, 325

Post Shores (Irving, Texas), *341*
Postconstruction, financing for, 151–52
Prairie Court (Oak Park, Illinois), *131*
Predevelopment. *See* Planning/predevelopment
Preliminary plans, 116, 121–23, 125
Prendergast & Associates, Inc., 258, 267
Prendergast, Pat, 258
Prepayment penalties, 135
Present value concept, 89
Preservation, 160. *See also* Historic properties
Price, 19, 23, 103, 163, 164
Prince George's County, Maryland, 69
Pritzger Residential (Celebration, Florida), *76*
Pritzker Apartments at King Farm (Rockville, Maryland), *52*
Privacy, 41, 104, 114–16, *115*, 168
Pro forma statements, 84–88, *85*, 89, 143, 145, 154, 187, 193, 272
Product types, 5–6, 23, 31, 341–43
Program/project: definition of, 119, 121; distinctiveness of, 170, 171, *179;* refining the, 123; viability of, 89, 96
Project data. *See specific case study*
Promenade at Aventura (southern Florida), *86, 119, 122*
Property lines, priorities for, *167*, **167**
Property management. *See* Management and operations; *specific case study*
Property value, 116, 145–47, 148
Prudential Insurance Company, 333
Pruitt Igoe (St. Louis, Missouri), 12
Public facilities, 75, 76, 118
Public housing, 12, 13, 14
Public services, 37–38, 51–55
Public space, 114
Public Works Authority, 10
Public/private partnerships, *153, 217, 339. See also* Gramercy on Garfield/ Greenwich on the Park
Purchase-money mortgage, 149

Queens, New York, 10
Queensland Department of Housing, 238
Queensland Department of Housing, Local Government, and Planning (DHLGP), 238–39, 240, 241

Race issues, 340, *340, 345, 345*
Radon, 48, 67
Rainbow Row (Charleston, South Carolina), 320
Ranch at Ridgeview (Plano, Texas), *339*
Rate lock fee, 135
Rate of return, 88–89, 157. *See also* Internal rate of return; Return
Rayner, Michael, 245
R&B Realty Group, 195, 198, 199, 204
Real estate investment trusts (REITs), 3, 13, *14*, 136, *138–39,* 139–42, *142,*

153–56, 176, 183, 188, 192, 230, 233, 293, 333, 346, 352
Real Page, 199
Real property administrator (RPA), 189
Recognition marketing, 171
Recreation. *See* Parks and recreation; *specific case study*
Redevelopment, and environmental issues, 66–67
Redlining, 59
Referendum, zoning by, 69–70
Regional forecasts, and trends, 343, 345
Regis Contractors, 297
Regulation, 3, 39, 44, 116, 118, 119, 121, 154, 158, 217. *See also* Approvals; Zoning
Rehabilitation and repositioning, 4, **63**, 72–73, *138*, 183, 212, 219–22, *220*, 224, 343. *See also* The Cotton Mill; Denver Dry Goods Building
REITs. *See* Mortgage REITs; Real estate investment trusts
ReLEASE, 179
Release dates, 170
Renovation. *See* Rehabilitation and repositioning
Rent: anticipated, 88, 143; deposits, 194–95; and design, 113, 114; and financial feasibility analysis, 83, *85*, 88, 97; and financing, 143, 159; fine-tuning, 193–95; and management and operations, 185–86, 187, 192–93, 202, 207; and market analysis, 23, 27, 31; and marketing, 164; overestimating, 97; restrictions on, 77–78; in Sacramento and Natomas, *28;* subsidies for, 224; surveys about, 164
Rent control, 77–78, 79
Rent.net, 176
Rent rolls, 192
Rental certificates, 68
Rental housing: declining profitability of, 80; and market analysis, 21, 23, *25,* 27, 31, 32; trends in, 339, 340–43, 348, 350. *See also specific topic or project*
Rental offices, 60
Rental services, 174–76
Rental vouchers, 68
Replacement of asset, 143
Reserve for replacements, 97
Residence Inn, 214, *214*
Resident relations, 187, 188, 197–205
Residents: problems with, 187; screening of, 187; services for, 3, 16, 110, 160, 173, 188, 190, 192, 200, 202–3, 211, 214–15, 223–24, 226, 343. *See also* Resident relations
Resolution Trust Corporation (RTC), 159
Reston, Virginia, 109
Restoration Hardware, 323
Retail space, *37, 105, 117, 206. See also* Denver Dry Goods Building; Mixed-use projects; Phillips Place
Retirement Research Foundation, 304

Return: cash-on-cash, 97, 101; on debt financing, 132; to developers, 130; to investors, 80, 83, 96–97, *100*, 129, 130, 135, 136, 142; and leverage, 135; and management and operations, 184
Richardson, Texas, *5, 53, 166, 194*
Rights-of-way, 118
Riis, Jacob, 6, 8
Ring, Gustave, 10
Risk, 129–30, 132–36, 142, 145, 147–51, 159, 353
River District (Portland, Oregon), 258, 259, *259*, 260, 262, 263, 264
Riverside (Atlanta, Georgia), *37, 104*
Riverside, California, *225*
Roads. *See* Streets/roads
Robert Taylor Homes (Chicago, Illinois), 12
Robert Waxman Camera Company, 276
Roberts, Jeffrey, 109
Rockville, Maryland, *52*
Rodriquez-Simon Design, 257
Rose, Jonathan F.P., 278
Royal Australian Institute of Architects, 241
Royal Australian Planning Institute, 241
RRH Associates, 311
RTKL Associates, 191
Ruby, Howard, 195, 207
Rural housing, 160

S corporations, 136, *138–39*, 139, 140, 141, 142
Sacramento, California, *26, 28, 29*
St. Charles, Illinois, *200, 201*
St. Louis, Missouri, 12
Sales & Marketing Magic Companies, 307
Sales/rental agents, 59
San Antonio, Texas, *115, 161, 187*
San Diego, California, 348. *See also* The Mercado Apartments
San Diego Gas and Electric, 253
San Diego Redevelopment Agency, 250, 254
San Francisco, California, 4, *64*
San Joaquin Hills Court (Newport Beach, California), 290
San Jose, California, *10, 37, 58, 74, 105, 133, 140, 162*
Sanborn Map Company (Pelham, New York), 65
Santa Cruz, California, *78*
Santa Monica, California, *12*, 188
Savings institutions, 156
Savings and loan institutions, 148, 156, 159
Scattered-site low-income housing, 107
Schools, 21, 23, 38, 39, 54, 76
Scruggs & Hammond, 332, 337
Seattle, Washington, 15, *36*, 79, *93*, 153, *182*, 184–85, *185*
Second mortgages, 160

Topographic surveys, 118, 122, 123
Toscana (Sunnyvale, California), *14, 27, 157, 196*
Towne-Place Suites, 214
Towne Properties, 244, 246, 247, 249
Townhouses, 106–7
Traffic, 3, 39, 169, 192, 348
Trammell Crow Residential, *189*
Transactions screen, 65
Transfer of development rights (TDR), 70, 71–72
Transportation: and development trends, 347, 348; and exactions and impact fees, 76; and market analysis, 21–22, *22;* and niche markets, 210; and senior housing, 226; and sites, 36, 39, 41, 107; and zoning, 68
Turner Construction, 249
Turnover, 185–86, 187, 188, 227
Typological coding, 71–72

■
UCLA University Village (Los Angeles, California), **229**, **326–31**, *327, 328, 329, 330*
Underground storage tanks, 67
Uniform Building Code, 72
United Dominion Realty Trust, Inc., *189*
United States Housing Authority (USHA), 10
Units: average size of new multifamily (1985 to 1999), *342;* design of, 113–14, 126; mix of, 103, 112, **112**, 126, 163, 166, 168, 174; with multiple bedrooms or baths (1985 to 1899), *342;* number of, 121, 126, 170; security of individual, 204; size of, 31, 103, **112**, *113*, 126, 163, *342;* types of, *164*, 168, 170, 175
University of California (UCLA). *See* UCLA University Village
UpREITs, 141, 153
Urban areas: and condominium conversions, 79; and development trends, 14, *15*, 343, 345, 346, 347–48, *347, 348, 350, 352;* financing for projects in, 154; and history of multifamily housing, 8–9, 12; industrial conversions in, *210;* and market analysis, 21, 22, 31; new construction case studies in, 229; and niche markets, 216; and rehabilitation and repositioning, 221; renovation case studies in, 229; and sites, 39, 41, 42, 105, 106, 107; typological coding in, 71–72, *72;* and zoning, 69. *See also specific case study*
Urban Design Group, 281
Urban renewal, 12
Use districts, 68
Utilities, 37–38, 51–55, **52**, 75, 110, 114, 122, 166, 169, 195, 202–3

■
Vacancies, 27–28, 112, 192, 345
Vegetation and wildlife, 50–51

Ventana Apartment Homes (San Antonio, Texas), *187*
Veterans Affairs, U.S. Department of, 10, 57
Victoria Manor (Riverside, California), *225*
View diagonal, 112
Villa Torino (San Jose, California), *37, 58, 140, 162*
Village of Euclid, Ohio v. *Ambler Realty Co.*, 68
Village Green at Cantera (Warrenville, Illinois), *11, 121*
Village Green Development and Construction, 109
Village Inn. *See* Franciscan Village
Villas at Cityplace (Dallas, Texas), *102, 105, 158*
Vine Restaurant, Market, and Catering, 284
VISTA Information Solutions, 65

■
Waiting list, 172, 177–78
Wakeland Housing and Development Corporation, 257
Walden Residential Properties, 333, 337
Warrenville, Illinois, *11, 121*
Washington, D.C. *See* District of Columbia
Water, *50*, 52, 76, 202–3. *See also* Hydrology; Utilities
Waterfront properties, 31
Web sites, 175–76, 179–80
West End Towers (New York City), *148*
West Park Village (Tampa, Florida), *67, 348*
Westlake Tower Apartments (Seattle, Washington), *93*
Wetlands, 63, *67*, 122
Wild and Scenic Rivers Act, 63
William Wilson Architects, 267
Wilson Building (Dallas, Texas), *216*
Wimbledon Apartments (Spring, Texas), **229**, **332–37**, *333, 334, 335, 336*
Wimbledon Estates, 332
Womack + Hampton, 311
Wright, Carroll, 8
Wright, Frank Lloyd, 9, *131*
Wright, Henry, 10

■
Xeriscaping, 110

■
The Yards (Portland, Oregon), *62*
Yield maintenance penalties, 135

■
ZOM Residential, 307, 308
Zoning, 6, 44, 47, 50, 67–70, *70*, 80, 106–7, 110, 118, 219, 220. *See also* Regulation